$AVING 80,000 GOLD IN ANOTHER WORLD FOR MY RETIREMENT

SAVING 80,000 GOLD IN ANOTHER WORLD FOR MY RETIREMENT

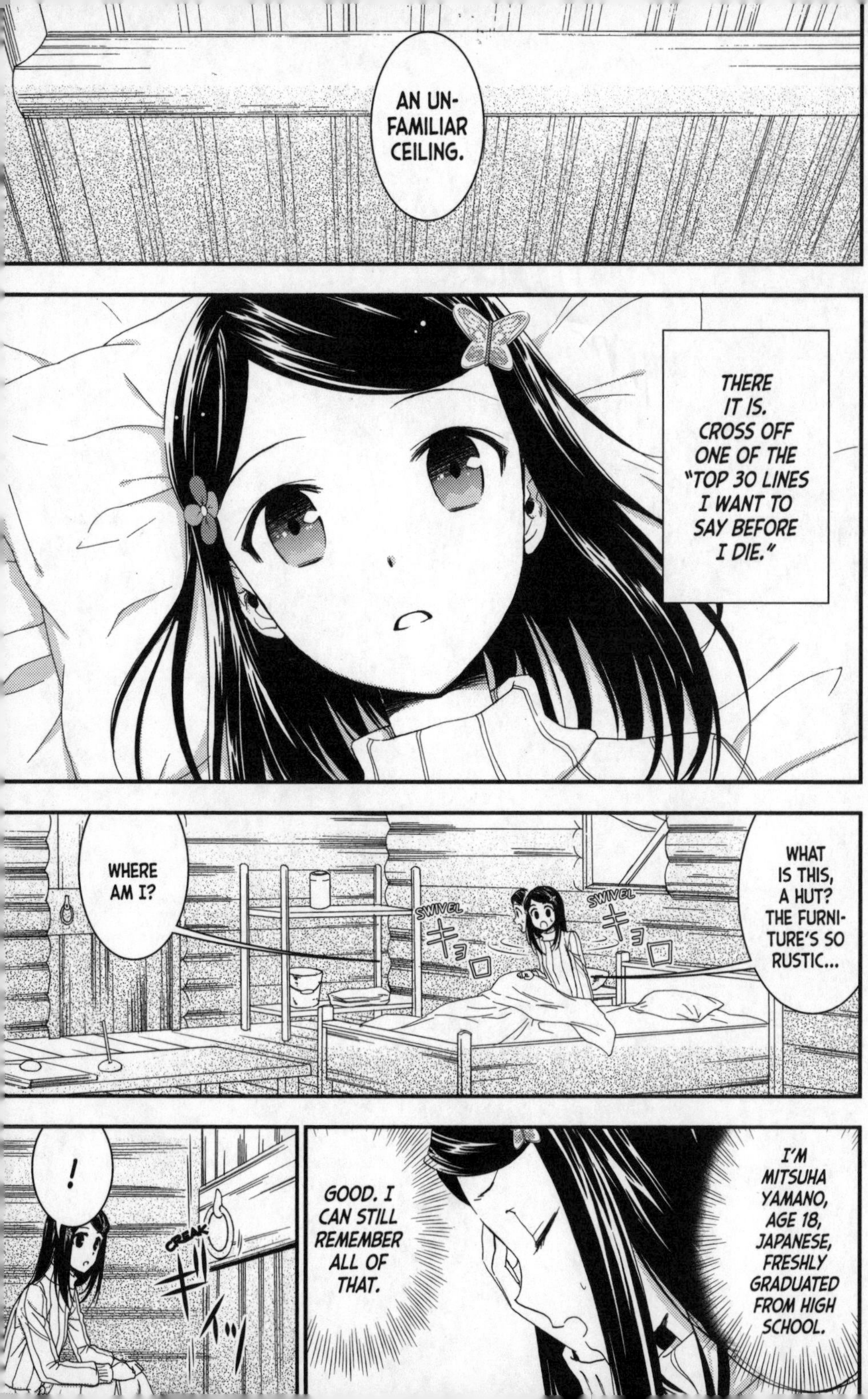
AN UN-FAMILIAR CEILING.
THERE IT IS. CROSS OFF ONE OF THE "TOP 30 LINES I WANT TO SAY BEFORE I DIE."
WHAT IS THIS, A HUT? THE FURNI-TURE'S SO RUSTIC...
SWIVEL
キョロ
SWIVEL
キョロ
WHERE AM I?
I'M MITSUHA YAMANO, AGE 18, JAPANESE, FRESHLY GRADUATED FROM HIGH SCHOOL.
GOOD. I CAN STILL REMEMBER ALL OF THAT.
!
CREAK
ギイッ

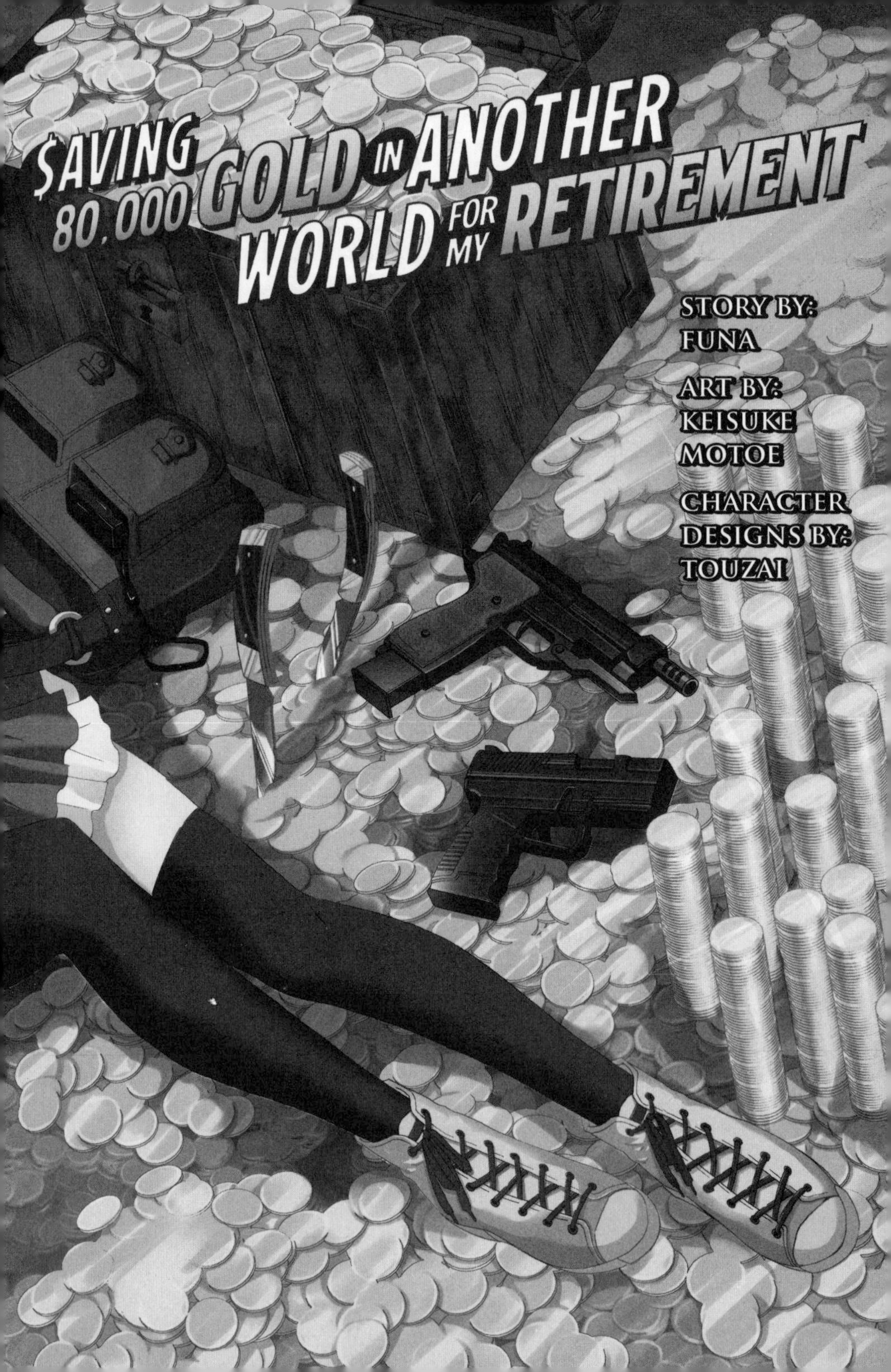
$AVING 80,000 GOLD IN ANOTHER WORLD FOR MY RETIREMENT
STORY BY:
FUNA
ART BY:
KEISUKE MOTOE
CHARACTER DESIGNS BY:
TOUZAI

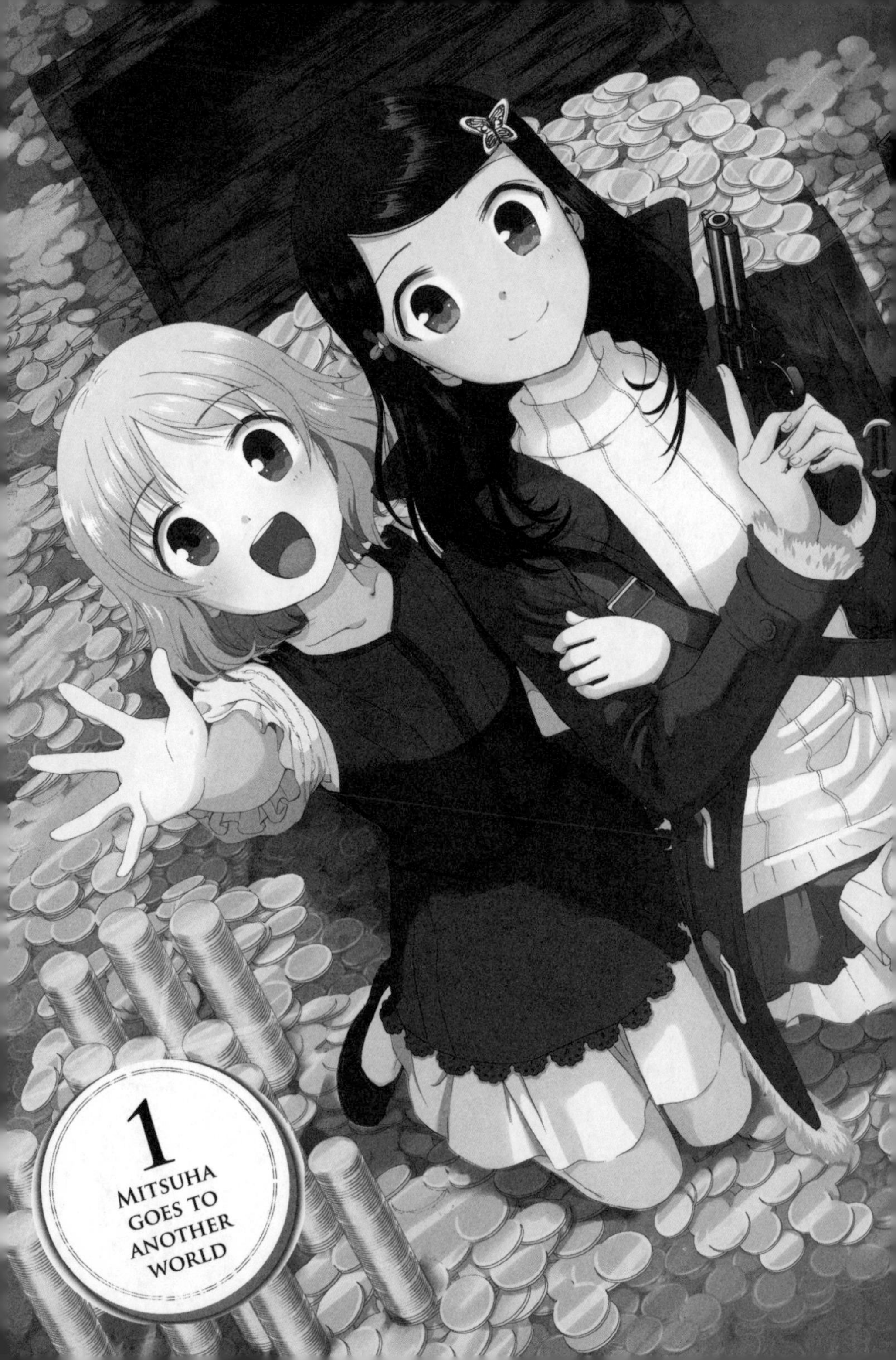
1
MITSUHA GOES TO ANOTHER WORLD

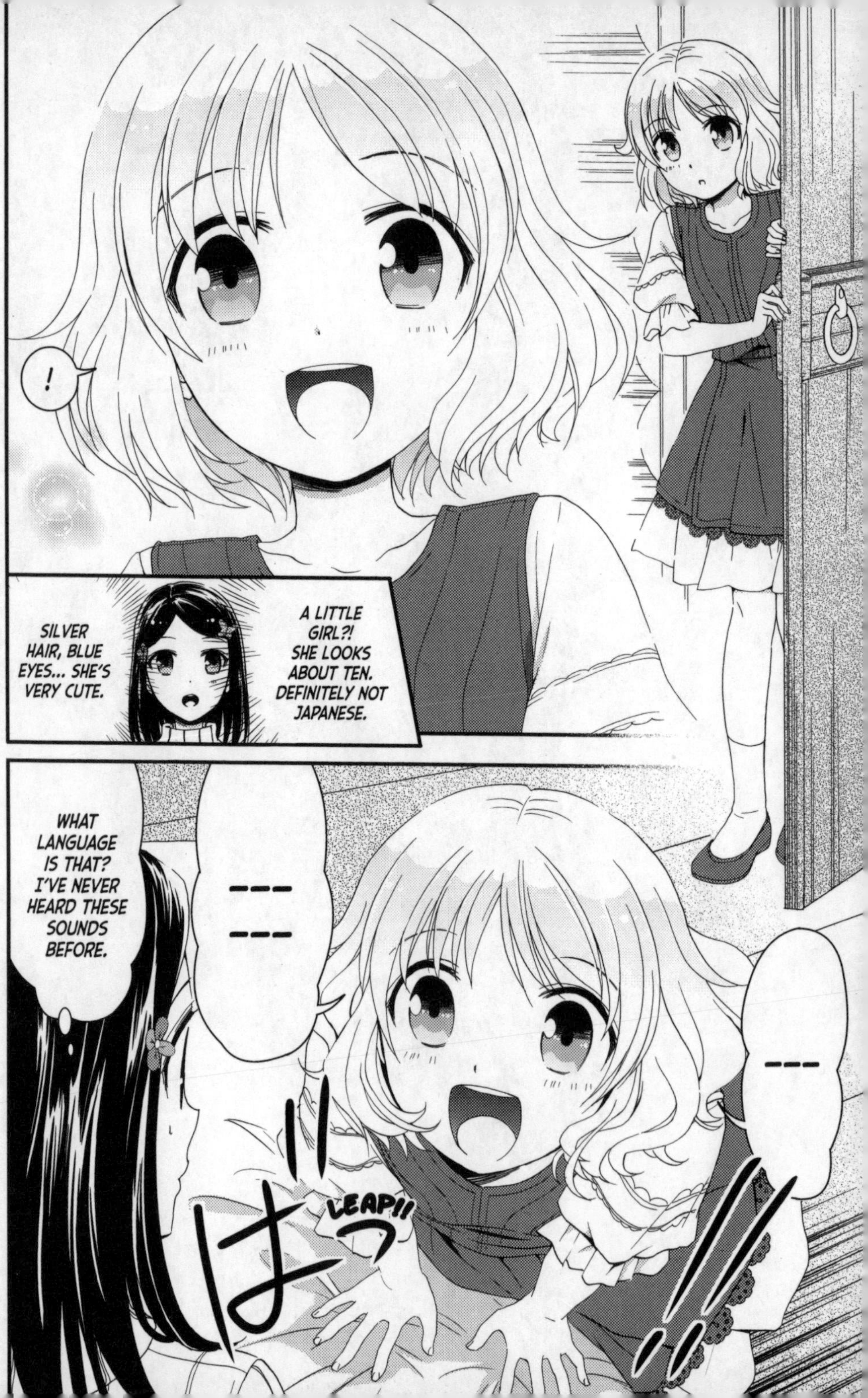
!
A LITTLE GIRL?! SHE LOOKS ABOUT TEN. DEFINITELY NOT JAPANESE.
SILVER HAIR, BLUE EYES... SHE'S VERY CUTE.
--- ---

WHAT LANGUAGE IS THAT? I'VE NEVER HEARD THESE SOUNDS BEFORE.
はっ
LEAP!!

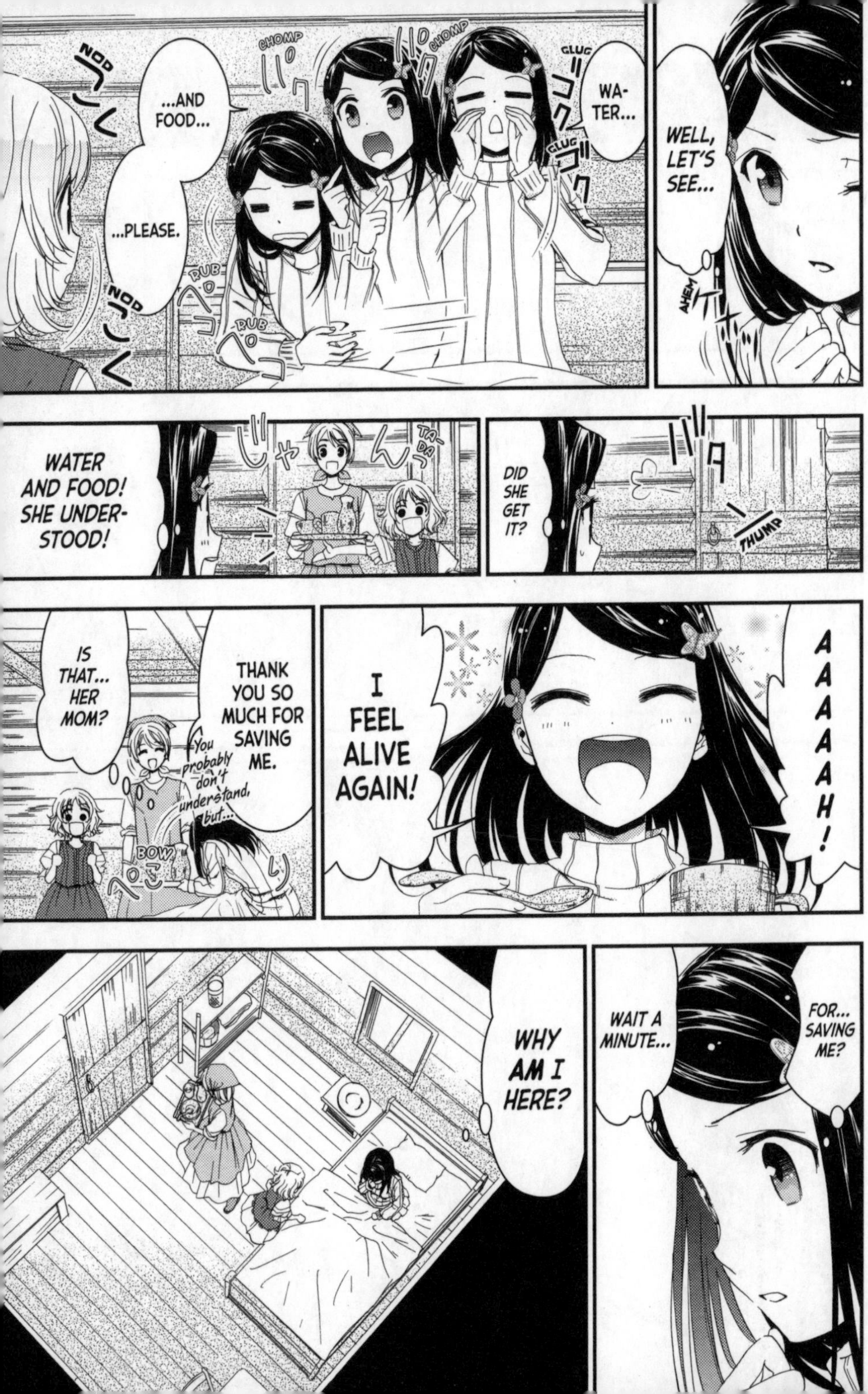
WELL, LET'S SEE...
AHEM
WA-TER...
GLUG
GLUG
CHOMP
CHOMP
...AND FOOD...
...PLEASE.
NOD
NOD
RUB
RUB
DID SHE GET IT?
THUMP
TA-DA
WATER AND FOOD! SHE UNDER-STOOD!
AAAAAAH!
I FEEL ALIVE AGAIN!
THANK YOU SO MUCH FOR SAVING ME.
You probably don't understand, but...
BOW
IS THAT... HER MOM?
FOR... SAVING ME?
WAIT A MINUTE...
WHY AM I HERE?

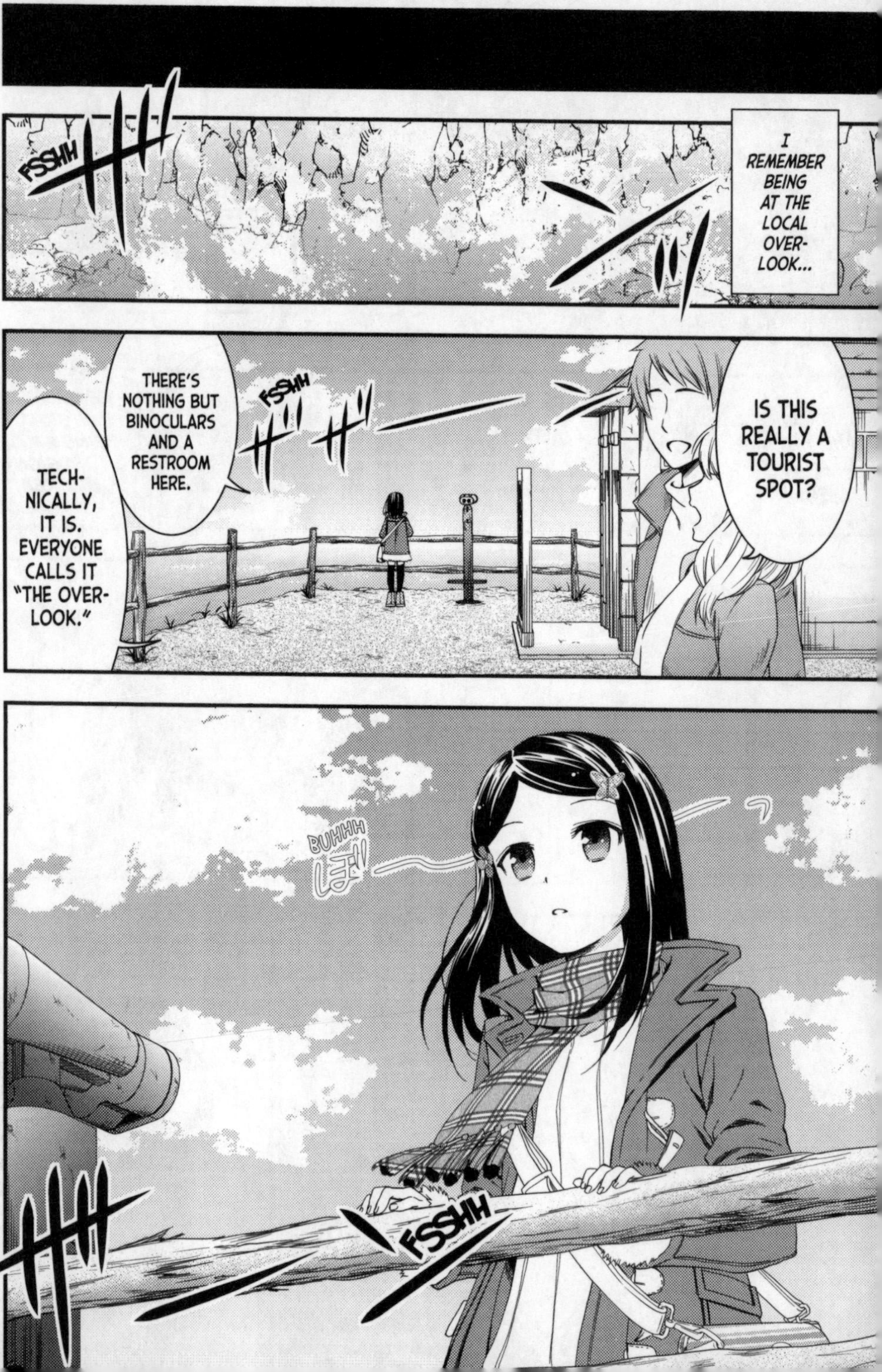
I REMEMBER BEING AT THE LOCAL OVER-LOOK...
FSSHH
IS THIS REALLY A TOURIST SPOT?
THERE'S NOTHING BUT BINOCULARS AND A RESTROOM HERE.
FSSHH
TECH-NICALLY, IT IS. EVERYONE CALLS IT "THE OVER-LOOK."
BUHHH
FSSHH

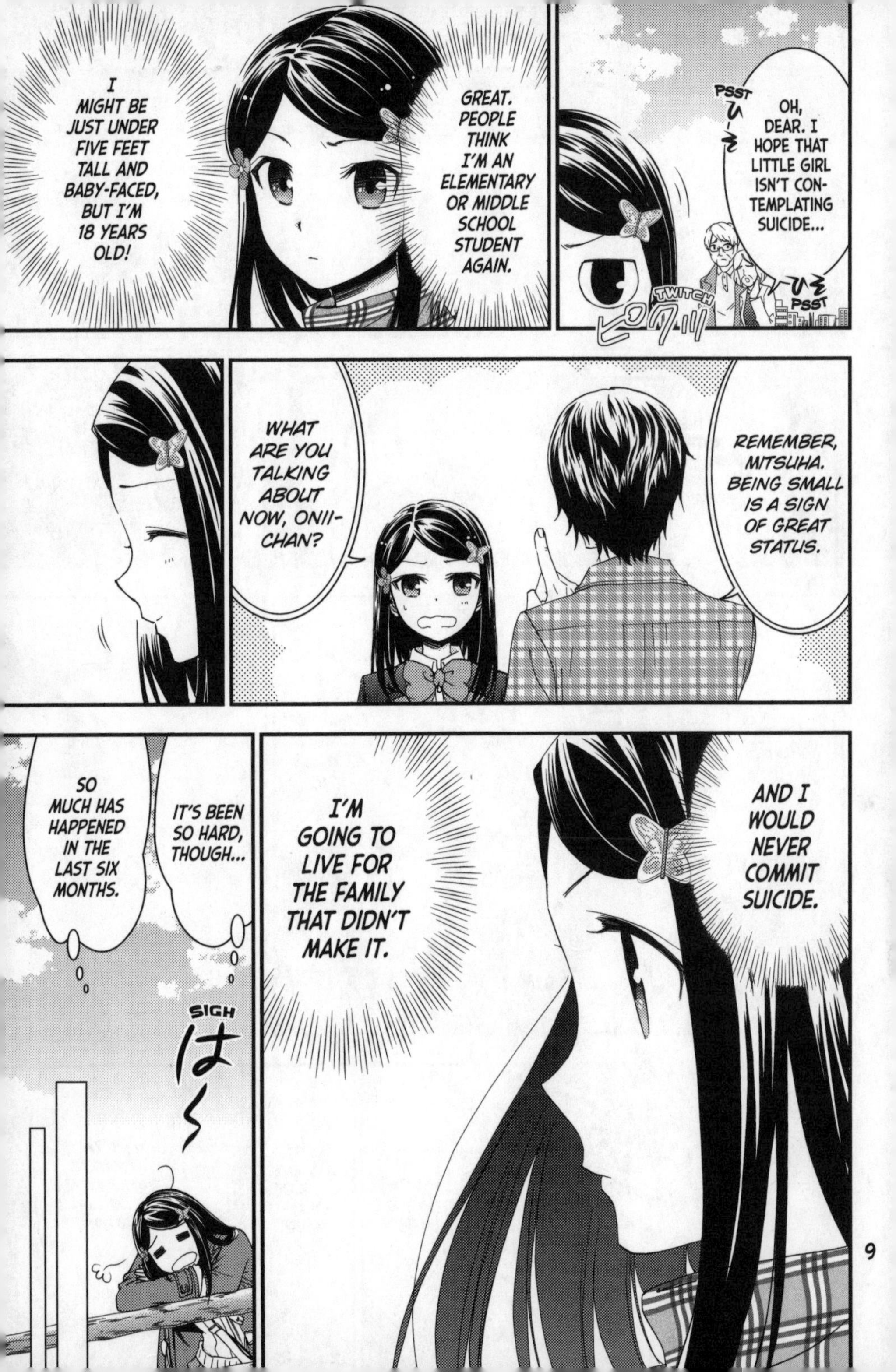
PSST
OH, DEAR. I HOPE THAT LITTLE GIRL ISN'T CONTEMPLATING SUICIDE...
PSST
TWITCH ピクッ
GREAT. PEOPLE THINK I'M AN ELEMENTARY OR MIDDLE SCHOOL STUDENT AGAIN.
I MIGHT BE JUST UNDER FIVE FEET TALL AND BABY-FACED, BUT I'M 18 YEARS OLD!
REMEMBER, MITSUHA. BEING SMALL IS A SIGN OF GREAT STATUS.
WHAT ARE YOU TALKING ABOUT NOW, ONII-CHAN?
AND I WOULD NEVER COMMIT SUICIDE.
I'M GOING TO LIVE FOR THE FAMILY THAT DIDN'T MAKE IT.
IT'S BEEN SO HARD, THOUGH...
SO MUCH HAS HAPPENED IN THE LAST SIX MONTHS.
SIGH

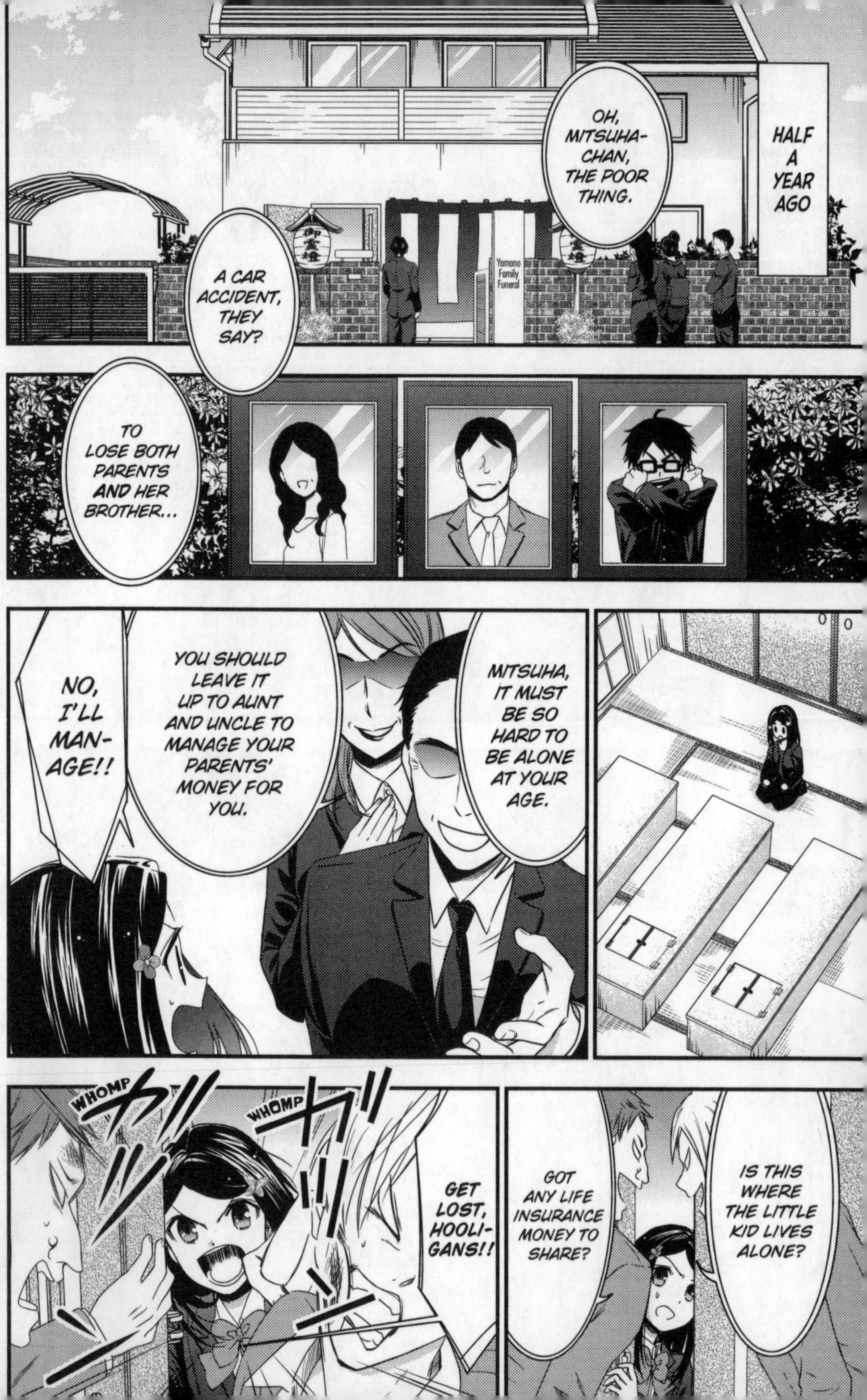
HALF A YEAR AGO
OH, MITSUHA-CHAN, THE POOR THING.
Yamano Family Funeral
A CAR ACCIDENT, THEY SAY?
TO LOSE BOTH PARENTS AND HER BROTHER...
MITSUHA, IT MUST BE SO HARD TO BE ALONE AT YOUR AGE.
YOU SHOULD LEAVE IT UP TO AUNT AND UNCLE TO MANAGE YOUR PARENTS' MONEY FOR YOU.
NO, I'LL MAN-AGE!!
IS THIS WHERE THE LITTLE KID LIVES ALONE?
GOT ANY LIFE INSURANCE MONEY TO SHARE?
GET LOST, HOOLI-GANS!!
WHOMP
WHOMP

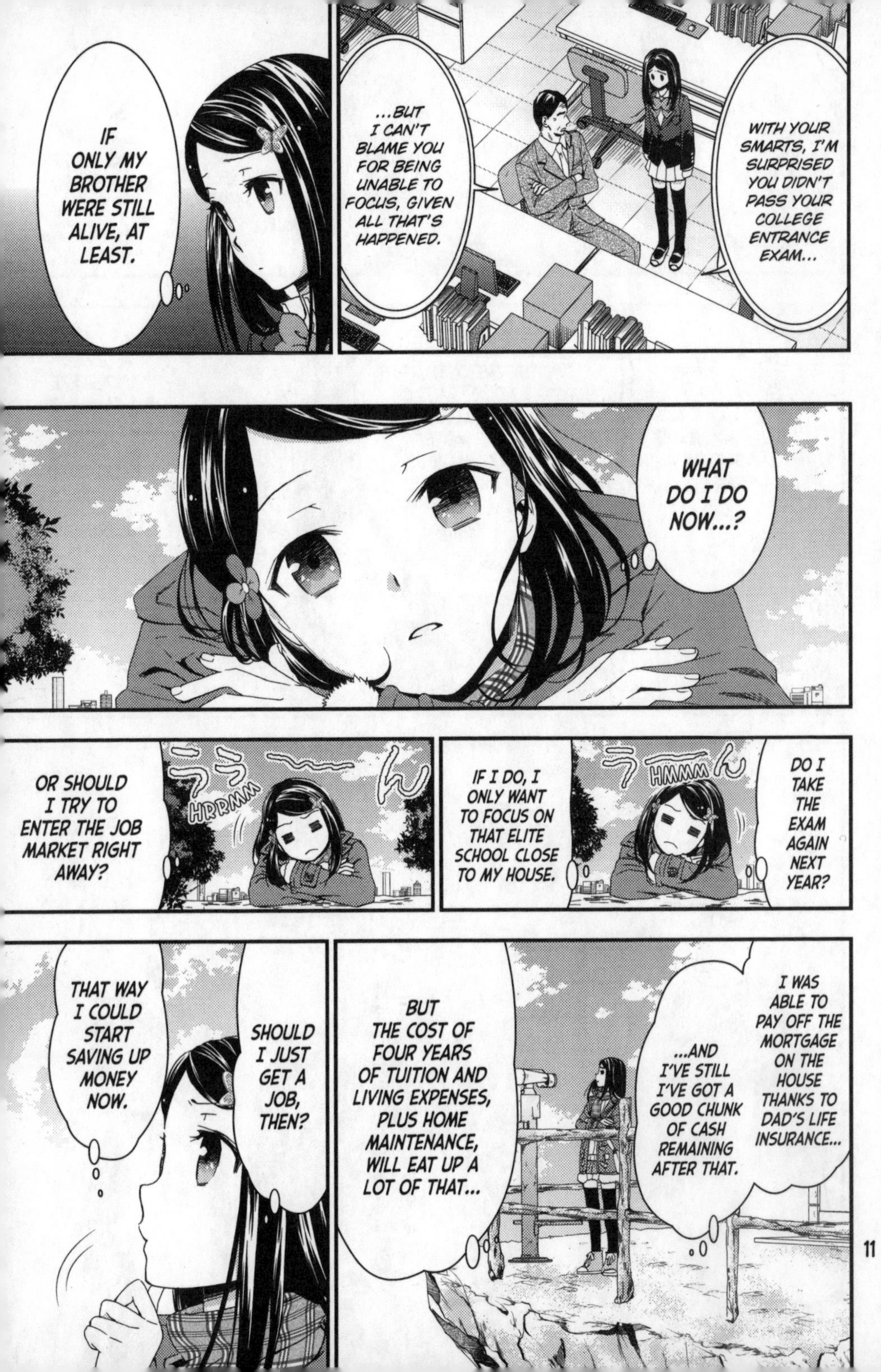
WITH YOUR SMARTS, I'M SURPRISED YOU DIDN'T PASS YOUR COLLEGE ENTRANCE EXAM...
...BUT I CAN'T BLAME YOU FOR BEING UNABLE TO FOCUS, GIVEN ALL THAT'S HAPPENED.
IF ONLY MY BROTHER WERE STILL ALIVE, AT LEAST.
WHAT DO I DO NOW...?
DO I TAKE THE EXAM AGAIN NEXT YEAR?
う〜ん
HMMM
IF I DO, I ONLY WANT TO FOCUS ON THAT ELITE SCHOOL CLOSE TO MY HOUSE.
うう〜ん
HRRMM
OR SHOULD I TRY TO ENTER THE JOB MARKET RIGHT AWAY?
I WAS ABLE TO PAY OFF THE MORTGAGE ON THE HOUSE THANKS TO DAD'S LIFE INSURANCE...
...AND I'VE STILL I'VE GOT A GOOD CHUNK OF CASH REMAINING AFTER THAT.
BUT THE COST OF FOUR YEARS OF TUITION AND LIVING EXPENSES, PLUS HOME MAINTENANCE, WILL EAT UP A LOT OF THAT...
SHOULD I JUST GET A JOB, THEN?
THAT WAY I COULD START SAVING UP MONEY NOW.

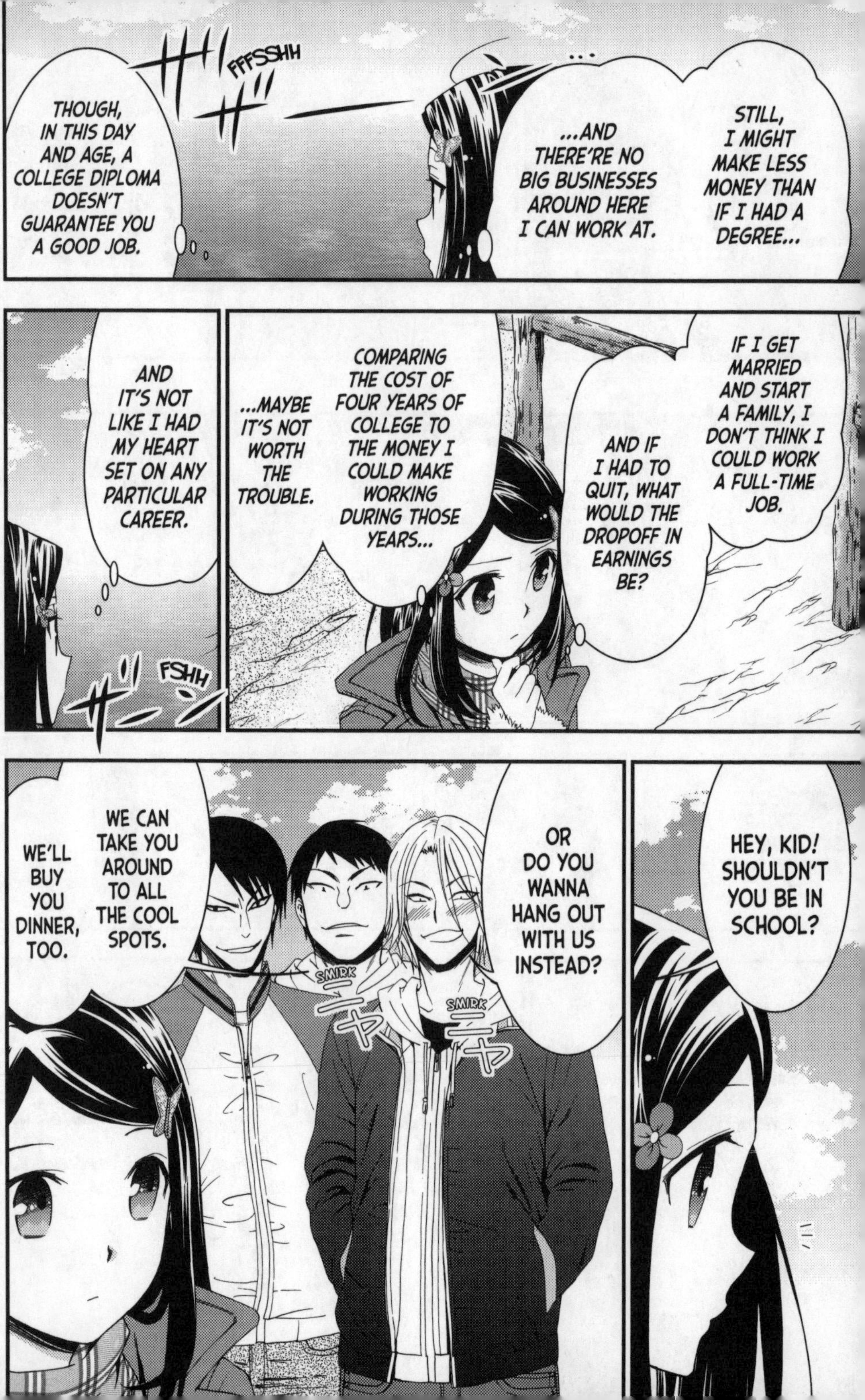
STILL, I MIGHT MAKE LESS MONEY THAN IF I HAD A DEGREE...
...
...AND THERE'RE NO BIG BUSINESSES AROUND HERE I CAN WORK AT.
FFFSSHH
THOUGH, IN THIS DAY AND AGE, A COLLEGE DIPLOMA DOESN'T GUARANTEE YOU A GOOD JOB.
IF I GET MARRIED AND START A FAMILY, I DON'T THINK I COULD WORK A FULL-TIME JOB.
AND IF I HAD TO QUIT, WHAT WOULD THE DROPOFF IN EARNINGS BE?
COMPARING THE COST OF FOUR YEARS OF COLLEGE TO THE MONEY I COULD MAKE WORKING DURING THOSE YEARS...
...MAYBE IT'S NOT WORTH THE TROUBLE.
AND IT'S NOT LIKE I HAD MY HEART SET ON ANY PARTICULAR CAREER.
FSHH
HEY, KID! SHOULDN'T YOU BE IN SCHOOL?
OR DO YOU WANNA HANG OUT WITH US INSTEAD?
SMIRK
SMIRK
WE CAN TAKE YOU AROUND TO ALL THE COOL SPOTS.
WE'LL BUY YOU DINNER, TOO.

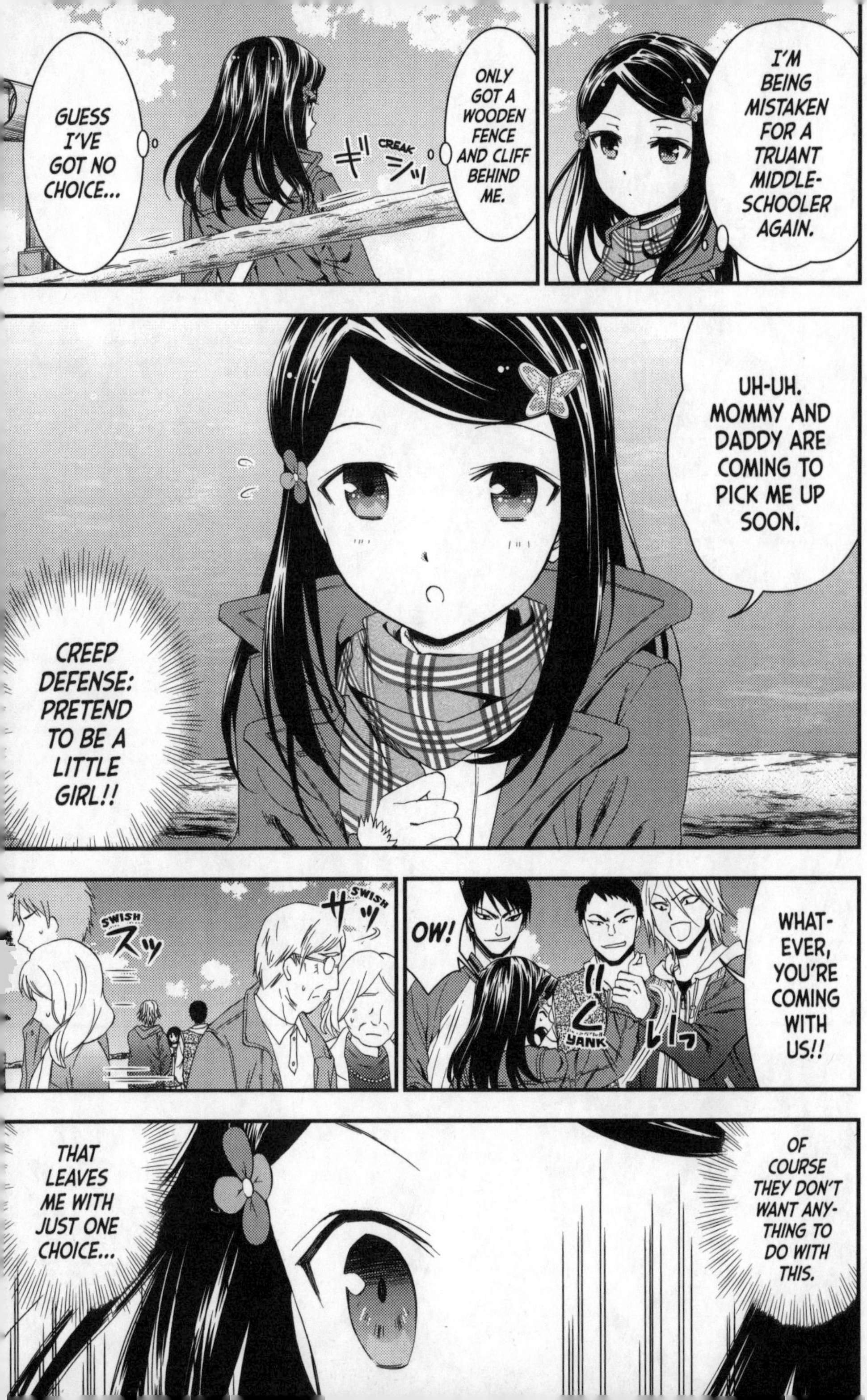
I'M BEING MISTAKEN FOR A TRUANT MIDDLE-SCHOOLER AGAIN.
ONLY GOT A WOODEN FENCE AND CLIFF BEHIND ME.
ギシッ CREAK
GUESS I'VE GOT NO CHOICE...
UH-UH. MOMMY AND DADDY ARE COMING TO PICK ME UP SOON.
CREEP DEFENSE: PRETEND TO BE A LITTLE GIRL!!
WHAT-EVER, YOU'RE COMING WITH US!!
ぐいっ YANK
OW!
ザッ SWISH
スッ SWISH
OF COURSE THEY DON'T WANT ANY-THING TO DO WITH THIS.
THAT LEAVES ME WITH JUST ONE CHOICE...

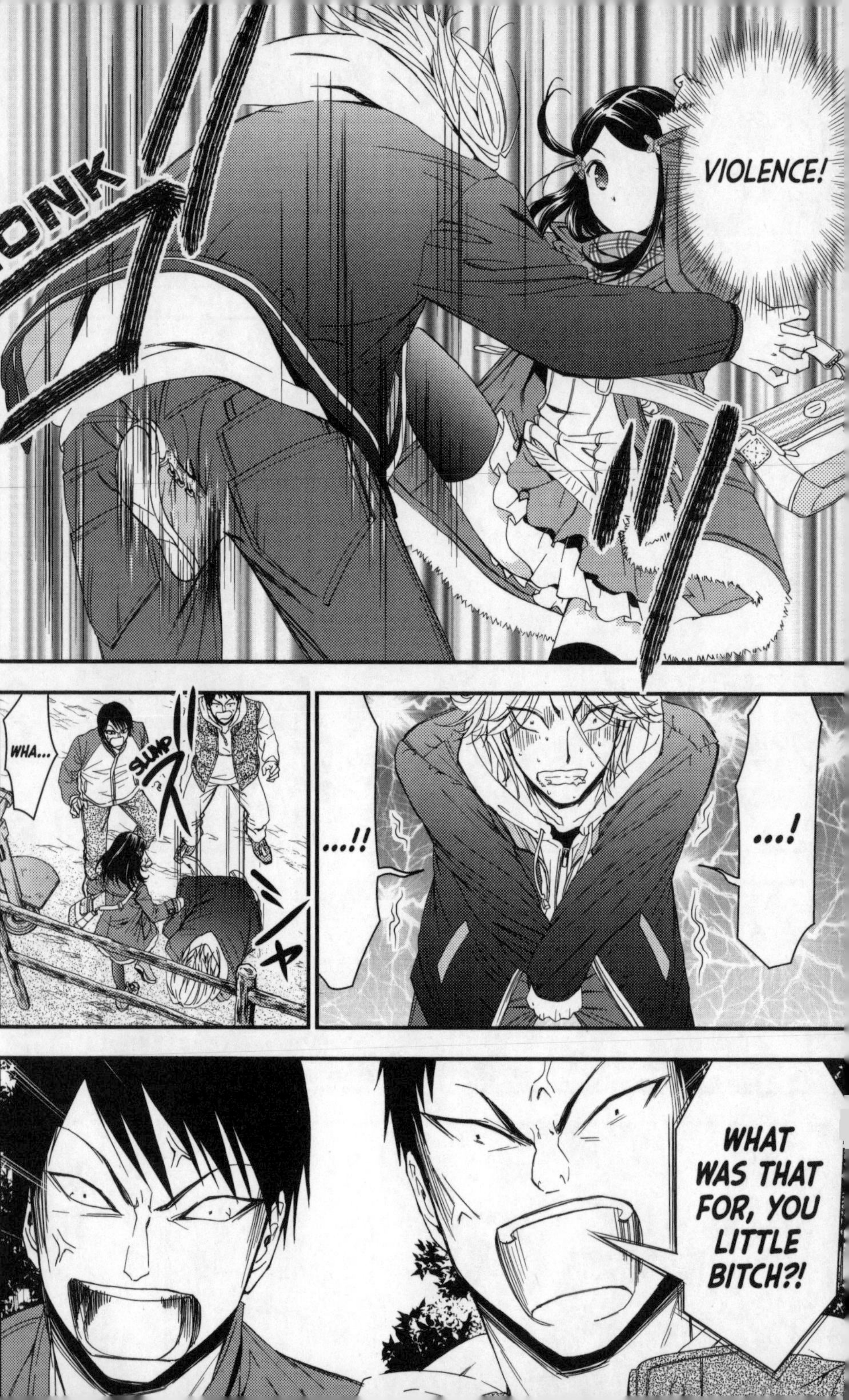
VIOLENCE!
GONK
...!
...!!
!!
WHA...
SLUMP
WHAT WAS THAT FOR, YOU LITTLE BITCH?!

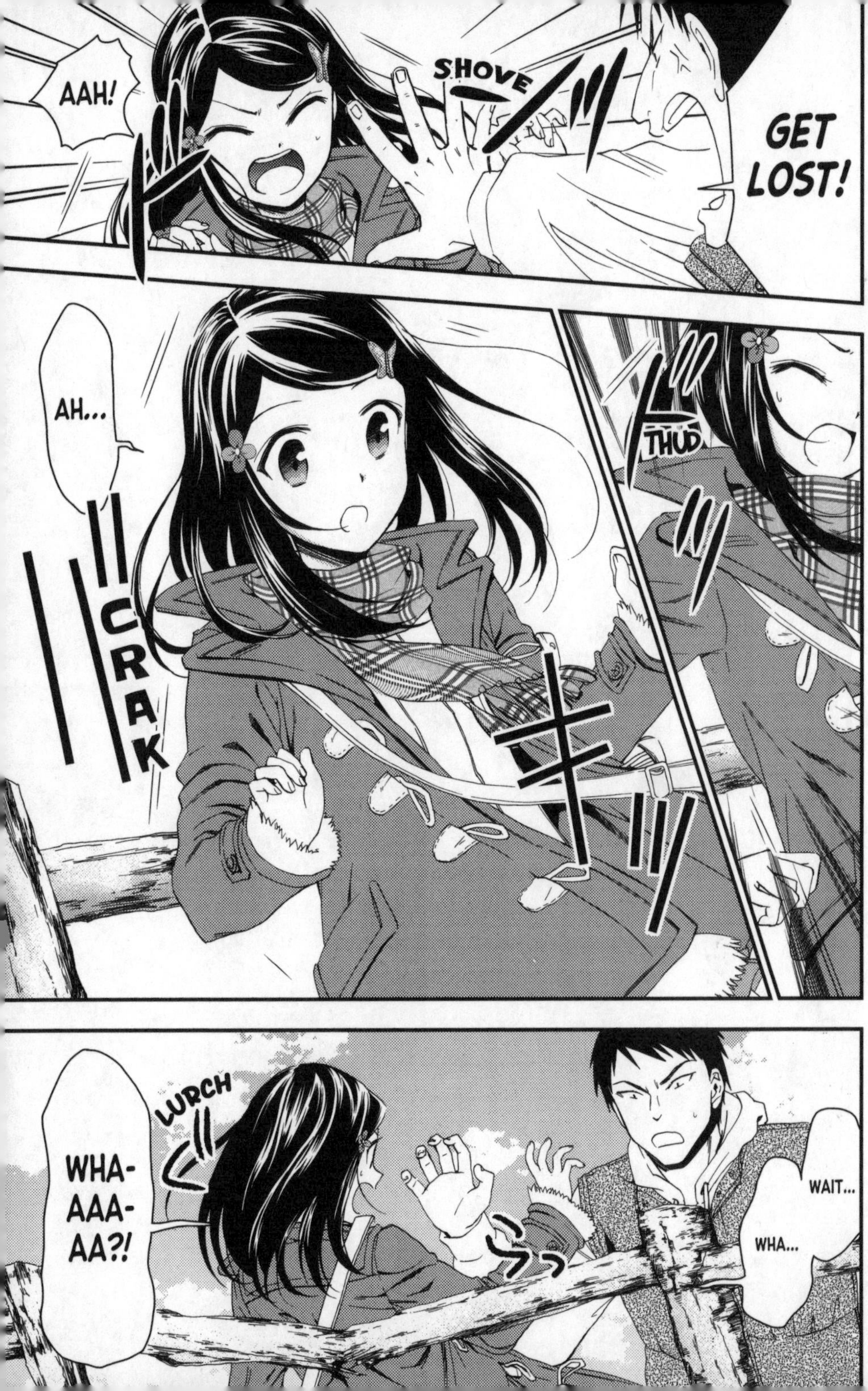
GET LOST!
SHOVE
AAH!
THUD
AH...
CRAK
WAIT...
WHA...
LURCH
WHA-AAA-AA?!

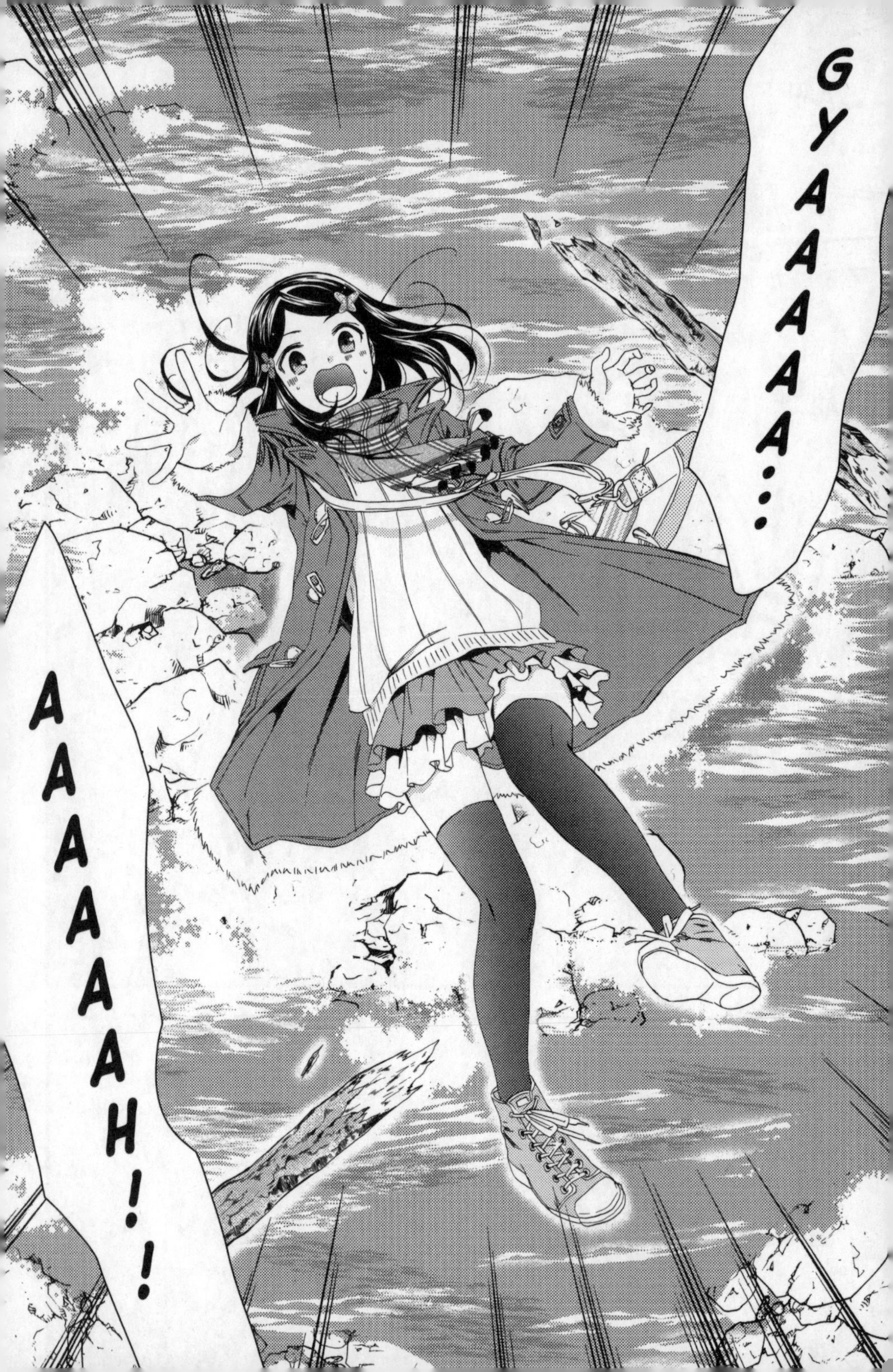
GYAAAAA...
AAAAAAH!!

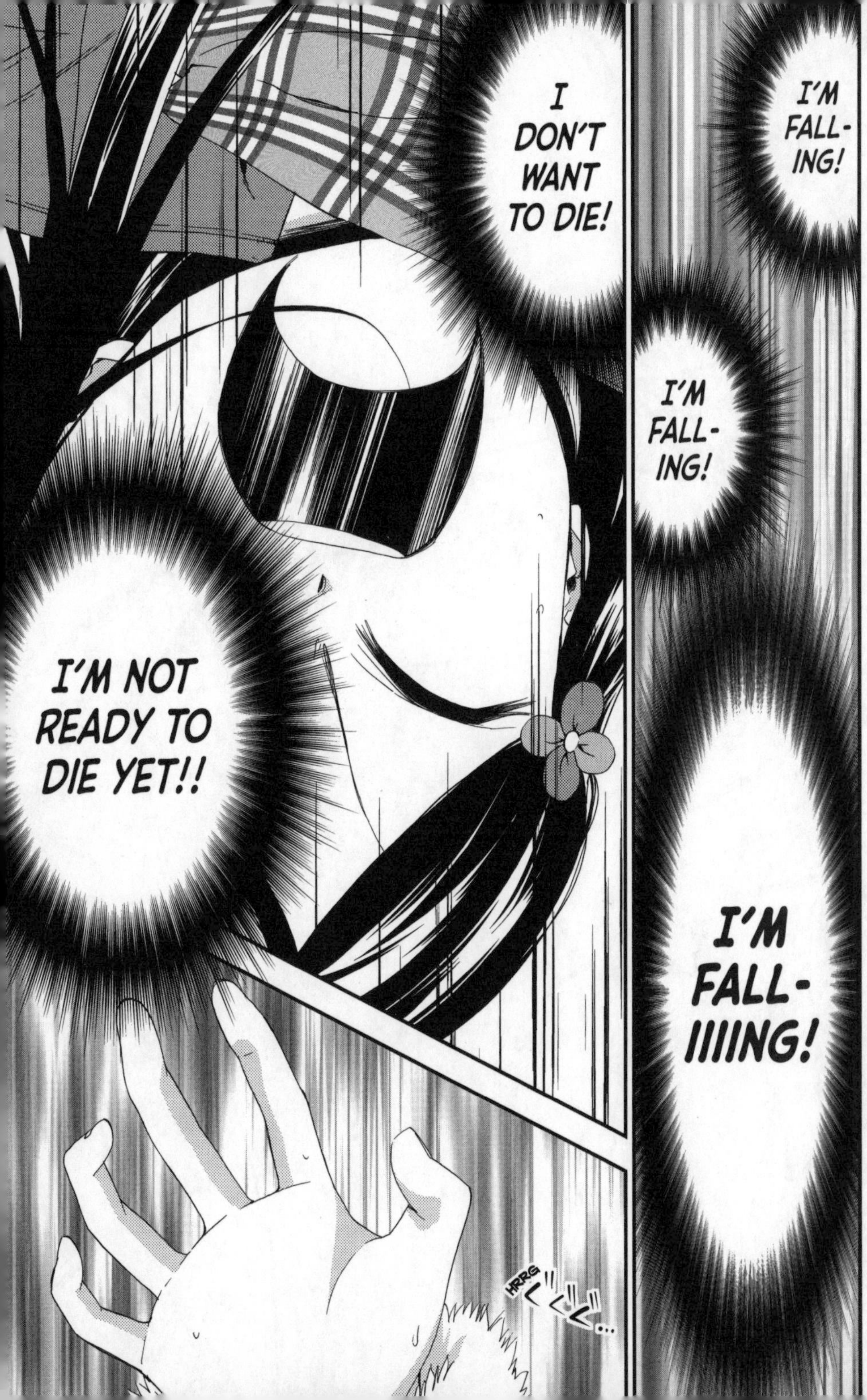
I'M FALLING!
I'M FALLING!
I'M FALLIIIING!
I DON'T WANT TO DIE!
I'M NOT READY TO DIE YET!!
HRRG

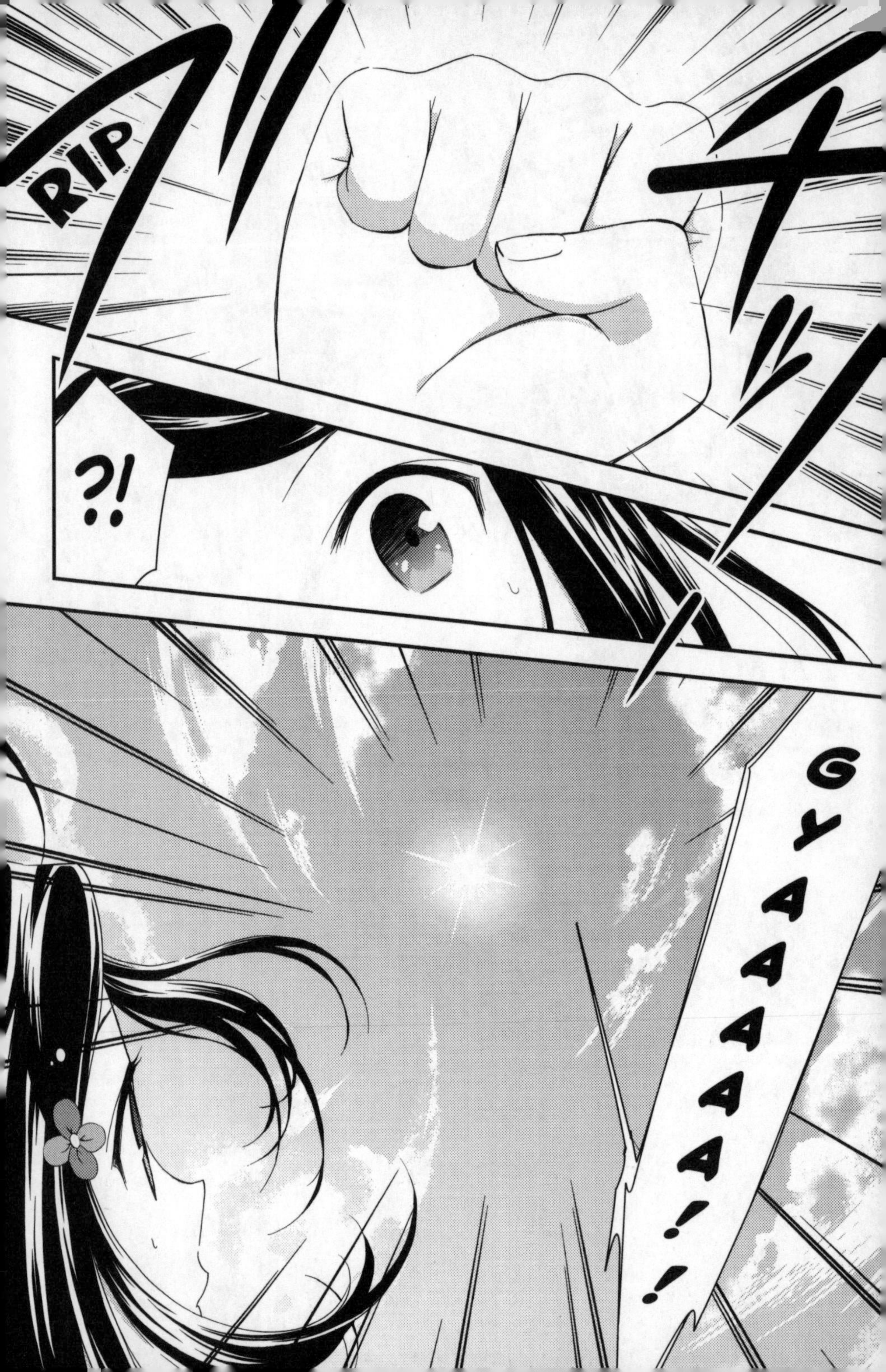
RIP
?!
GYAAAAAA!!

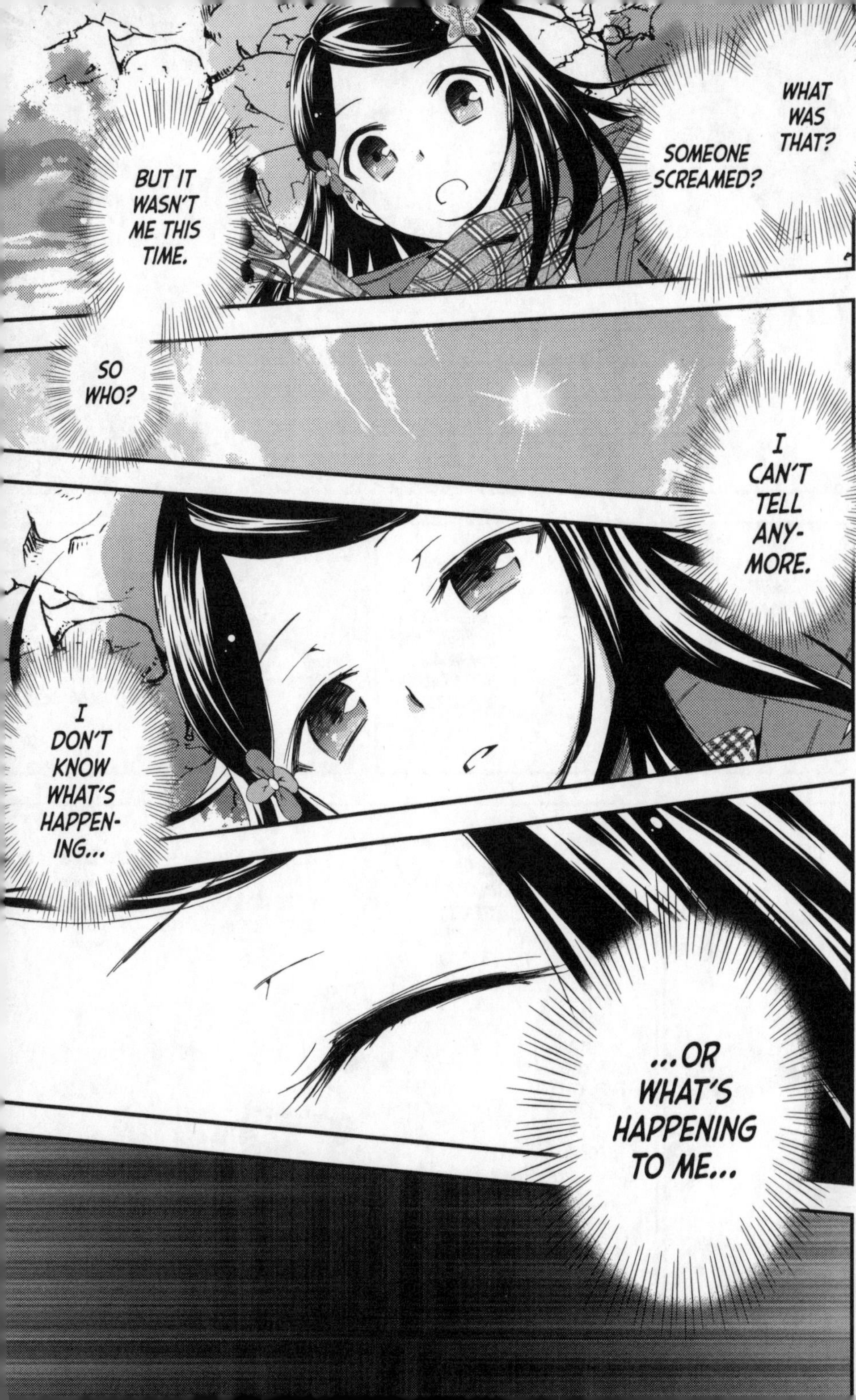
WHAT WAS THAT?
SOMEONE SCREAMED?
BUT IT WASN'T ME THIS TIME.
SO WHO?
I CAN'T TELL ANY-MORE.
I DON'T KNOW WHAT'S HAPPEN-ING...
...OR WHAT'S HAPPENING TO ME...

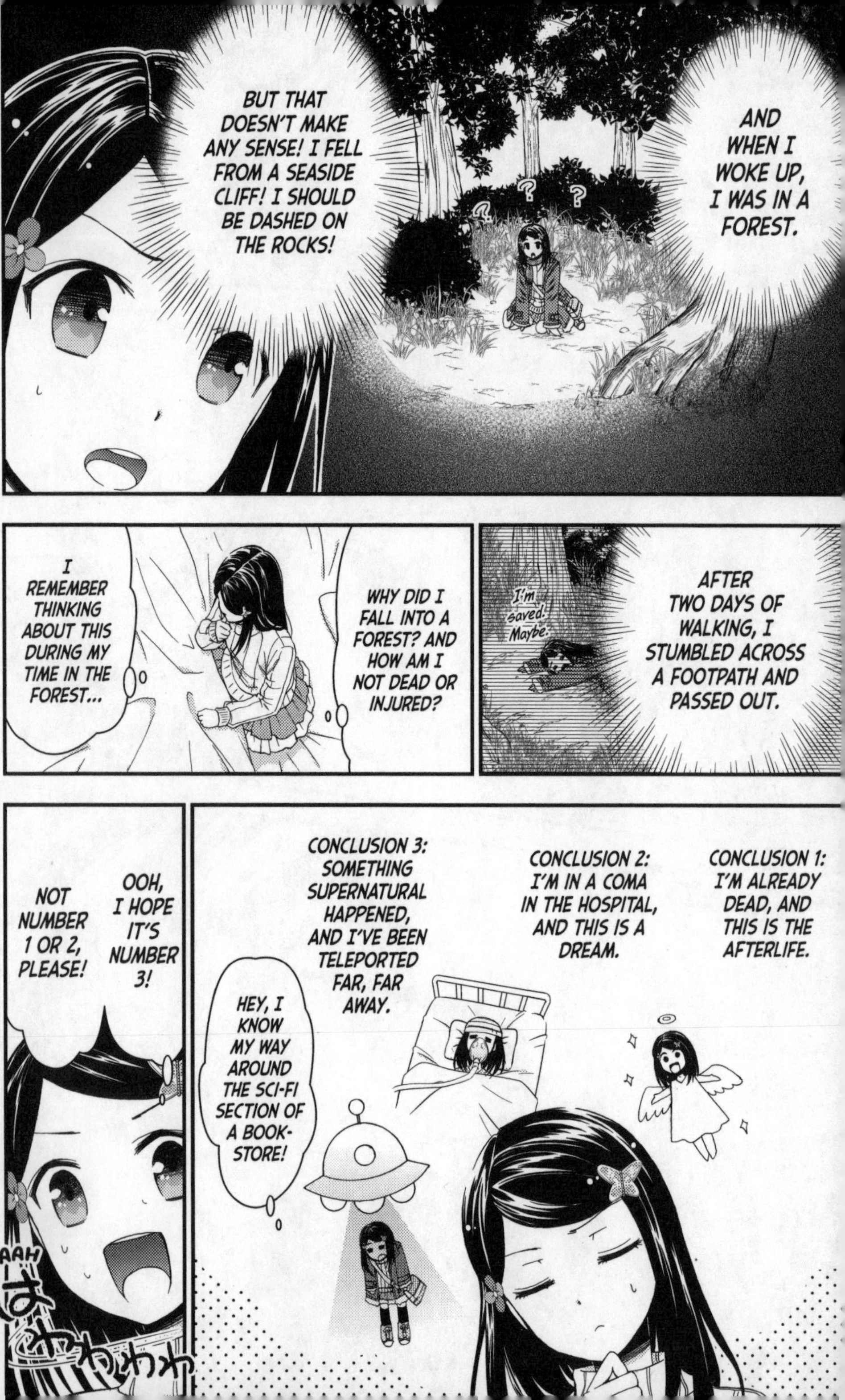
AND WHEN I WOKE UP, I WAS IN A FOREST.
BUT THAT DOESN'T MAKE ANY SENSE! I FELL FROM A SEASIDE CLIFF! I SHOULD BE DASHED ON THE ROCKS!
AFTER TWO DAYS OF WALKING, I STUMBLED ACROSS A FOOTPATH AND PASSED OUT.
I'm saved. Maybe.
WHY DID I FALL INTO A FOREST? AND HOW AM I NOT DEAD OR INJURED?
I REMEMBER THINKING ABOUT THIS DURING MY TIME IN THE FOREST...
CONCLUSION 1: I'M ALREADY DEAD, AND THIS IS THE AFTERLIFE.
CONCLUSION 2: I'M IN A COMA IN THE HOSPITAL, AND THIS IS A DREAM.
CONCLUSION 3: SOMETHING SUPERNATURAL HAPPENED, AND I'VE BEEN TELEPORTED FAR, FAR AWAY.
HEY, I KNOW MY WAY AROUND THE SCI-FI SECTION OF A BOOK-STORE!
OOH, I HOPE IT'S NUMBER 3!
NOT NUMBER 1 OR 2, PLEASE!
GAAAH

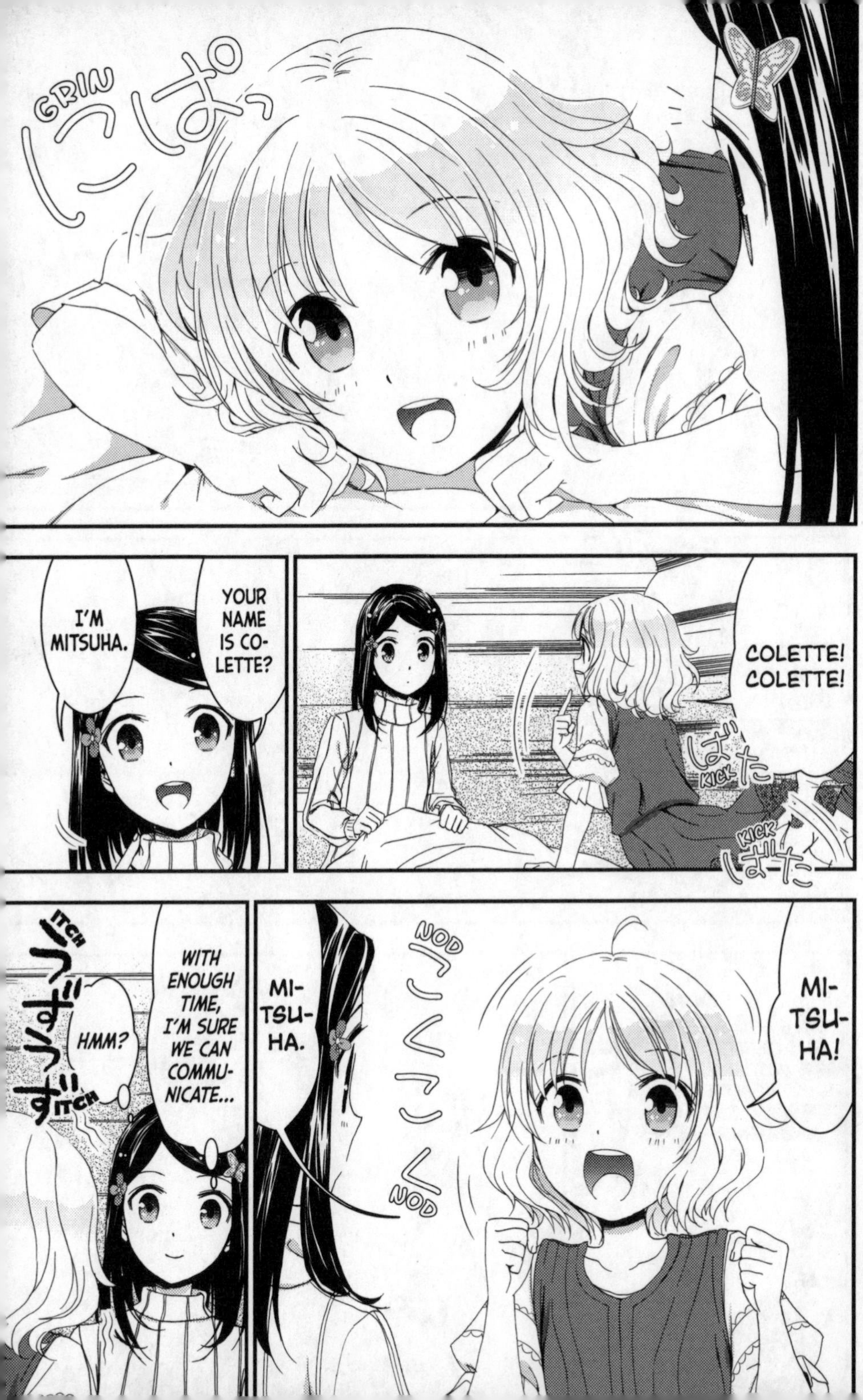
GRIN
にぱっ
COLETTE! COLETTE!
KICK
ばた
KICK
ばた
YOUR NAME IS CO-LETTE?
I'M MITSUHA.
MI-TSU-HA!
NOD
こくこく
NOD
MI-TSU-HA.
WITH ENOUGH TIME, I'M SURE WE CAN COMMU-NICATE...
HMM?
ITCH
ITCH

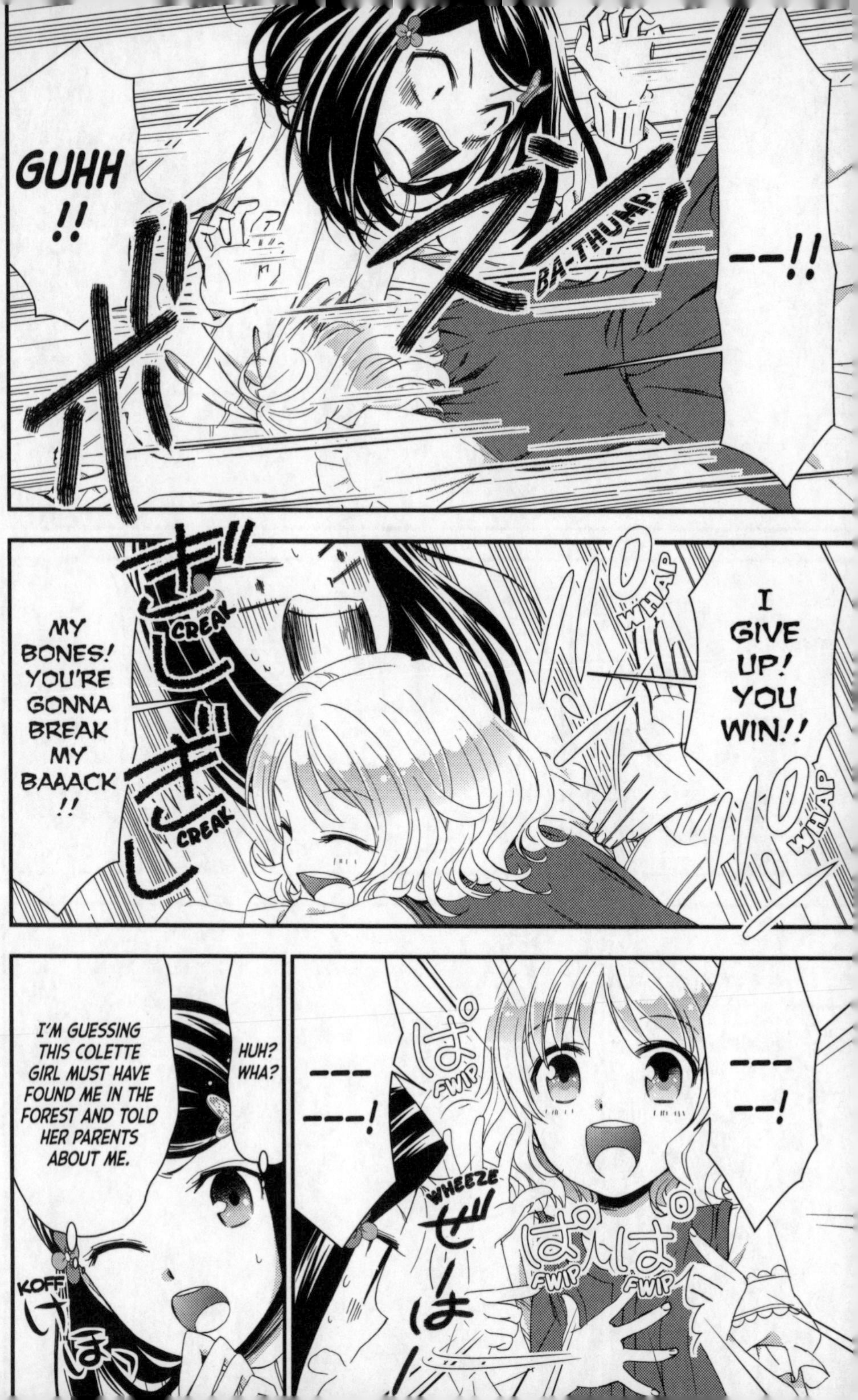
--!!
BA-THUMP
GUHH !!
I GIVE UP! YOU WIN!!
WHAP
WHAP
CREAK
CREAK
MY BONES! YOU'RE GONNA BREAK MY BAAACK!!
--- --!
FWIP
--- ---!
WHEEZE
FWIP
FWIP
HUH? WHA?
I'M GUESSING THIS COLETTE GIRL MUST HAVE FOUND ME IN THE FOREST AND TOLD HER PARENTS ABOUT ME.
KOFF

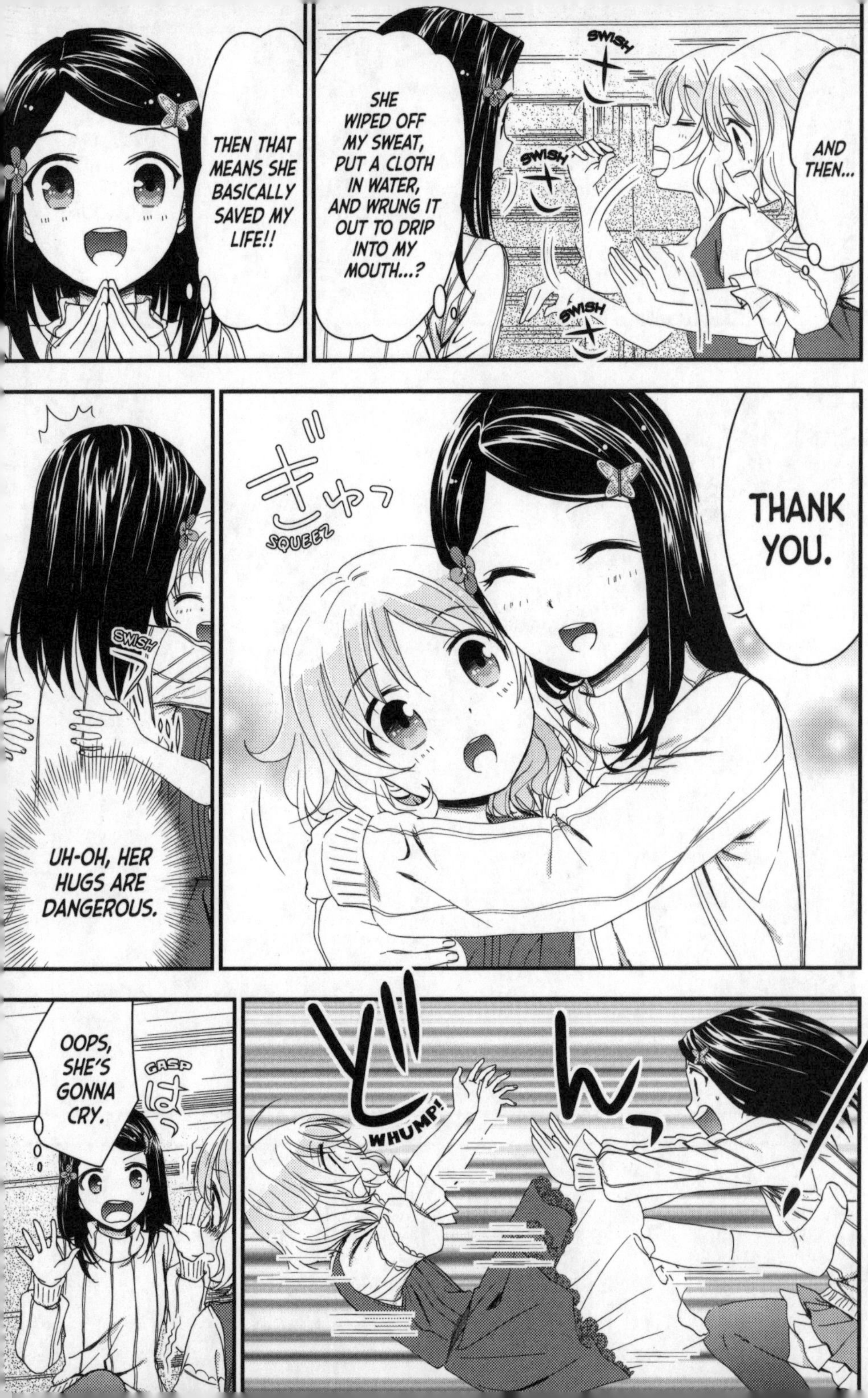
AND THEN...
SWISH
SWISH
SWISH
SHE WIPED OFF MY SWEAT, PUT A CLOTH IN WATER, AND WRUNG IT OUT TO DRIP INTO MY MOUTH...?
THEN THAT MEANS SHE BASICALLY SAVED MY LIFE!!
THANK YOU.
ぎゅっ
SQUEEZ
SWISH
UH-OH, HER HUGS ARE DANGEROUS.
どんっ
WHUMP!
OOPS, SHE'S GONNA CRY.
は、
GASP

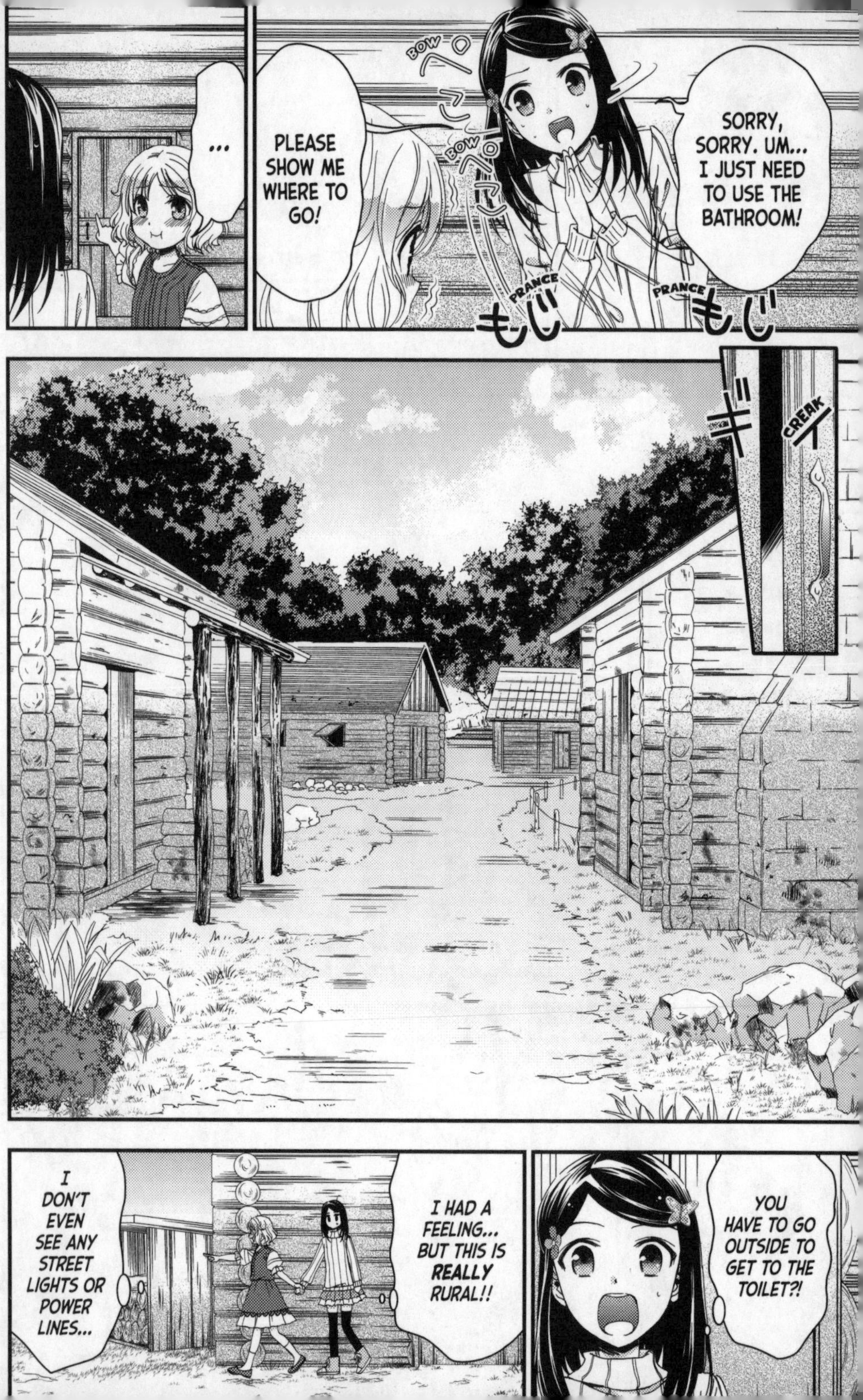
SORRY, SORRY. UM... I JUST NEED TO USE THE BATHROOM!
BOW
BOW
PRANCE
PRANCE
PLEASE SHOW ME WHERE TO GO!
...
CREAK
YOU HAVE TO GO OUTSIDE TO GET TO THE TOILET?!
I HAD A FEELING... BUT THIS IS **REALLY** RURAL!!
I DON'T EVEN SEE ANY STREET LIGHTS OR POWER LINES...

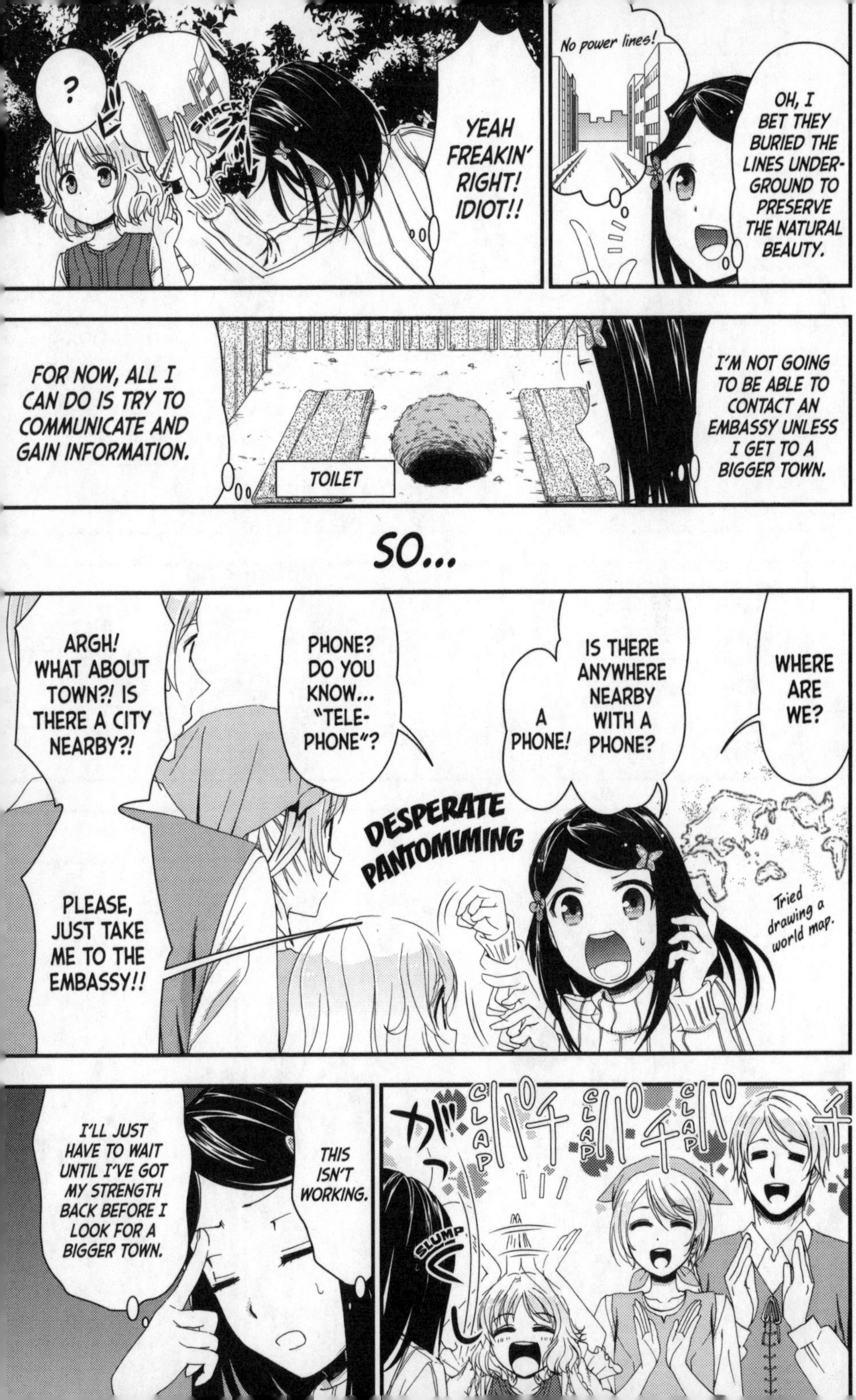
No power lines!
OH, I BET THEY BURIED THE LINES UNDERGROUND TO PRESERVE THE NATURAL BEAUTY.
YEAH FREAKIN' RIGHT! IDIOT!!
SMACK
?
I'M NOT GOING TO BE ABLE TO CONTACT AN EMBASSY UNLESS I GET TO A BIGGER TOWN.
TOILET
FOR NOW, ALL I CAN DO IS TRY TO COMMUNICATE AND GAIN INFORMATION.
SO...
WHERE ARE WE?
IS THERE ANYWHERE NEARBY WITH A PHONE?
A PHONE!
PHONE? DO YOU KNOW... "TELE-PHONE"?
ARGH! WHAT ABOUT TOWN?! IS THERE A CITY NEARBY?!
DESPERATE PANTOMIMING
Tried drawing a world map.
PLEASE, JUST TAKE ME TO THE EMBASSY!!
CLAP
CLAP
CLAP
SLUMP
THIS ISN'T WORKING.
I'LL JUST HAVE TO WAIT UNTIL I'VE GOT MY STRENGTH BACK BEFORE I LOOK FOR A BIGGER TOWN.

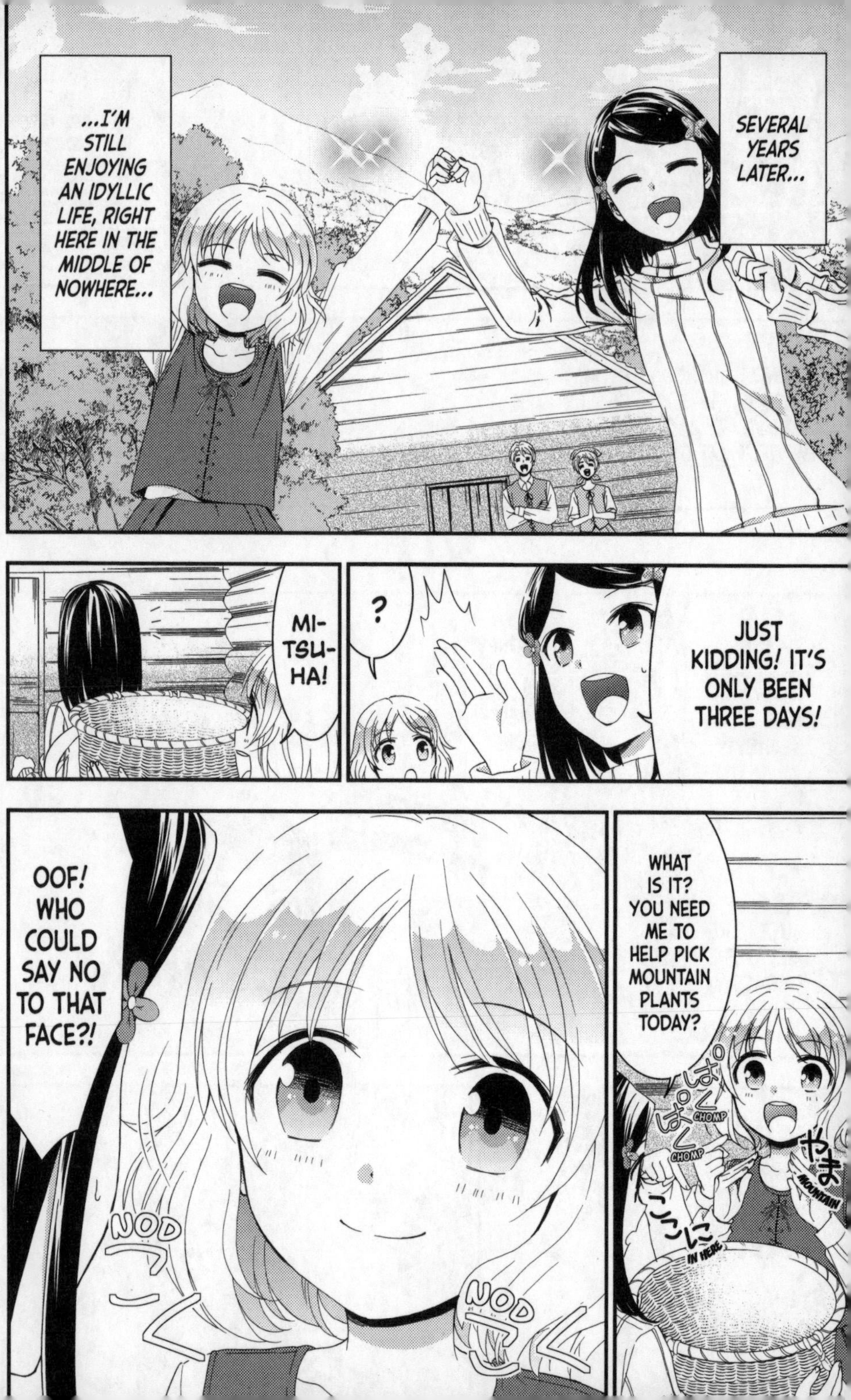
SEVERAL YEARS LATER...
...I'M STILL ENJOYING AN IDYLLIC LIFE, RIGHT HERE IN THE MIDDLE OF NOWHERE...
JUST KIDDING! IT'S ONLY BEEN THREE DAYS!
?
MI-TSU-HA!
WHAT IS IT? YOU NEED ME TO HELP PICK MOUNTAIN PLANTS TODAY?
ぱく ぱく
CHOMP CHOMP
やま
MOUNTAIN
ここに
IN HERE
OOF! WHO COULD SAY NO TO THAT FACE?!
NOD
NOD

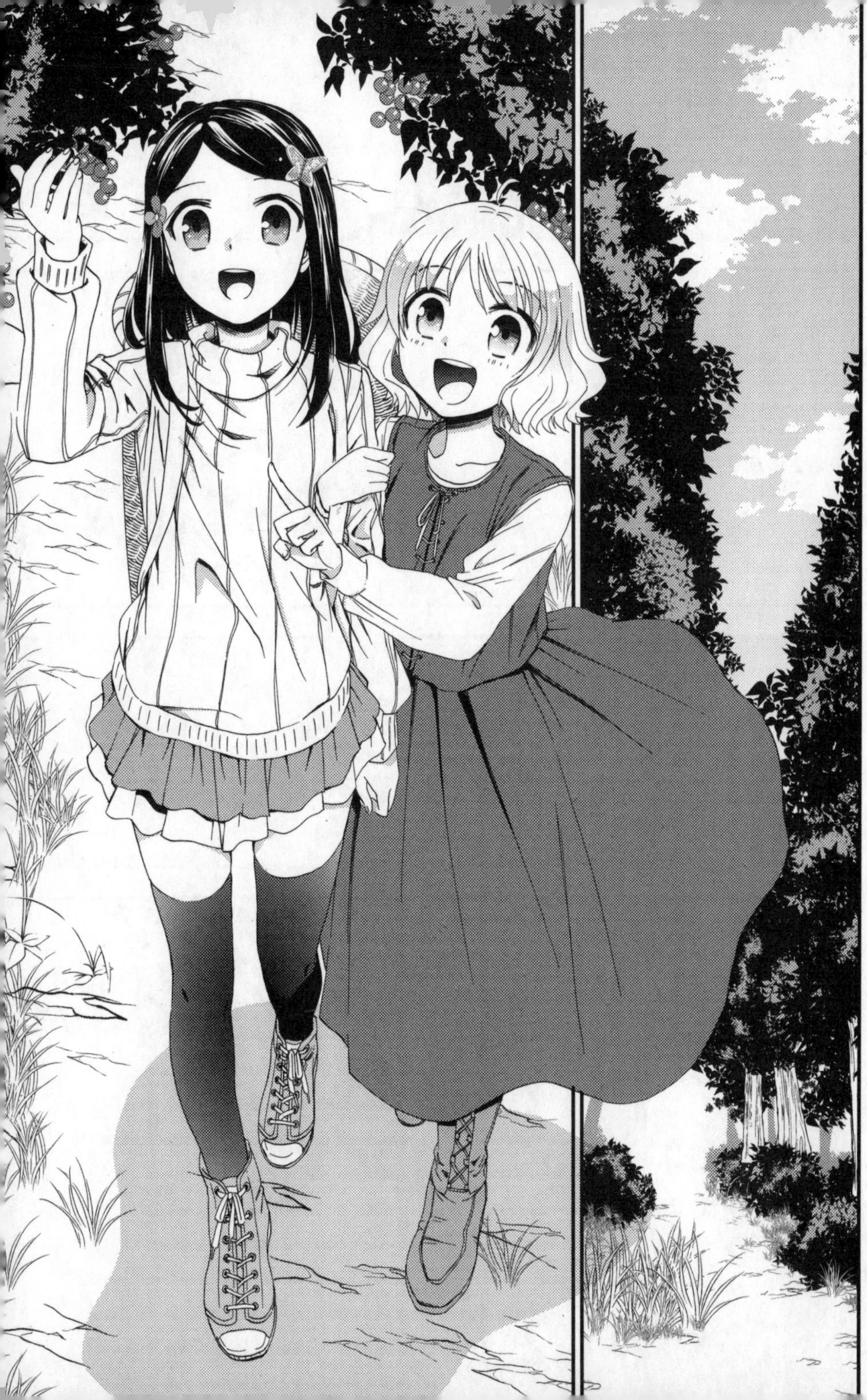

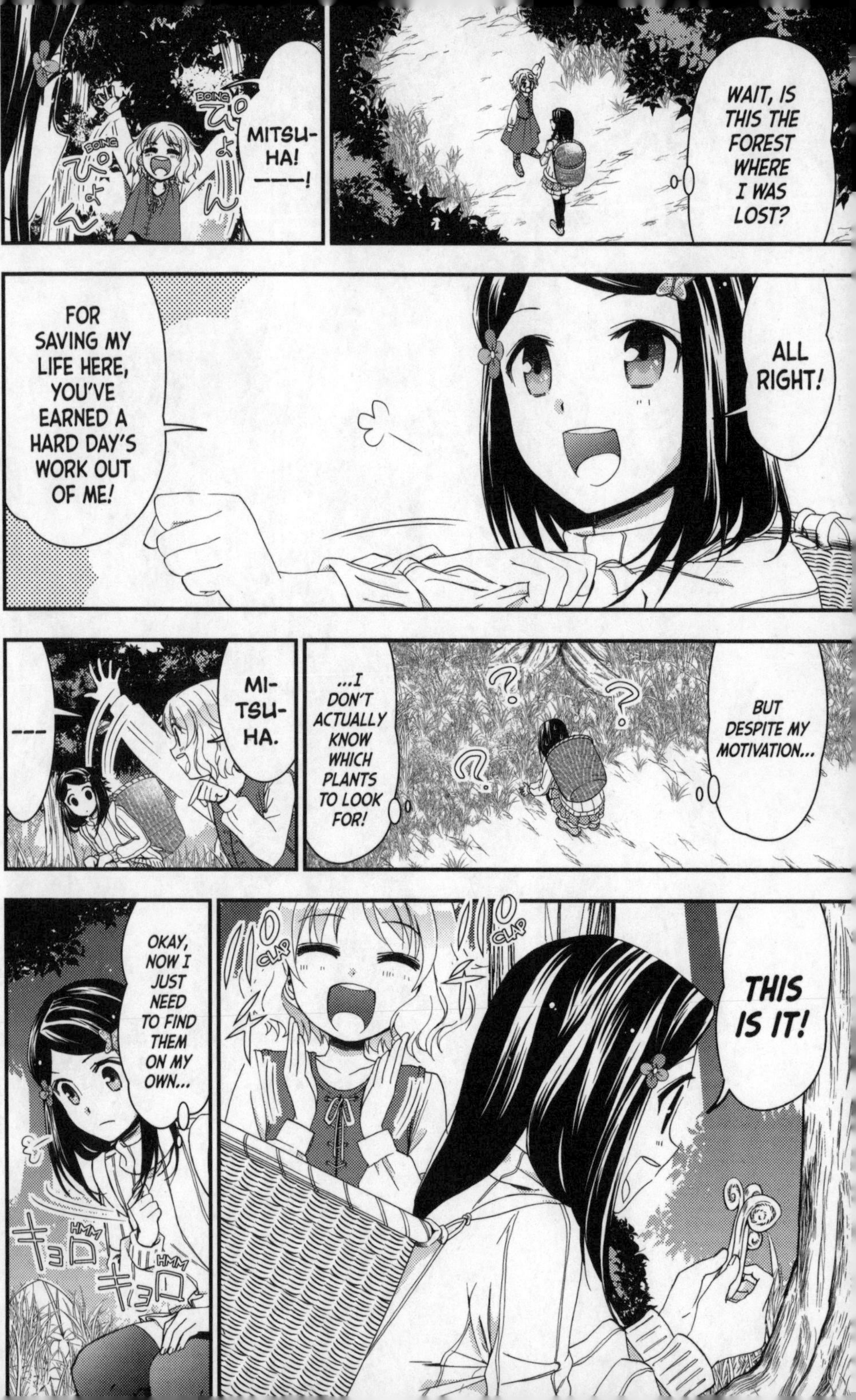
WAIT, IS THIS THE FOREST WHERE I WAS LOST?
BOING BOING
ぴょんぴょん
MITSU-HA! ———!
ALL RIGHT!
FOR SAVING MY LIFE HERE, YOU'VE EARNED A HARD DAY'S WORK OUT OF ME!
BUT DESPITE MY MOTIVATION...
...I DON'T ACTUALLY KNOW WHICH PLANTS TO LOOK FOR!
MI-TSU-HA.
———
THIS IS IT!
CLAP CLAP
OKAY, NOW I JUST NEED TO FIND THEM ON MY OWN...
HMM HMM
キョロキョロ

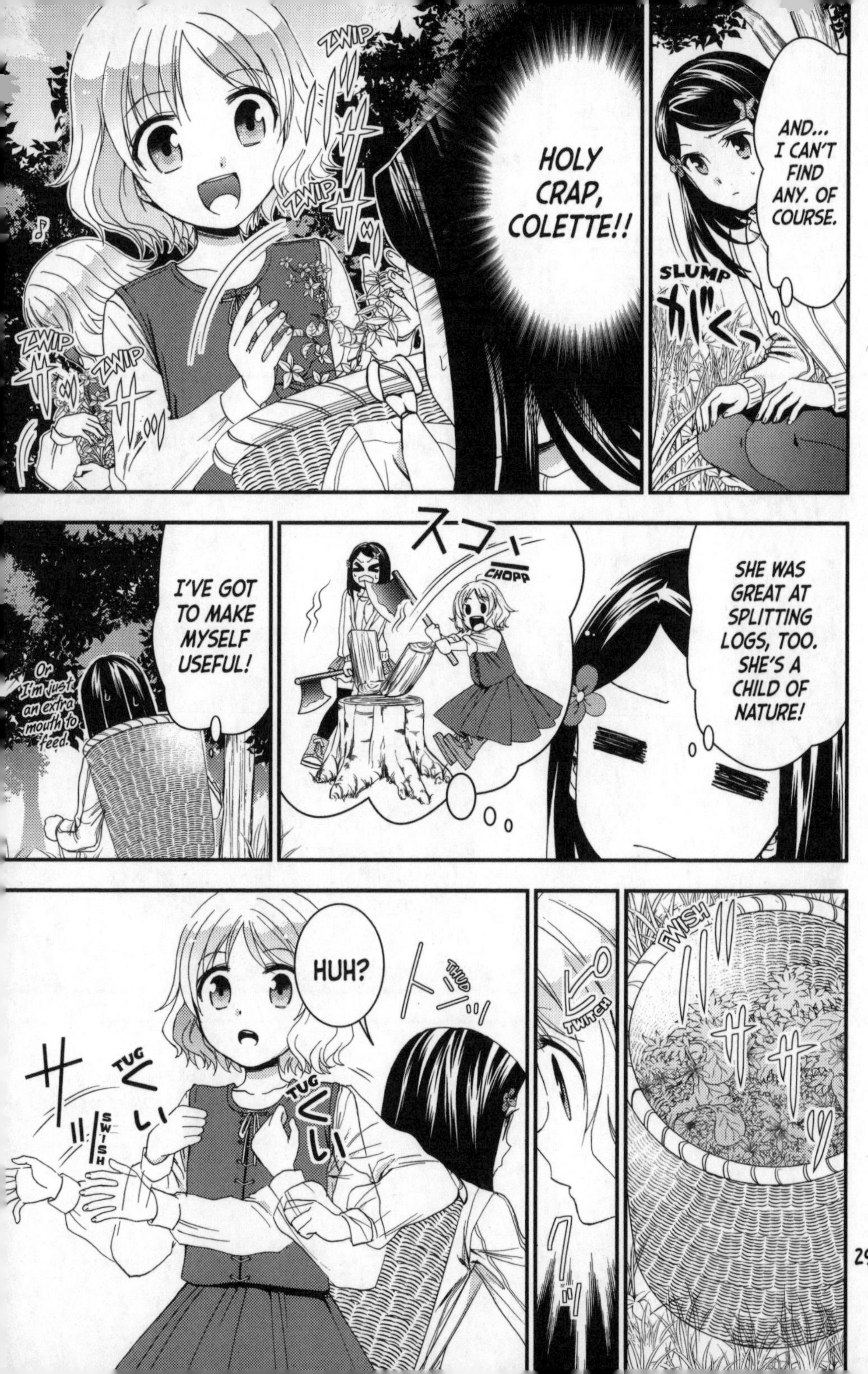

AND... I CAN'T FIND ANY. OF COURSE.
SLUMP
HOLY CRAP, COLETTE!!
ZWIP
ZWIP
ZWIP
ZWIP
SHE WAS GREAT AT SPLITTING LOGS, TOO. SHE'S A CHILD OF NATURE!
CHOPP
I'VE GOT TO MAKE MYSELF USEFUL!
Or I'm just an extra mouth to feed.
FWISH
TWITCH
HUH?
THUD
TUG
TUG
SWISH

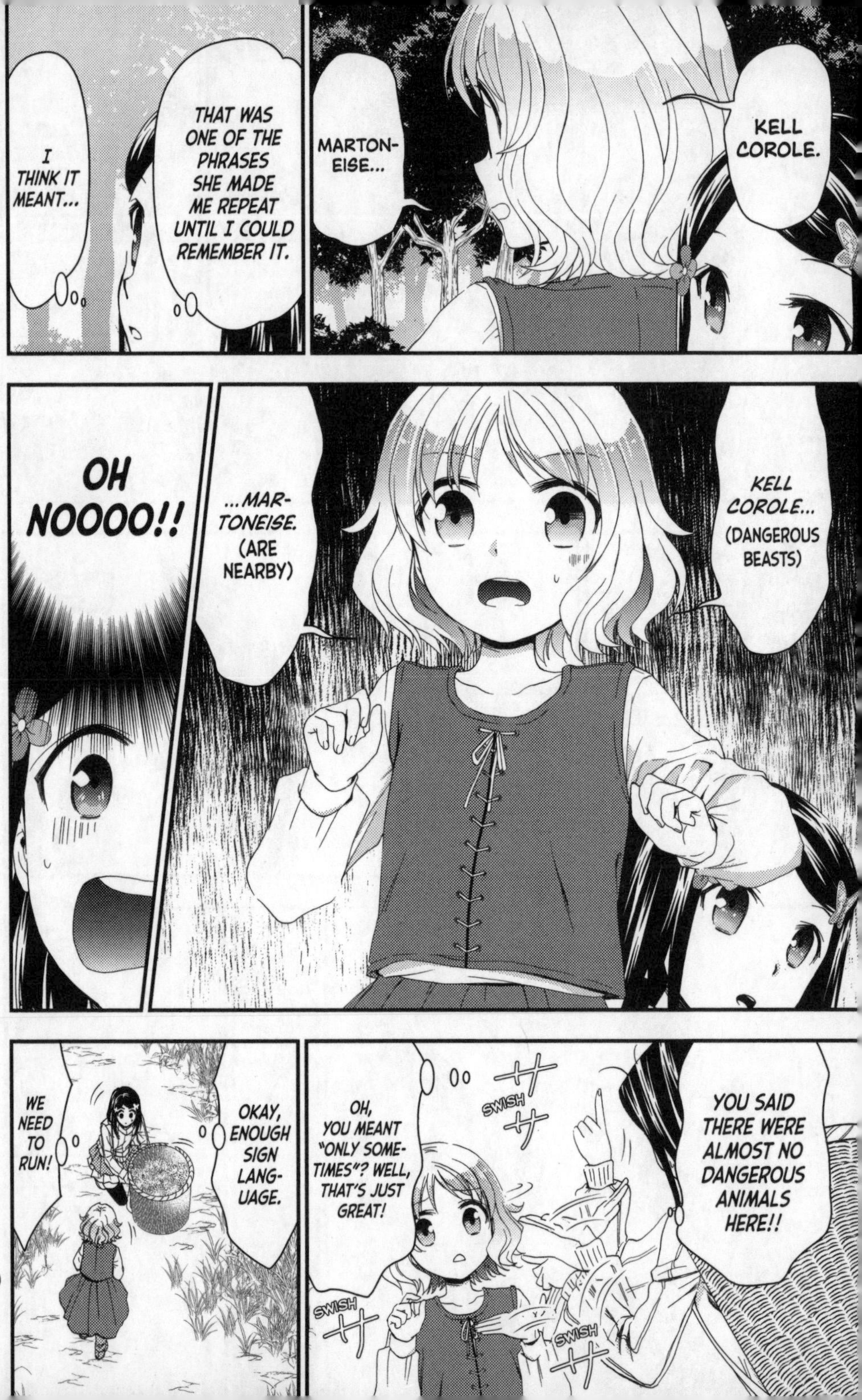
KELL COROLE.
MARTON-EISE...
THAT WAS ONE OF THE PHRASES SHE MADE ME REPEAT UNTIL I COULD REMEMBER IT.
I THINK IT MEANT...
KELL COROLE... (DANGEROUS BEASTS)
...MAR-TONEISE. (ARE NEARBY)
OH NOOOO!!
YOU SAID THERE WERE ALMOST NO DANGEROUS ANIMALS HERE!!
SWISH
OH, YOU MEANT "ONLY SOME-TIMES"? WELL, THAT'S JUST GREAT!
SWISH
SWISH
OKAY, ENOUGH SIGN LANG-UAGE.
WE NEED TO RUN!

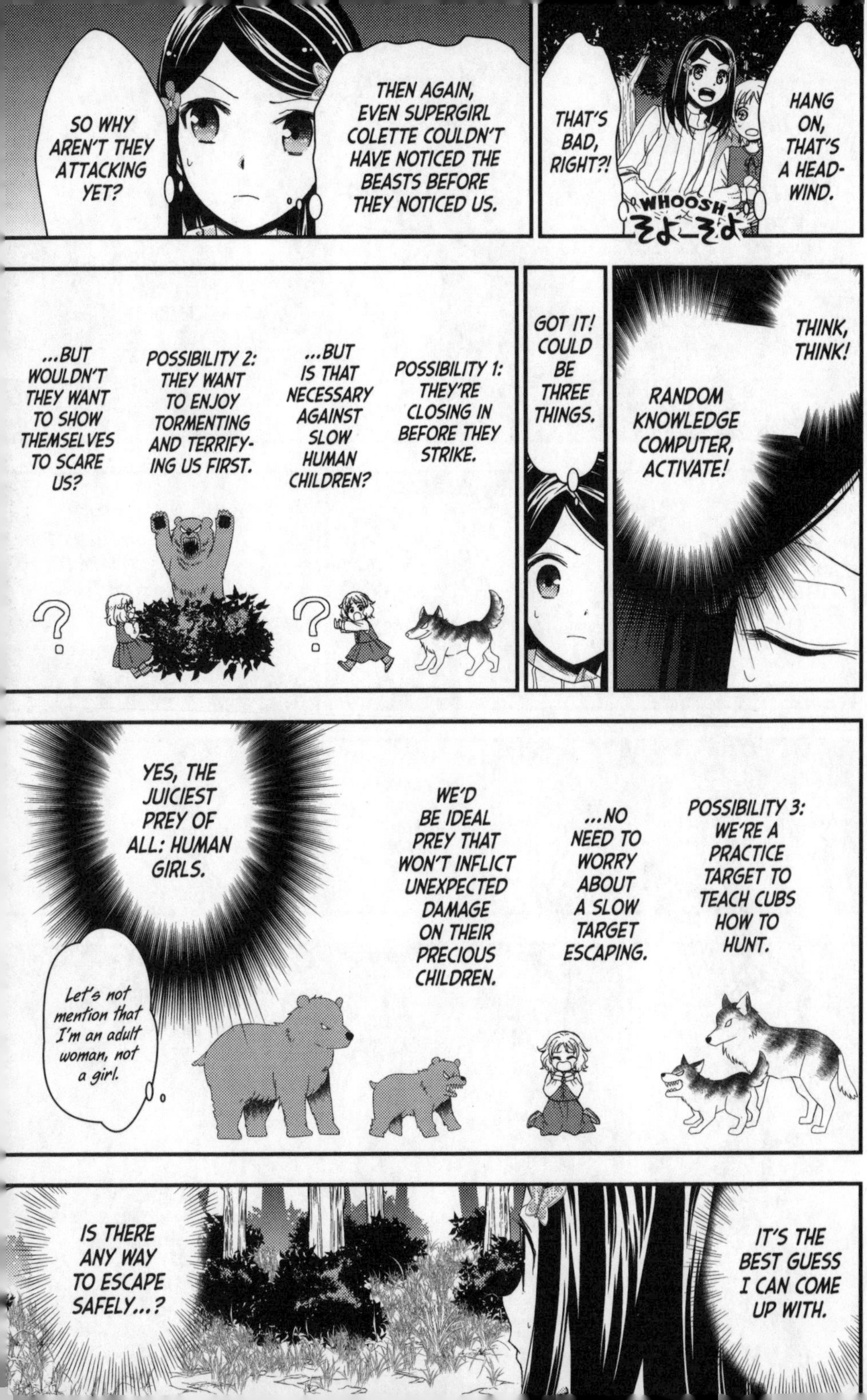
HANG ON, THAT'S A HEAD-WIND.
THAT'S BAD, RIGHT?!
WHOOSH
そよ そよ
THEN AGAIN, EVEN SUPERGIRL COLETTE COULDN'T HAVE NOTICED THE BEASTS BEFORE THEY NOTICED US.
SO WHY AREN'T THEY ATTACKING YET?
THINK, THINK!
RANDOM KNOWLEDGE COMPUTER, ACTIVATE!
GOT IT! COULD BE THREE THINGS.
POSSIBILITY 1: THEY'RE CLOSING IN BEFORE THEY STRIKE.
...BUT IS THAT NECESSARY AGAINST SLOW HUMAN CHILDREN?
POSSIBILITY 2: THEY WANT TO ENJOY TORMENTING AND TERRIFY-ING US FIRST.
...BUT WOULDN'T THEY WANT TO SHOW THEMSELVES TO SCARE US?
POSSIBILITY 3: WE'RE A PRACTICE TARGET TO TEACH CUBS HOW TO HUNT.
...NO NEED TO WORRY ABOUT A SLOW TARGET ESCAPING.
WE'D BE IDEAL PREY THAT WON'T INFLICT UNEXPECTED DAMAGE ON THEIR PRECIOUS CHILDREN.
YES, THE JUICIEST PREY OF ALL: HUMAN GIRLS.
Let's not mention that I'm an adult woman, not a girl.
IT'S THE BEST GUESS I CAN COME UP WITH.
IS THERE ANY WAY TO ESCAPE SAFELY...?

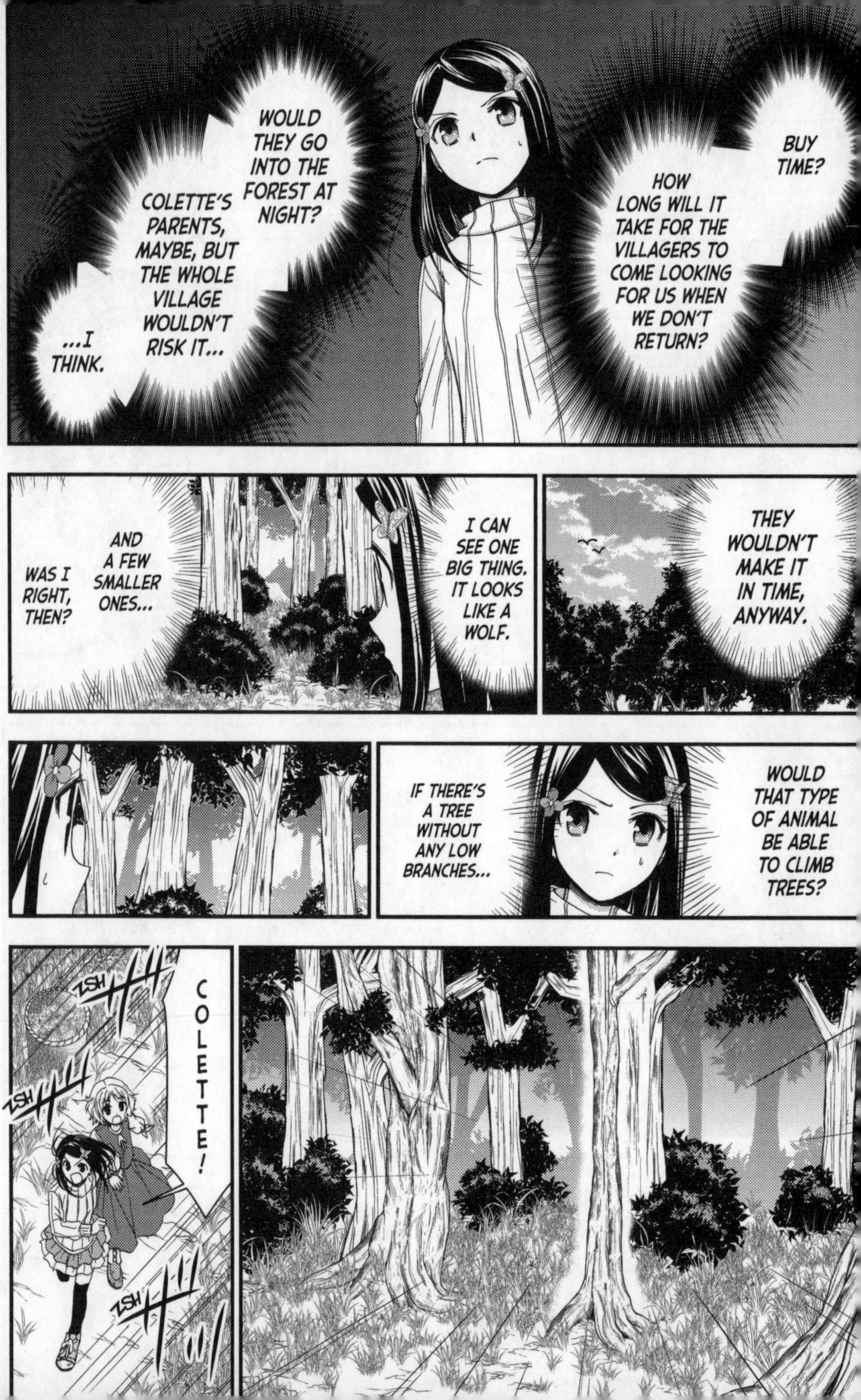
BUY TIME?
HOW LONG WILL IT TAKE FOR THE VILLAGERS TO COME LOOKING FOR US WHEN WE DON'T RETURN?
WOULD THEY GO INTO THE FOREST AT NIGHT?
COLETTE'S PARENTS, MAYBE, BUT THE WHOLE VILLAGE WOULDN'T RISK IT...
...I THINK.
THEY WOULDN'T MAKE IT IN TIME, ANYWAY.
I CAN SEE ONE BIG THING. IT LOOKS LIKE A WOLF.
AND A FEW SMALLER ONES...
WAS I RIGHT, THEN?
WOULD THAT TYPE OF ANIMAL BE ABLE TO CLIMB TREES?
IF THERE'S A TREE WITHOUT ANY LOW BRANCHES...
COLETTE!
ZSH
ZSH
ZSH

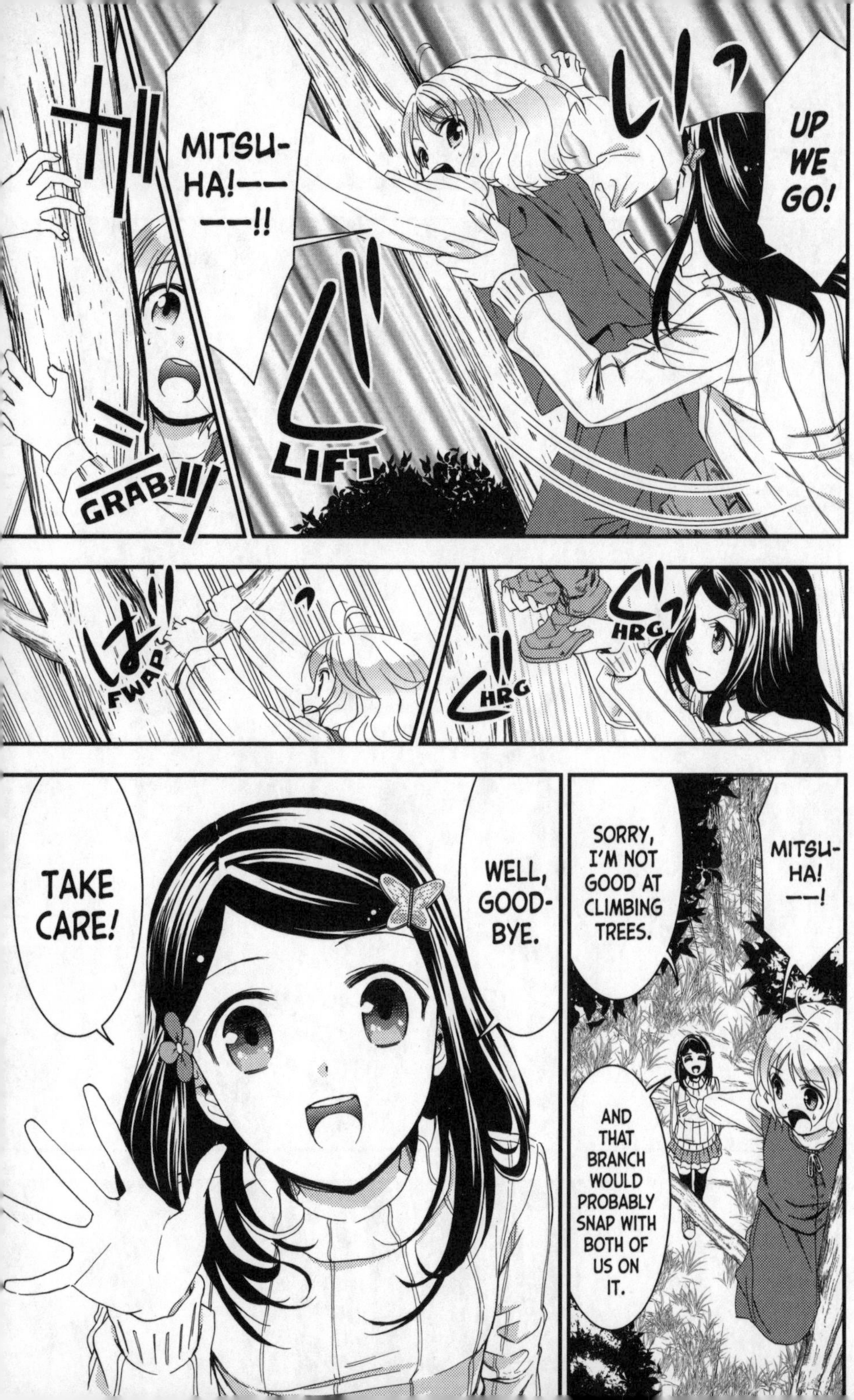
UP WE GO!
LIFT
MITSU-HA!——
——!!
GRAB
HRG
HRG
FWAP
MITSU-HA! ——!
SORRY, I'M NOT GOOD AT CLIMBING TREES.
AND THAT BRANCH WOULD PROBABLY SNAP WITH BOTH OF US ON IT.
WELL, GOOD-BYE.
TAKE CARE!

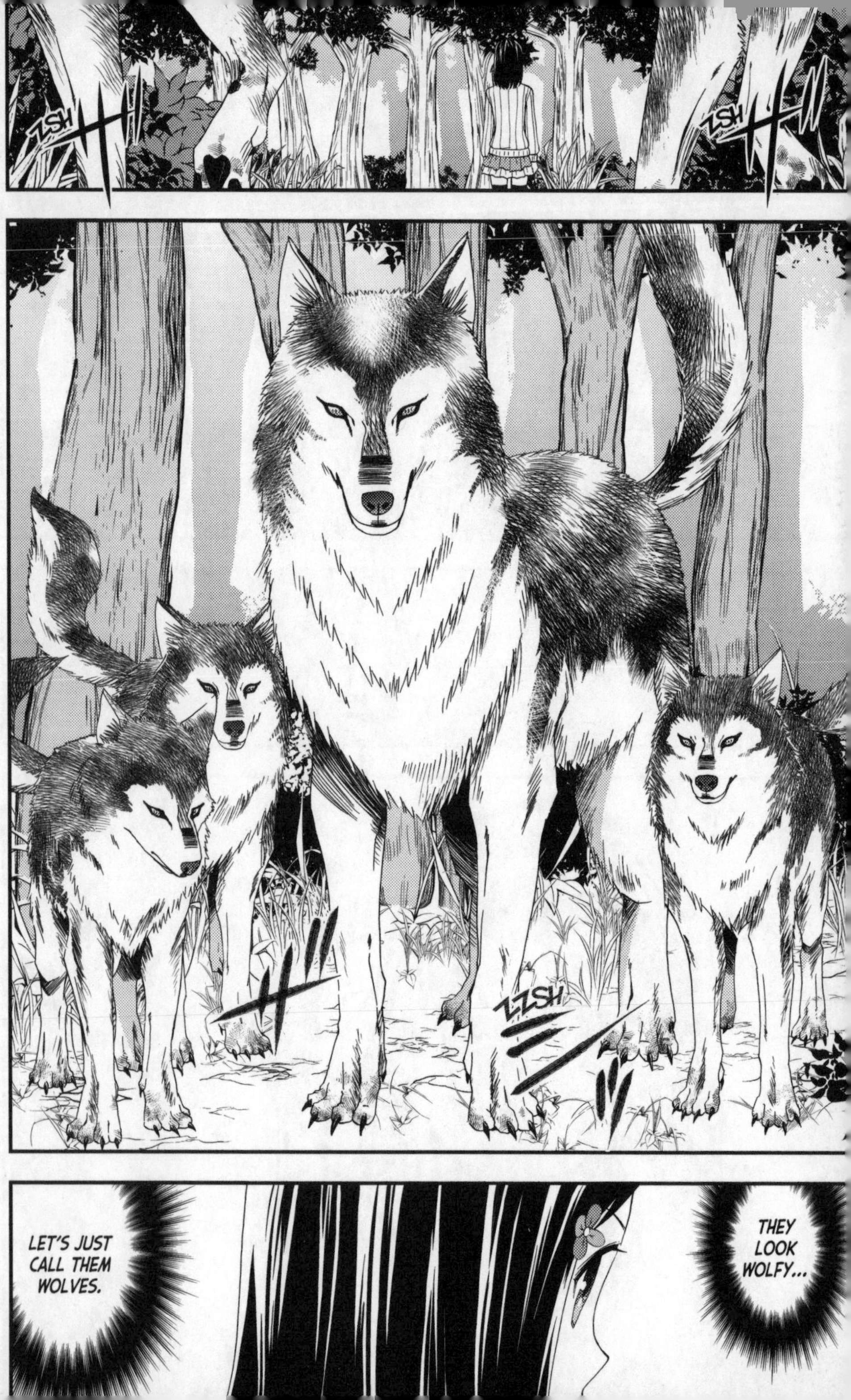
ZSH
ZSH
ZZSH
THEY LOOK WOLFY...
LET'S JUST CALL THEM WOLVES.

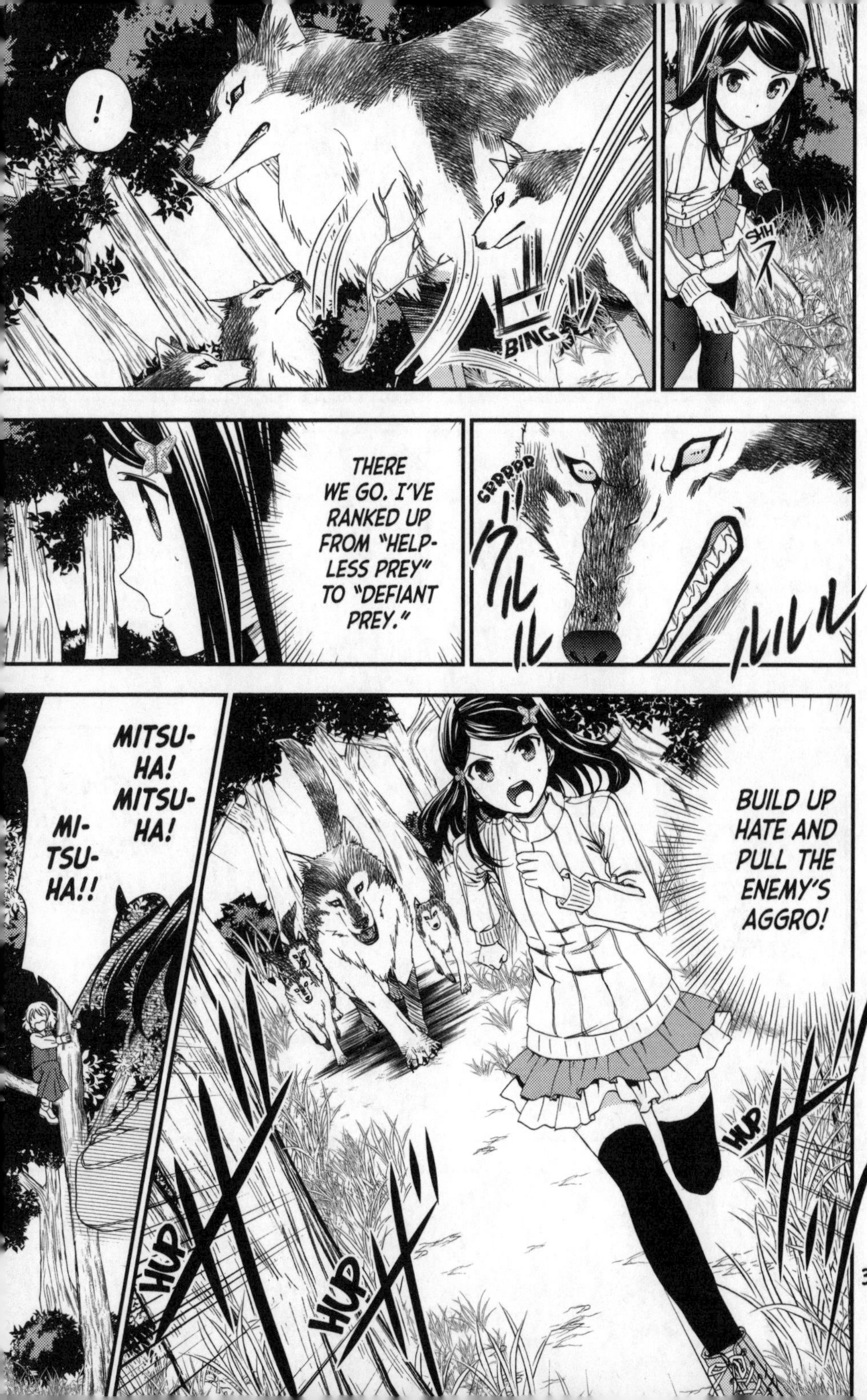
SHH
!
BING
GRRRRR
THERE WE GO. I'VE RANKED UP FROM "HELPLESS PREY" TO "DEFIANT PREY."
BUILD UP HATE AND PULL THE ENEMY'S AGGRO!
MITSU-HA! MITSU-HA!
MI-TSU-HA!!
HUP
HUP
HUP

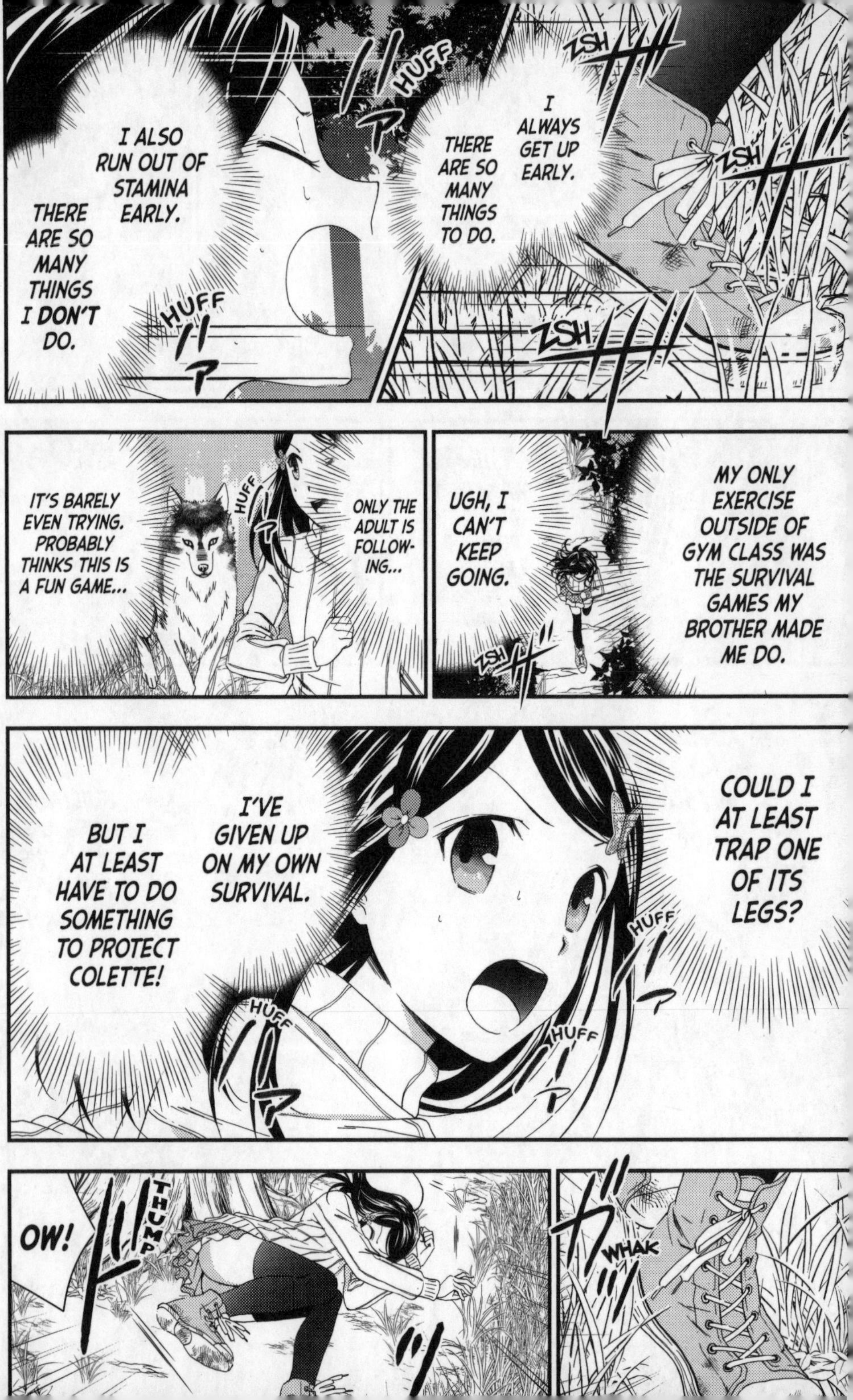
ZSH
I ALWAYS GET UP EARLY.
ZSH
HUFF
THERE ARE SO MANY THINGS TO DO.
I ALSO RUN OUT OF STAMINA EARLY.
THERE ARE SO MANY THINGS I DON'T DO.
HUFF
ZSH
MY ONLY EXERCISE OUTSIDE OF GYM CLASS WAS THE SURVIVAL GAMES MY BROTHER MADE ME DO.
UGH, I CAN'T KEEP GOING.
ZSH
ONLY THE ADULT IS FOLLOW-ING...
HUFF
IT'S BARELY EVEN TRYING. PROBABLY THINKS THIS IS A FUN GAME...
COULD I AT LEAST TRAP ONE OF ITS LEGS?
HUFF
I'VE GIVEN UP ON MY OWN SURVIVAL.
BUT I AT LEAST HAVE TO DO SOMETHING TO PROTECT COLETTE!
HUFF
HUFF
WHAK
THUMP
OW!

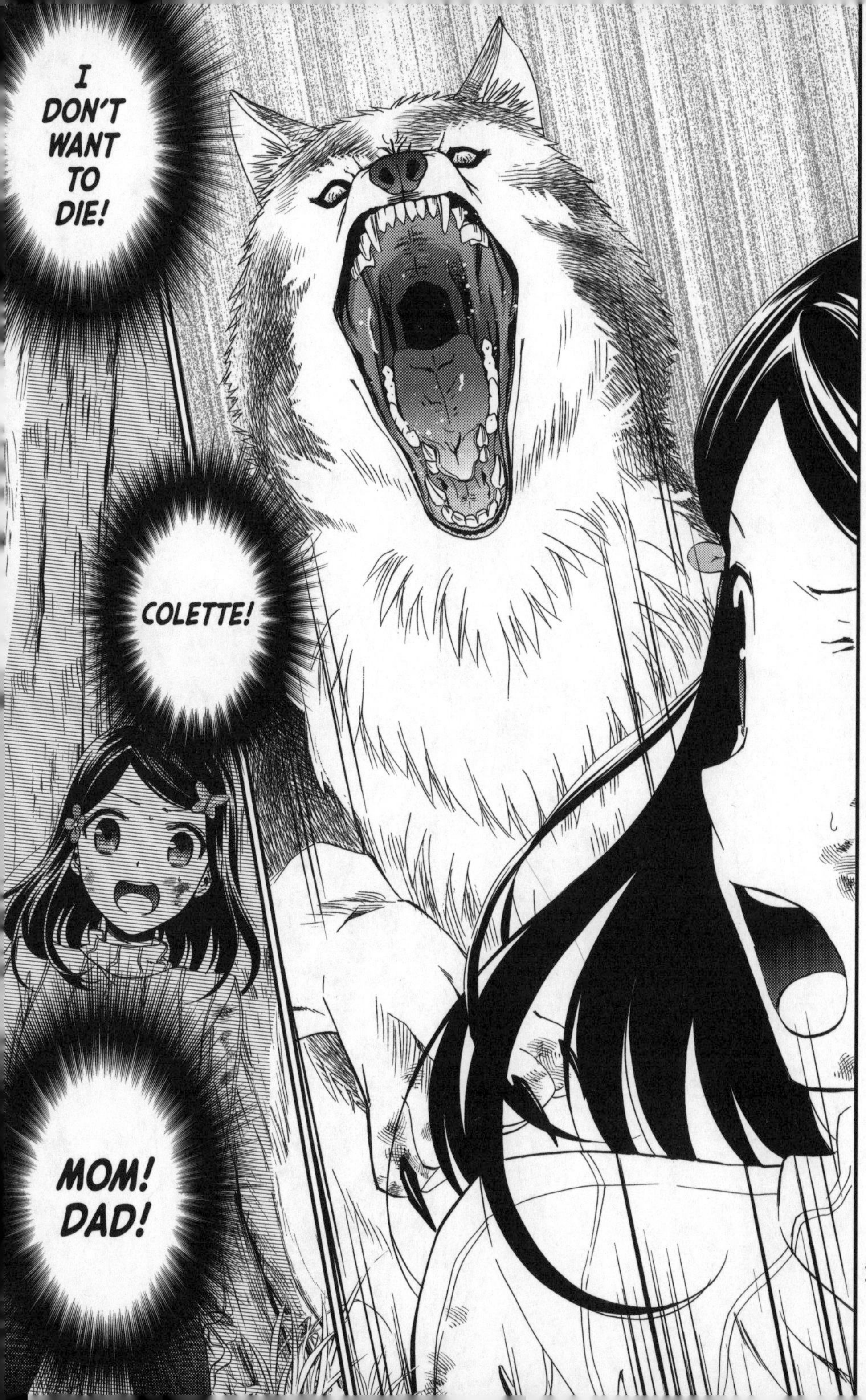
I DON'T WANT TO DIE!
COLETTE!
MOM! DAD!

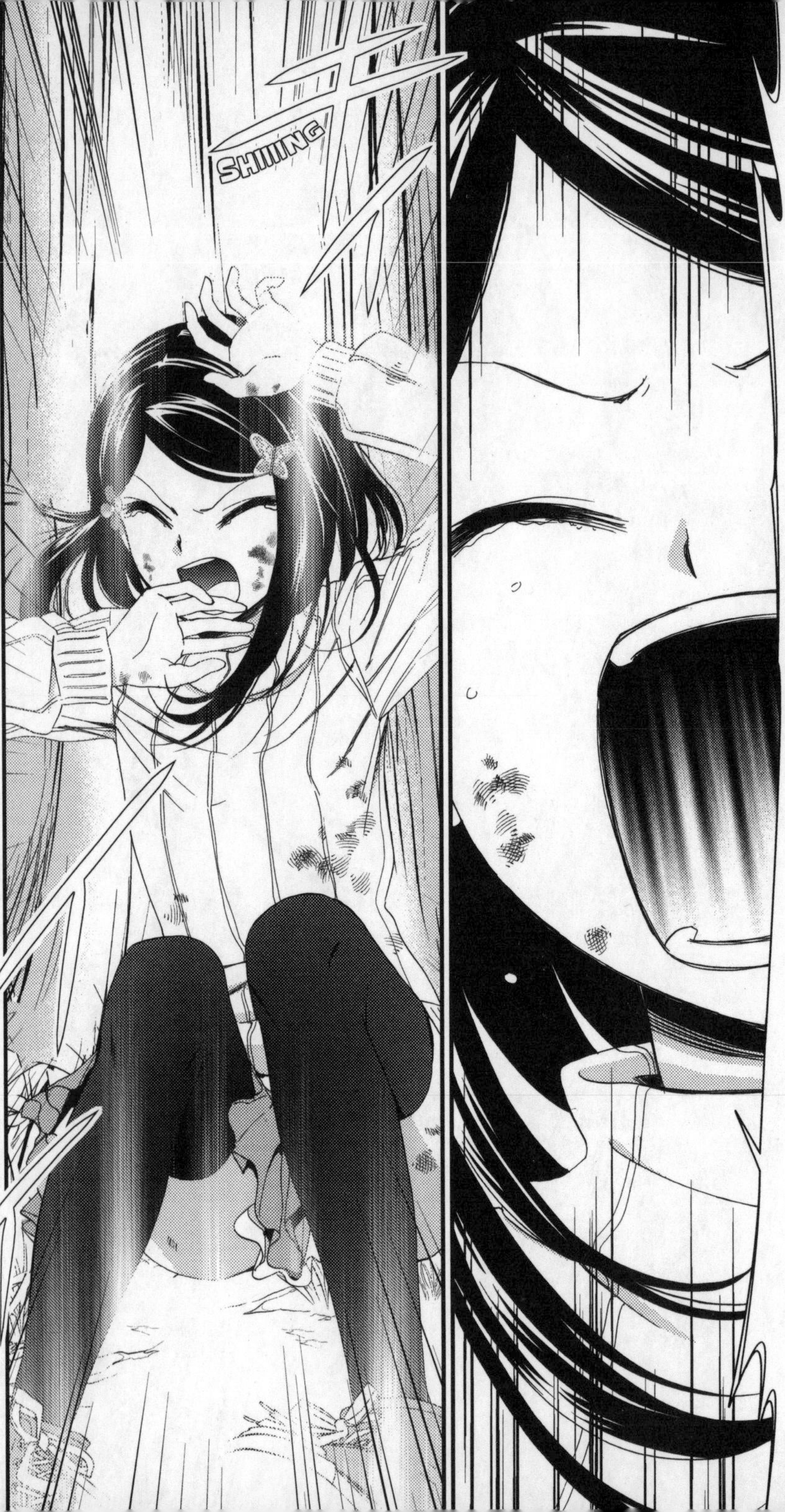
ONII-CHAAAAAAN!!
SHIIIING

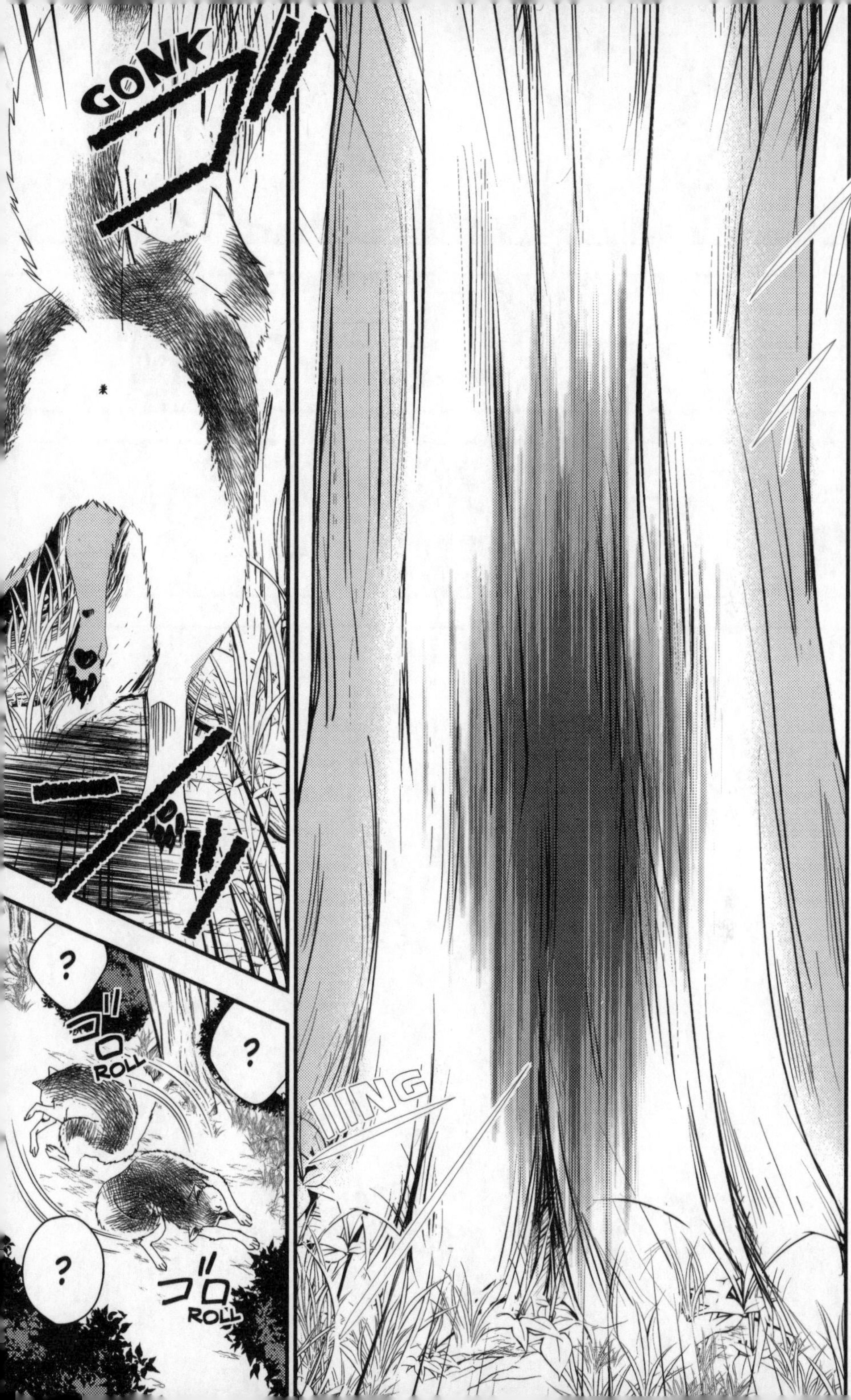

IIING
GONK
?
ゴロ ROLL
?
?
ゴロ ROLL

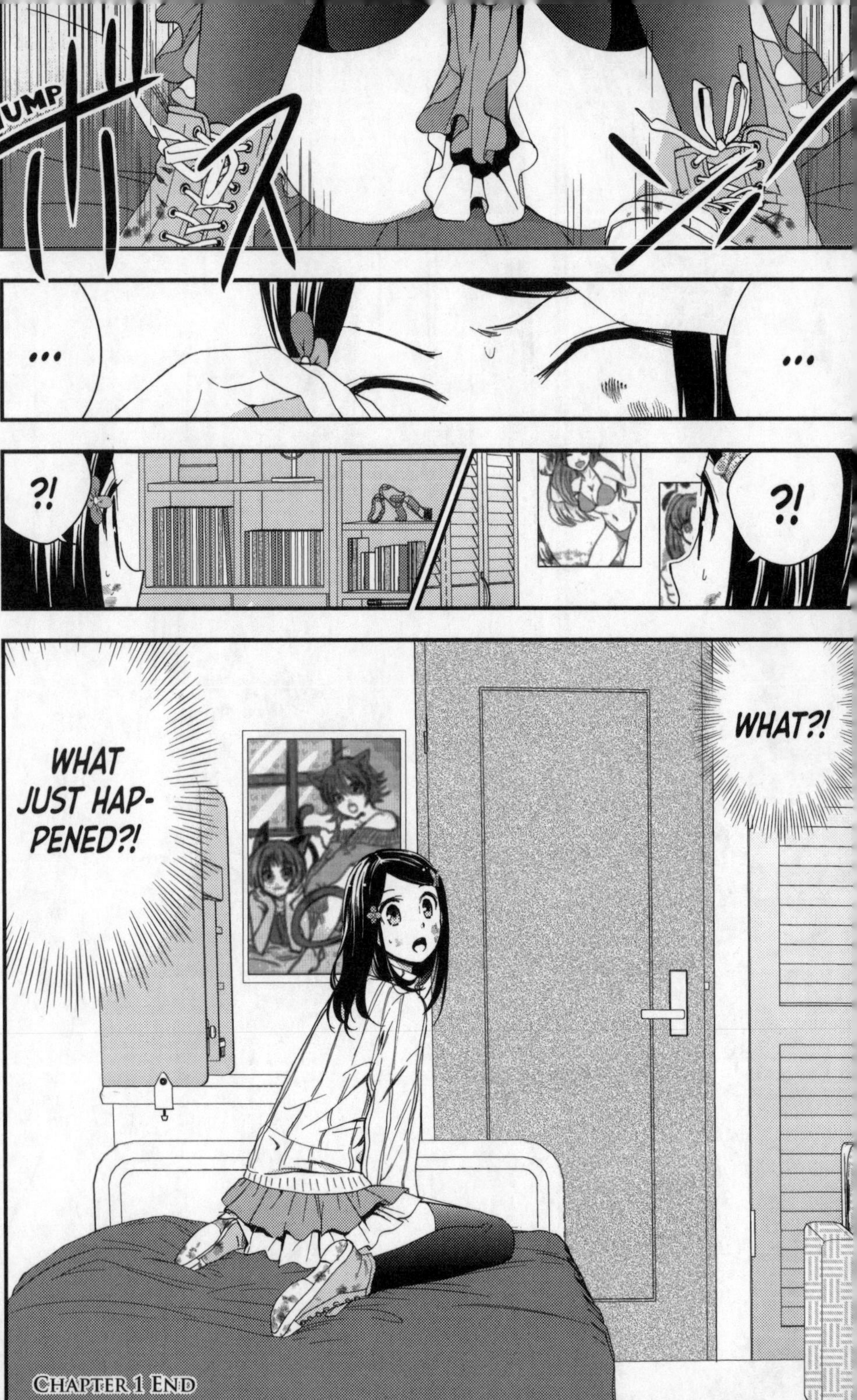
FWUMP
...
...
?!
?!
WHAT?!
WHAT JUST HAP-PENED?!
Chapter 1 End

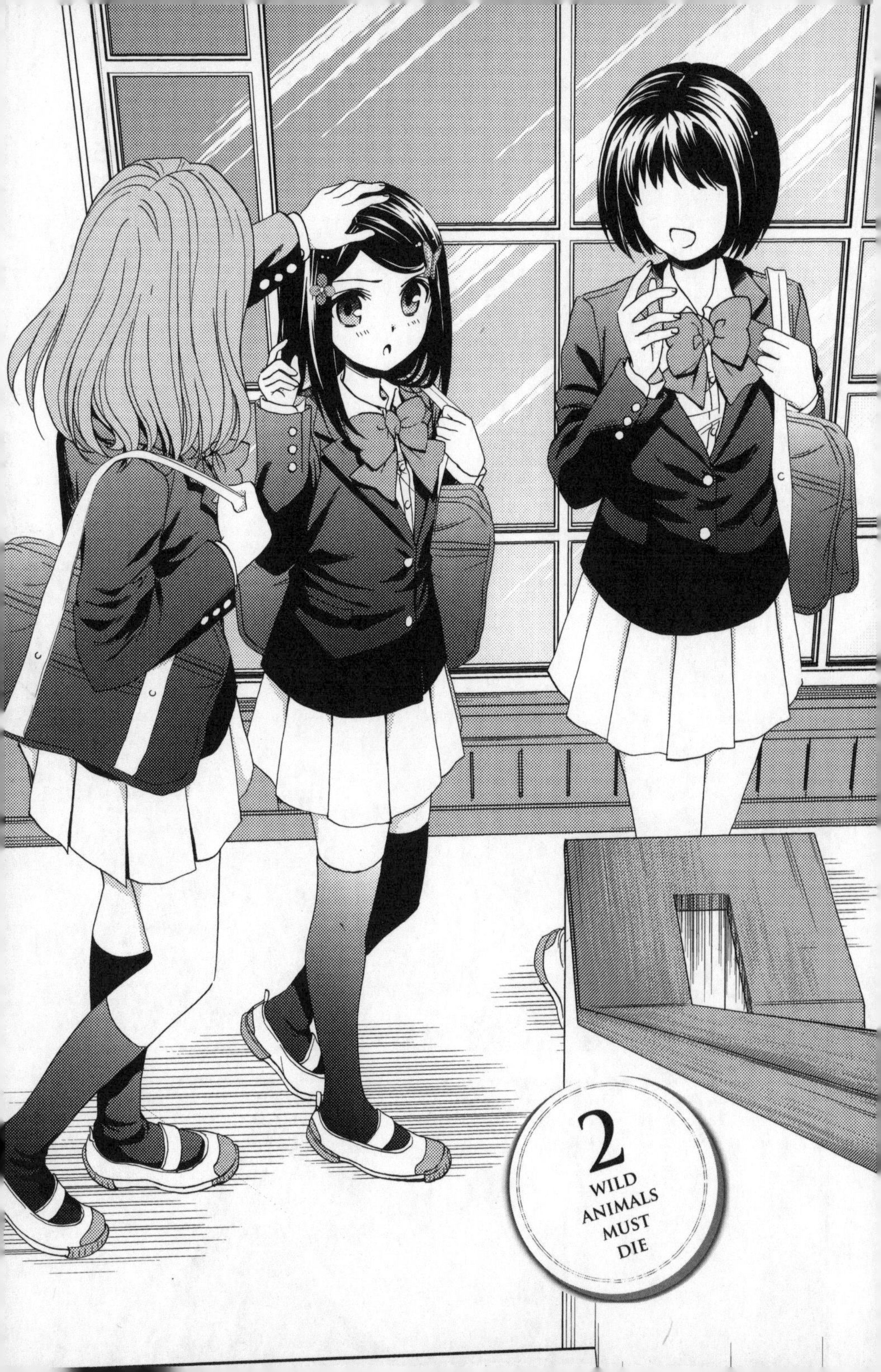
2
WILD ANIMALS MUST DIE

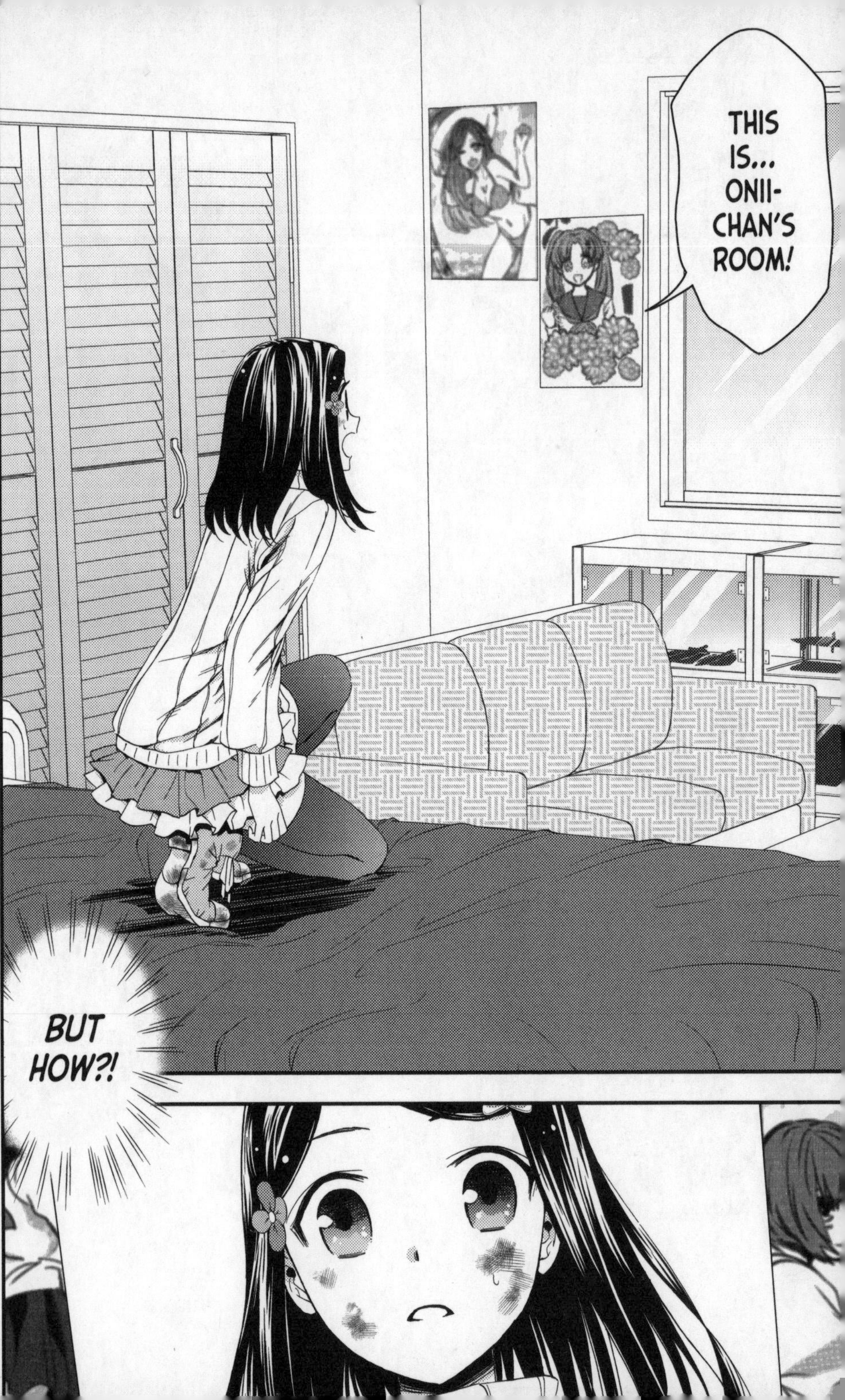
THIS IS... ONII-CHAN'S ROOM!
BUT HOW?!

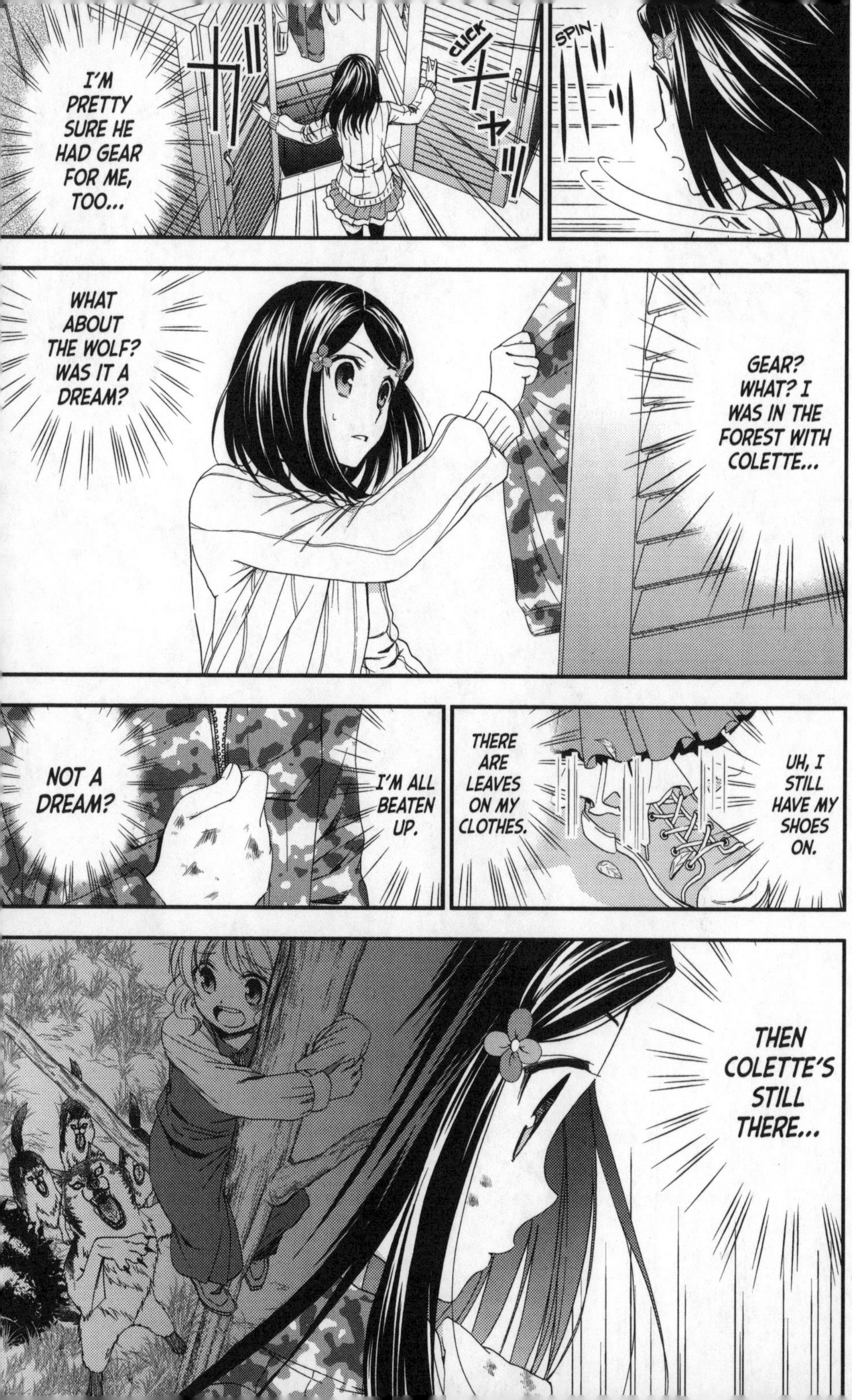
SPIN
CLICK
I'M PRETTY SURE HE HAD GEAR FOR ME, TOO...
GEAR? WHAT? I WAS IN THE FOREST WITH COLETTE...
WHAT ABOUT THE WOLF? WAS IT A DREAM?
UH, I STILL HAVE MY SHOES ON.
THERE ARE LEAVES ON MY CLOTHES.
I'M ALL BEATEN UP.
NOT A DREAM?
THEN COLETTE'S STILL THERE...

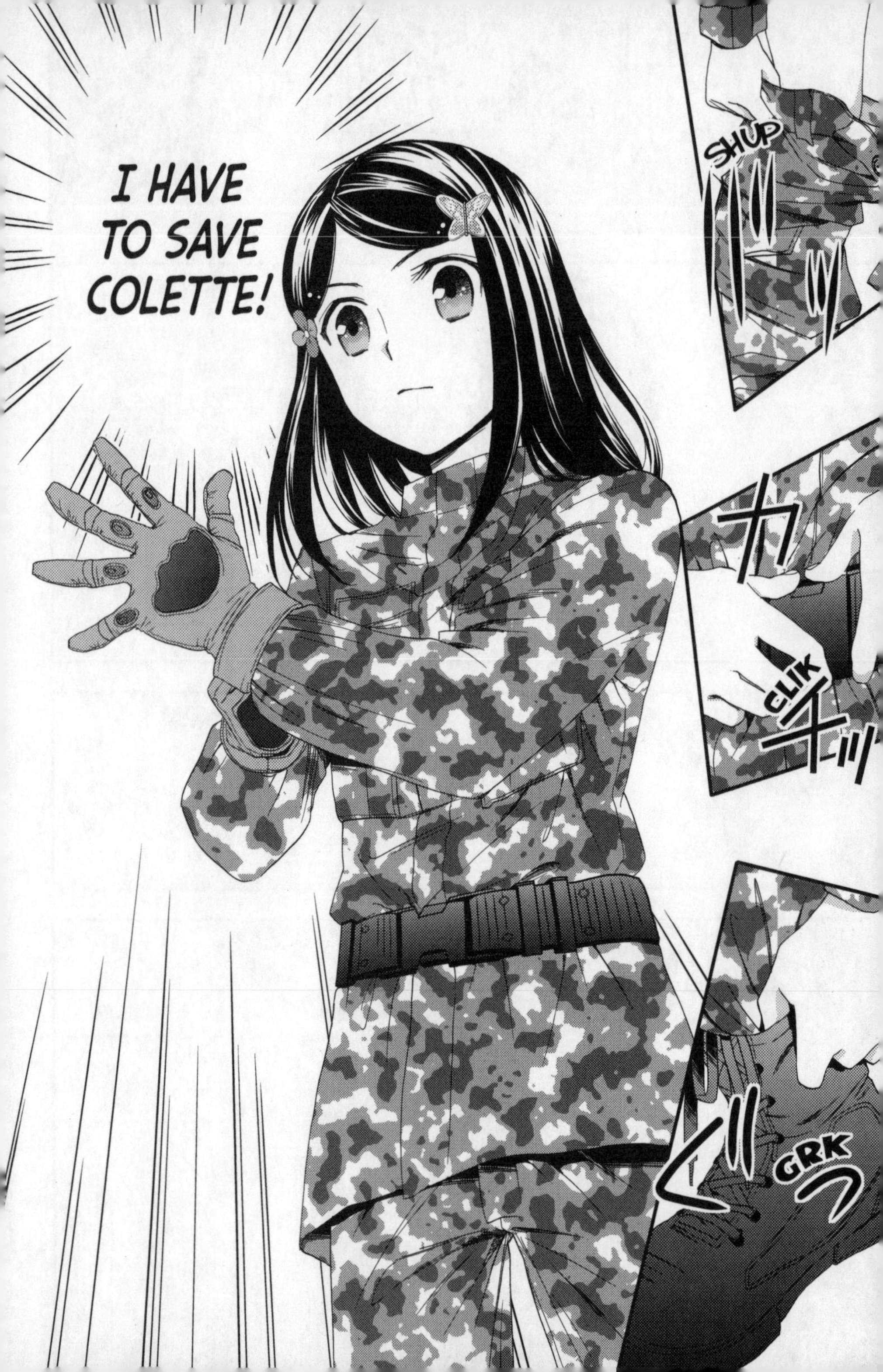
SHUP
CLIK
GRK
I HAVE TO SAVE COLETTE!

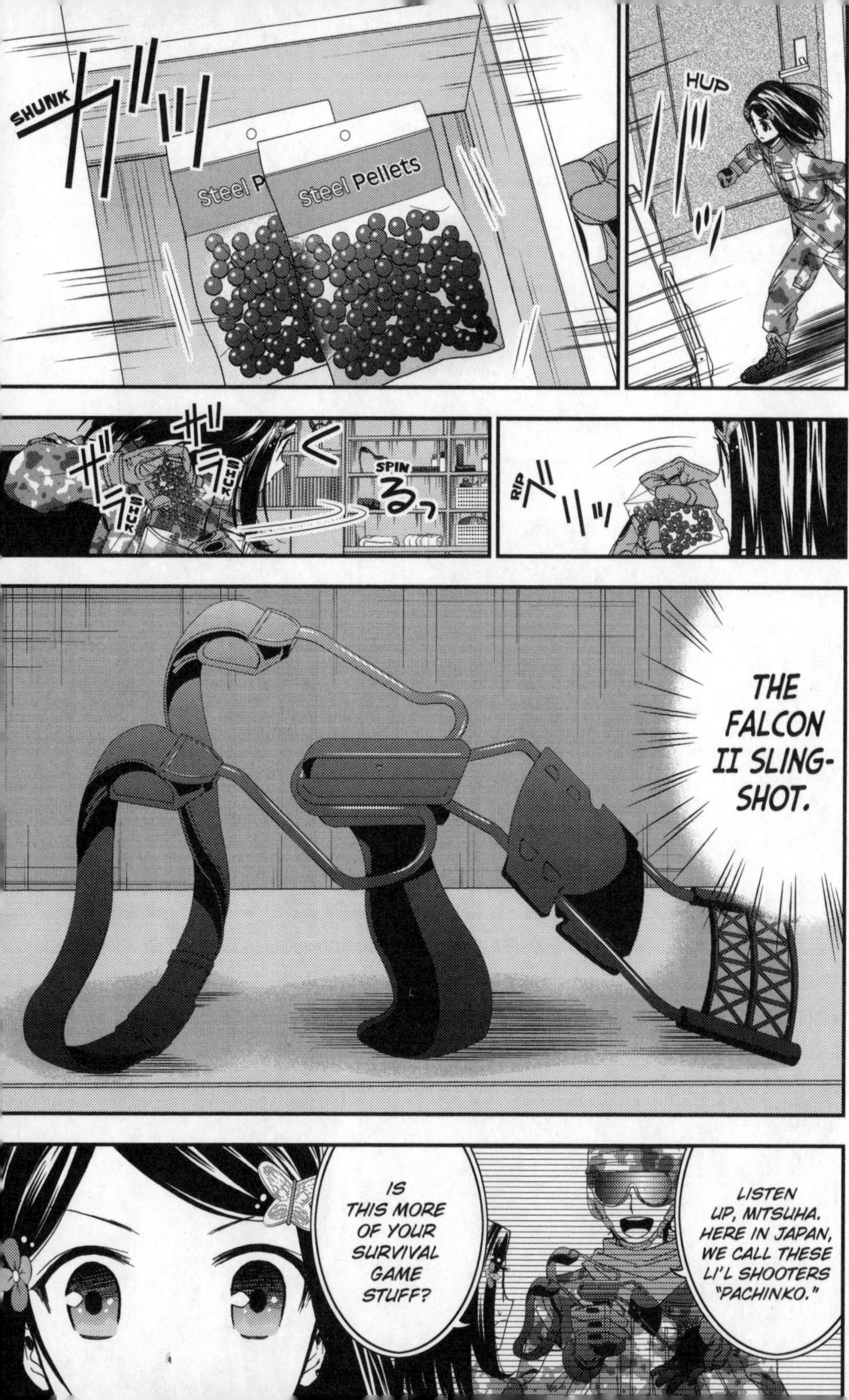
HUP
SHUNK
RIP
ベリッ
SPIN
るっ
く
ザラ
SHUK
ザラ
SHUK
Steel Pellets
THE FALCON II SLING-SHOT.
LISTEN UP, MITSUHA. HERE IN JAPAN, WE CALL THESE LI'L SHOOTERS "PACHINKO."
IS THIS MORE OF YOUR SURVIVAL GAME STUFF?

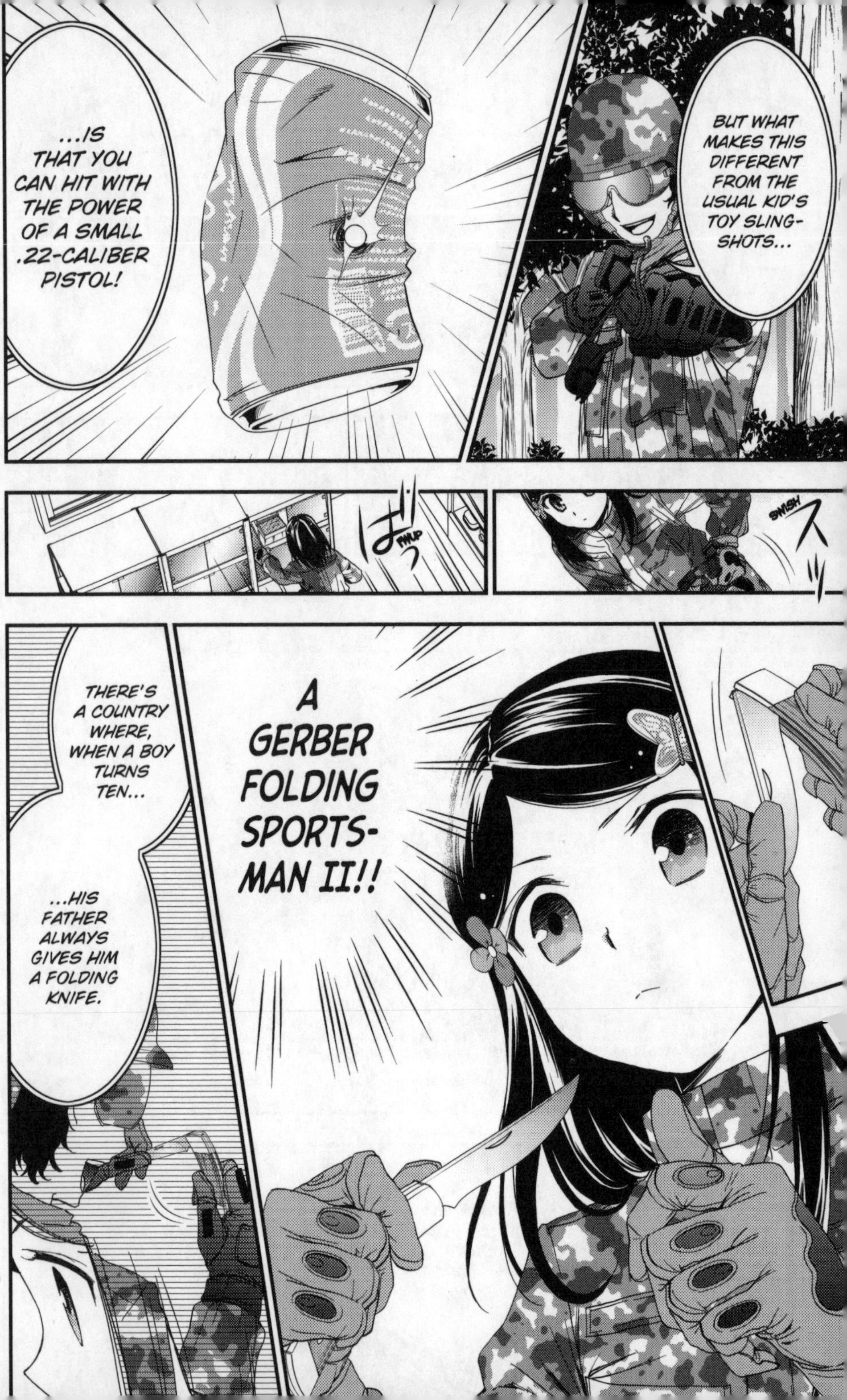
BUT WHAT MAKES THIS DIFFERENT FROM THE USUAL KID'S TOY SLING-SHOTS...
...IS THAT YOU CAN HIT WITH THE POWER OF A SMALL .22-CALIBER PISTOL!
SWISH
スッ
FWUP
A GERBER FOLDING SPORTS-MAN II!!
THERE'S A COUNTRY WHERE, WHEN A BOY TURNS TEN...
...HIS FATHER ALWAYS GIVES HIM A FOLDING KNIFE.

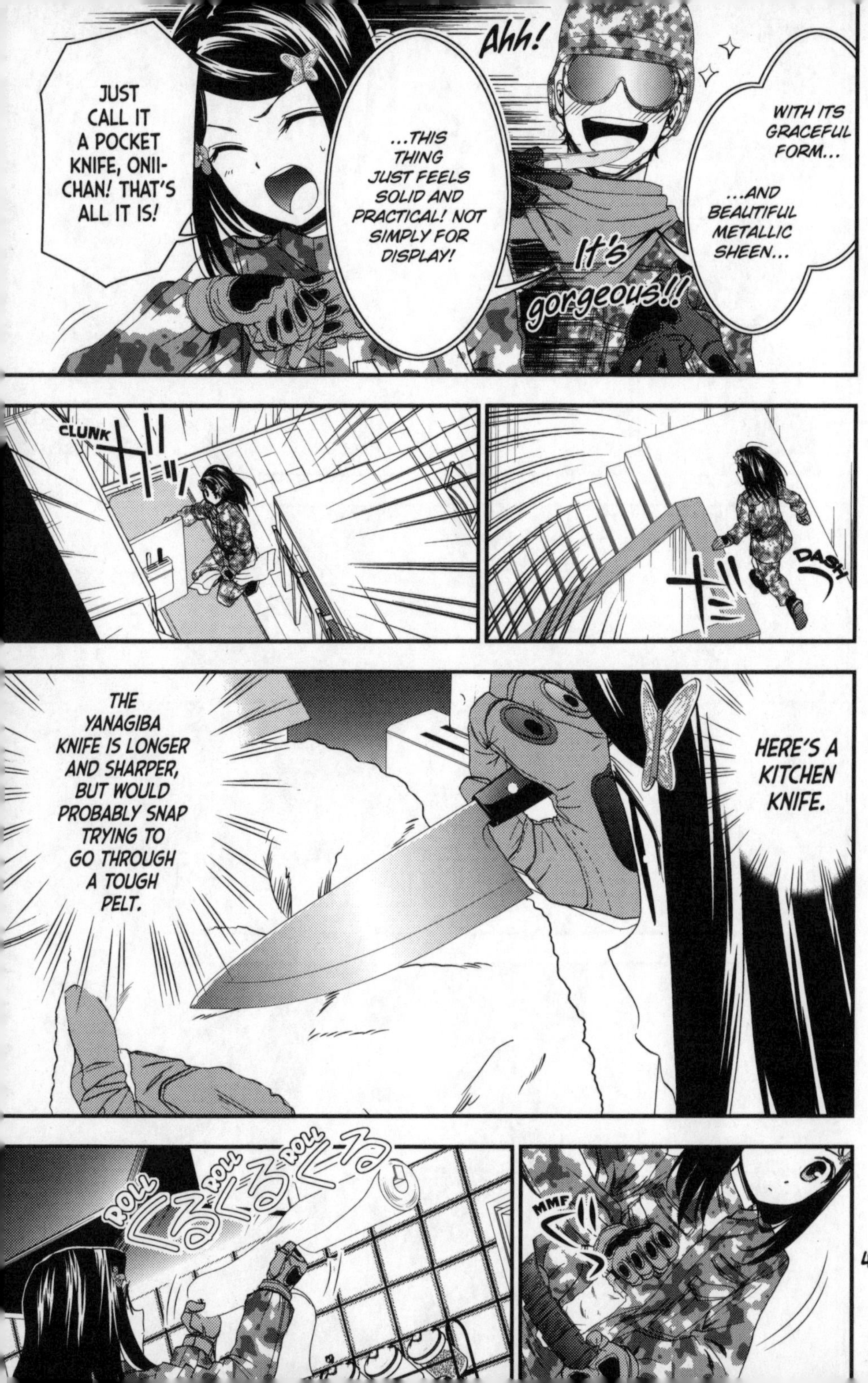

Ahh!
WITH ITS GRACEFUL FORM...
...AND BEAUTIFUL METALLIC SHEEN...
It's gorgeous!!
...THIS THING JUST FEELS SOLID AND PRACTICAL! NOT SIMPLY FOR DISPLAY!
JUST CALL IT A POCKET KNIFE, ONII-CHAN! THAT'S ALL IT IS!
DASH
CLUNK
HERE'S A KITCHEN KNIFE.
THE YANAGIBA KNIFE IS LONGER AND SHARPER, BUT WOULD PROBABLY SNAP TRYING TO GO THROUGH A TOUGH PELT.
MMF
ROLL ROLL ROLL

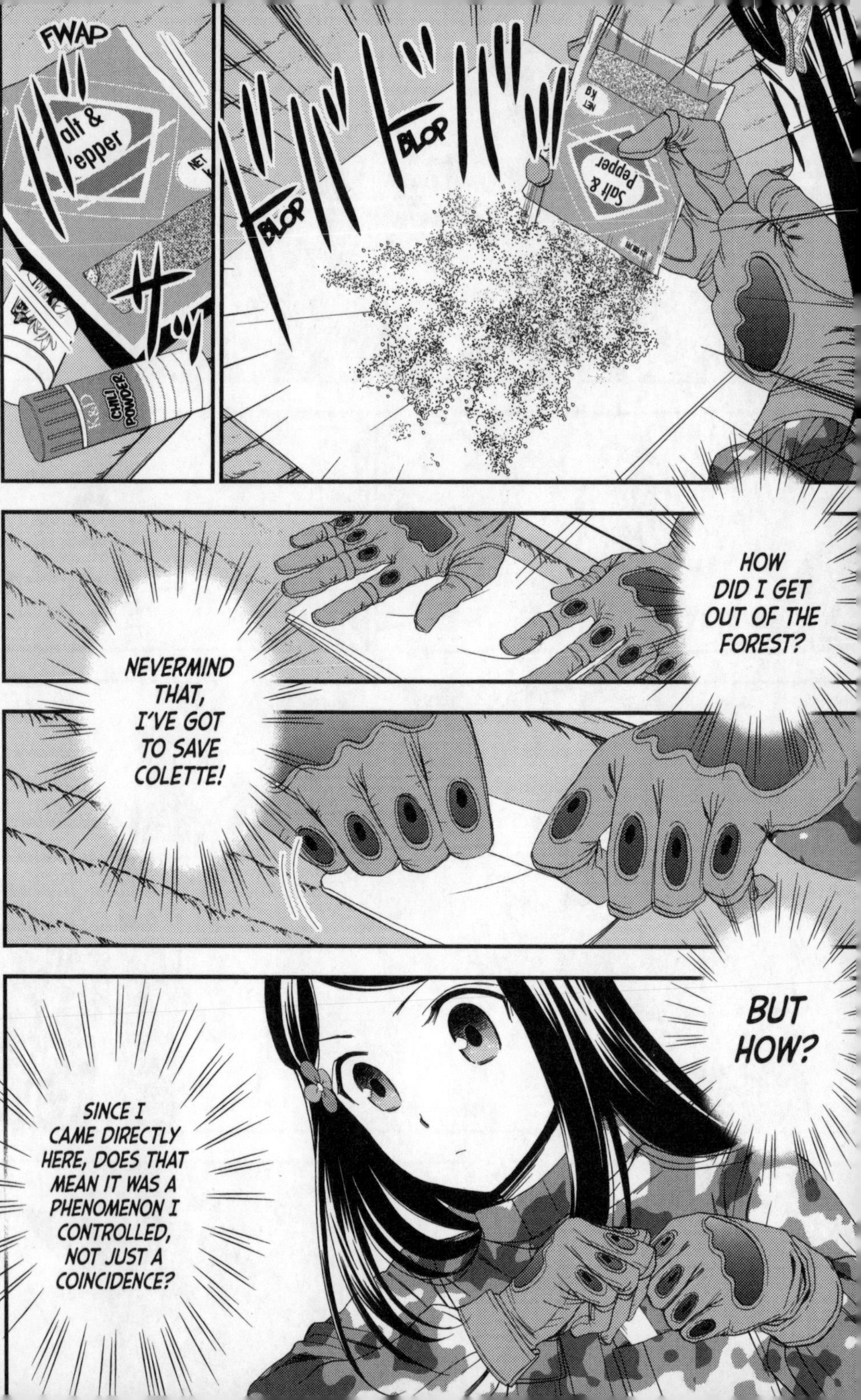
BLOP
BLOP
Salt & Pepper
FWAP
CHILI POWDER
HOW DID I GET OUT OF THE FOREST?
NEVERMIND THAT, I'VE GOT TO SAVE COLETTE!
BUT HOW?
SINCE I CAME DIRECTLY HERE, DOES THAT MEAN IT WAS A PHENOMENON I CONTROLLED, NOT JUST A COINCIDENCE?

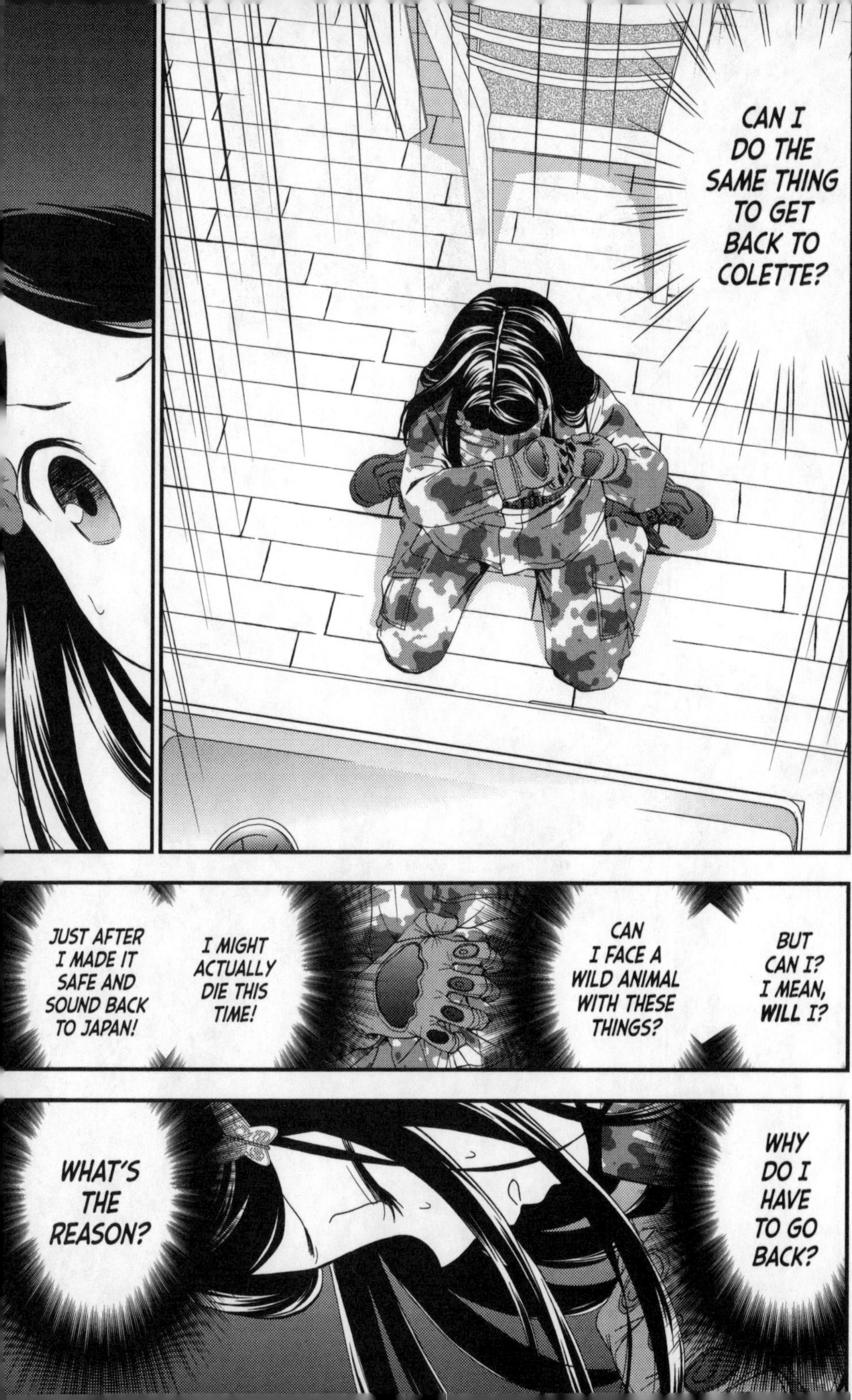
CAN I DO THE SAME THING TO GET BACK TO COLETTE?
BUT CAN I? I MEAN, WILL I?
CAN I FACE A WILD ANIMAL WITH THESE THINGS?
I MIGHT ACTUALLY DIE THIS TIME!
JUST AFTER I MADE IT SAFE AND SOUND BACK TO JAPAN!
WHY DO I HAVE TO GO BACK?
WHAT'S THE REASON?

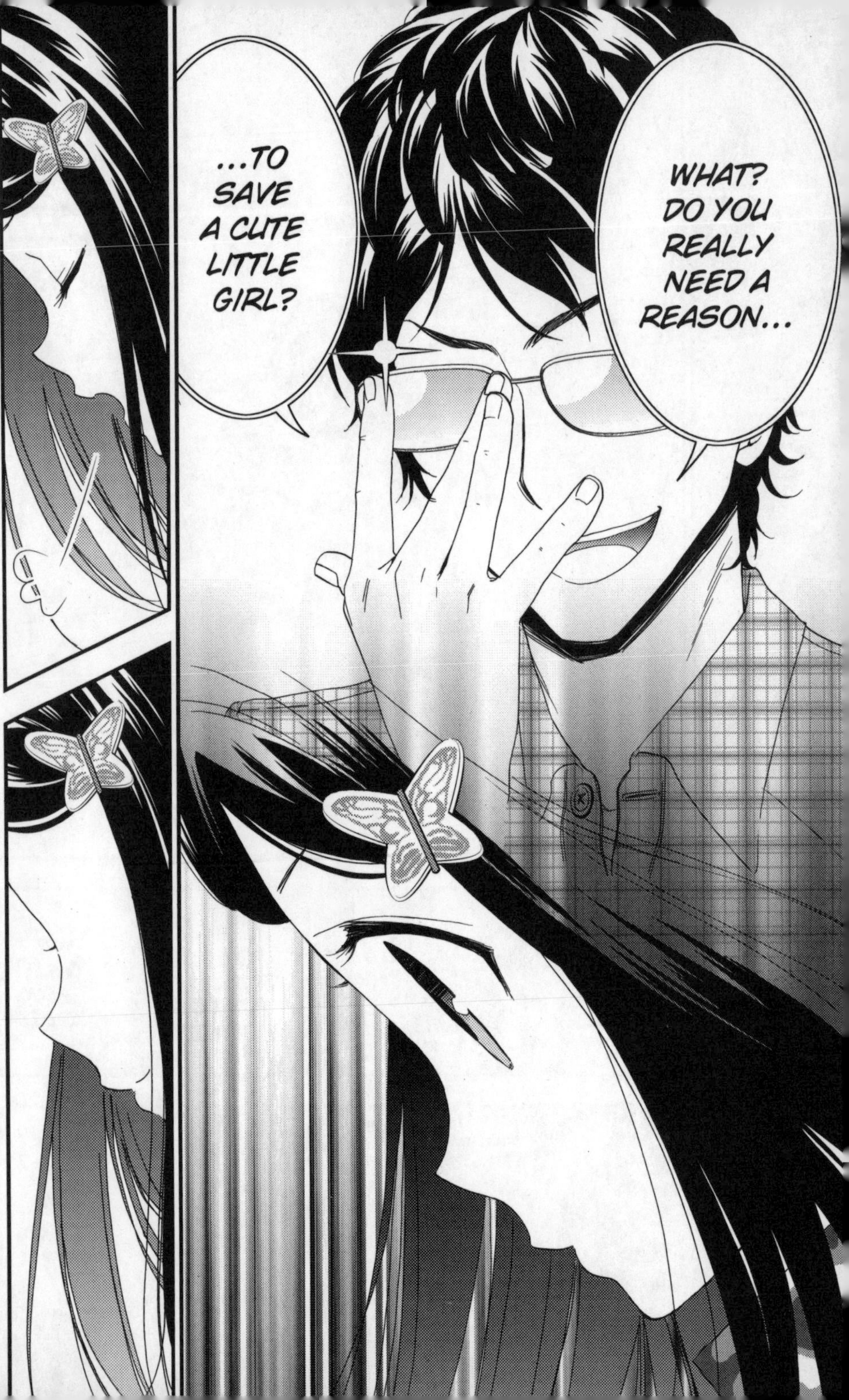
WHAT? DO YOU REALLY NEED A REASON...
...TO SAVE A CUTE LITTLE GIRL?

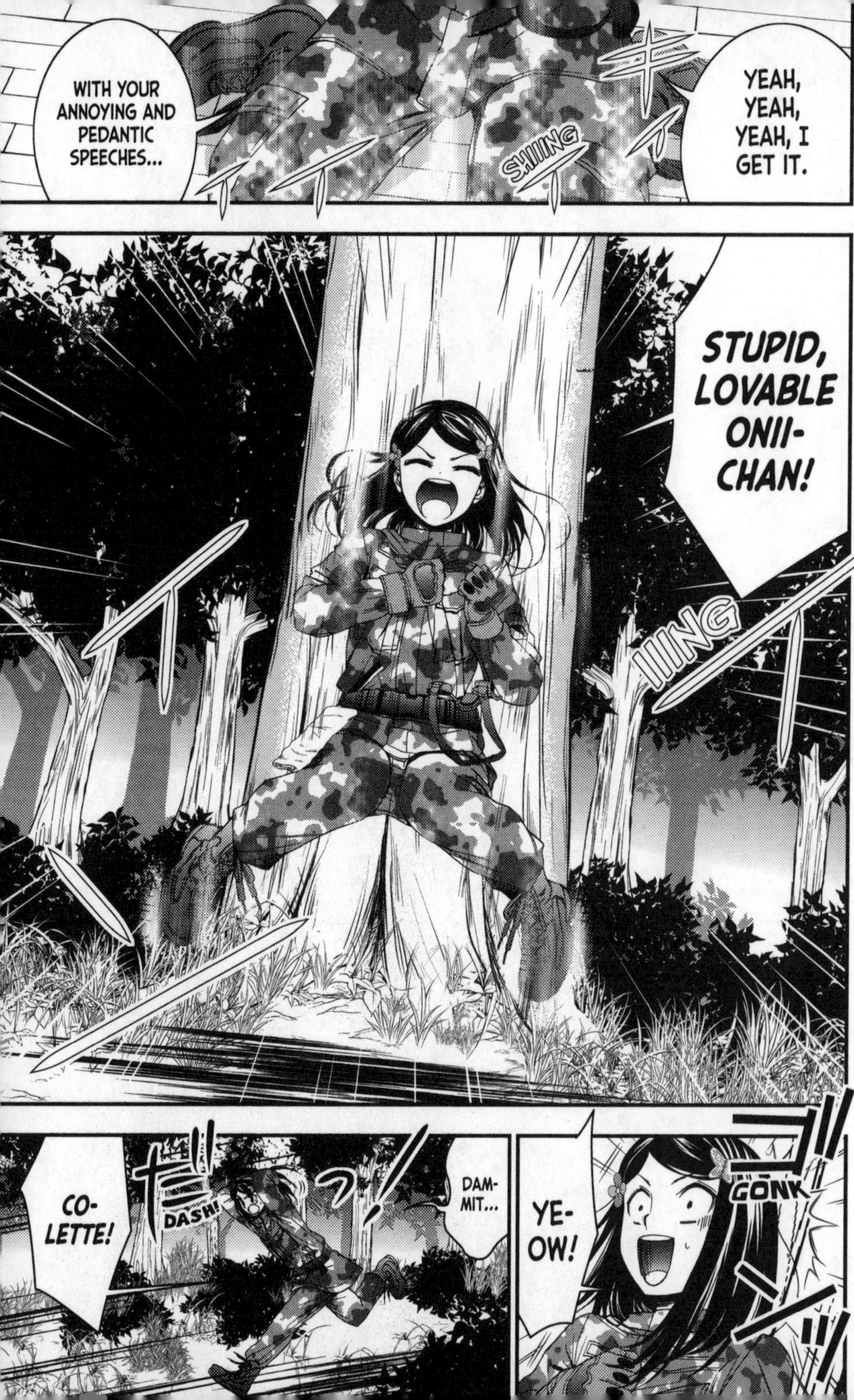
YEAH, YEAH, YEAH, I GET IT.
SHIIING
WITH YOUR ANNOYING AND PEDANTIC SPEECHES...
STUPID, LOVABLE ONII-CHAN!
IIING
GONK
YE-OW!
DAM-MIT...
DASH!
CO-LETTE!

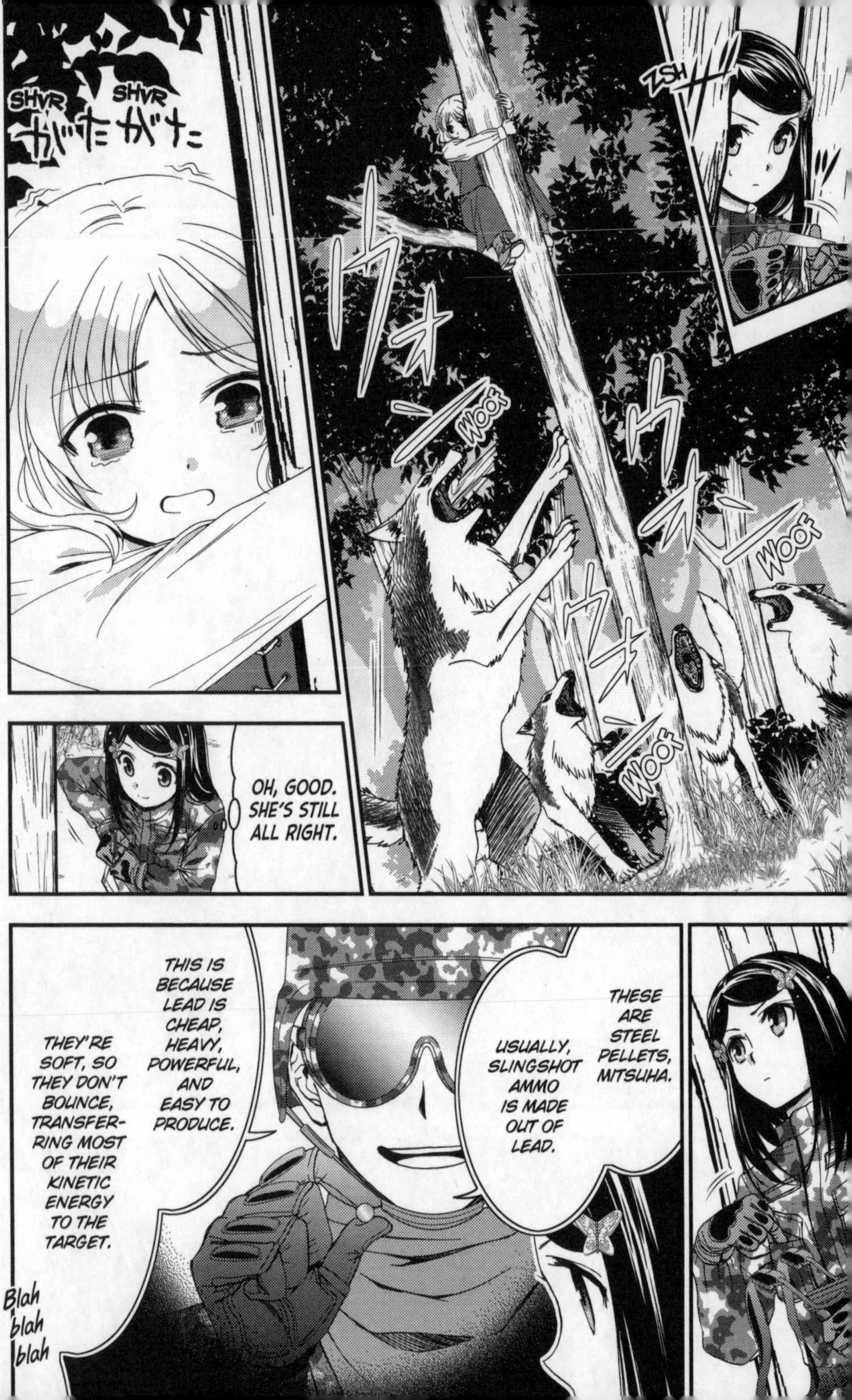

ZSH
WOOF
WOOF
WOOF
SHVR SHVR
がたがた
OH, GOOD. SHE'S STILL ALL RIGHT.
THESE ARE STEEL PELLETS, MITSUHA.
USUALLY, SLINGSHOT AMMO IS MADE OUT OF LEAD.
THIS IS BECAUSE LEAD IS CHEAP, HEAVY, POWERFUL, AND EASY TO PRODUCE.
THEY'RE SOFT, SO THEY DON'T BOUNCE, TRANSFERRING MOST OF THEIR KINETIC ENERGY TO THE TARGET.
Blah blah blah

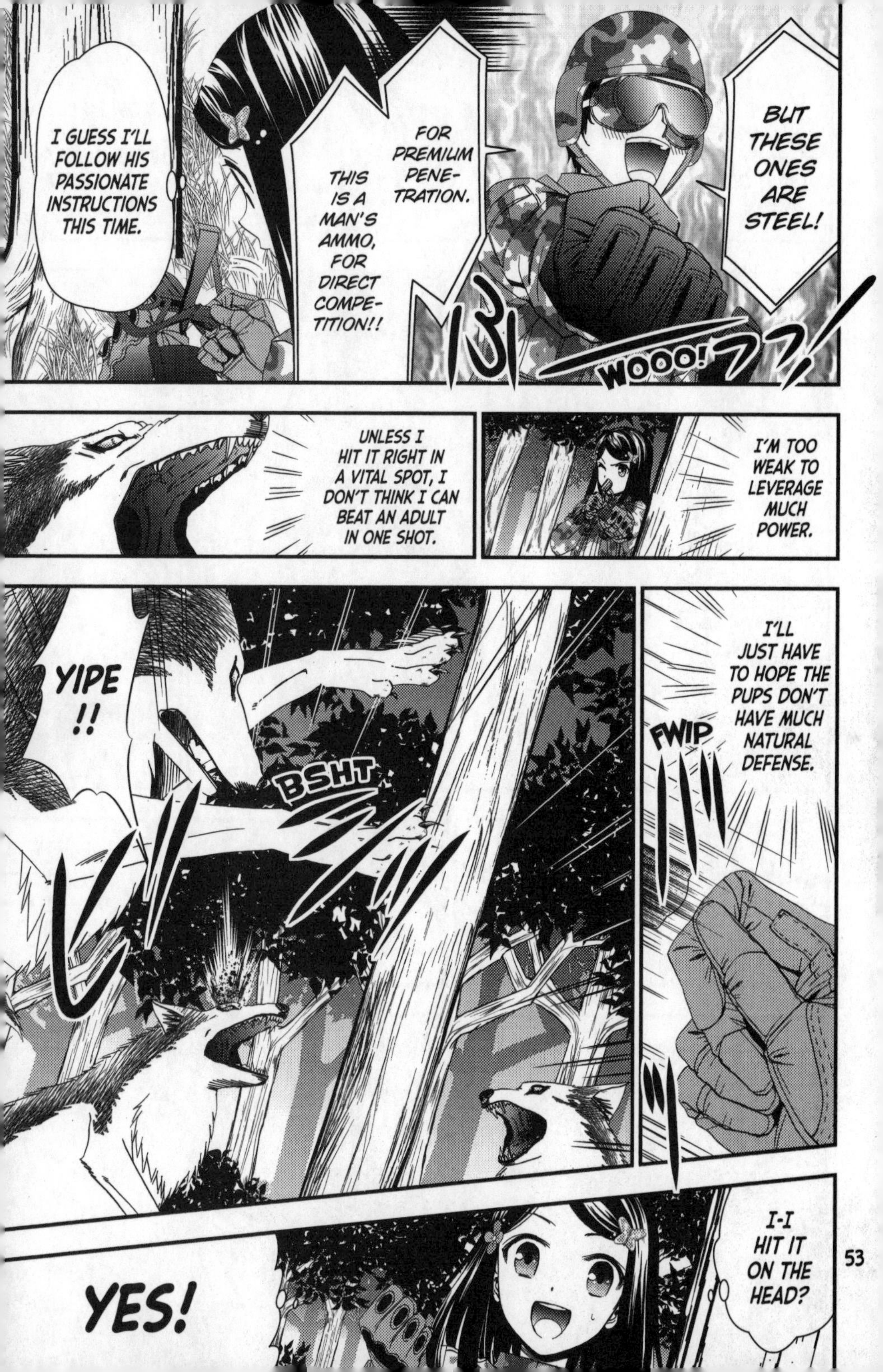
BUT THESE ONES ARE STEEL!
WOOO!
FOR PREMIUM PENE-TRATION.
THIS IS A MAN'S AMMO, FOR DIRECT COMPE-TITION!!
I GUESS I'LL FOLLOW HIS PASSIONATE INSTRUCTIONS THIS TIME.
I'M TOO WEAK TO LEVERAGE MUCH POWER.
UNLESS I HIT IT RIGHT IN A VITAL SPOT, I DON'T THINK I CAN BEAT AN ADULT IN ONE SHOT.
I'LL JUST HAVE TO HOPE THE PUPS DON'T HAVE MUCH NATURAL DEFENSE.
FWIP
BSHT
YIPE !!
I-I HIT IT ON THE HEAD?
YES!

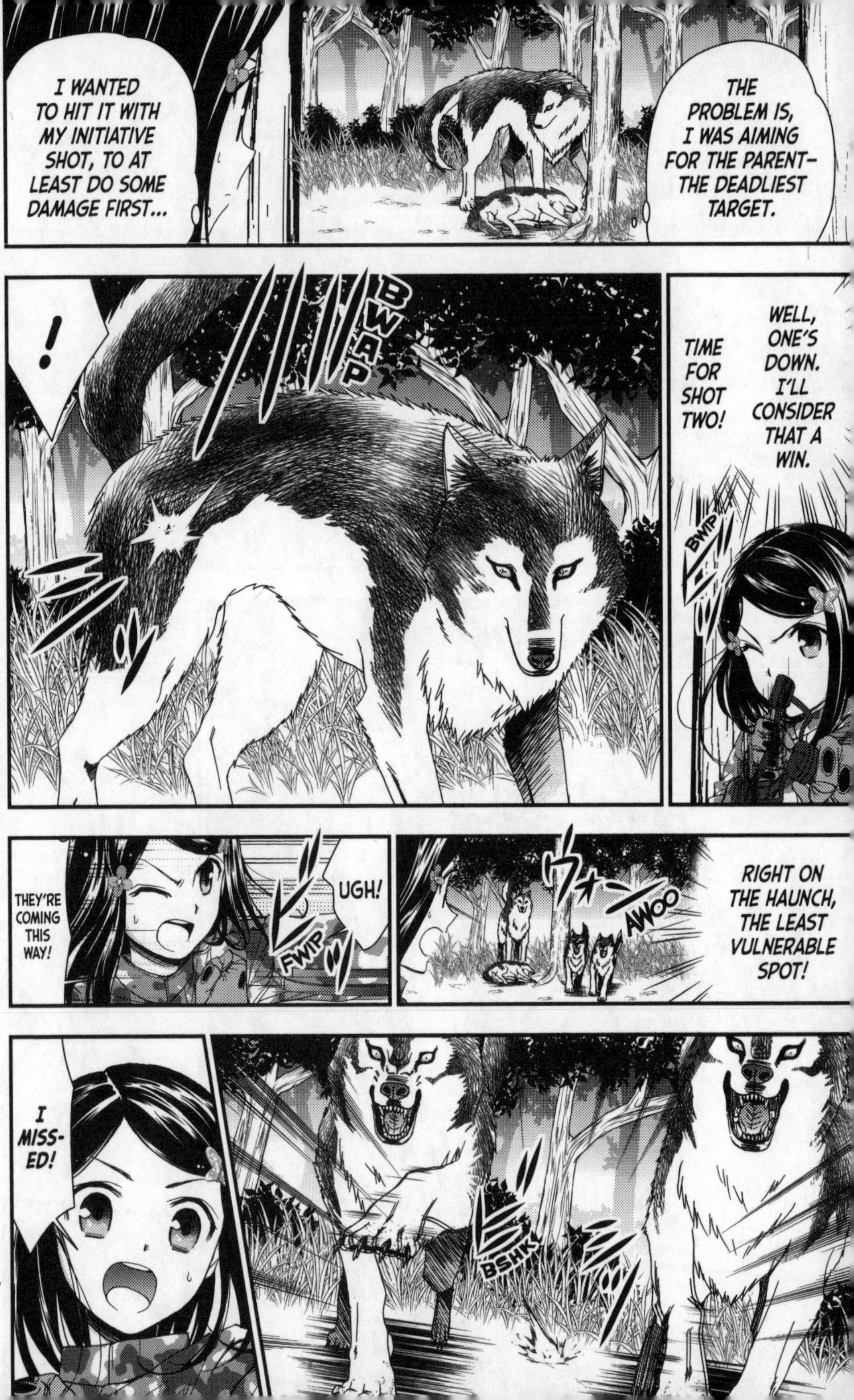
THE PROBLEM IS, I WAS AIMING FOR THE PARENT—THE DEADLIEST TARGET.
I WANTED TO HIT IT WITH MY INITIATIVE SHOT, TO AT LEAST DO SOME DAMAGE FIRST...
WELL, ONE'S DOWN. I'LL CONSIDER THAT A WIN.
TIME FOR SHOT TWO!
BWIP
BWAP
!
RIGHT ON THE HAUNCH, THE LEAST VULNERABLE SPOT!
AWOO
UGH!
FWIP
THEY'RE COMING THIS WAY!
BSHK
I MISS-ED!

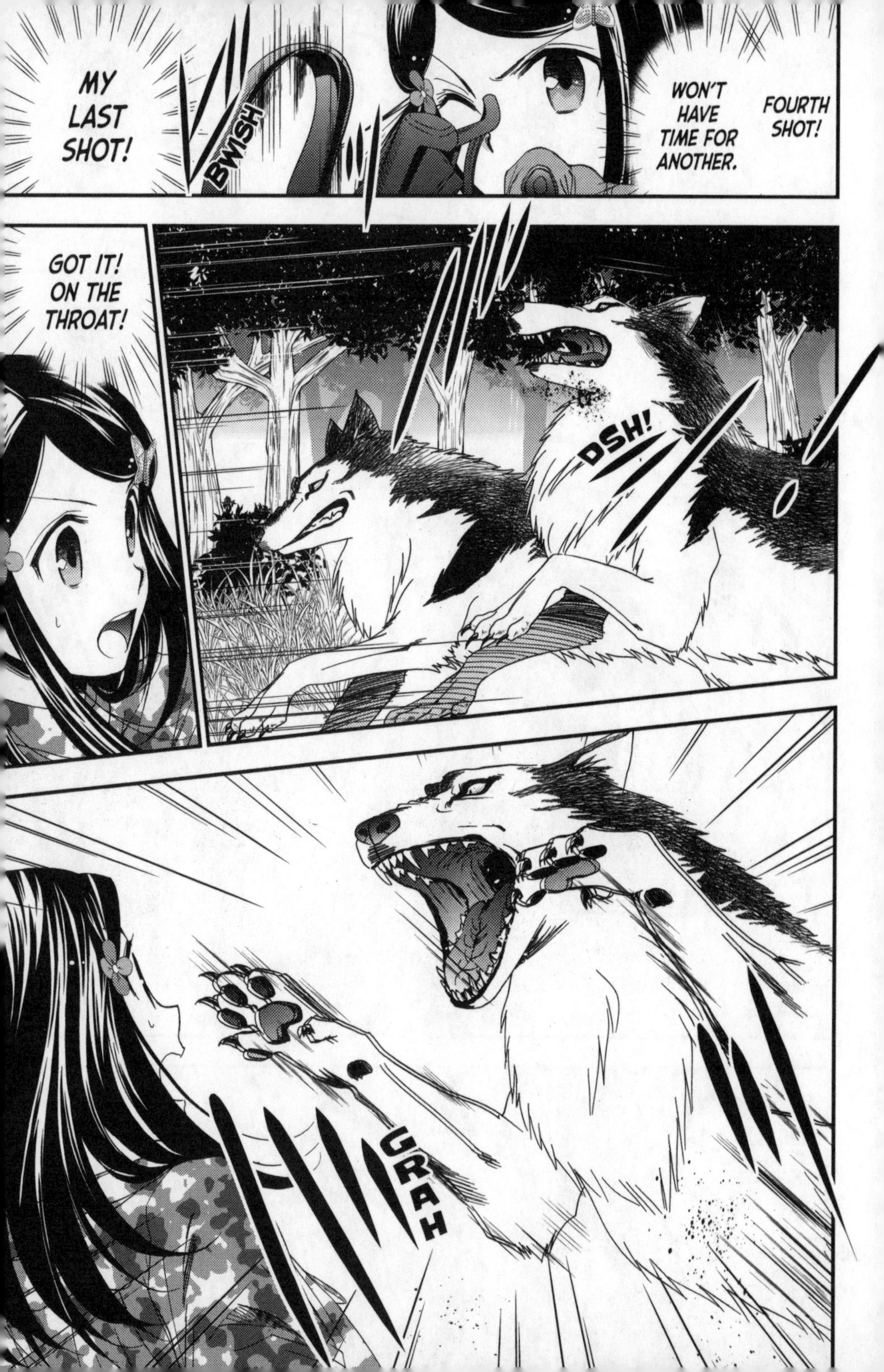
FOURTH SHOT!
WON'T HAVE TIME FOR ANOTHER.
BWISH
MY LAST SHOT!
DSH!
GOT IT! ON THE THROAT!
GRAH

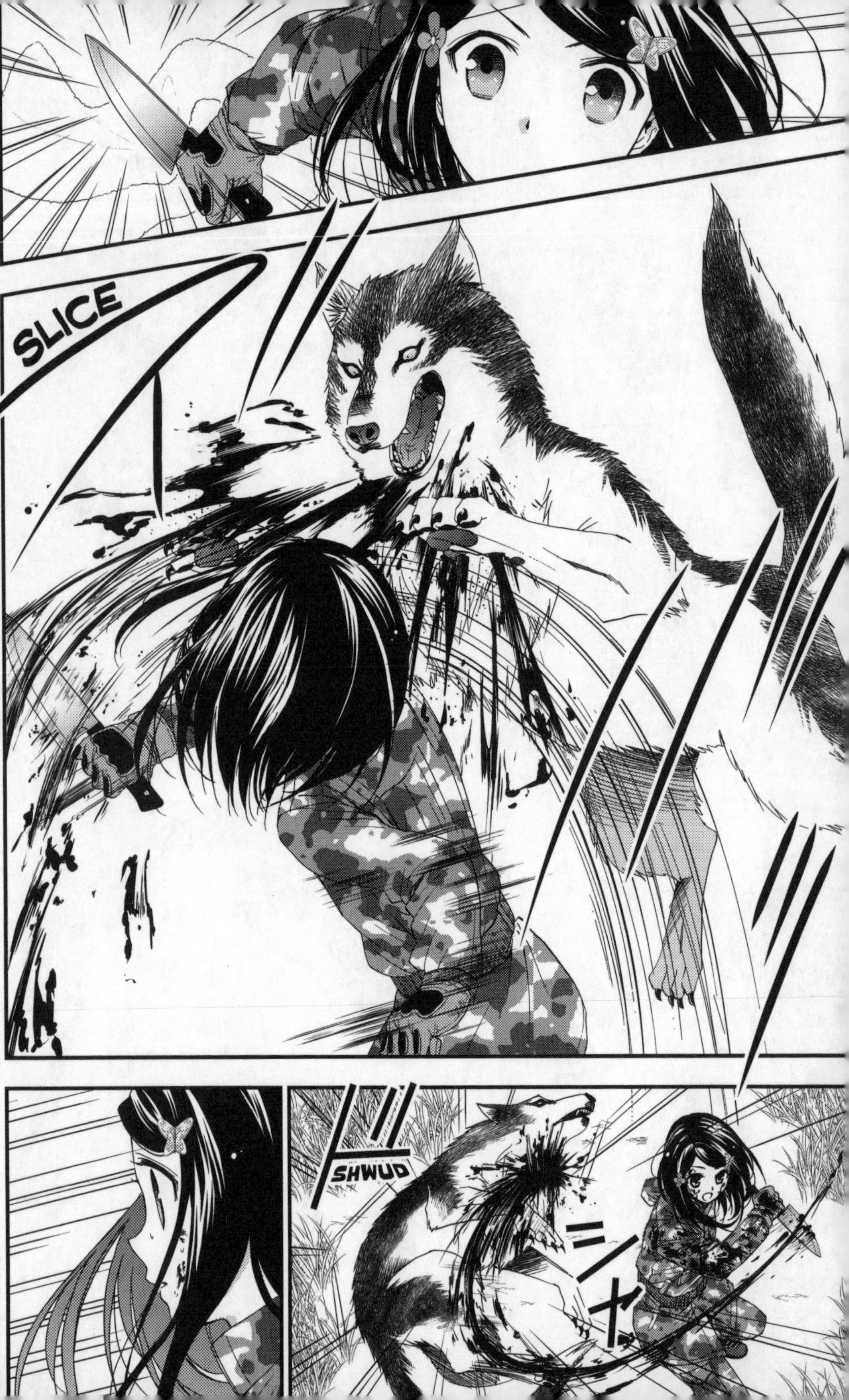
SLICE
SHWUD

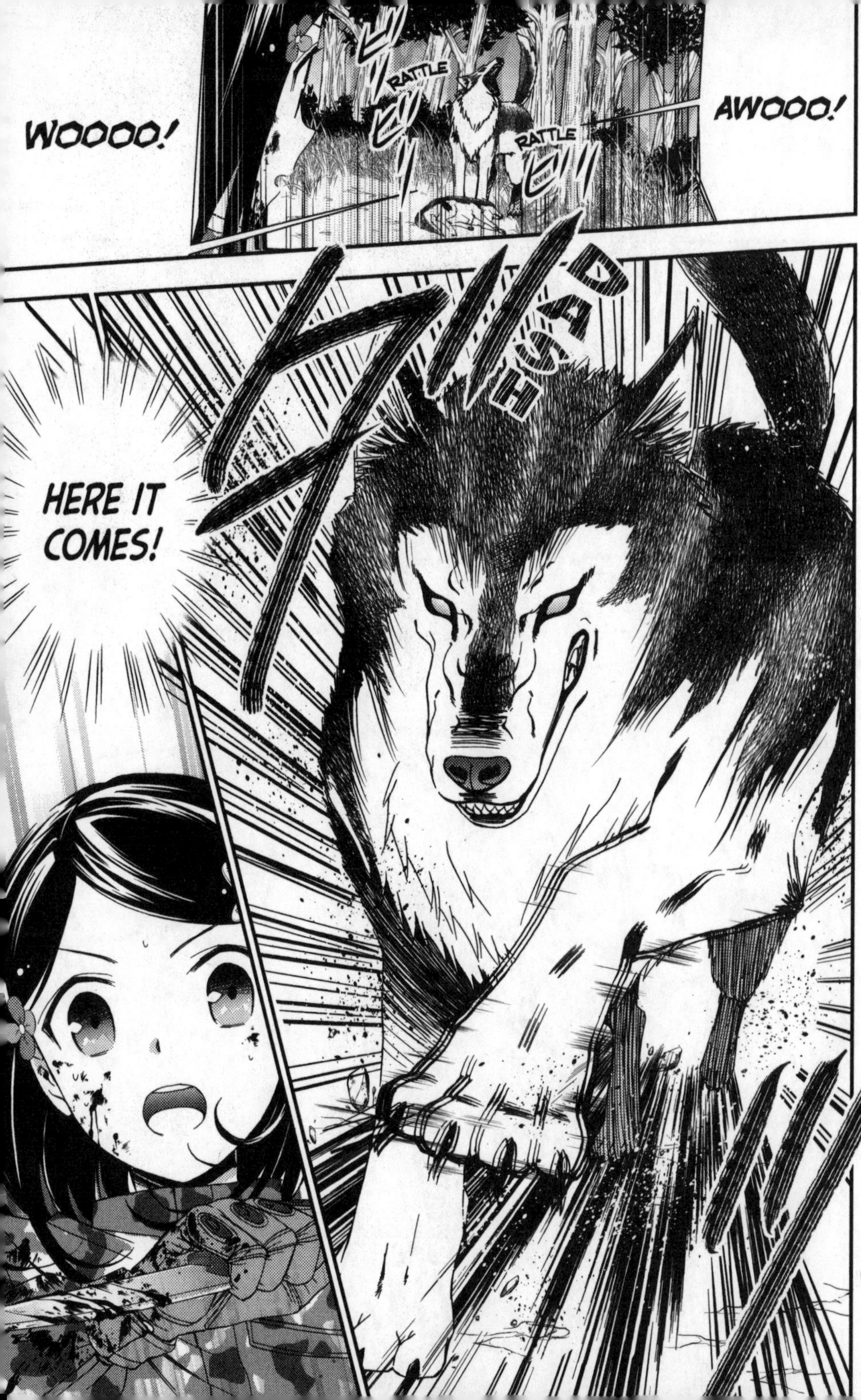
AWOOO!
RATTLE
RATTLE
WOOOO!
DASH
HERE IT COMES!

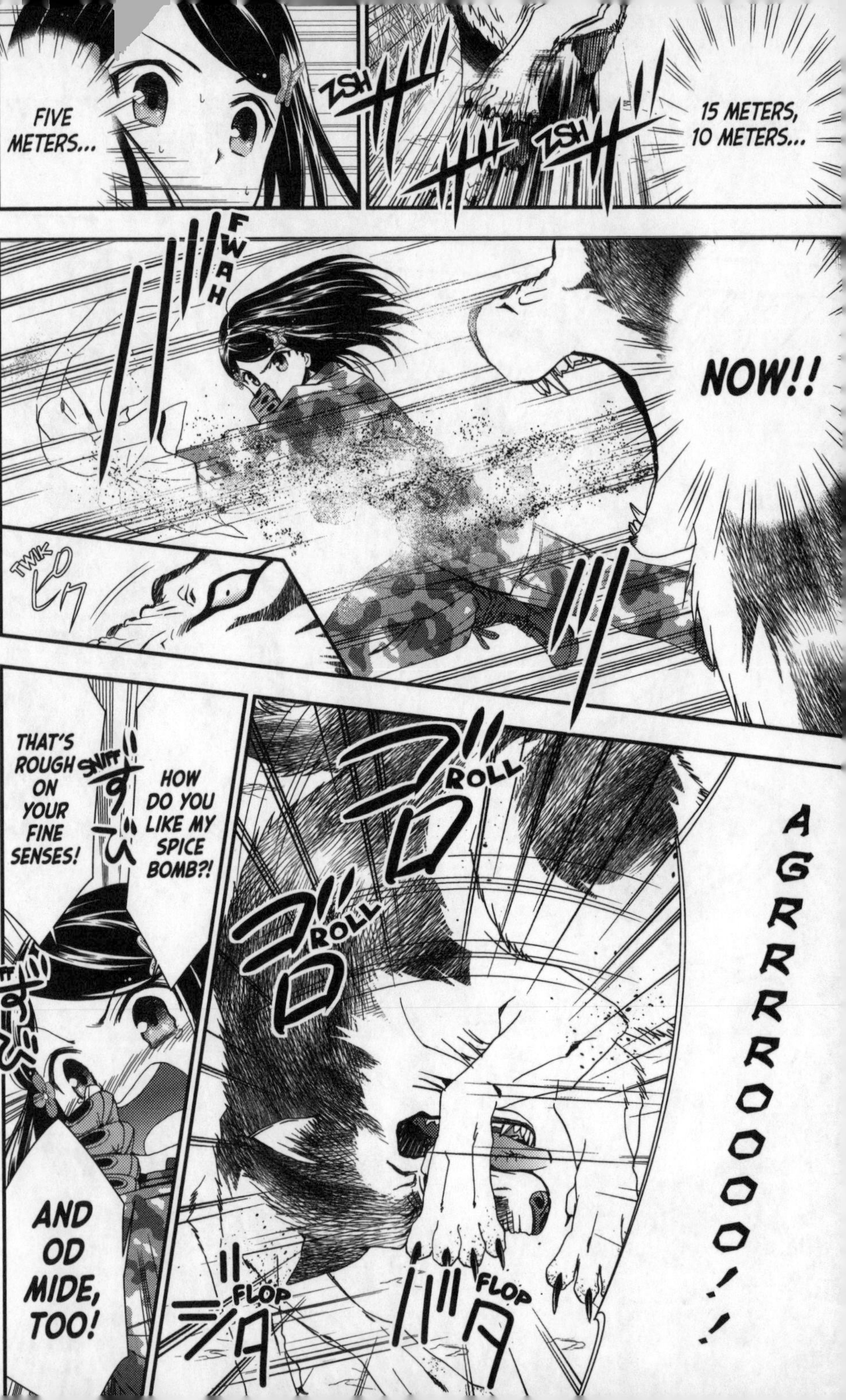

ZSH
ZSH
15 METERS, 10 METERS...
FIVE METERS...
FWAH
NOW!!
TWIK
AGRRRROOOOOO!!
ROLL
ROLL
FLOP
FLOP
HOW DO YOU LIKE MY SPICE BOMB?!
SNIFF
THAT'S ROUGH ON YOUR FINE SENSES!
SNIFF
AND OD MIDE, TOO!

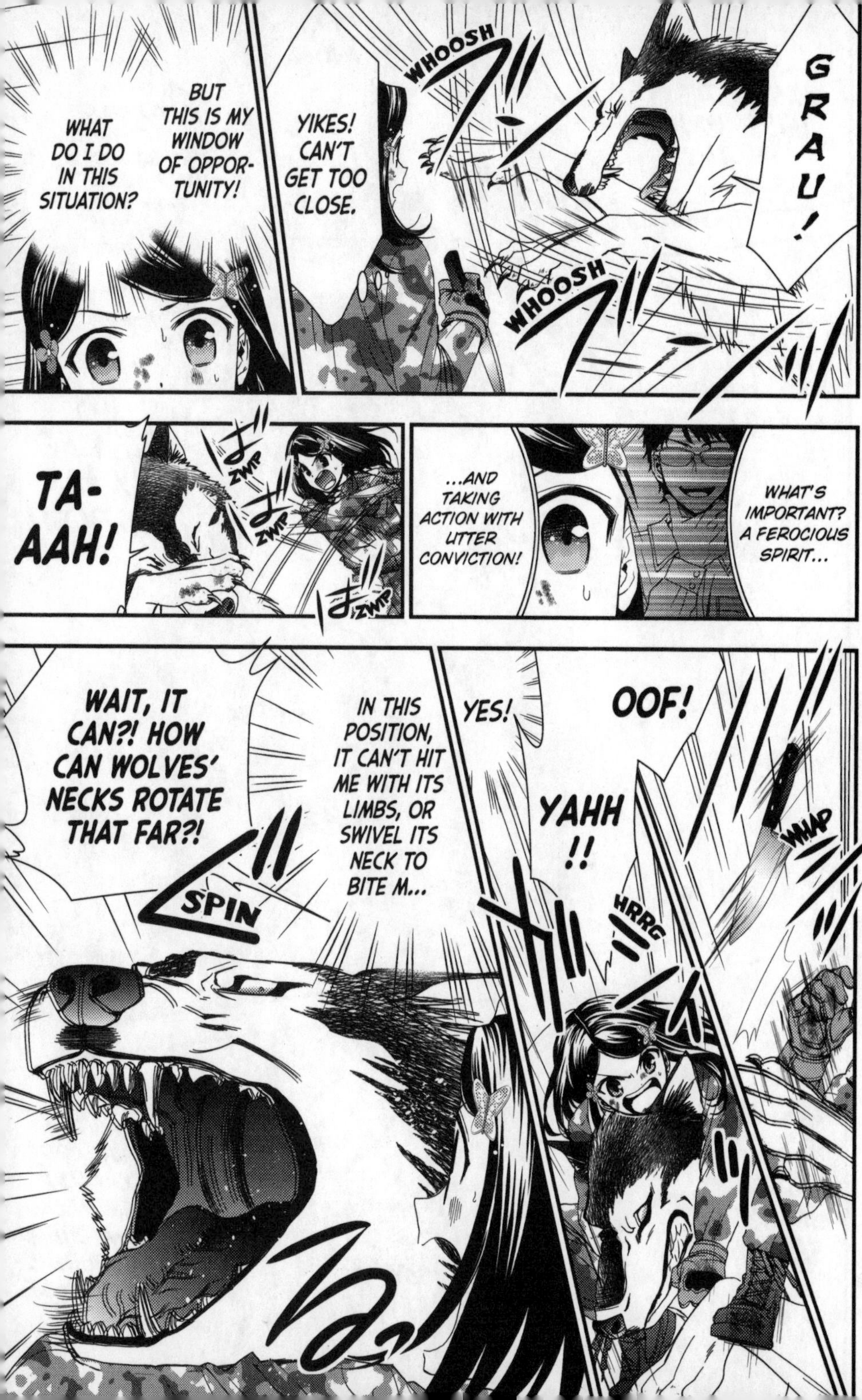
GRAU!
WHOOSH
WHOOSH
YIKES! CAN'T GET TOO CLOSE.
BUT THIS IS MY WINDOW OF OPPOR-TUNITY!
WHAT DO I DO IN THIS SITUATION?
WHAT'S IMPORTANT? A FEROCIOUS SPIRIT...
...AND TAKING ACTION WITH UTTER CONVICTION!
ZWIP
ZWIP
ZWIP
TA-AAH!
OOF!
YES!
YAHH!!
WHAP
HRRG
IN THIS POSITION, IT CAN'T HIT ME WITH ITS LIMBS, OR SWIVEL ITS NECK TO BITE M...
SPIN
WAIT, IT CAN?! HOW CAN WOLVES' NECKS ROTATE THAT FAR?!

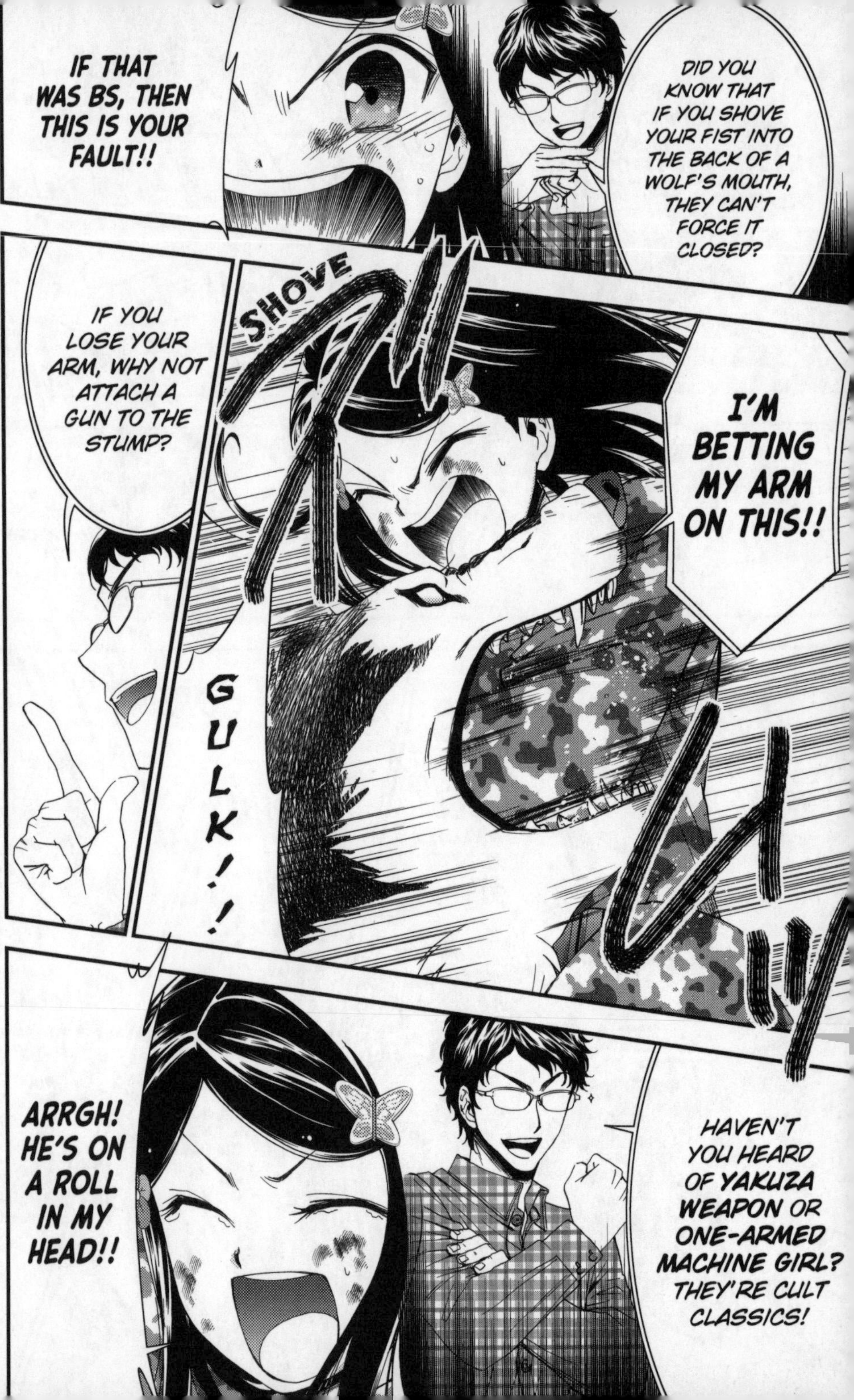
DID YOU KNOW THAT IF YOU SHOVE YOUR FIST INTO THE BACK OF A WOLF'S MOUTH, THEY CAN'T FORCE IT CLOSED?
IF THAT WAS BS, THEN THIS IS YOUR FAULT!!
SHOVE
I'M BETTING MY ARM ON THIS!!
GULK!!
IF YOU LOSE YOUR ARM, WHY NOT ATTACH A GUN TO THE STUMP?
HAVEN'T YOU HEARD OF YAKUZA WEAPON OR ONE-ARMED MACHINE GIRL? THEY'RE CULT CLASSICS!
ARRGH! HE'S ON A ROLL IN MY HEAD!!

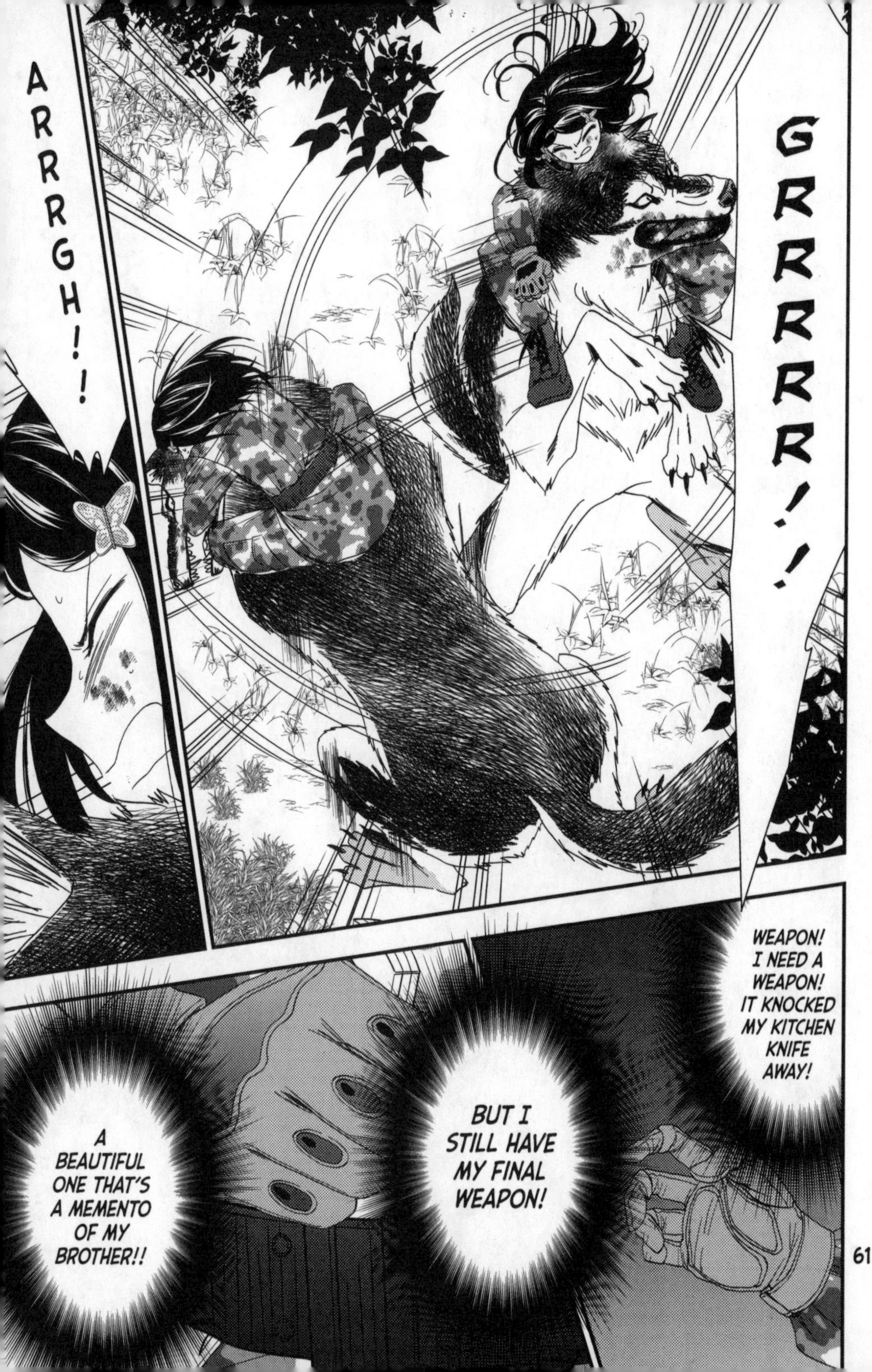
GRRRRR!!
ARRRGH!!
WEAPON! I NEED A WEAPON! IT KNOCKED MY KITCHEN KNIFE AWAY!
BUT I STILL HAVE MY FINAL WEAPON!
A BEAUTIFUL ONE THAT'S A MEMENTO OF MY BROTHER!!

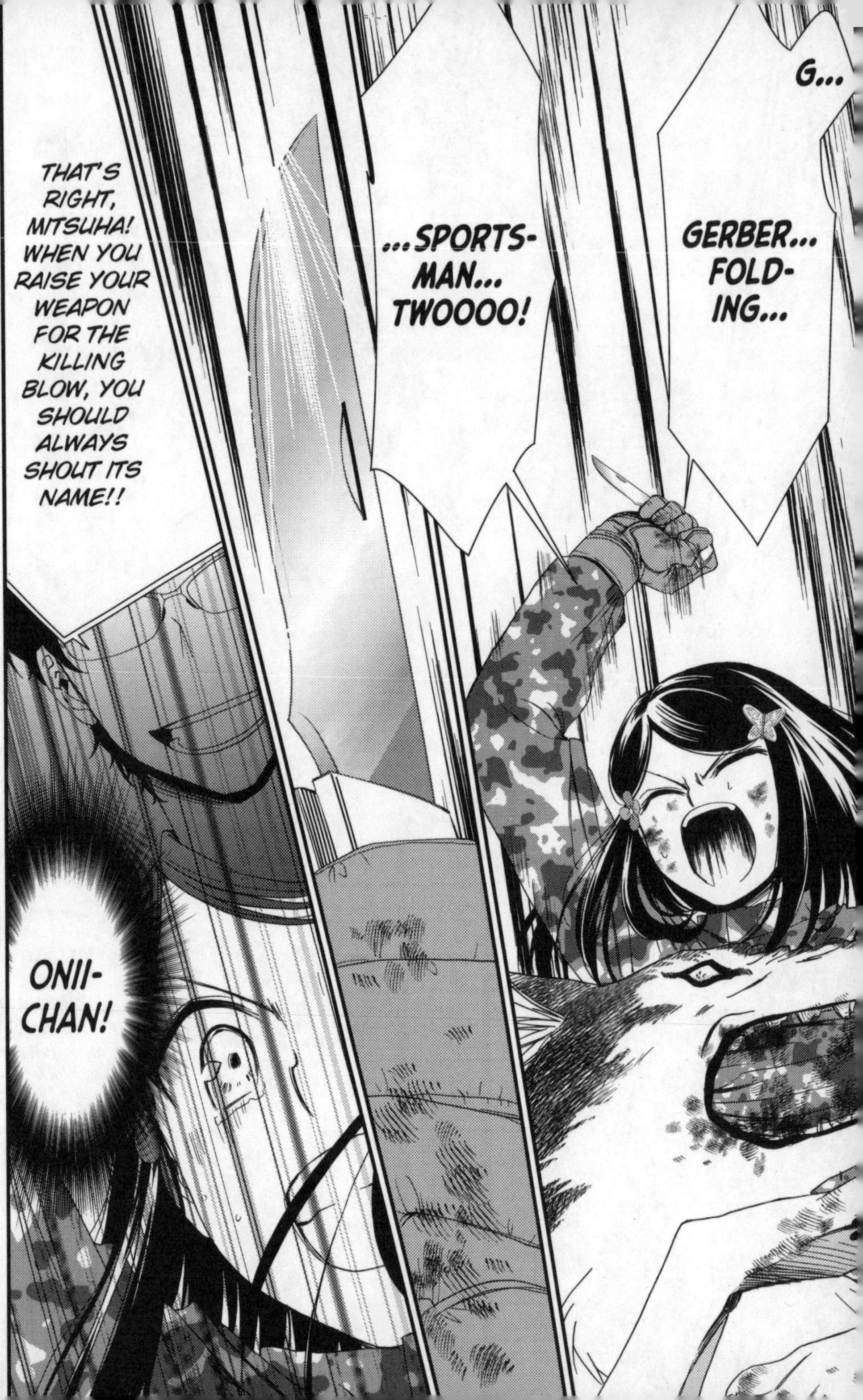
G...
GERBER... FOLD-ING...
...SPORTS-MAN... TWOOOO!
THAT'S RIGHT, MITSUHA! WHEN YOU RAISE YOUR WEAPON FOR THE KILLING BLOW, YOU SHOULD ALWAYS SHOUT ITS NAME!!
ONII-CHAN!

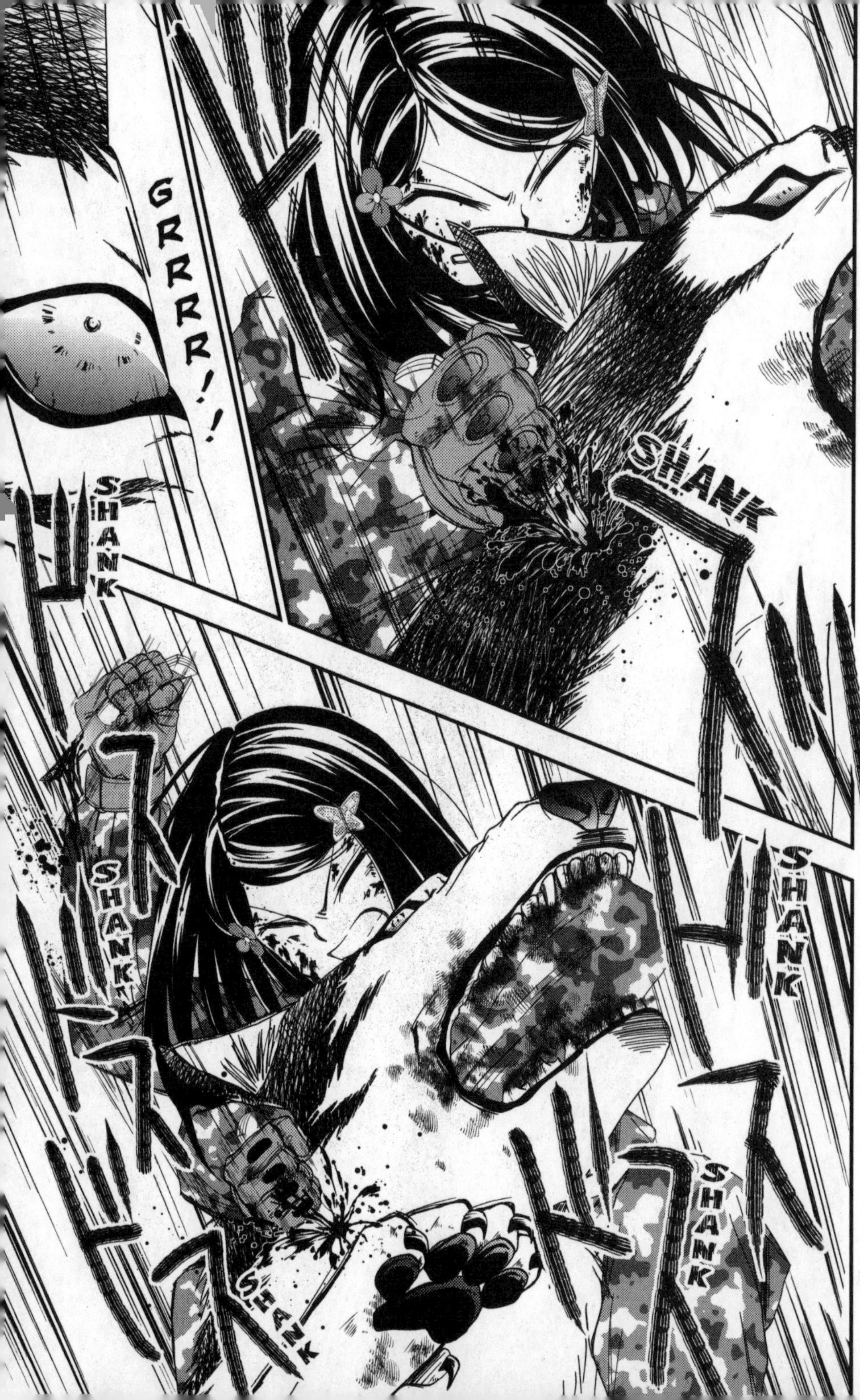
SHANK
GRRRR!!
SHANK
SHANK
SHANK
SHANK
SHANK

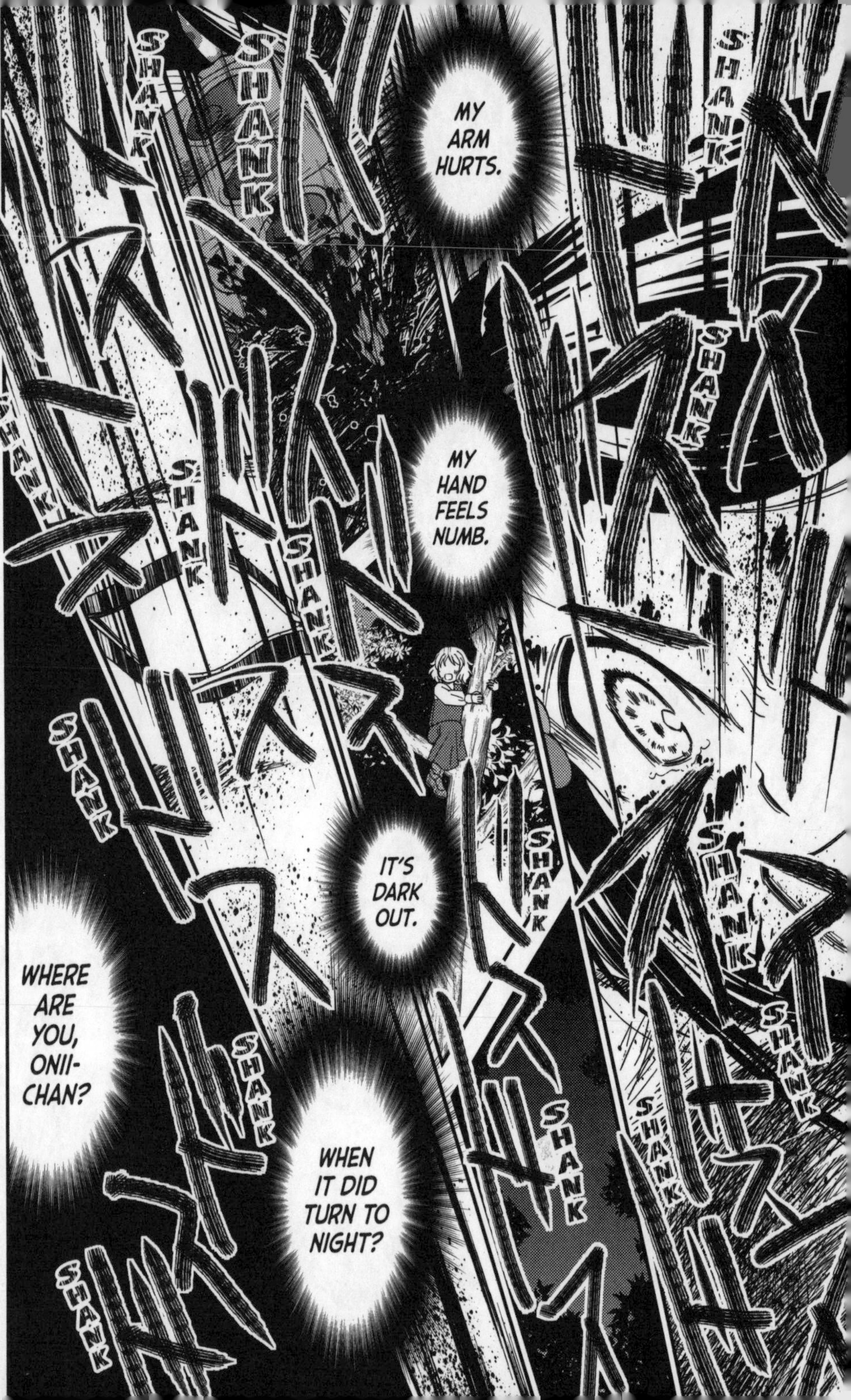
SHANK
SHANK
SHANK
MY ARM HURTS.
SHANK
MY HAND FEELS NUMB.
SHANK
SHANK
SHANK
SHANK
SHANK
SHANK
IT'S DARK OUT.
SHANK
SHANK
SHANK
WHEN IT DID TURN TO NIGHT?
SHANK
WHERE ARE YOU, ONII-CHAN?
SHANK

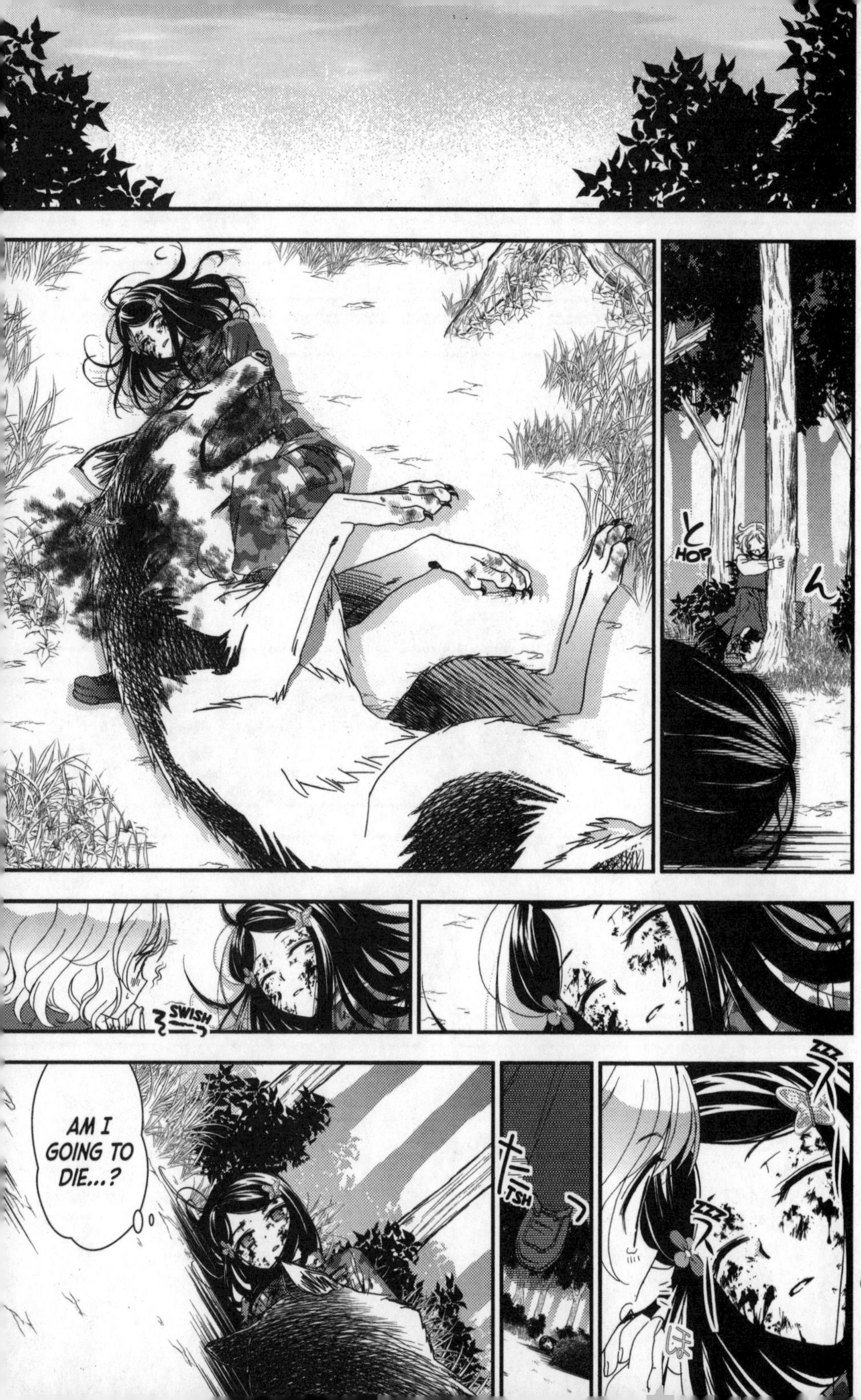
と
HOP
ん
SWISH
ほ
TSH
AM I GOING TO DIE...?

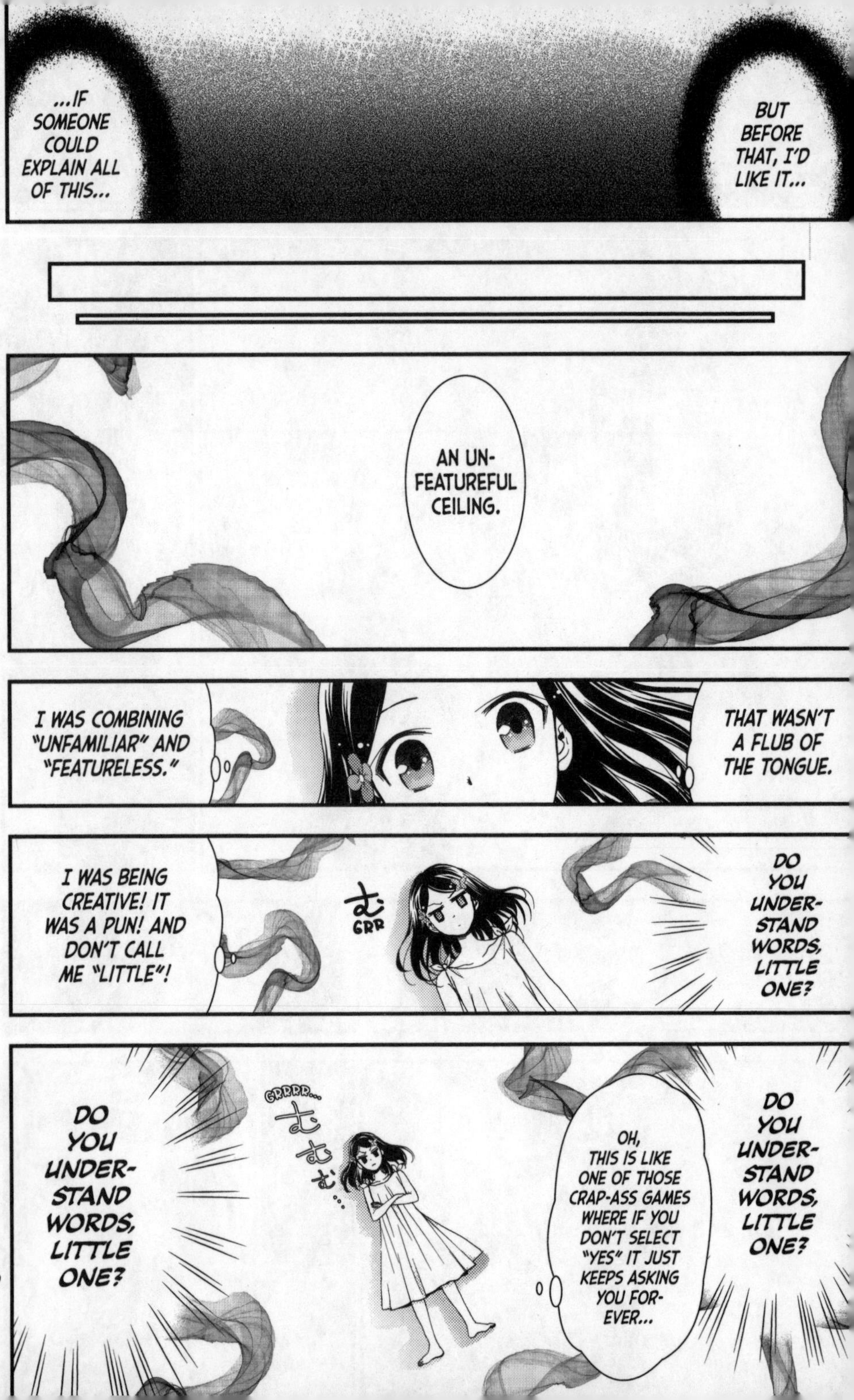

BUT BEFORE THAT, I'D LIKE IT...
...IF SOMEONE COULD EXPLAIN ALL OF THIS...
AN UN-FEATUREFUL CEILING.
THAT WASN'T A FLUB OF THE TONGUE.
I WAS COMBINING "UNFAMILIAR" AND "FEATURELESS."
DO YOU UNDER-STAND WORDS, LITTLE ONE?
GRR
I WAS BEING CREATIVE! IT WAS A PUN! AND DON'T CALL ME "LITTLE"!
DO YOU UNDER-STAND WORDS, LITTLE ONE?
OH, THIS IS LIKE ONE OF THOSE CRAP-ASS GAMES WHERE IF YOU DON'T SELECT "YES" IT JUST KEEPS ASKING YOU FOR-EVER...
GRRRR...
DO YOU UNDER-STAND WORDS, LITTLE ONE?

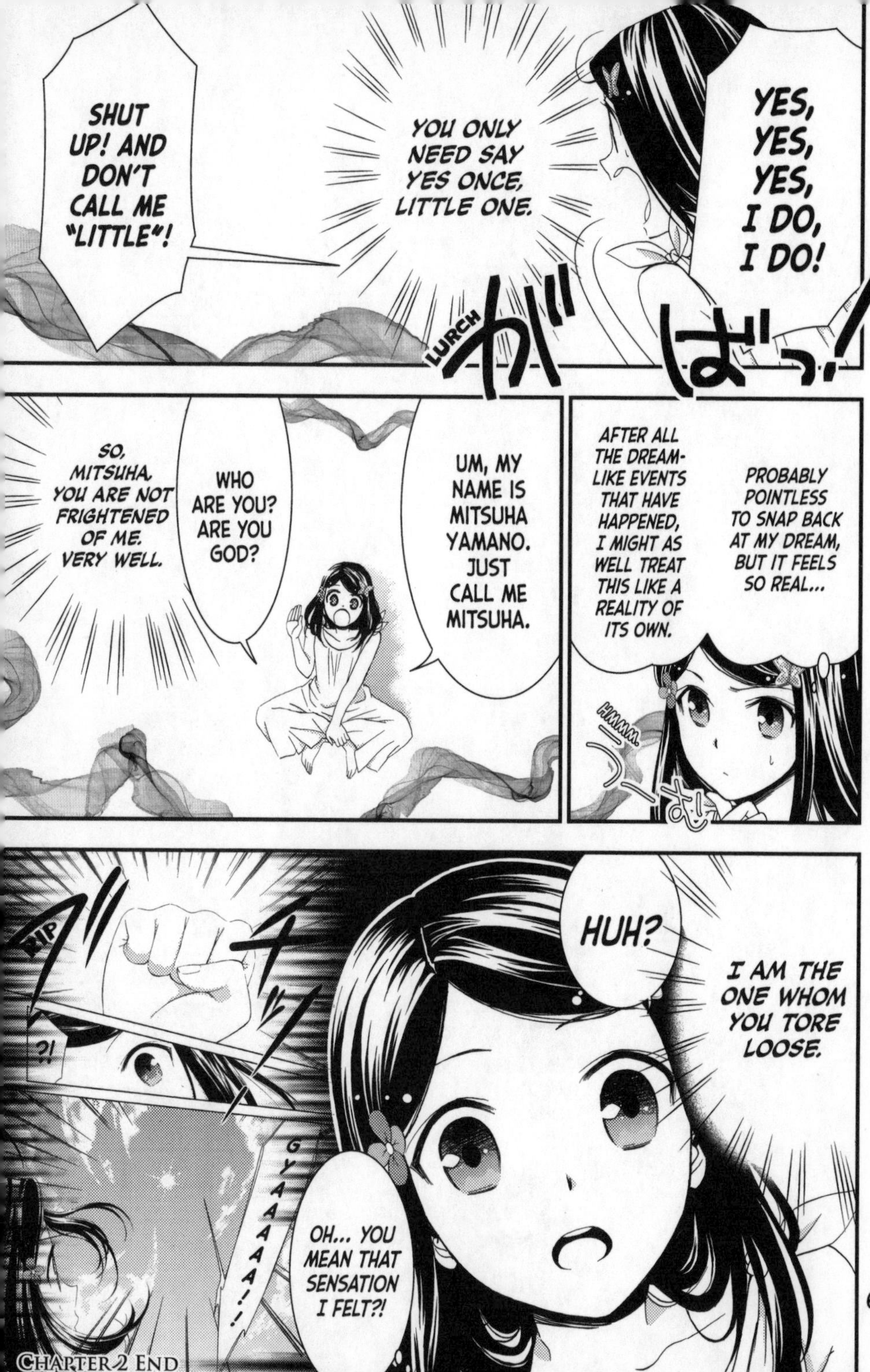
YES, YES, YES, I DO, I DO!
LURCH
YOU ONLY NEED SAY YES ONCE, LITTLE ONE.
SHUT UP! AND DON'T CALL ME "LITTLE"!
PROBABLY POINTLESS TO SNAP BACK AT MY DREAM, BUT IT FEELS SO REAL...
AFTER ALL THE DREAM-LIKE EVENTS THAT HAVE HAPPENED, I MIGHT AS WELL TREAT THIS LIKE A REALITY OF ITS OWN.
HMMM.
UM, MY NAME IS MITSUHA YAMANO. JUST CALL ME MITSUHA.
WHO ARE YOU? ARE YOU GOD?
SO, MITSUHA, YOU ARE NOT FRIGHTENED OF ME. VERY WELL.
HUH?
I AM THE ONE WHOM YOU TORE LOOSE.
OH... YOU MEAN THAT SENSATION I FELT?!
RIP
?!
GYAAAAAA!!
CHAPTER 2 END

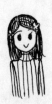

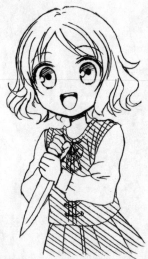

Oh, the two cubs were still alive, so I finished them off.
That's the wild child Colette I know—skillful and merciless.

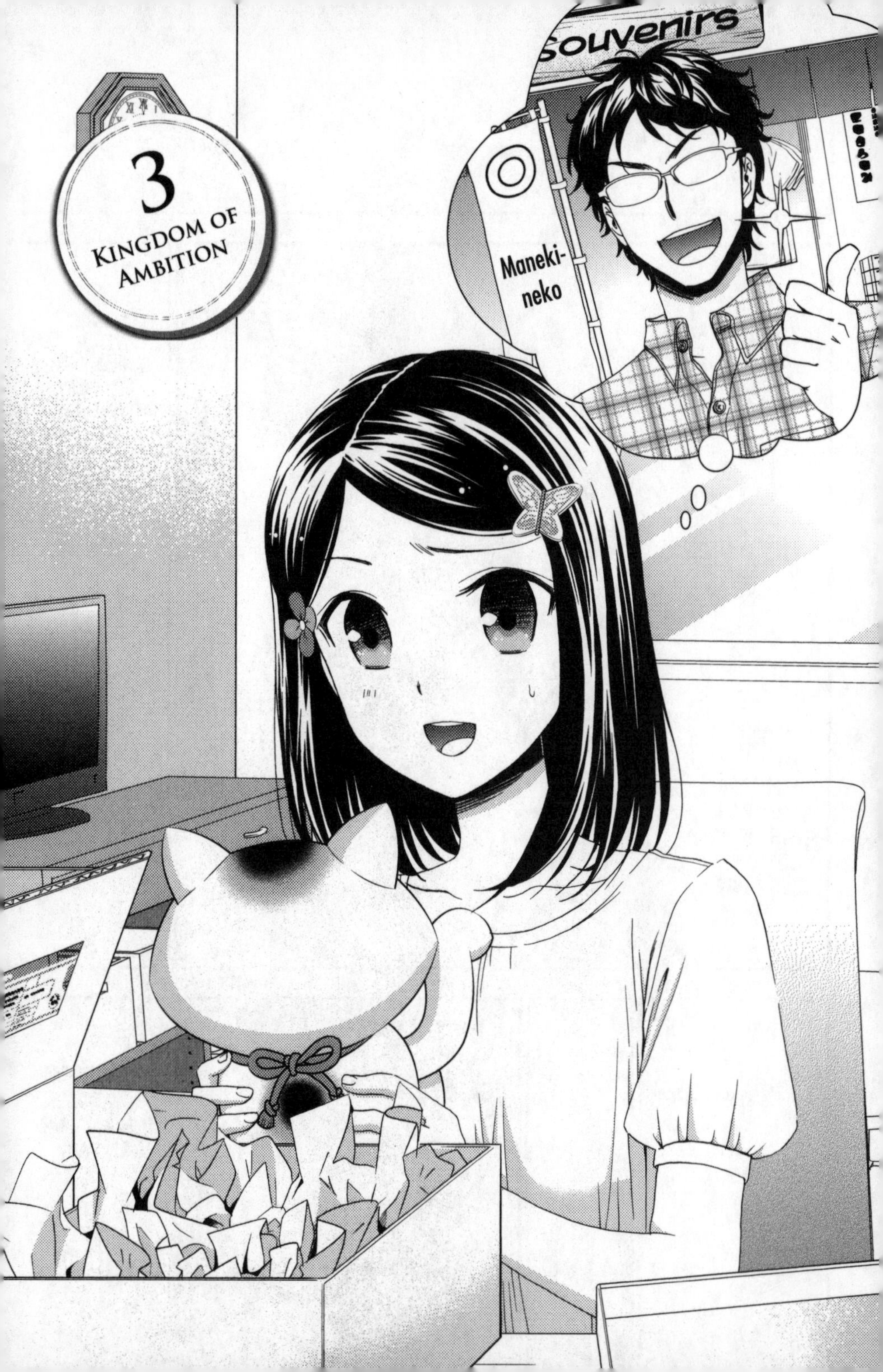
3
Kingdom of Ambition
Souvenirs
Maneki-neko

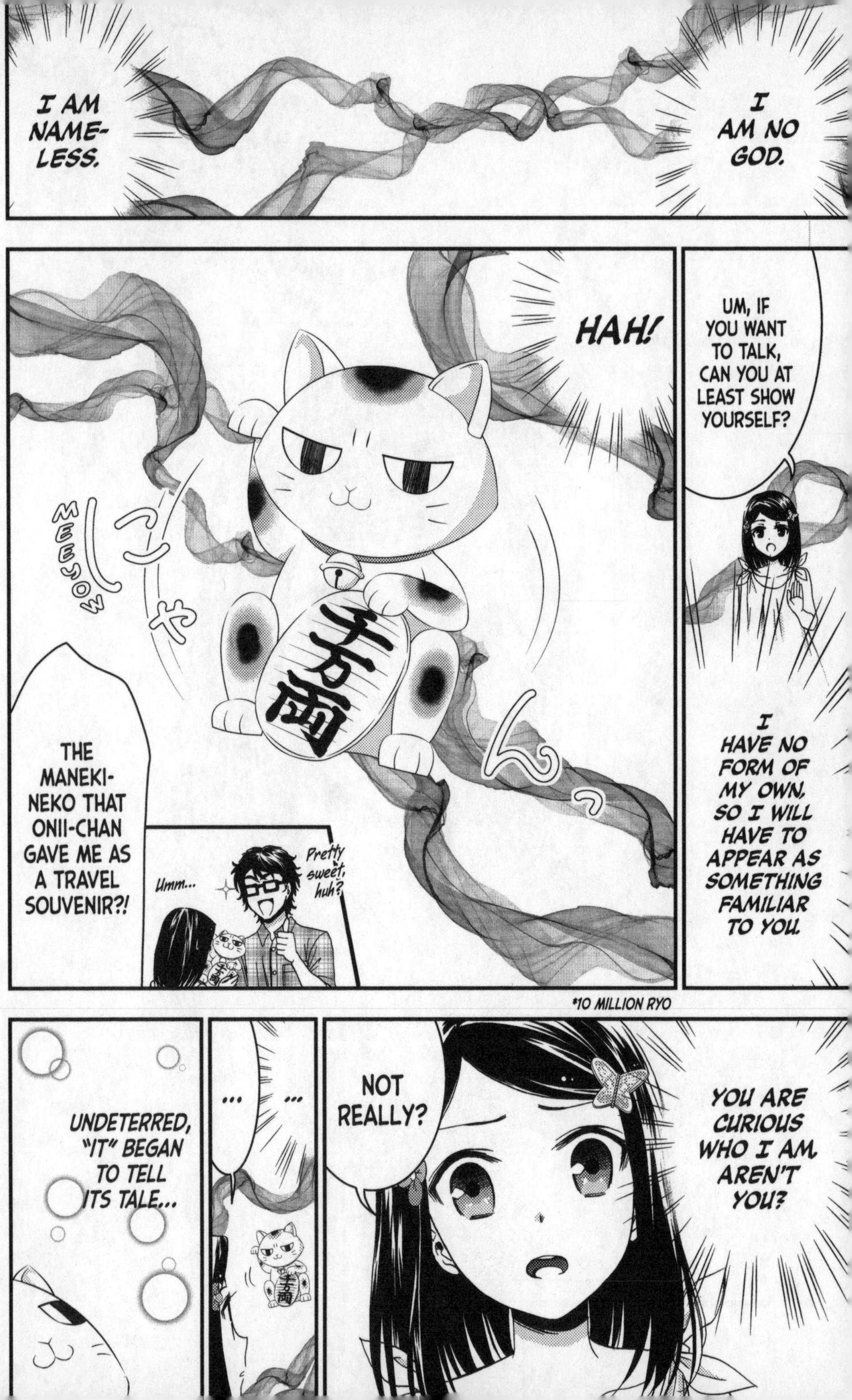
I AM NO GOD.
I AM NAMELESS.
UM, IF YOU WANT TO TALK, CAN YOU AT LEAST SHOW YOURSELF?
I HAVE NO FORM OF MY OWN, SO I WILL HAVE TO APPEAR AS SOMETHING FAMILIAR TO YOU.
HAH!
千万両
MEEYOW
THE MANEKI-NEKO THAT ONII-CHAN GAVE ME AS A TRAVEL SOUVENIR?!
Pretty sweet, huh?
Umm...
*10 MILLION RYO
YOU ARE CURIOUS WHO I AM, AREN'T YOU?
NOT REALLY?
... ...
UNDETERRED, "IT" BEGAN TO TELL ITS TALE...

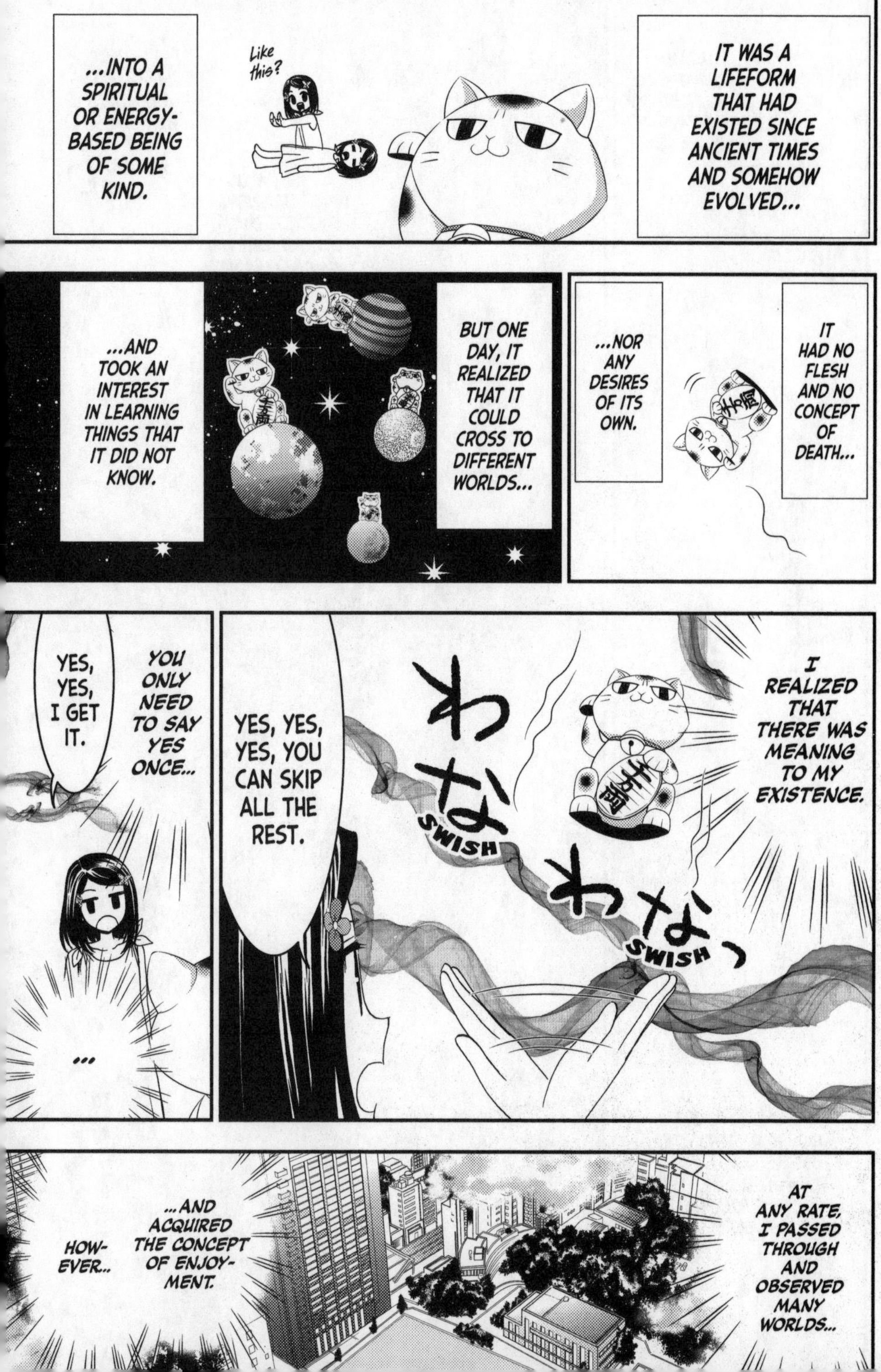
IT WAS A LIFEFORM THAT HAD EXISTED SINCE ANCIENT TIMES AND SOMEHOW EVOLVED...
Like this?
...INTO A SPIRITUAL OR ENERGY-BASED BEING OF SOME KIND.
IT HAD NO FLESH AND NO CONCEPT OF DEATH...
...NOR ANY DESIRES OF ITS OWN.
BUT ONE DAY, IT REALIZED THAT IT COULD CROSS TO DIFFERENT WORLDS...
...AND TOOK AN INTEREST IN LEARNING THINGS THAT IT DID NOT KNOW.
I REALIZED THAT THERE WAS MEANING TO MY EXISTENCE.
わな SWISH
わなっ SWISH
YES, YES, YES, YOU CAN SKIP ALL THE REST.
YOU ONLY NEED TO SAY YES ONCE...
YES, YES, I GET IT.
...
AT ANY RATE, I PASSED THROUGH AND OBSERVED MANY WORLDS...
...AND ACQUIRED THE CONCEPT OF ENJOY-MENT.
HOW-EVER...

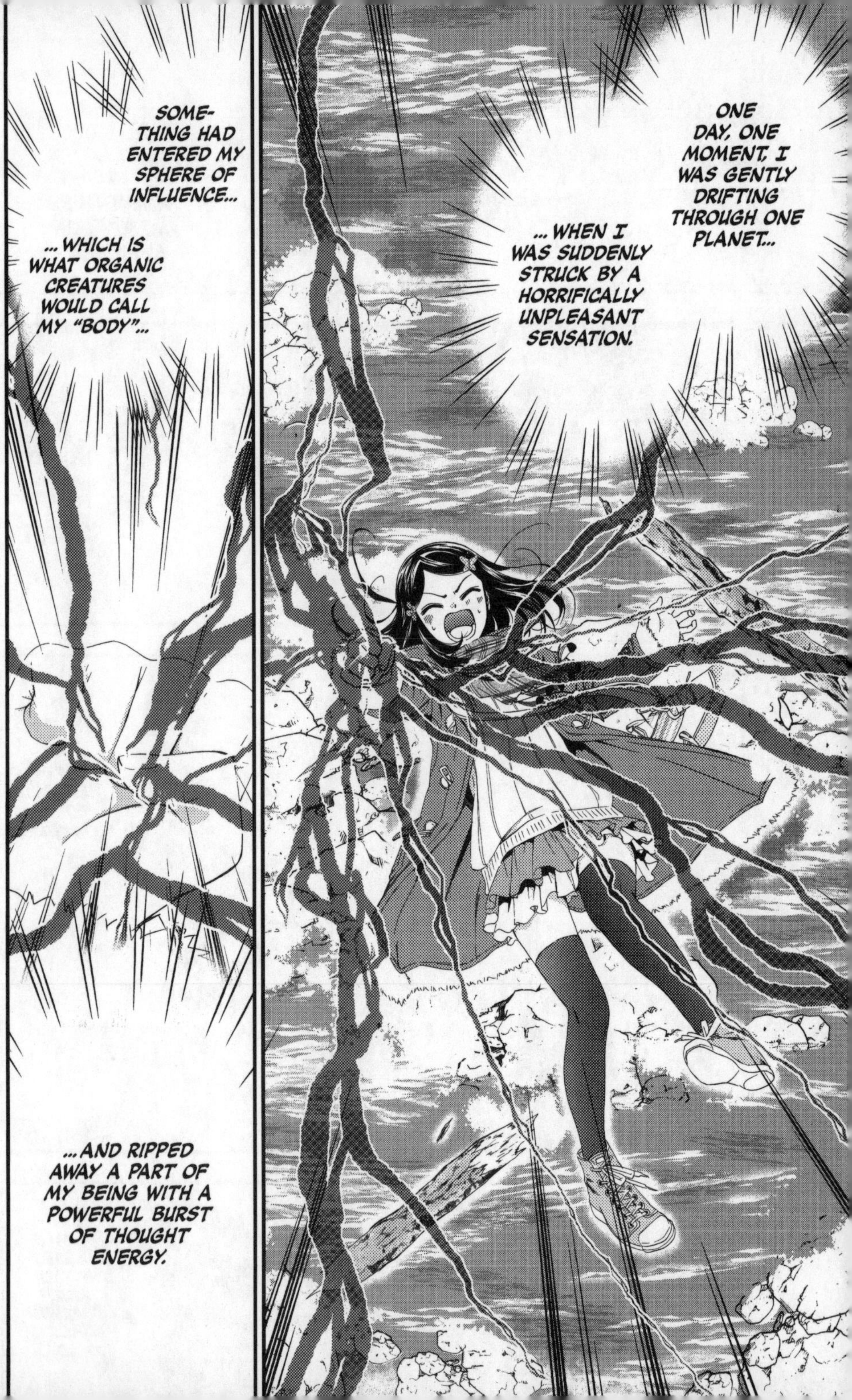
ONE DAY, ONE MOMENT, I WAS GENTLY DRIFTING THROUGH ONE PLANET...
...WHEN I WAS SUDDENLY STRUCK BY A HORRIFICALLY UNPLEASANT SENSATION.
SOME-THING HAD ENTERED MY SPHERE OF INFLUENCE...
...WHICH IS WHAT ORGANIC CREATURES WOULD CALL MY "BODY"...
...AND RIPPED AWAY A PART OF MY BEING WITH A POWERFUL BURST OF THOUGHT ENERGY.

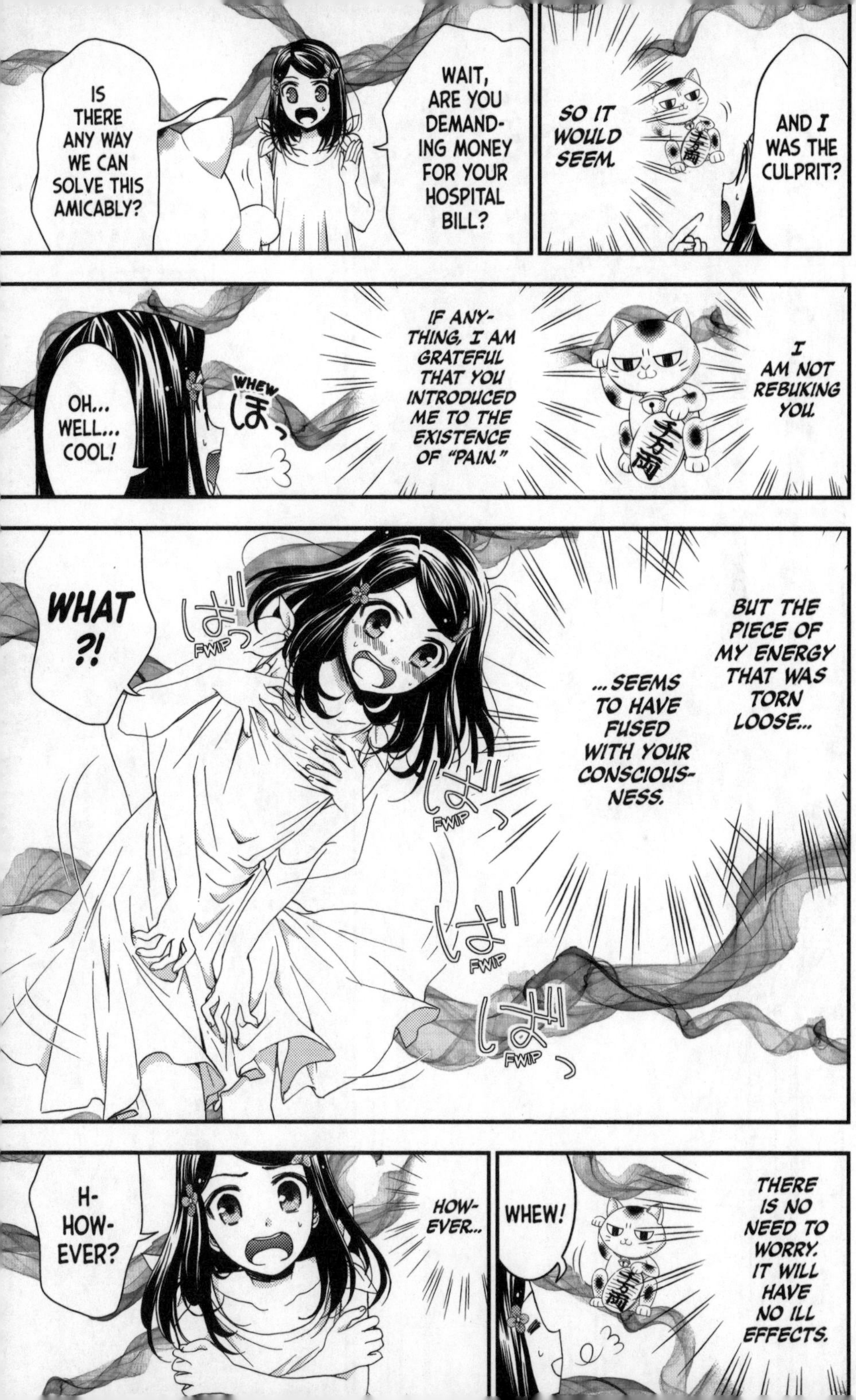
AND I WAS THE CULPRIT?
SO IT WOULD SEEM.
WAIT, ARE YOU DEMANDING MONEY FOR YOUR HOSPITAL BILL?
IS THERE ANY WAY WE CAN SOLVE THIS AMICABLY?
I AM NOT REBUKING YOU.
IF ANYTHING, I AM GRATEFUL THAT YOU INTRODUCED ME TO THE EXISTENCE OF "PAIN."
ほっ WHEW
OH... WELL... COOL!
BUT THE PIECE OF MY ENERGY THAT WAS TORN LOOSE...
...SEEMS TO HAVE FUSED WITH YOUR CONSCIOUSNESS.
ばっ FWIP
ばっ FWIP
ばっ FWIP
ばっ FWIP
WHAT?!
THERE IS NO NEED TO WORRY. IT WILL HAVE NO ILL EFFECTS.
WHEW!
HOWEVER...
H-HOWEVER?

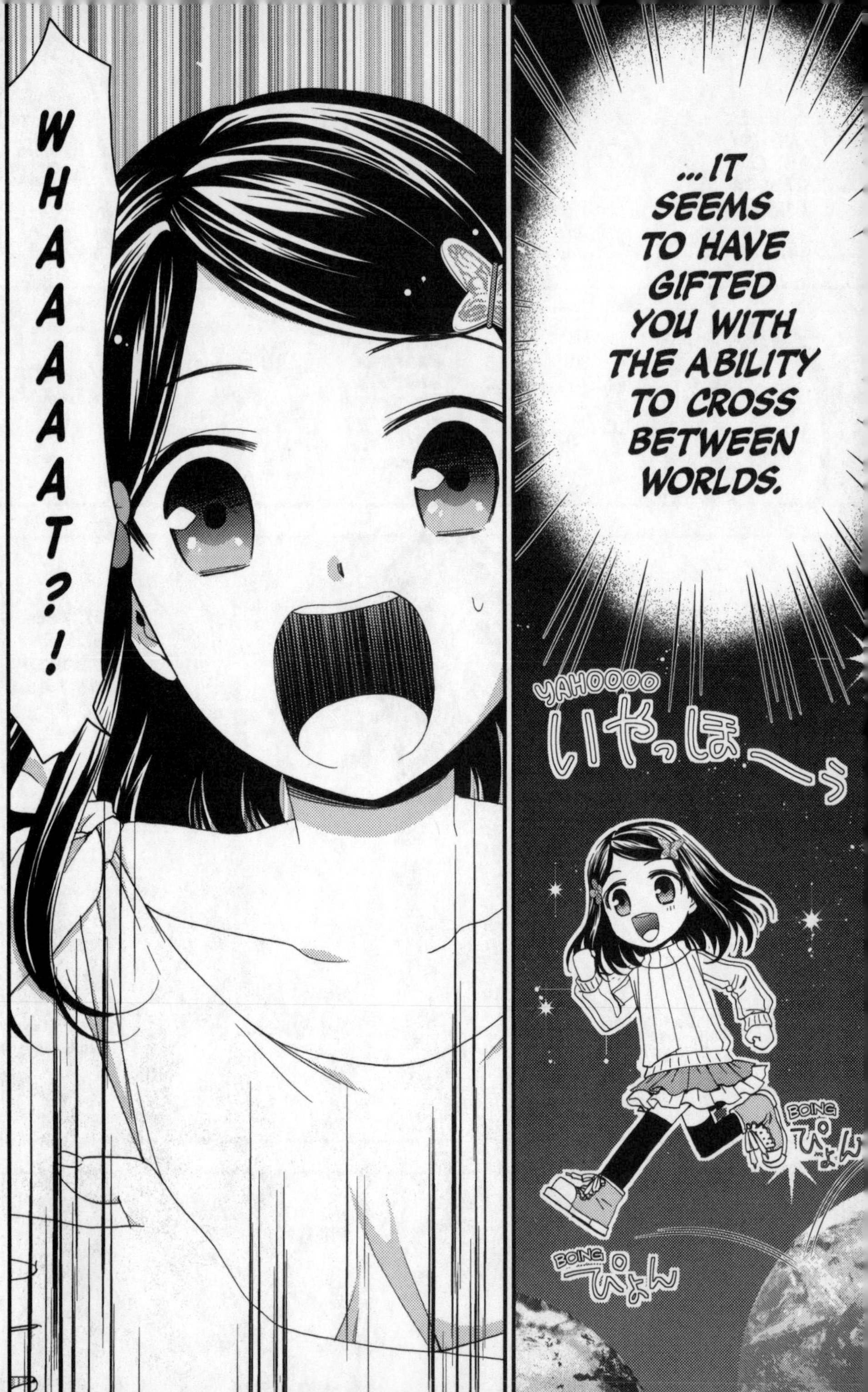
...IT SEEMS TO HAVE GIFTED YOU WITH THE ABILITY TO CROSS BETWEEN WORLDS.
YAHOOOO
いやっほ～う
BOING
ぴょん
BOING
ぴょん
WHAAAAAT?!

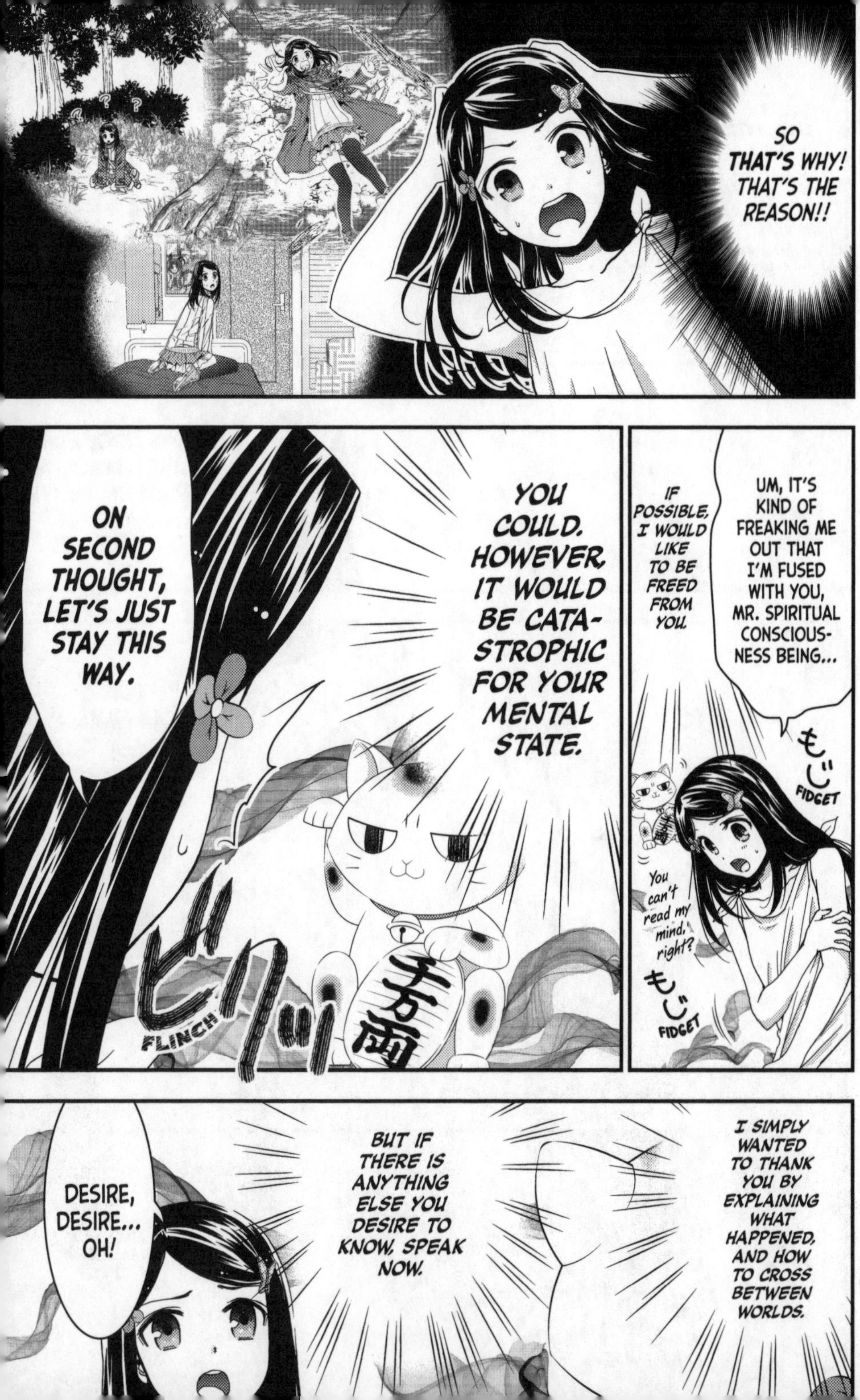
SO THAT'S WHY! THAT'S THE REASON!!
UM, IT'S KIND OF FREAKING ME OUT THAT I'M FUSED WITH YOU, MR. SPIRITUAL CONSCIOUSNESS BEING...
IF POSSIBLE, I WOULD LIKE TO BE FREED FROM YOU.
もじ FIDGET
You can't read my mind, right?
もじ FIDGET
YOU COULD. HOWEVER, IT WOULD BE CATA-STROPHIC FOR YOUR MENTAL STATE.
ON SECOND THOUGHT, LET'S JUST STAY THIS WAY.
ビクッ FLINCH
千万両
I SIMPLY WANTED TO THANK YOU BY EXPLAINING WHAT HAPPENED, AND HOW TO CROSS BETWEEN WORLDS.
BUT IF THERE IS ANYTHING ELSE YOU DESIRE TO KNOW, SPEAK NOW.
DESIRE, DESIRE... OH!

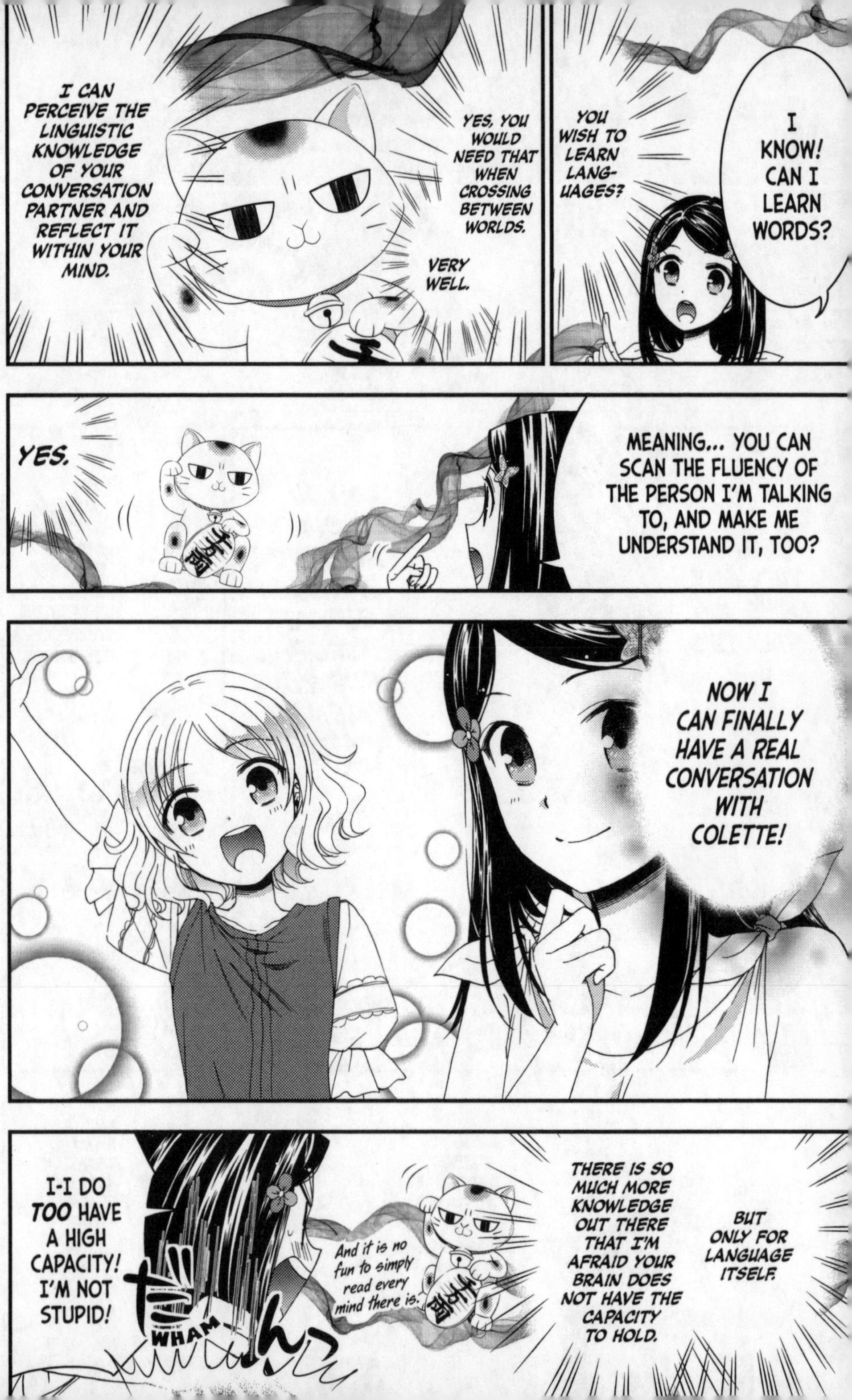
I KNOW! CAN I LEARN WORDS?
YOU WISH TO LEARN LANG-UAGES?
YES, YOU WOULD NEED THAT WHEN CROSSING BETWEEN WORLDS.
VERY WELL.
I CAN PERCEIVE THE LINGUISTIC KNOWLEDGE OF YOUR CONVERSATION PARTNER AND REFLECT IT WITHIN YOUR MIND.
MEANING... YOU CAN SCAN THE FLUENCY OF THE PERSON I'M TALKING TO, AND MAKE ME UNDERSTAND IT, TOO?
YES.
NOW I CAN FINALLY HAVE A REAL CONVERSATION WITH COLETTE!
BUT ONLY FOR LANGUAGE ITSELF.
THERE IS SO MUCH MORE KNOWLEDGE OUT THERE THAT I'M AFRAID YOUR BRAIN DOES NOT HAVE THE CAPACITY TO HOLD.
And it is no fun to simply read every mind there is.
I-I DO *TOO* HAVE A HIGH CAPACITY! I'M NOT STUPID!
WHAM

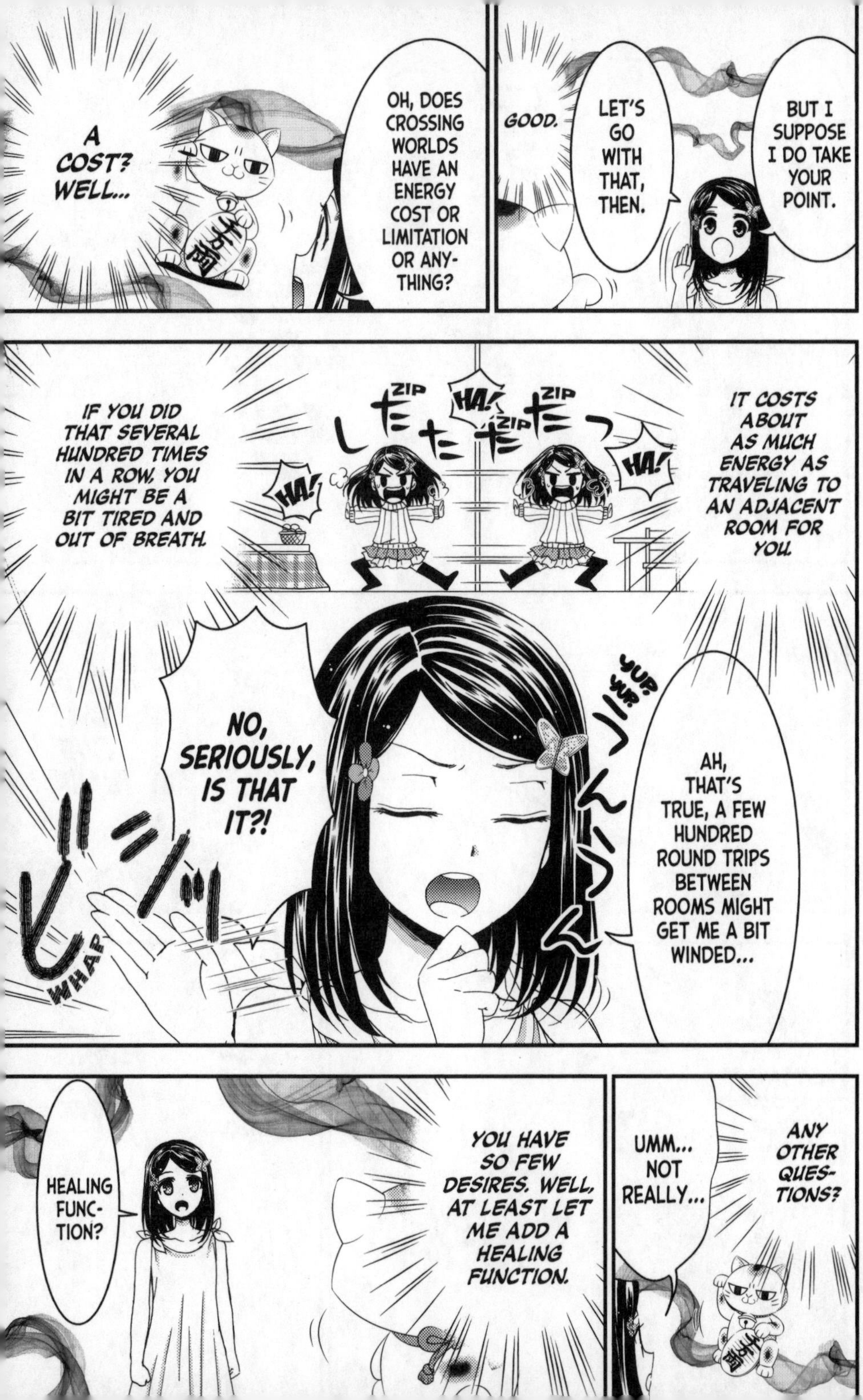
BUT I SUPPOSE I DO TAKE YOUR POINT.
LET'S GO WITH THAT, THEN.
GOOD.
OH, DOES CROSSING WORLDS HAVE AN ENERGY COST OR LIMITATION OR ANYTHING?
A COST? WELL...
IT COSTS ABOUT AS MUCH ENERGY AS TRAVELING TO AN ADJACENT ROOM FOR YOU.
ZIP
HA!
ZIP
ZIP
HA!
HA!
IF YOU DID THAT SEVERAL HUNDRED TIMES IN A ROW, YOU MIGHT BE A BIT TIRED AND OUT OF BREATH.
YUP YUP
AH, THAT'S TRUE, A FEW HUNDRED ROUND TRIPS BETWEEN ROOMS MIGHT GET ME A BIT WINDED...
NO, SERIOUSLY, IS THAT IT?!
WHAP
ANY OTHER QUESTIONS?
UMM... NOT REALLY...
YOU HAVE SO FEW DESIRES. WELL, AT LEAST LET ME ADD A HEALING FUNCTION.
HEALING FUNCTION?

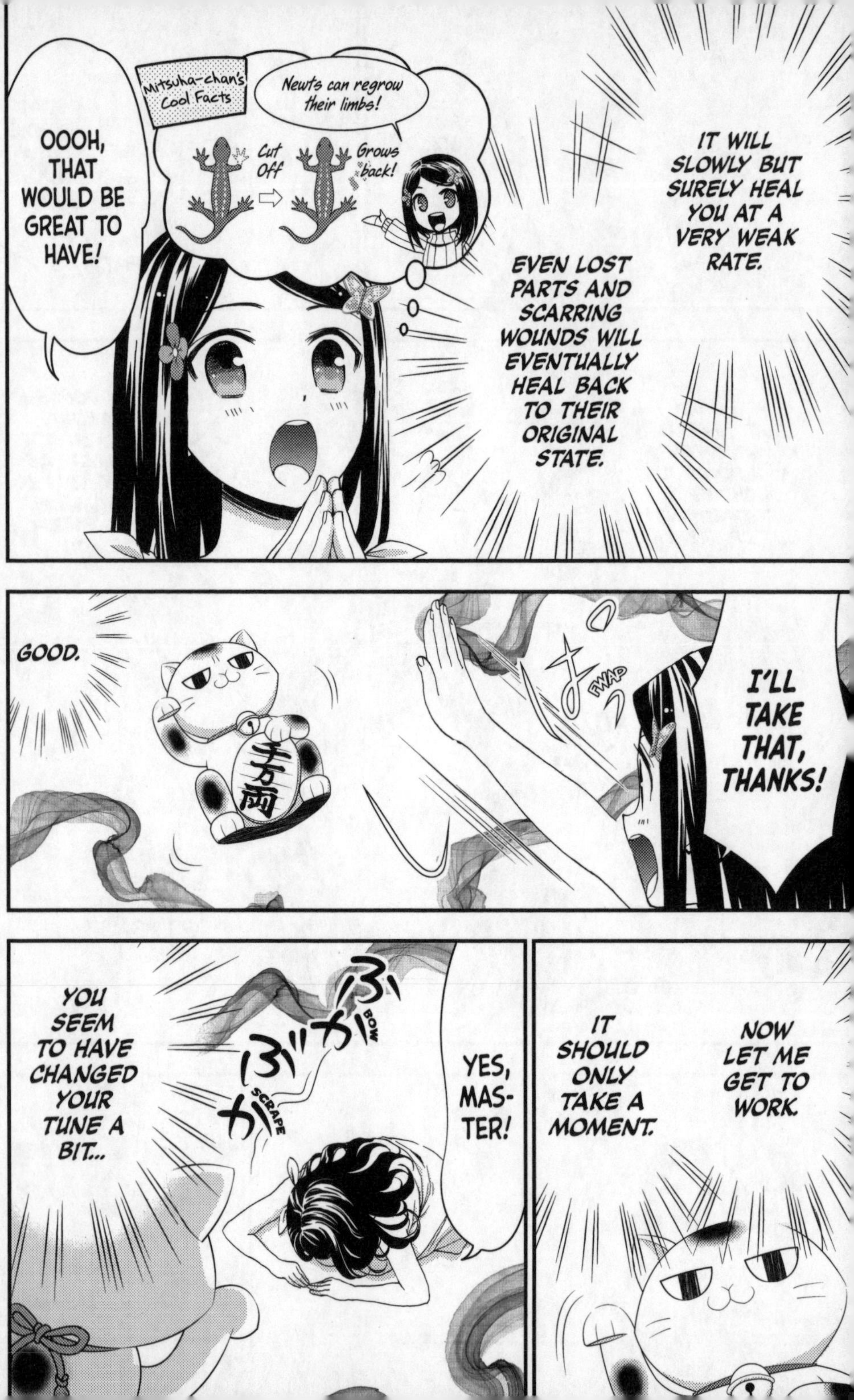
IT WILL SLOWLY BUT SURELY HEAL YOU AT A VERY WEAK RATE.
EVEN LOST PARTS AND SCARRING WOUNDS WILL EVENTUALLY HEAL BACK TO THEIR ORIGINAL STATE.
Mitsuha-chan's Cool Facts
Newts can regrow their limbs!
Cut Off
Grows back!
OOOH, THAT WOULD BE GREAT TO HAVE!
I'LL TAKE THAT, THANKS!
FWAP
GOOD.
千万両
NOW LET ME GET TO WORK.
IT SHOULD ONLY TAKE A MOMENT.
YES, MASTER!
BOW
SCRAPE
YOU SEEM TO HAVE CHANGED YOUR TUNE A BIT...

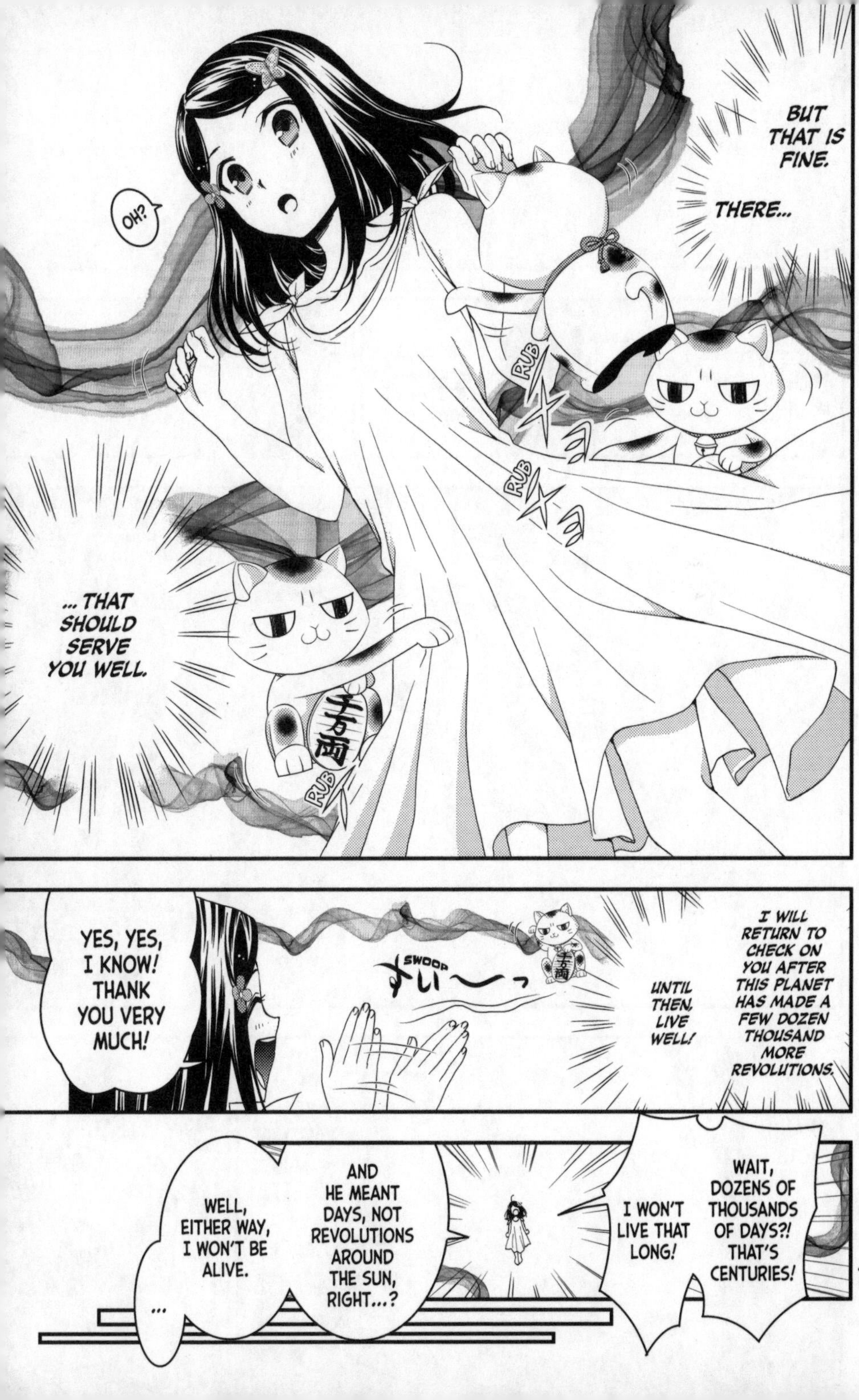
BUT THAT IS FINE.
THERE...
OH?
RUB
RUB
... THAT SHOULD SERVE YOU WELL.
RUB
I WILL RETURN TO CHECK ON YOU AFTER THIS PLANET HAS MADE A FEW DOZEN THOUSAND MORE REVOLUTIONS.
UNTIL THEN, LIVE WELL!
SWOOP
YES, YES, I KNOW! THANK YOU VERY MUCH!
WAIT, DOZENS OF THOUSANDS OF DAYS?! THAT'S CENTURIES!
I WON'T LIVE THAT LONG!
AND HE MEANT DAYS, NOT REVOLUTIONS AROUND THE SUN, RIGHT...?
WELL, EITHER WAY, I WON'T BE ALIVE.
...

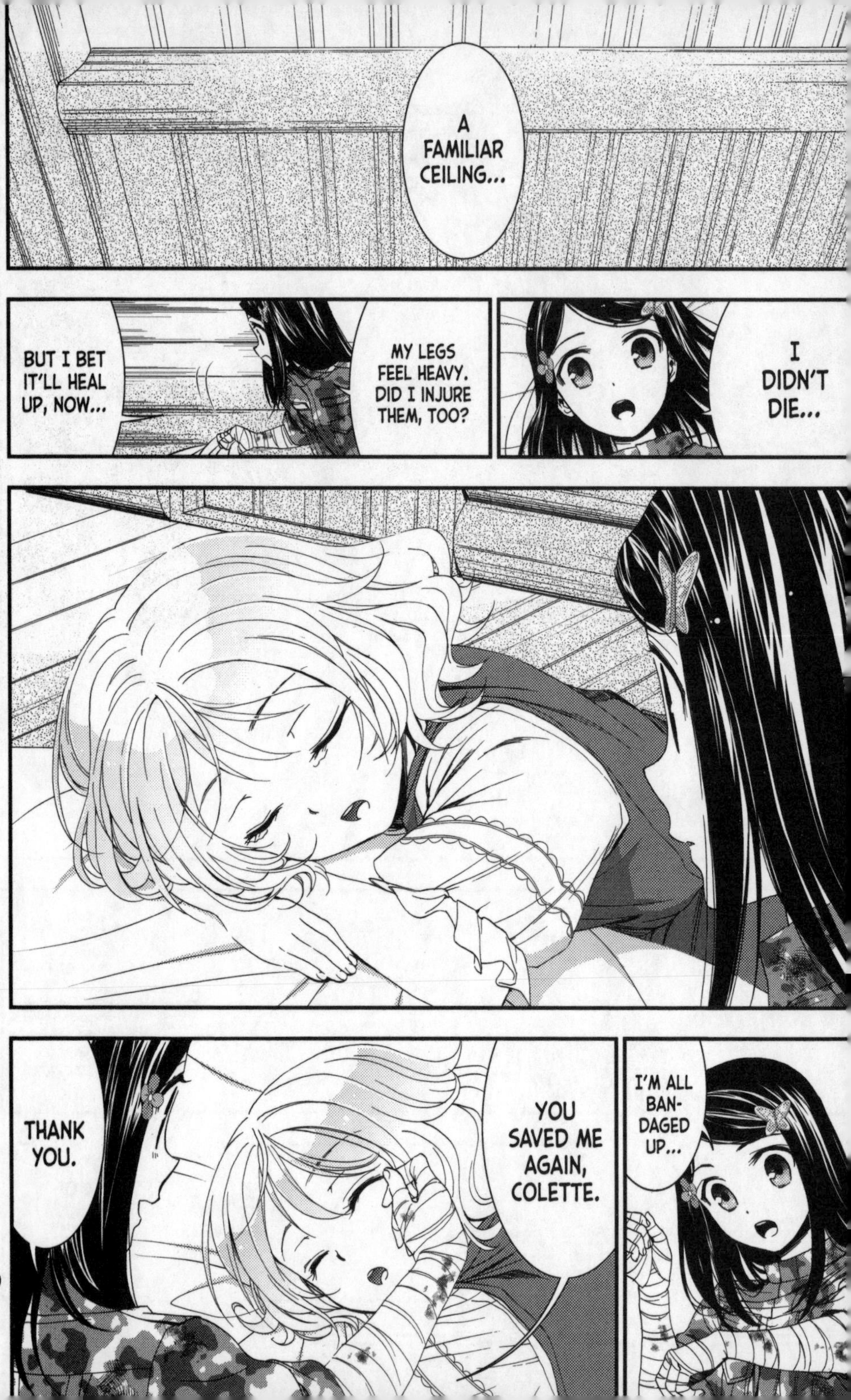
A FAMILIAR CEILING...
I DIDN'T DIE...
MY LEGS FEEL HEAVY. DID I INJURE THEM, TOO?
BUT I BET IT'LL HEAL UP, NOW...
I'M ALL BAN-DAGED UP...
YOU SAVED ME AGAIN, COLETTE.
THANK YOU.

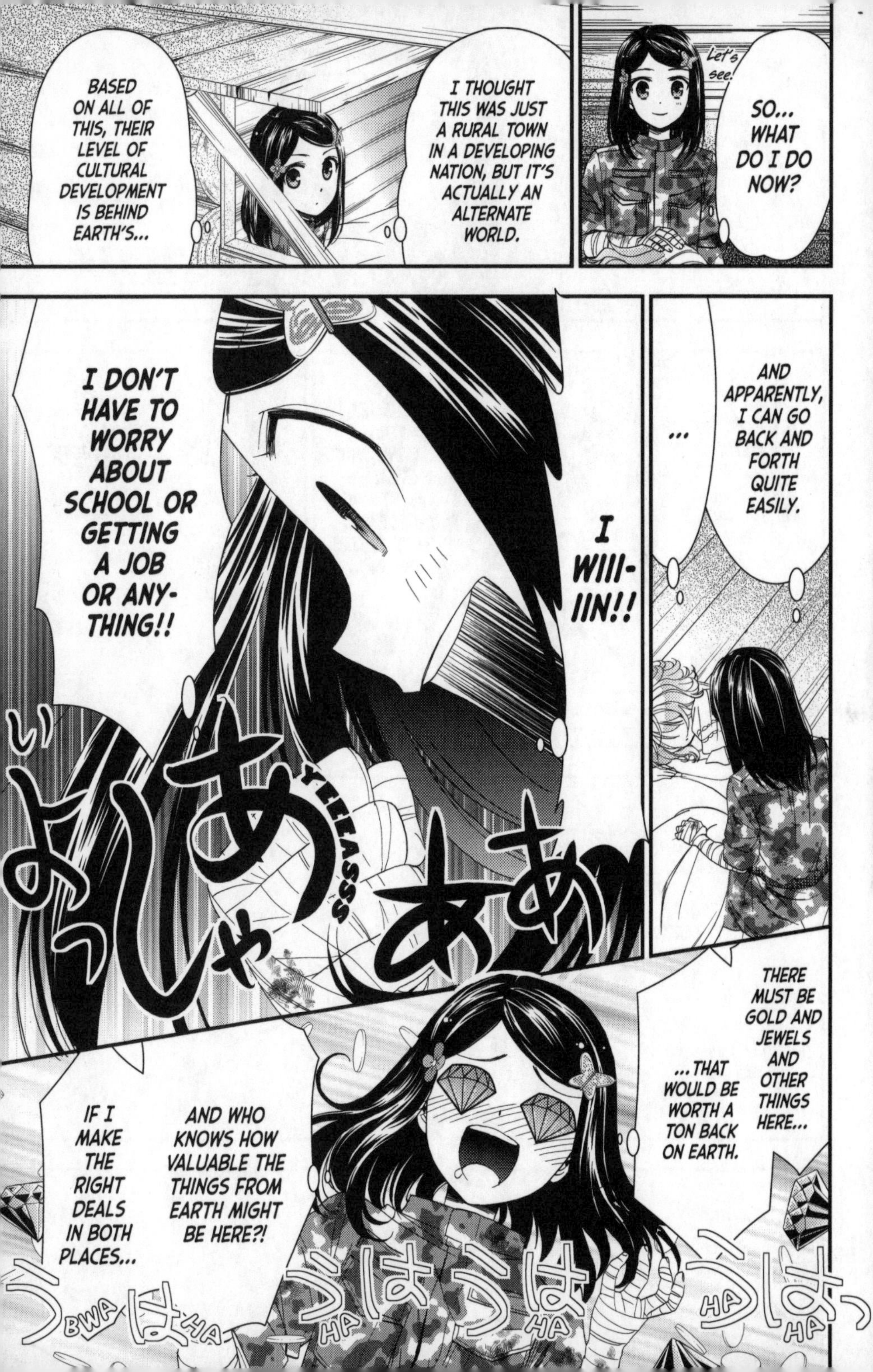
Let's see!
SO... WHAT DO I DO NOW?
I THOUGHT THIS WAS JUST A RURAL TOWN IN A DEVELOPING NATION, BUT IT'S ACTUALLY AN ALTERNATE WORLD.
BASED ON ALL OF THIS, THEIR LEVEL OF CULTURAL DEVELOPMENT IS BEHIND EARTH'S...
AND APPARENTLY, I CAN GO BACK AND FORTH QUITE EASILY.
...
I WIIII-IIN!!
I DON'T HAVE TO WORRY ABOUT SCHOOL OR GETTING A JOB OR ANY-THING!!
YEEEASSS
THERE MUST BE GOLD AND JEWELS AND OTHER THINGS HERE...
...THAT WOULD BE WORTH A TON BACK ON EARTH.
AND WHO KNOWS HOW VALUABLE THE THINGS FROM EARTH MIGHT BE HERE?!
IF I MAKE THE RIGHT DEALS IN BOTH PLACES...
BWA HA HA HA HA HA

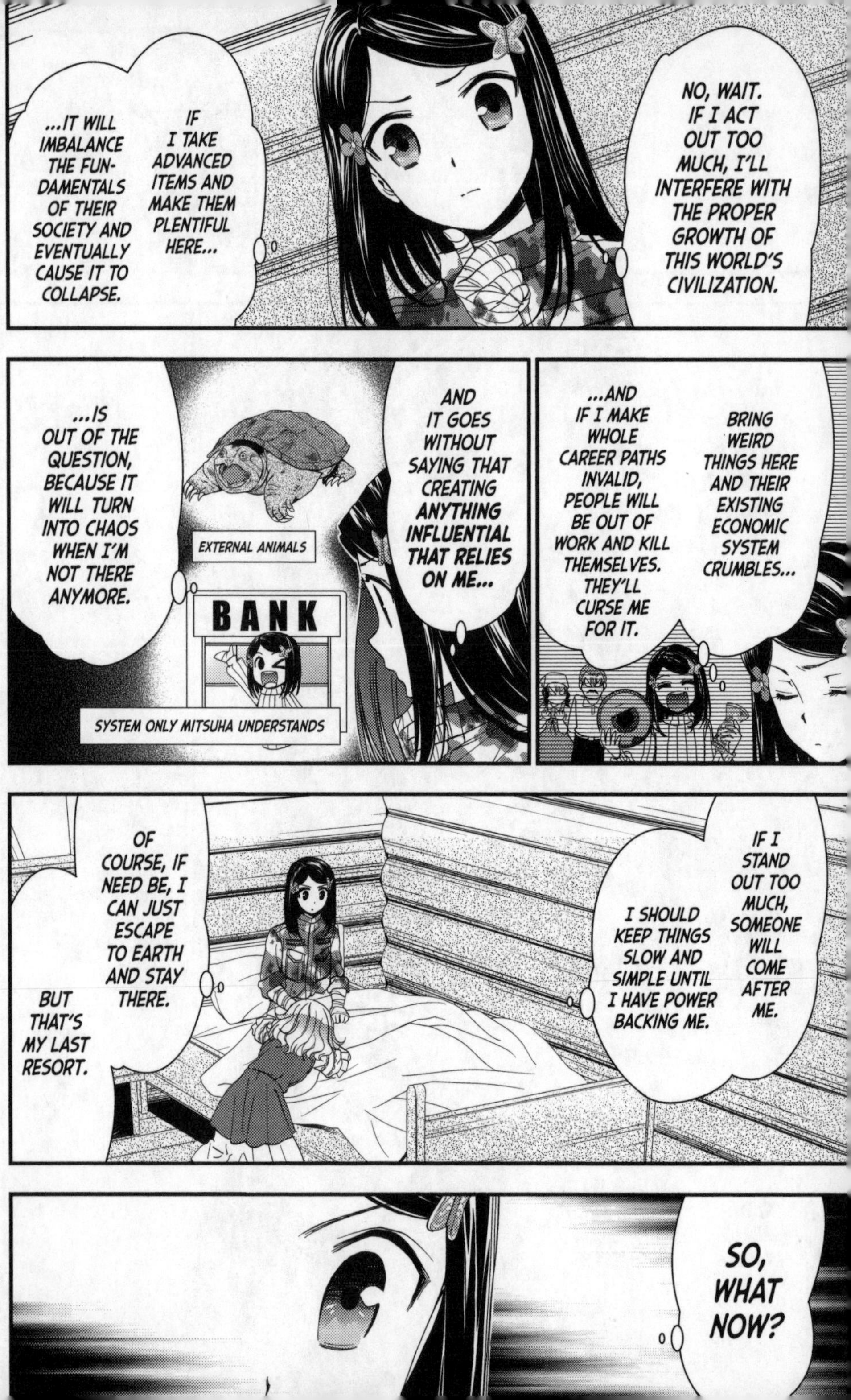
NO, WAIT. IF I ACT OUT TOO MUCH, I'LL INTERFERE WITH THE PROPER GROWTH OF THIS WORLD'S CIVILIZATION.
IF I TAKE ADVANCED ITEMS AND MAKE THEM PLENTIFUL HERE...
...IT WILL IMBALANCE THE FUN-DAMENTALS OF THEIR SOCIETY AND EVENTUALLY CAUSE IT TO COLLAPSE.
BRING WEIRD THINGS HERE AND THEIR EXISTING ECONOMIC SYSTEM CRUMBLES...
...AND IF I MAKE WHOLE CAREER PATHS INVALID, PEOPLE WILL BE OUT OF WORK AND KILL THEMSELVES. THEY'LL CURSE ME FOR IT.
AND IT GOES WITHOUT SAYING THAT CREATING ANYTHING INFLUENTIAL THAT RELIES ON ME...
EXTERNAL ANIMALS
BANK
SYSTEM ONLY MITSUHA UNDERSTANDS
...IS OUT OF THE QUESTION, BECAUSE IT WILL TURN INTO CHAOS WHEN I'M NOT THERE ANYMORE.
IF I STAND OUT TOO MUCH, SOMEONE WILL COME AFTER ME.
I SHOULD KEEP THINGS SLOW AND SIMPLE UNTIL I HAVE POWER BACKING ME.
OF COURSE, IF NEED BE, I CAN JUST ESCAPE TO EARTH AND STAY THERE.
BUT THAT'S MY LAST RESORT.
SO, WHAT NOW?

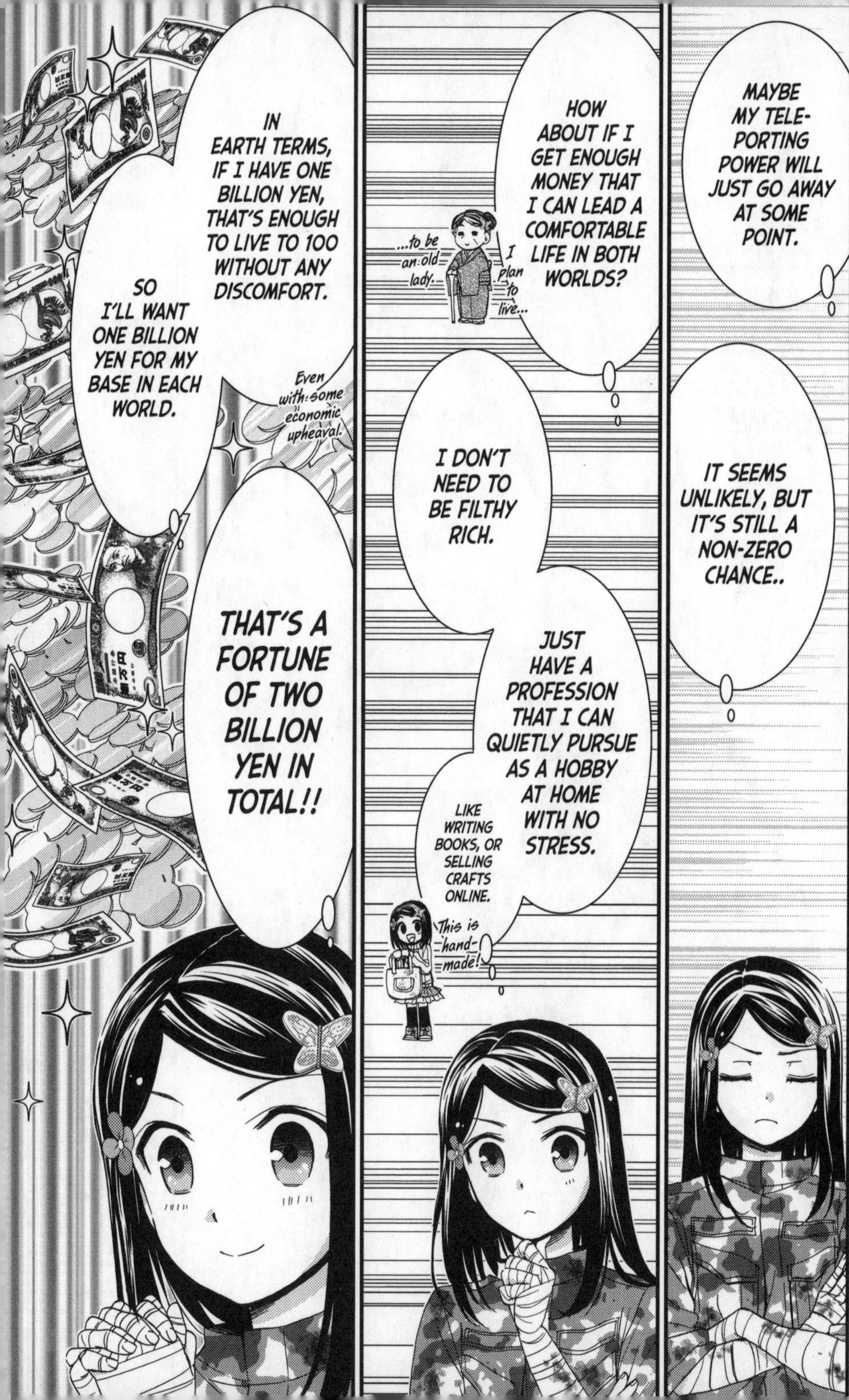
MAYBE MY TELE-PORTING POWER WILL JUST GO AWAY AT SOME POINT.
IT SEEMS UNLIKELY, BUT IT'S STILL A NON-ZERO CHANCE..
HOW ABOUT IF I GET ENOUGH MONEY THAT I CAN LEAD A COMFORTABLE LIFE IN BOTH WORLDS?
I plan to live...
...to be an old lady.
I DON'T NEED TO BE FILTHY RICH.
JUST HAVE A PROFESSION THAT I CAN QUIETLY PURSUE AS A HOBBY AT HOME WITH NO STRESS.
LIKE WRITING BOOKS, OR SELLING CRAFTS ONLINE.
This is hand-made!
IN EARTH TERMS, IF I HAVE ONE BILLION YEN, THAT'S ENOUGH TO LIVE TO 100 WITHOUT ANY DISCOMFORT.
SO I'LL WANT ONE BILLION YEN FOR MY BASE IN EACH WORLD.
Even with some economic upheaval.
THAT'S A FORTUNE OF TWO BILLION YEN IN TOTAL!!

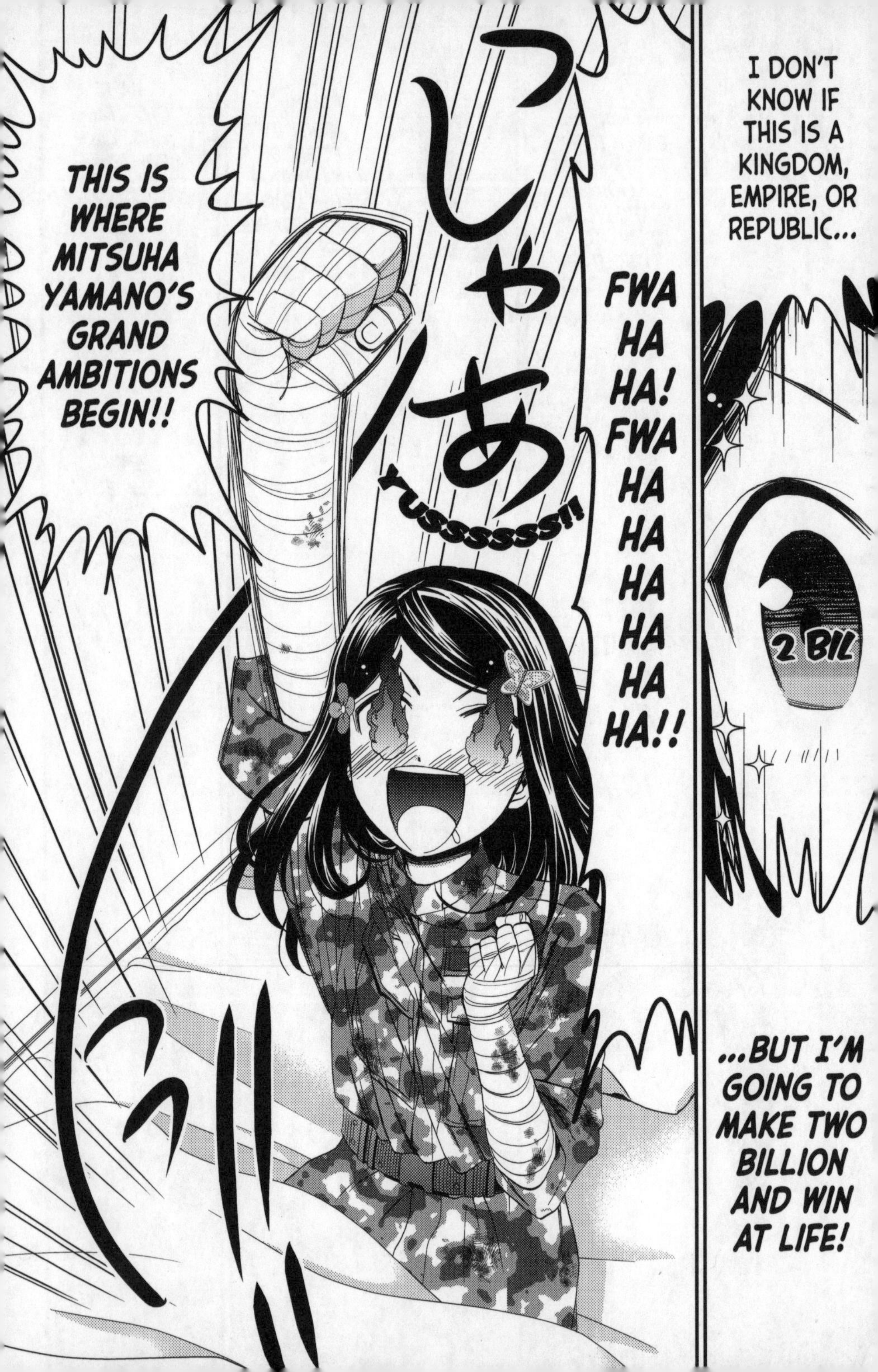
I DON'T KNOW IF THIS IS A KINGDOM, EMPIRE, OR REPUBLIC...
2 BIL
...BUT I'M GOING TO MAKE TWO BILLION AND WIN AT LIFE!
FWA HA HA! FWA HA HA HA HA HA HA HA!!
っしゃあ
YUSSSSSSS!!
THIS IS WHERE MITSUHA YAMANO'S GRAND AMBITIONS BEGIN!!

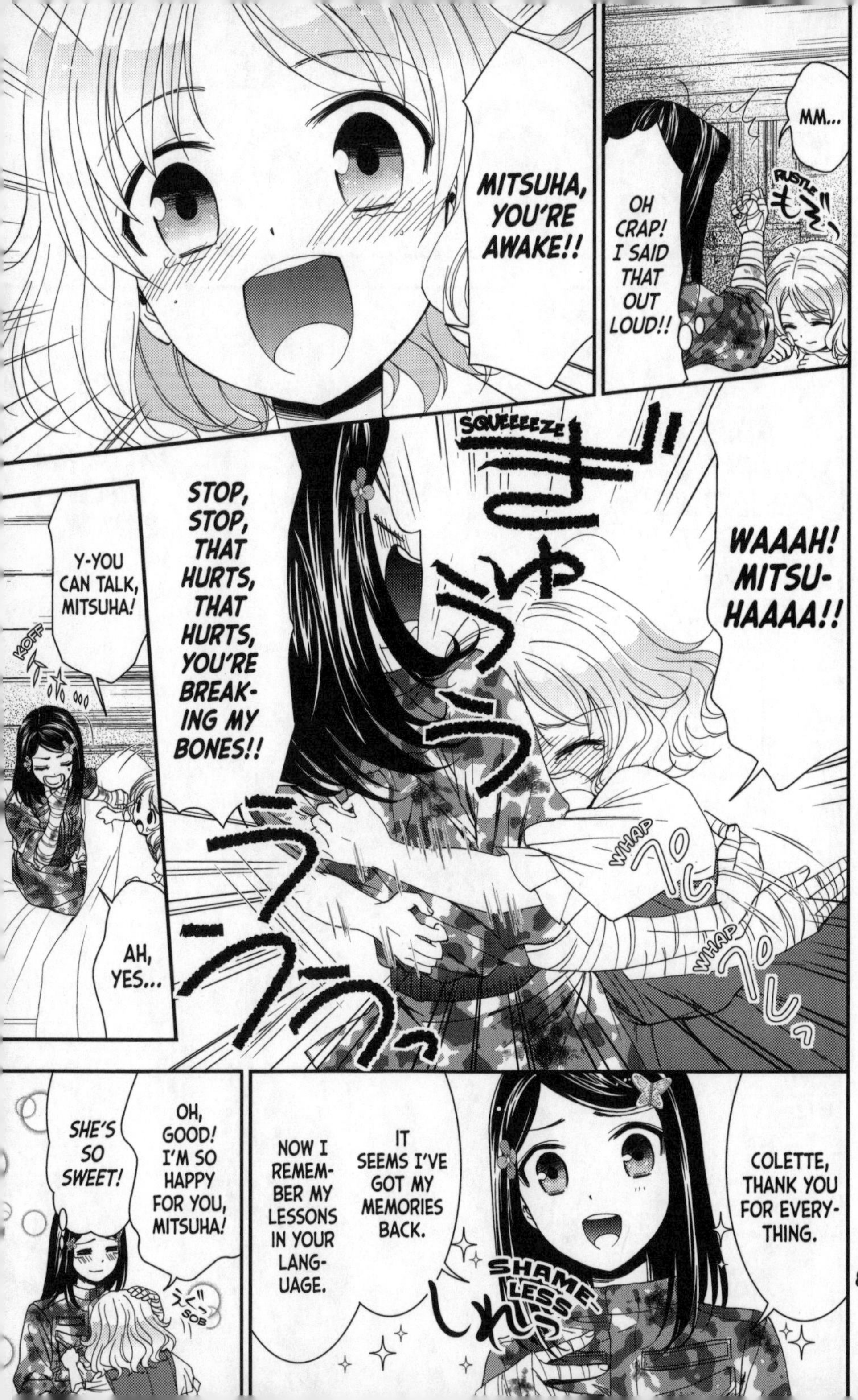
MM...
RUSTLE
OH CRAP! I SAID THAT OUT LOUD!!
MITSUHA, YOU'RE AWAKE!!
WAAAH! MITSU-HAAAA!!
SQUEEEEZE
STOP, STOP, THAT HURTS, THAT HURTS, YOU'RE BREAK-ING MY BONES!!
WHAP
WHAP
Y-YOU CAN TALK, MITSUHA!
KOFF
AH, YES...
COLETTE, THANK YOU FOR EVERY-THING.
IT SEEMS I'VE GOT MY MEMORIES BACK.
NOW I REMEM-BER MY LESSONS IN YOUR LANG-UAGE.
SHAME-LESS
OH, GOOD! I'M SO HAPPY FOR YOU, MITSUHA!
SHE'S SO SWEET!
SOB

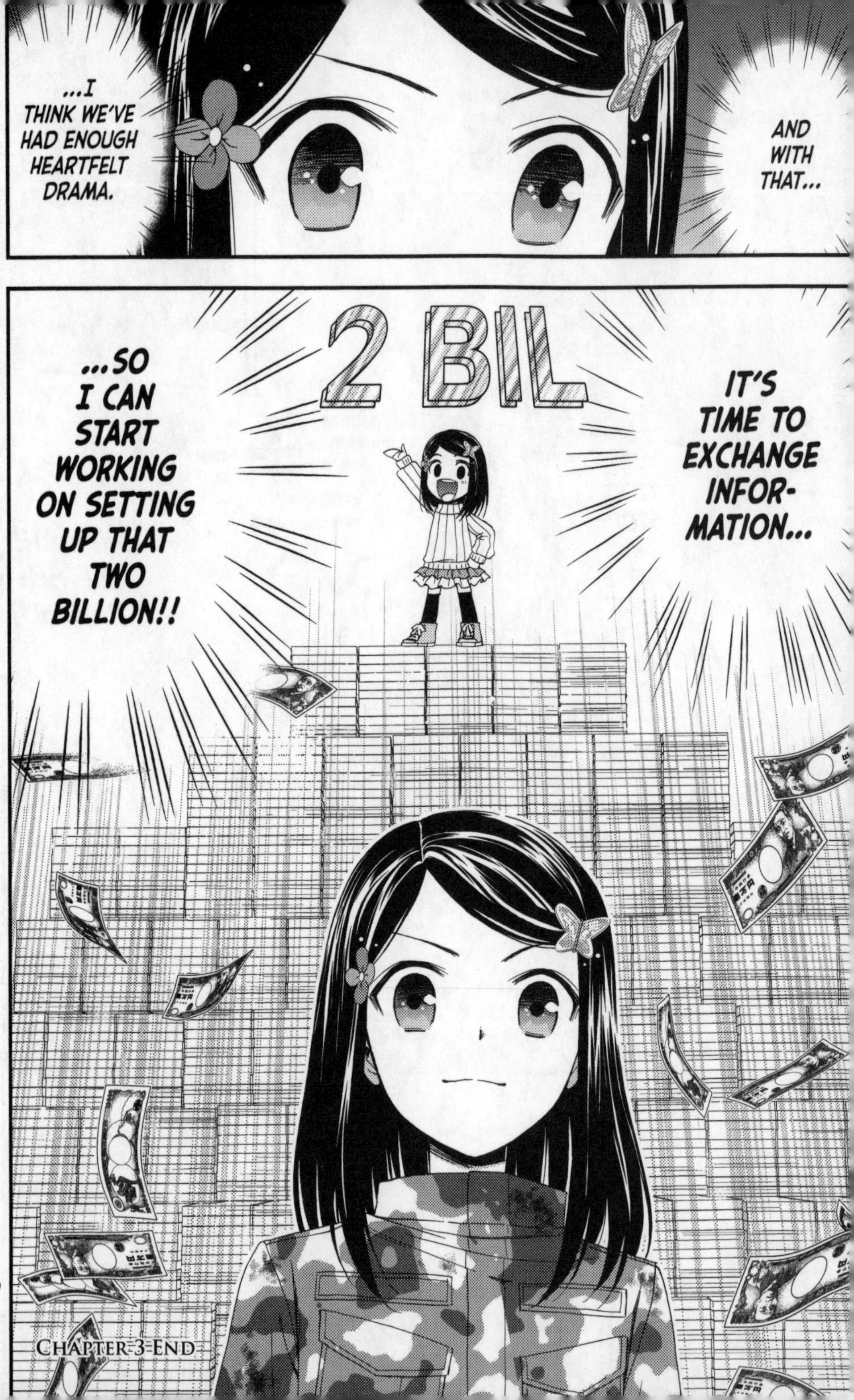
...I THINK WE'VE HAD ENOUGH HEARTFELT DRAMA.
AND WITH THAT...
2 BIL
IT'S TIME TO EXCHANGE INFOR-MATION...
...SO I CAN START WORKING ON SETTING UP THAT TWO BILLION!!
CHAPTER 3 END

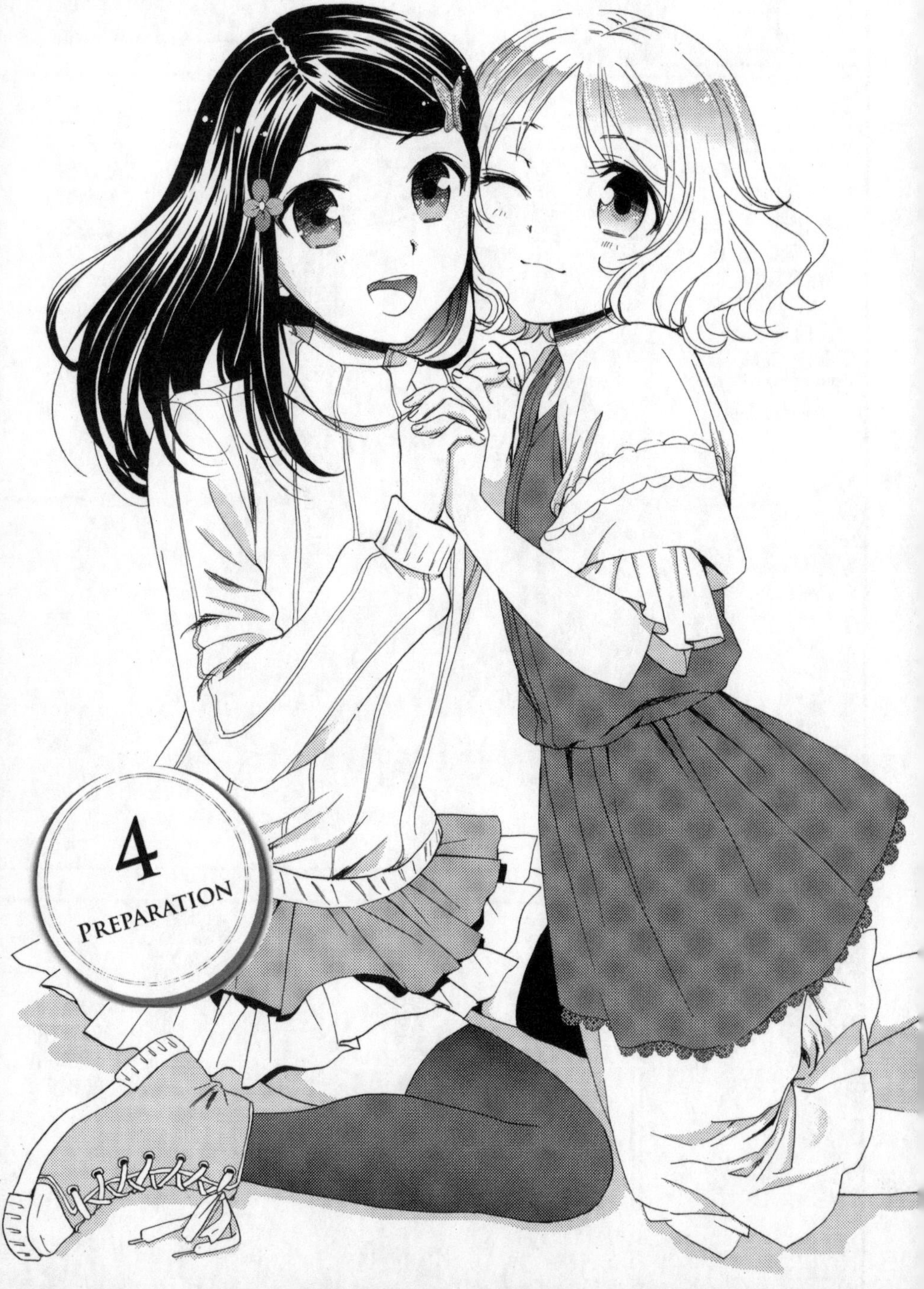
4
PREPARATION

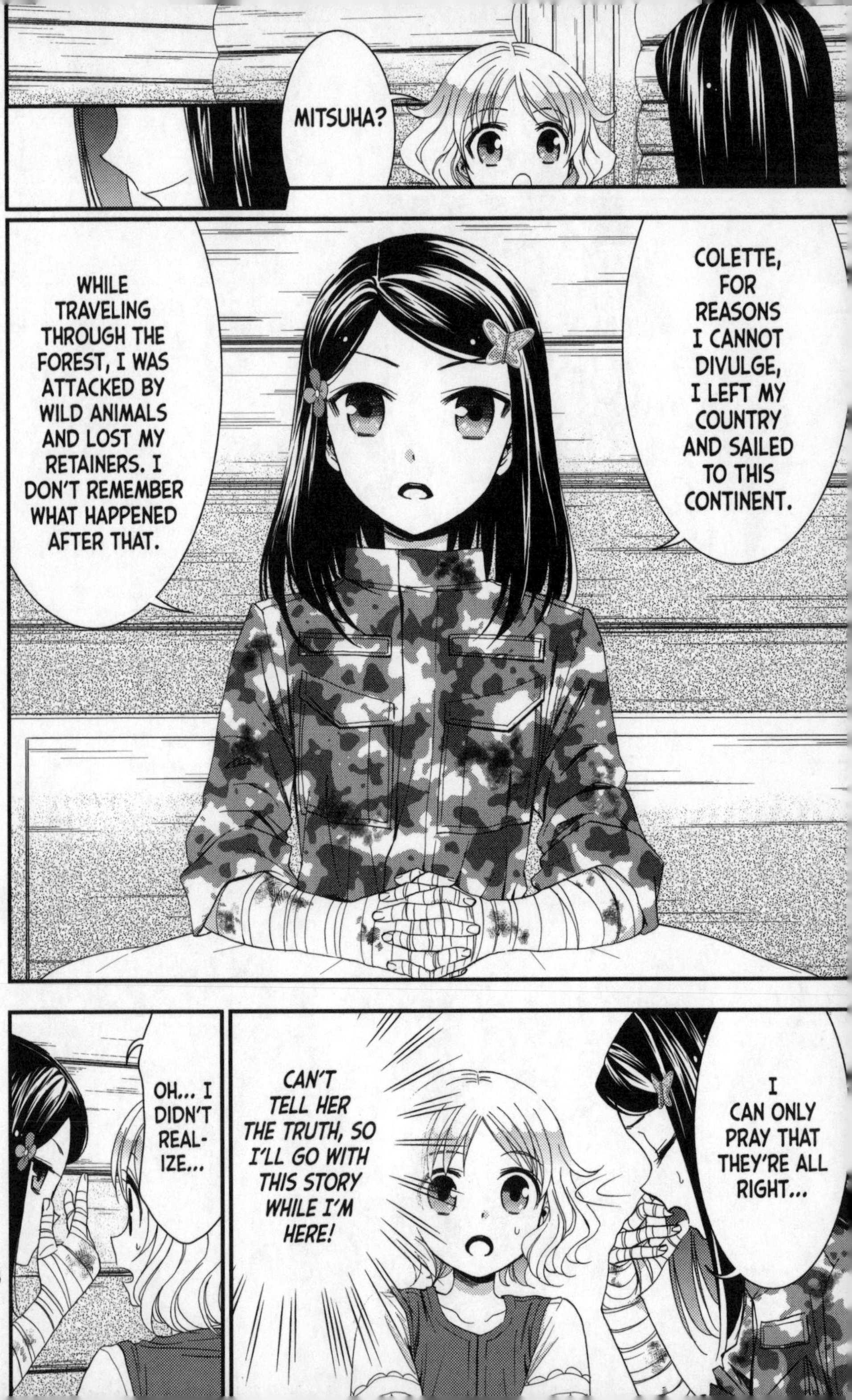
MITSUHA?
COLETTE, FOR REASONS I CANNOT DIVULGE, I LEFT MY COUNTRY AND SAILED TO THIS CONTINENT.
WHILE TRAVELING THROUGH THE FOREST, I WAS ATTACKED BY WILD ANIMALS AND LOST MY RETAINERS. I DON'T REMEMBER WHAT HAPPENED AFTER THAT.
I CAN ONLY PRAY THAT THEY'RE ALL RIGHT...
CAN'T TELL HER THE TRUTH, SO I'LL GO WITH THIS STORY WHILE I'M HERE!
OH... I DIDN'T REAL-IZE...

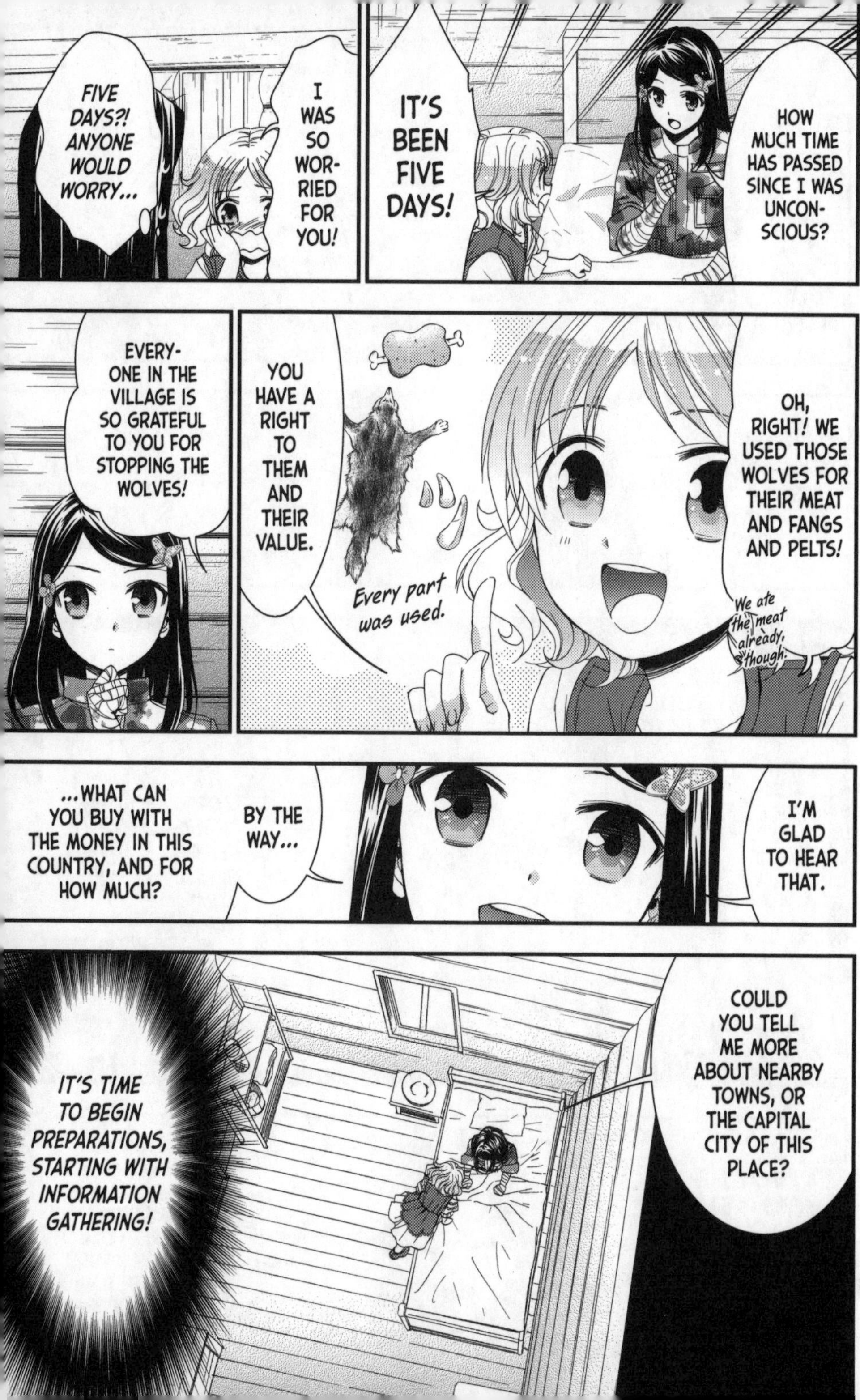
HOW MUCH TIME HAS PASSED SINCE I WAS UNCON-SCIOUS?
IT'S BEEN FIVE DAYS!
I WAS SO WOR-RIED FOR YOU!
FIVE DAYS?! ANYONE WOULD WORRY...
OH, RIGHT! WE USED THOSE WOLVES FOR THEIR MEAT AND FANGS AND PELTS!
We ate the meat already, though.
Every part was used.
YOU HAVE A RIGHT TO THEM AND THEIR VALUE.
EVERY-ONE IN THE VILLAGE IS SO GRATEFUL TO YOU FOR STOPPING THE WOLVES!
I'M GLAD TO HEAR THAT.
BY THE WAY...
...WHAT CAN YOU BUY WITH THE MONEY IN THIS COUNTRY, AND FOR HOW MUCH?
COULD YOU TELL ME MORE ABOUT NEARBY TOWNS, OR THE CAPITAL CITY OF THIS PLACE?
IT'S TIME TO BEGIN PREPARATIONS, STARTING WITH INFORMATION GATHERING!

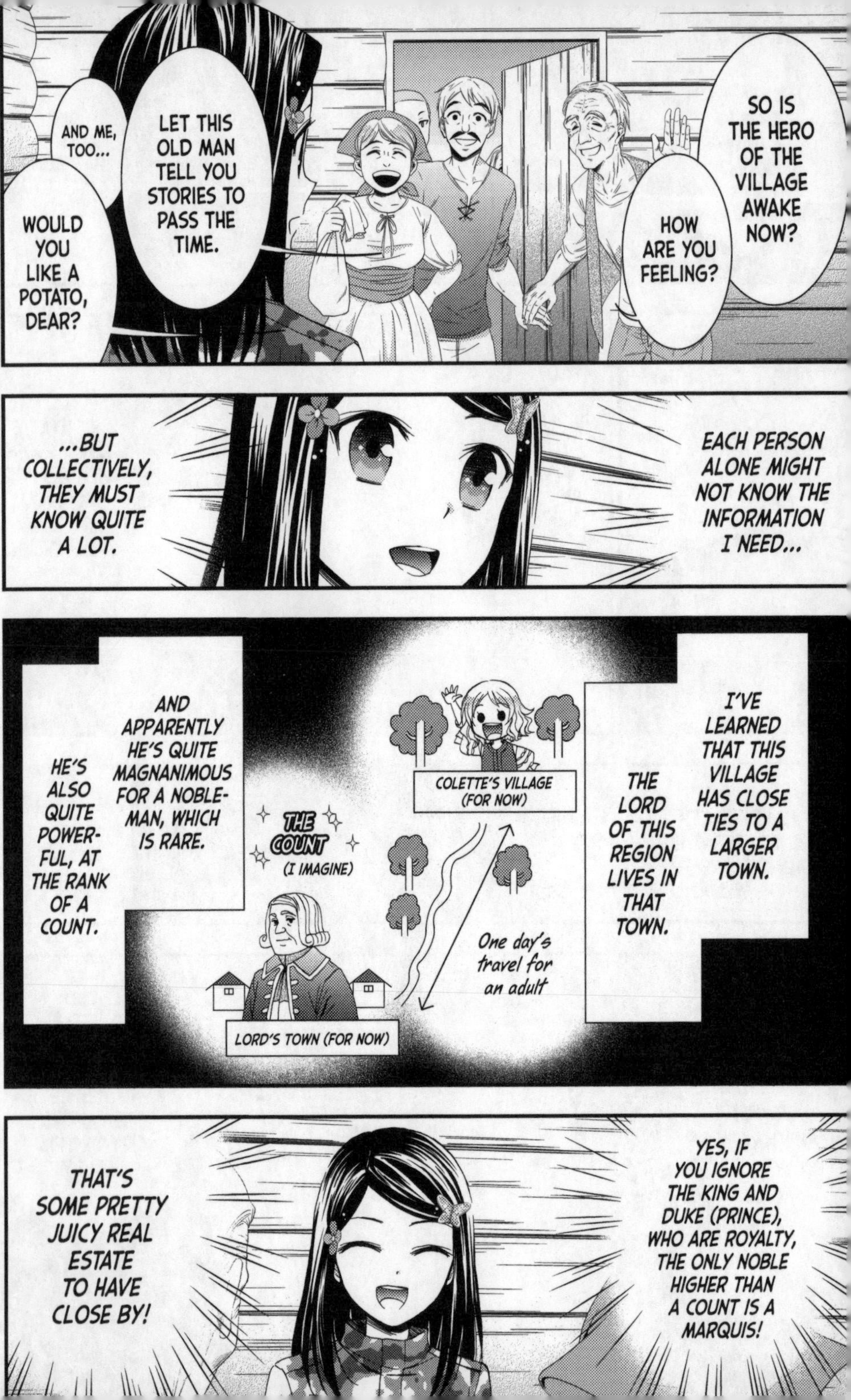
SO IS THE HERO OF THE VILLAGE AWAKE NOW?
HOW ARE YOU FEELING?
LET THIS OLD MAN TELL YOU STORIES TO PASS THE TIME.
AND ME, TOO...
WOULD YOU LIKE A POTATO, DEAR?
EACH PERSON ALONE MIGHT NOT KNOW THE INFORMATION I NEED...
...BUT COLLECTIVELY, THEY MUST KNOW QUITE A LOT.
I'VE LEARNED THAT THIS VILLAGE HAS CLOSE TIES TO A LARGER TOWN.
THE LORD OF THIS REGION LIVES IN THAT TOWN.
COLETTE'S VILLAGE (FOR NOW)
One day's travel for an adult
THE COUNT
(I IMAGINE)
LORD'S TOWN (FOR NOW)
AND APPARENTLY HE'S QUITE MAGNANIMOUS FOR A NOBLE- MAN, WHICH IS RARE.
HE'S ALSO QUITE POWER- FUL, AT THE RANK OF A COUNT.
YES, IF YOU IGNORE THE KING AND DUKE (PRINCE), WHO ARE ROYALTY, THE ONLY NOBLE HIGHER THAN A COUNT IS A MARQUIS!
THAT'S SOME PRETTY JUICY REAL ESTATE TO HAVE CLOSE BY!

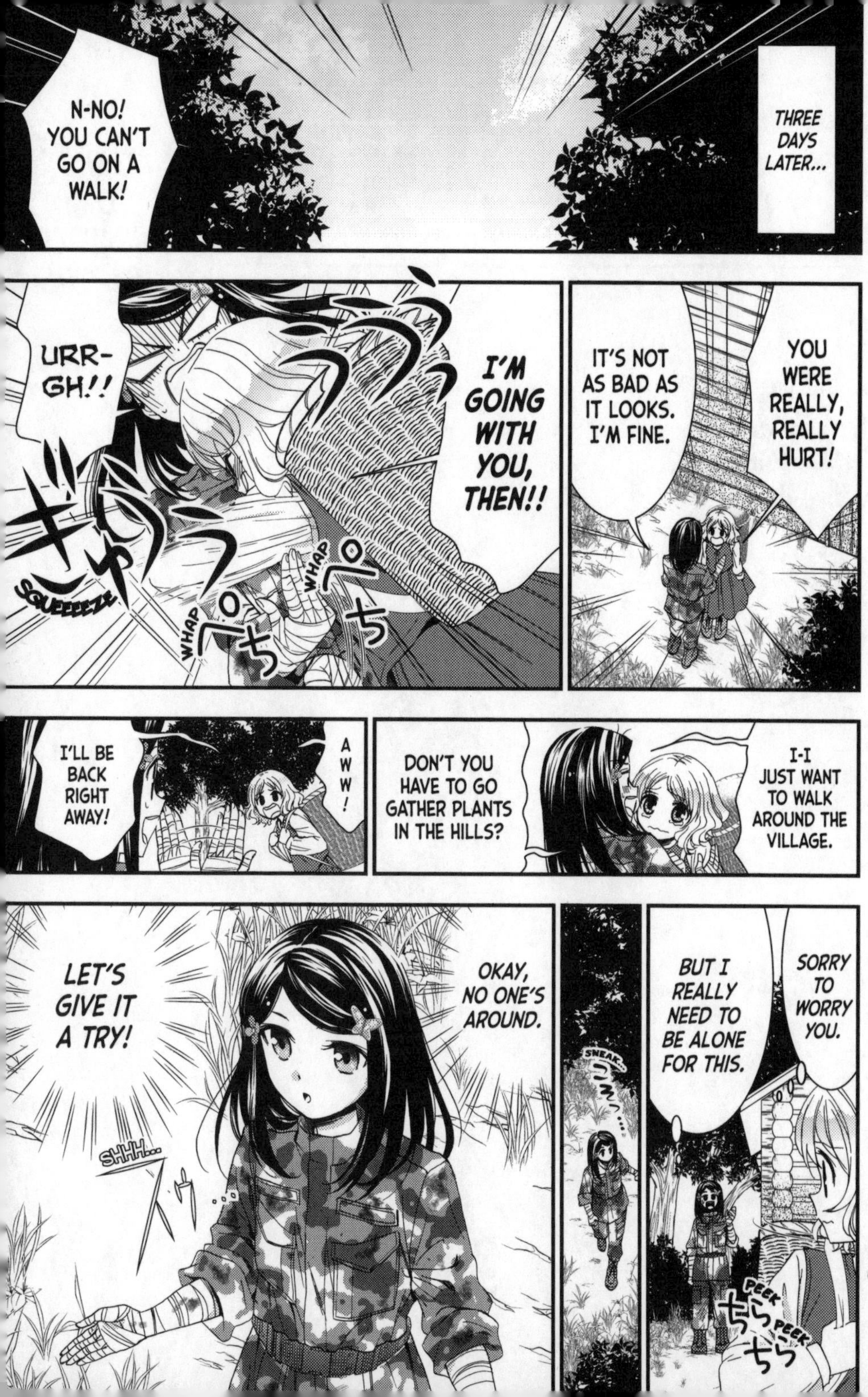
THREE DAYS LATER...
N-NO! YOU CAN'T GO ON A WALK!
YOU WERE REALLY, REALLY HURT!
IT'S NOT AS BAD AS IT LOOKS. I'M FINE.
I'M GOING WITH YOU, THEN!!
URR-GH!!
SQUEEEEEZE
WHAP
WHAP
I-I JUST WANT TO WALK AROUND THE VILLAGE.
DON'T YOU HAVE TO GO GATHER PLANTS IN THE HILLS?
AWW!
I'LL BE BACK RIGHT AWAY!
SORRY TO WORRY YOU.
BUT I REALLY NEED TO BE ALONE FOR THIS.
PEEK
PEEK
SNEAK...
OKAY, NO ONE'S AROUND.
LET'S GIVE IT A TRY!
SHHH...

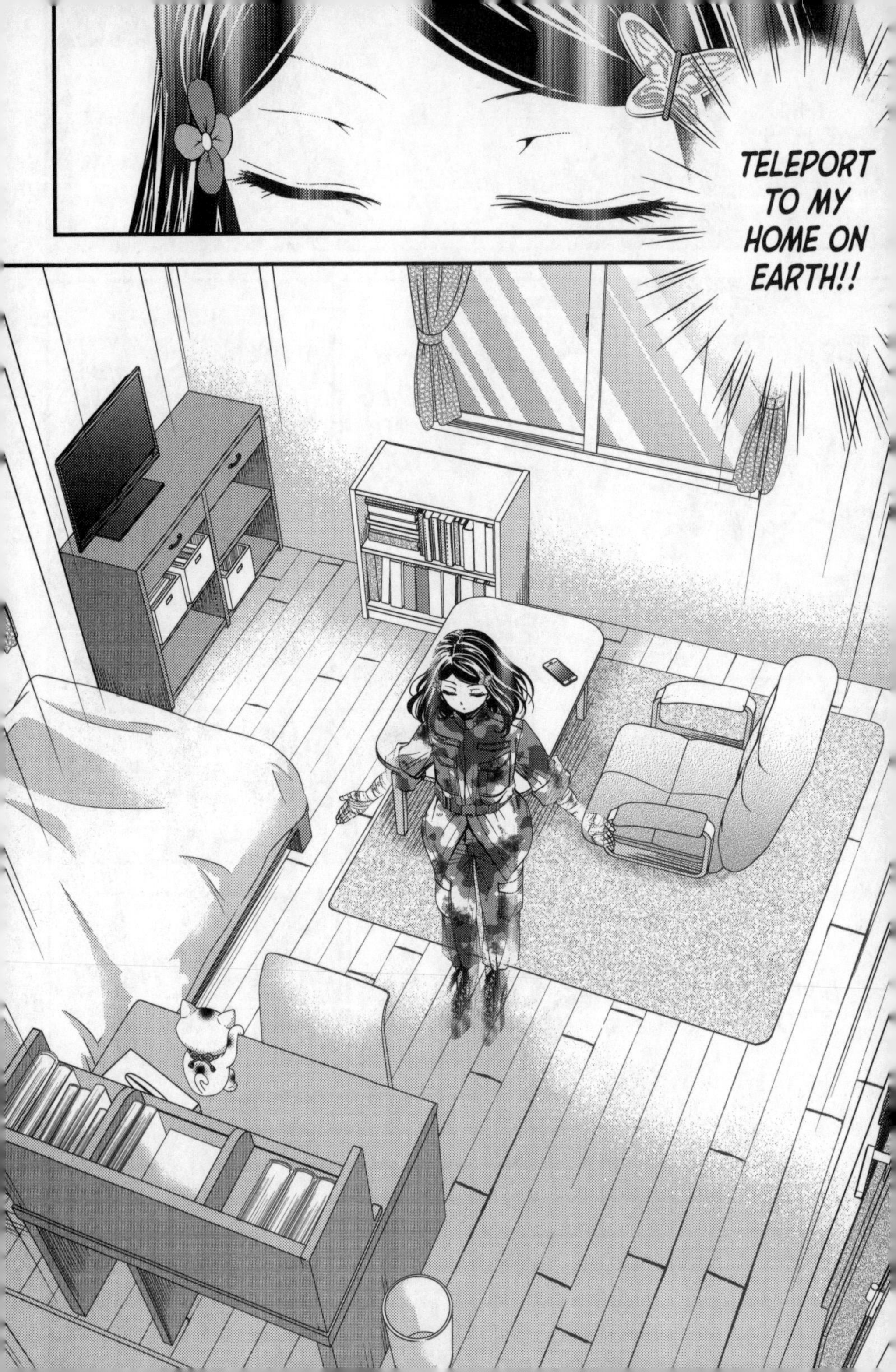
TELEPORT TO MY HOME ON EARTH!!

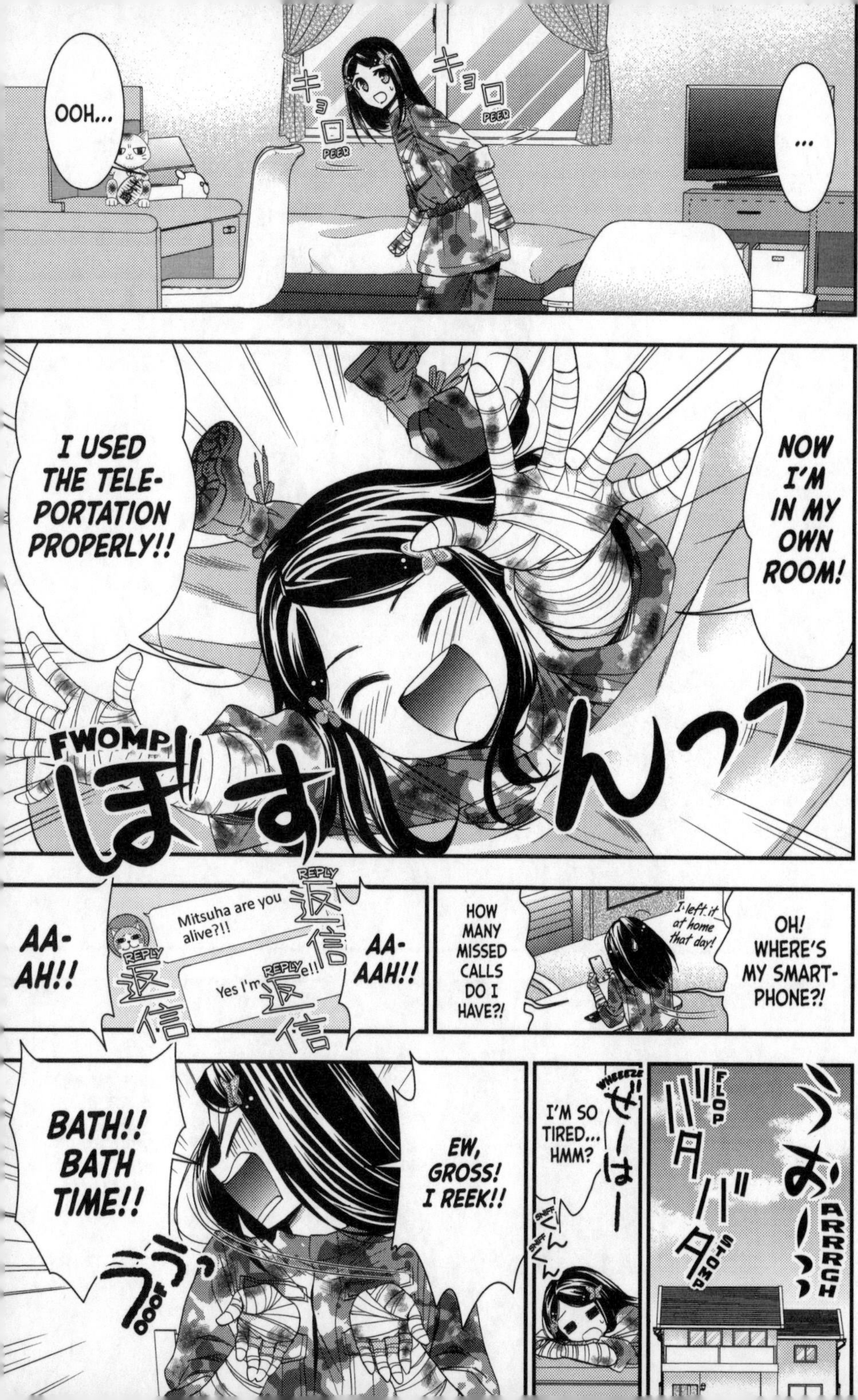
...
キョロ
PEER
キョロ
PEER
OOH...
NOW I'M IN MY OWN ROOM!
I USED THE TELE-PORTATION PROPERLY!!
FWOMP
ぼすんっ
OH! WHERE'S MY SMART-PHONE?!
I left it at home that day!
HOW MANY MISSED CALLS DO I HAVE?!
AA-AAH!!
REPLY
返信
Mitsuha are you alive?!!
Yes I'm
REPLY
返信
REPLY
返信
AA-AH!!
うおーっっ
ARRRGH
バタバタ
FLOP
STOMP
I'M SO TIRED... HMM?
ぜーはー
WHEEZE
くんくん
SNIFF
SNIFF
EW, GROSS! I REEK!!
BATH!! BATH TIME!!
うぅっ

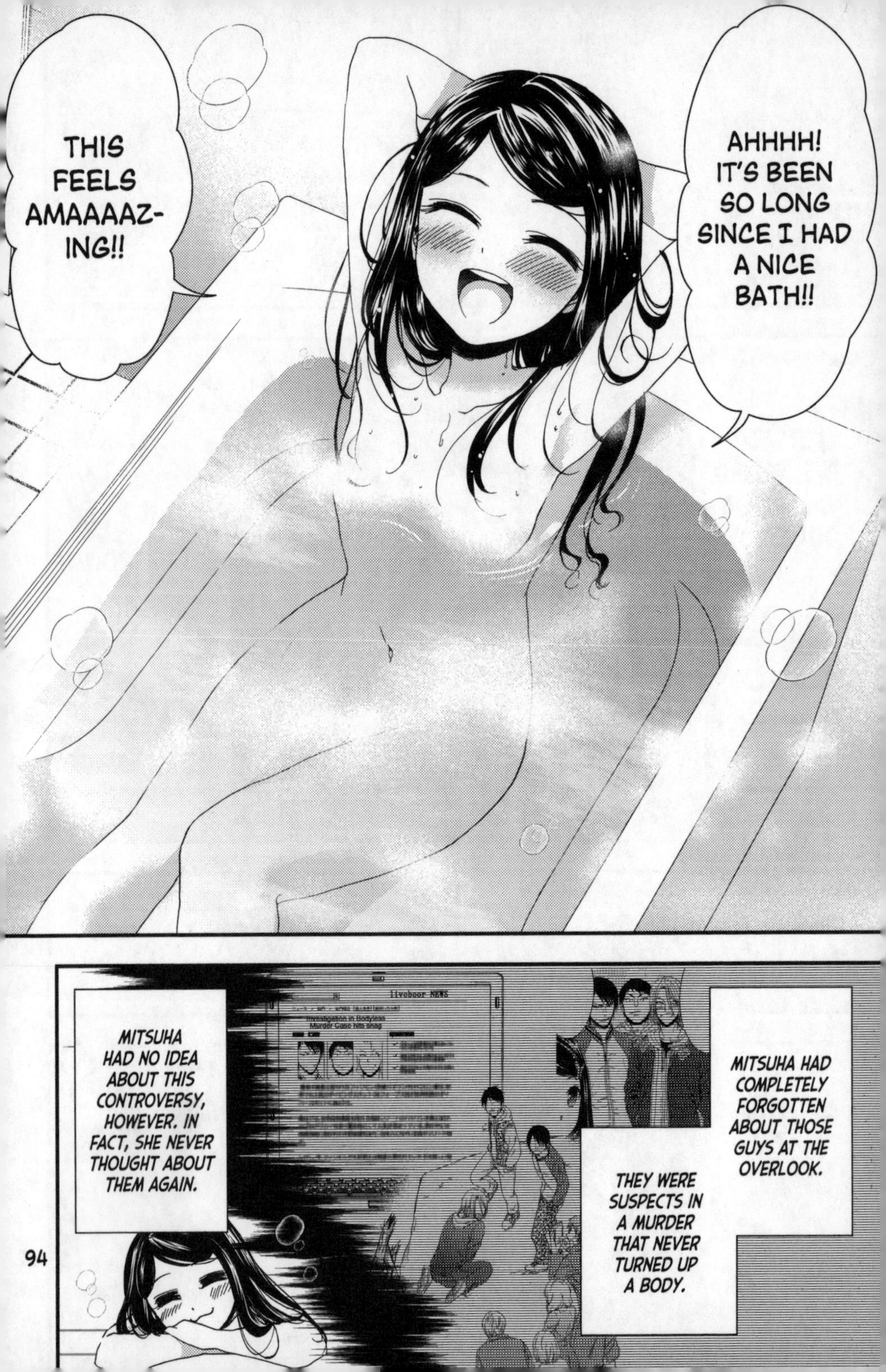
AHHHH! IT'S BEEN SO LONG SINCE I HAD A NICE BATH!!
THIS FEELS AMAAAAZ-ING!!
MITSUHA HAD COMPLETELY FORGOTTEN ABOUT THOSE GUYS AT THE OVERLOOK.
THEY WERE SUSPECTS IN A MURDER THAT NEVER TURNED UP A BODY.
Investigation in Bodyless Murder Case hits snag
MITSUHA HAD NO IDEA ABOUT THIS CONTROVERSY, HOWEVER. IN FACT, SHE NEVER THOUGHT ABOUT THEM AGAIN.

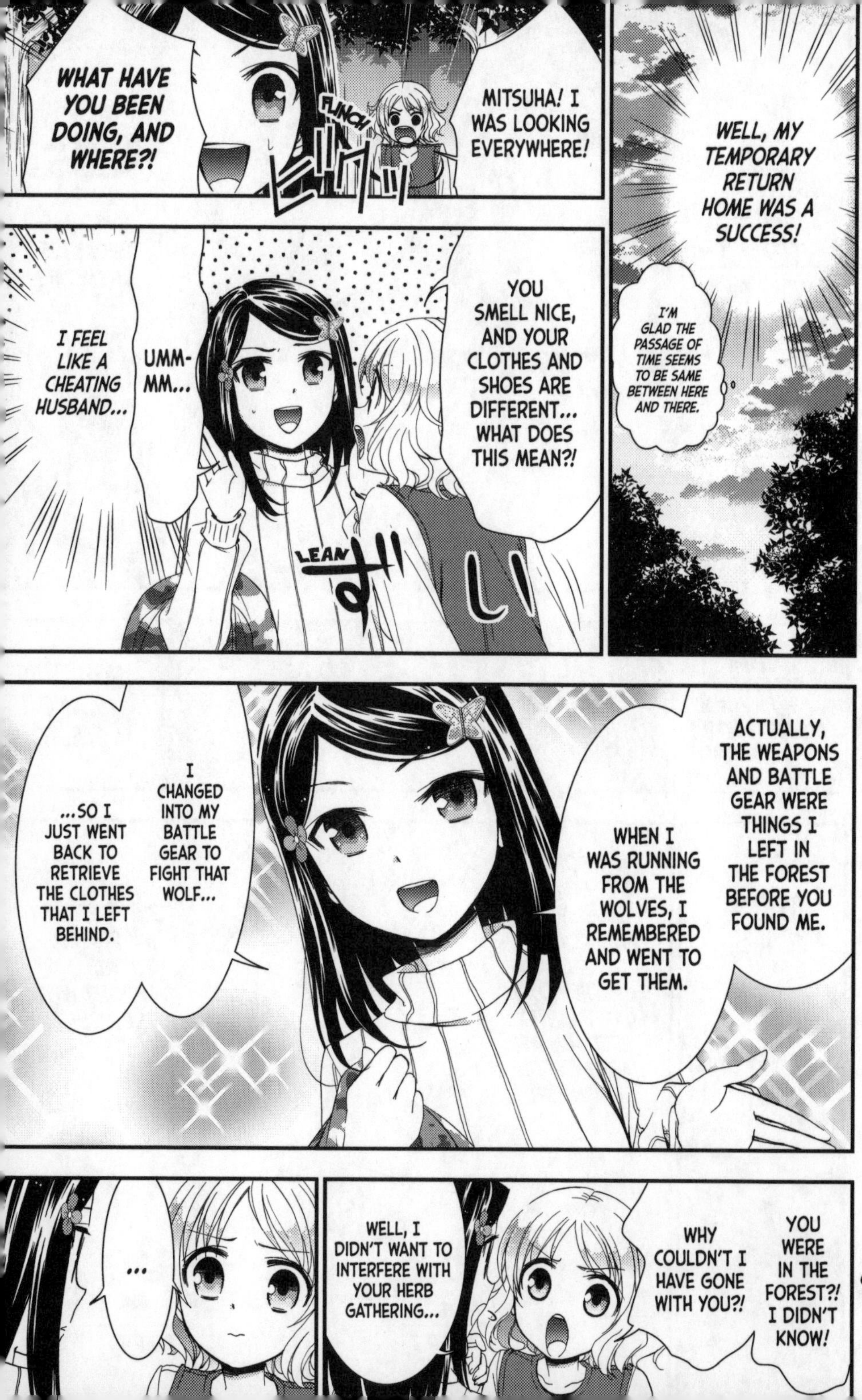
WELL, MY TEMPORARY RETURN HOME WAS A SUCCESS!
I'M GLAD THE PASSAGE OF TIME SEEMS TO BE SAME BETWEEN HERE AND THERE.
MITSUHA! I WAS LOOKING EVERYWHERE!
FLINCH
WHAT HAVE YOU BEEN DOING, AND WHERE?!
YOU SMELL NICE, AND YOUR CLOTHES AND SHOES ARE DIFFERENT... WHAT DOES THIS MEAN?!
LEAN
UMM-MM...
I FEEL LIKE A CHEATING HUSBAND...
ACTUALLY, THE WEAPONS AND BATTLE GEAR WERE THINGS I LEFT IN THE FOREST BEFORE YOU FOUND ME.
WHEN I WAS RUNNING FROM THE WOLVES, I REMEMBERED AND WENT TO GET THEM.
I CHANGED INTO MY BATTLE GEAR TO FIGHT THAT WOLF...
...SO I JUST WENT BACK TO RETRIEVE THE CLOTHES THAT I LEFT BEHIND.
YOU WERE IN THE FOREST?! I DIDN'T KNOW!
WHY COULDN'T I HAVE GONE WITH YOU?!
WELL, I DIDN'T WANT TO INTERFERE WITH YOUR HERB GATHERING...
...

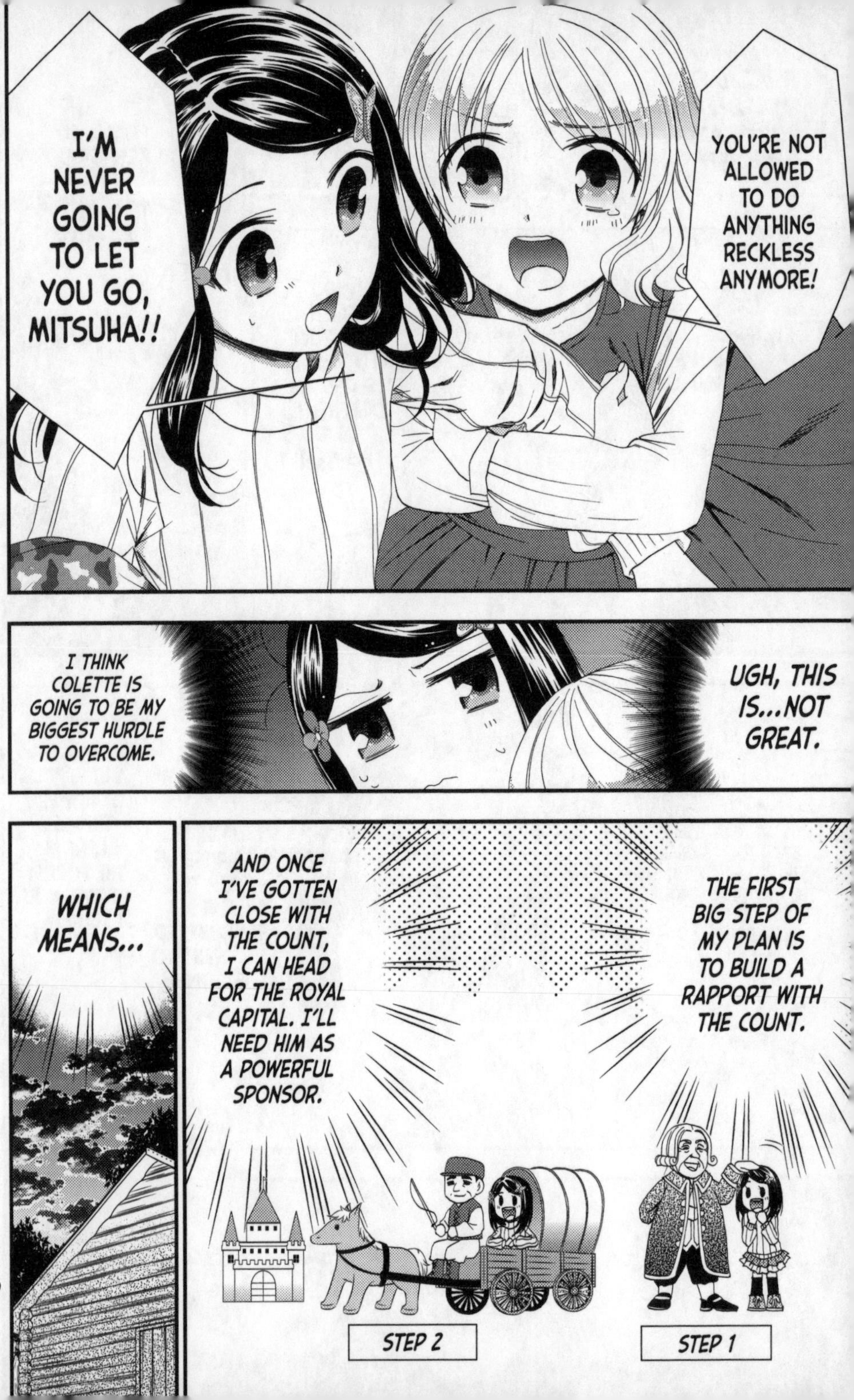
YOU'RE NOT ALLOWED TO DO ANYTHING RECKLESS ANYMORE!
I'M NEVER GOING TO LET YOU GO, MITSUHA!!
UGH, THIS IS...NOT GREAT.
I THINK COLETTE IS GOING TO BE MY BIGGEST HURDLE TO OVERCOME.
THE FIRST BIG STEP OF MY PLAN IS TO BUILD A RAPPORT WITH THE COUNT.
AND ONCE I'VE GOTTEN CLOSE WITH THE COUNT, I CAN HEAD FOR THE ROYAL CAPITAL. I'LL NEED HIM AS A POWERFUL SPONSOR.
STEP 1
STEP 2
WHICH MEANS...

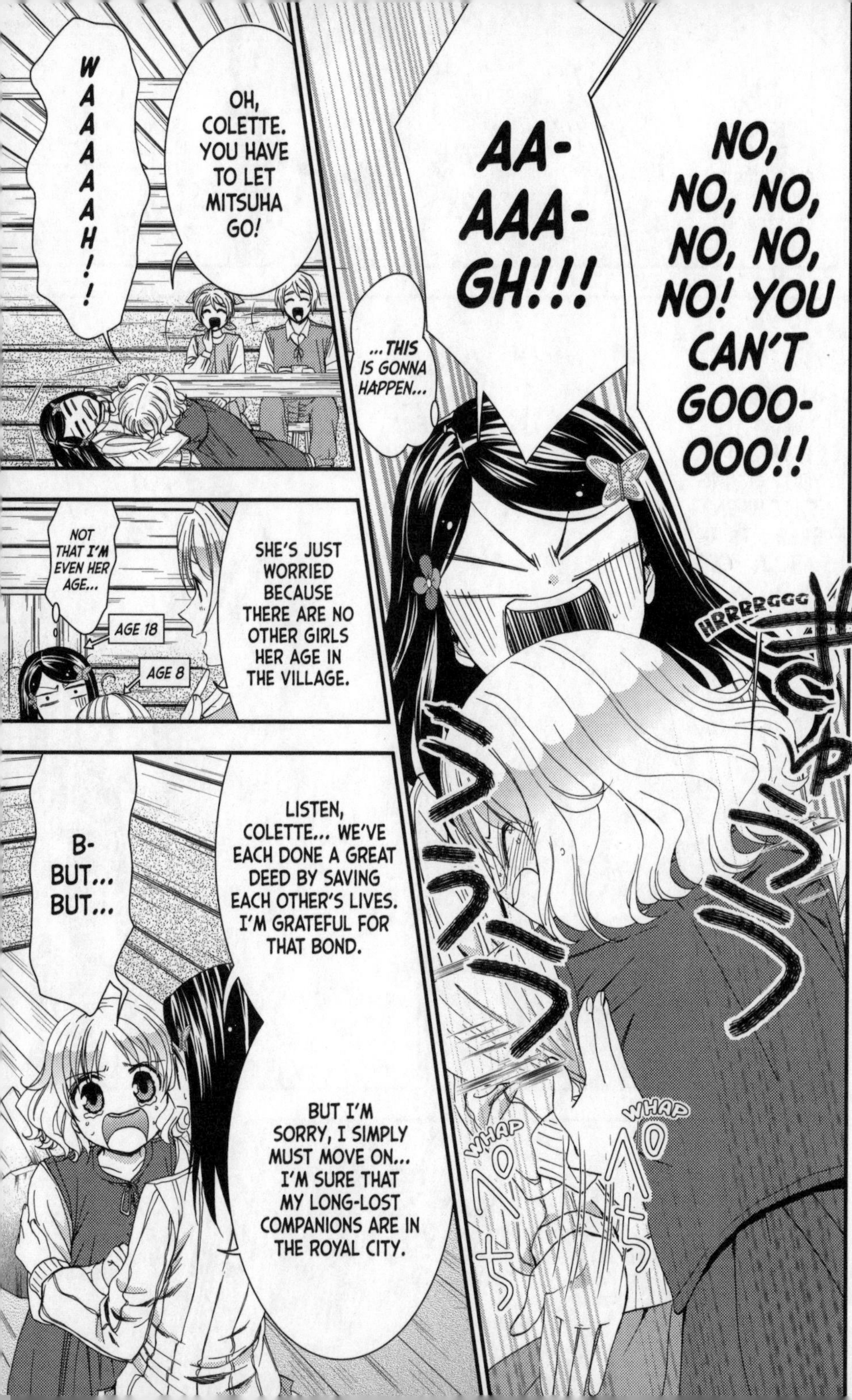
NO, NO, NO, NO, NO, NO! YOU CAN'T GOOOOOO!!
AA-AAA-GH!!!
...THIS IS GONNA HAPPEN...
HRRRRGGG
WHAP
WHAP
OH, COLETTE. YOU HAVE TO LET MITSUHA GO!
WAAAAAAH!!
SHE'S JUST WORRIED BECAUSE THERE ARE NO OTHER GIRLS HER AGE IN THE VILLAGE.
NOT THAT I'M EVEN HER AGE...
AGE 18
AGE 8
LISTEN, COLETTE... WE'VE EACH DONE A GREAT DEED BY SAVING EACH OTHER'S LIVES. I'M GRATEFUL FOR THAT BOND.
B-BUT... BUT...
BUT I'M SORRY, I SIMPLY MUST MOVE ON... I'M SURE THAT MY LONG-LOST COMPANIONS ARE IN THE ROYAL CITY.

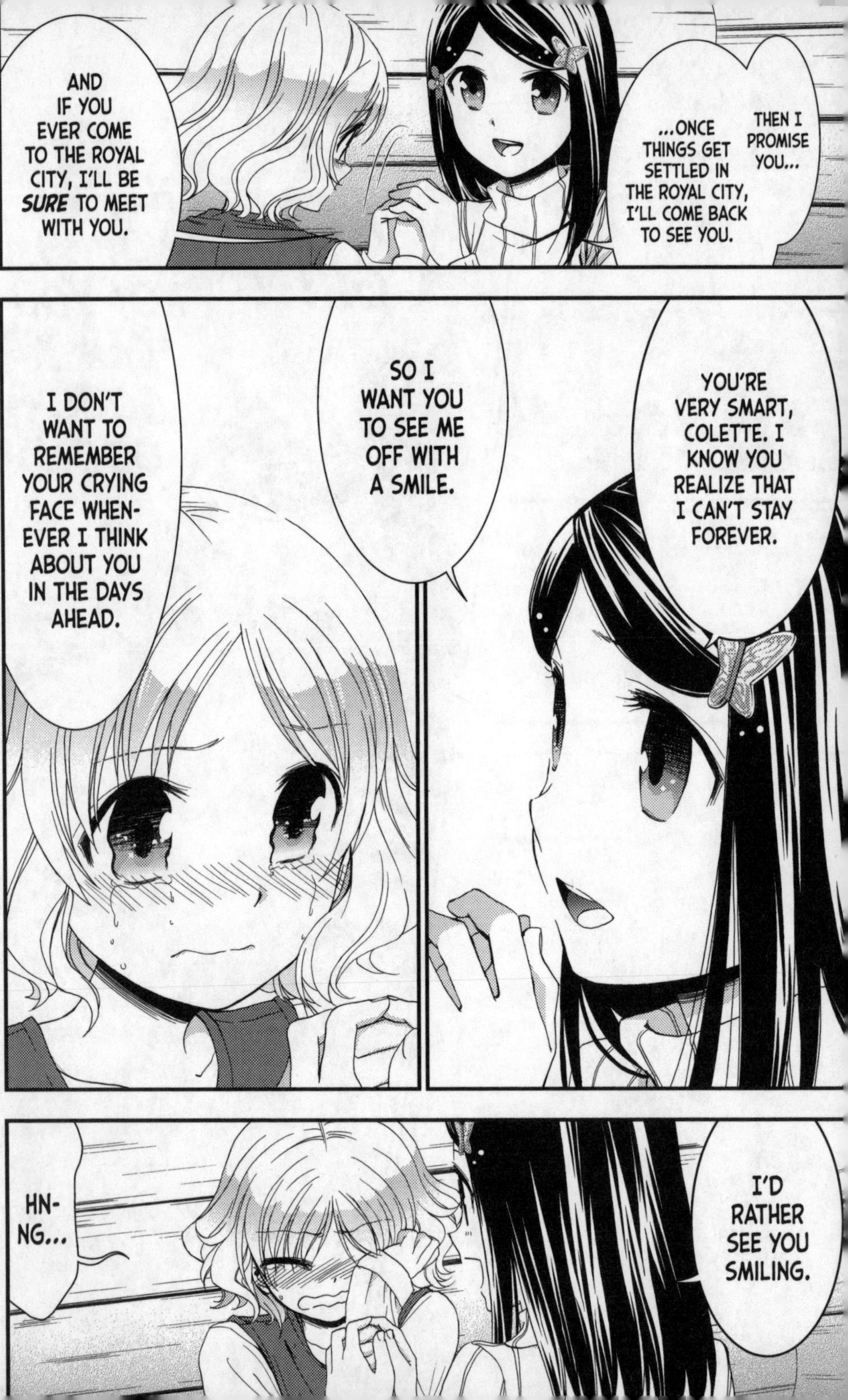
THEN I PROMISE YOU...
...ONCE THINGS GET SETTLED IN THE ROYAL CITY, I'LL COME BACK TO SEE YOU.
AND IF YOU EVER COME TO THE ROYAL CITY, I'LL BE *SURE* TO MEET WITH YOU.
YOU'RE VERY SMART, COLETTE. I KNOW YOU REALIZE THAT I CAN'T STAY FOREVER.
SO I WANT YOU TO SEE ME OFF WITH A SMILE.
I DON'T WANT TO REMEMBER YOUR CRYING FACE WHENEVER I THINK ABOUT YOU IN THE DAYS AHEAD.
I'D RATHER SEE YOU SMILING.
HN-NG...

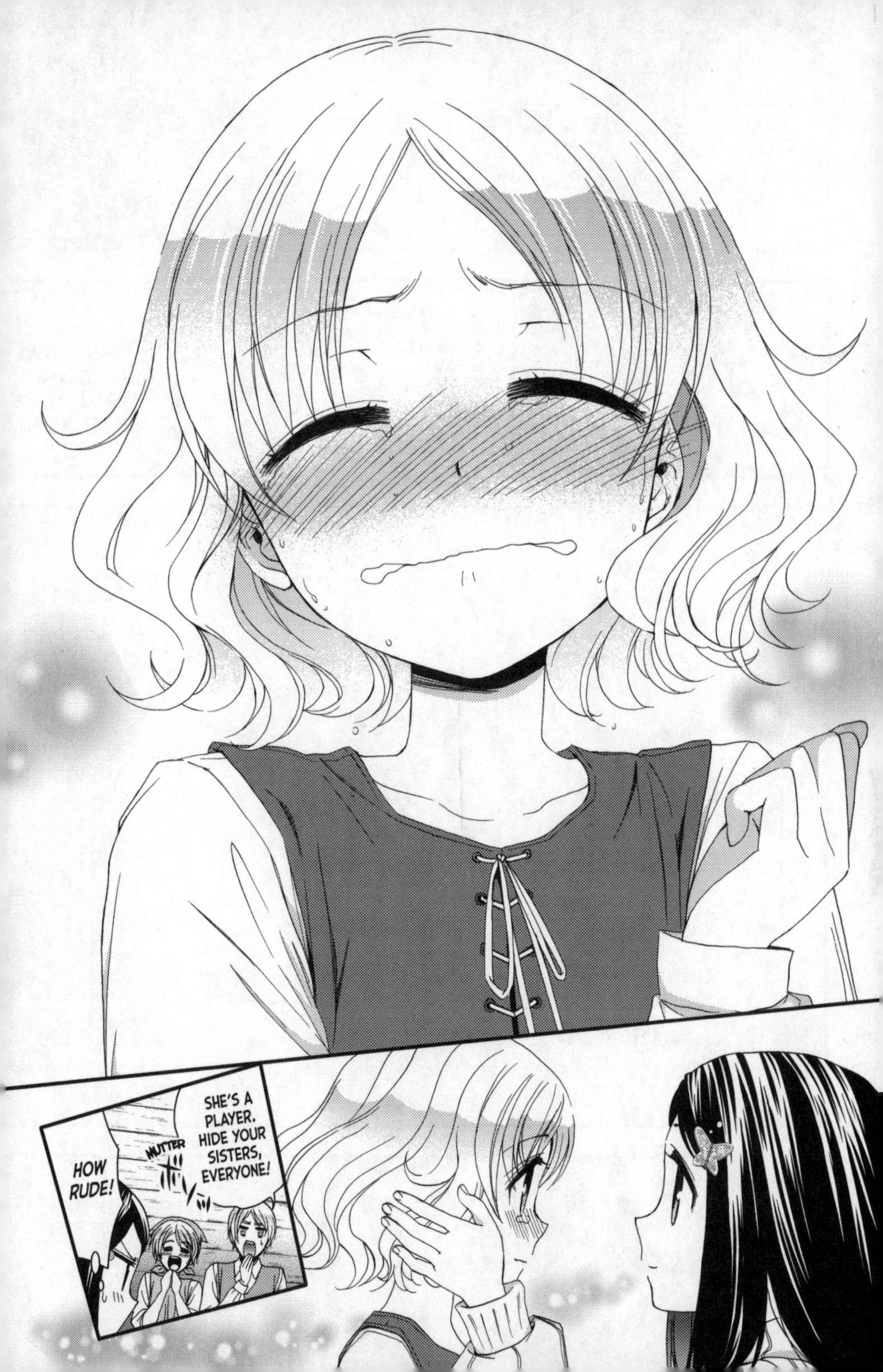
SHE'S A PLAYER. HIDE YOUR SISTERS, EVERYONE!
MUTTER
HOW RUDE!

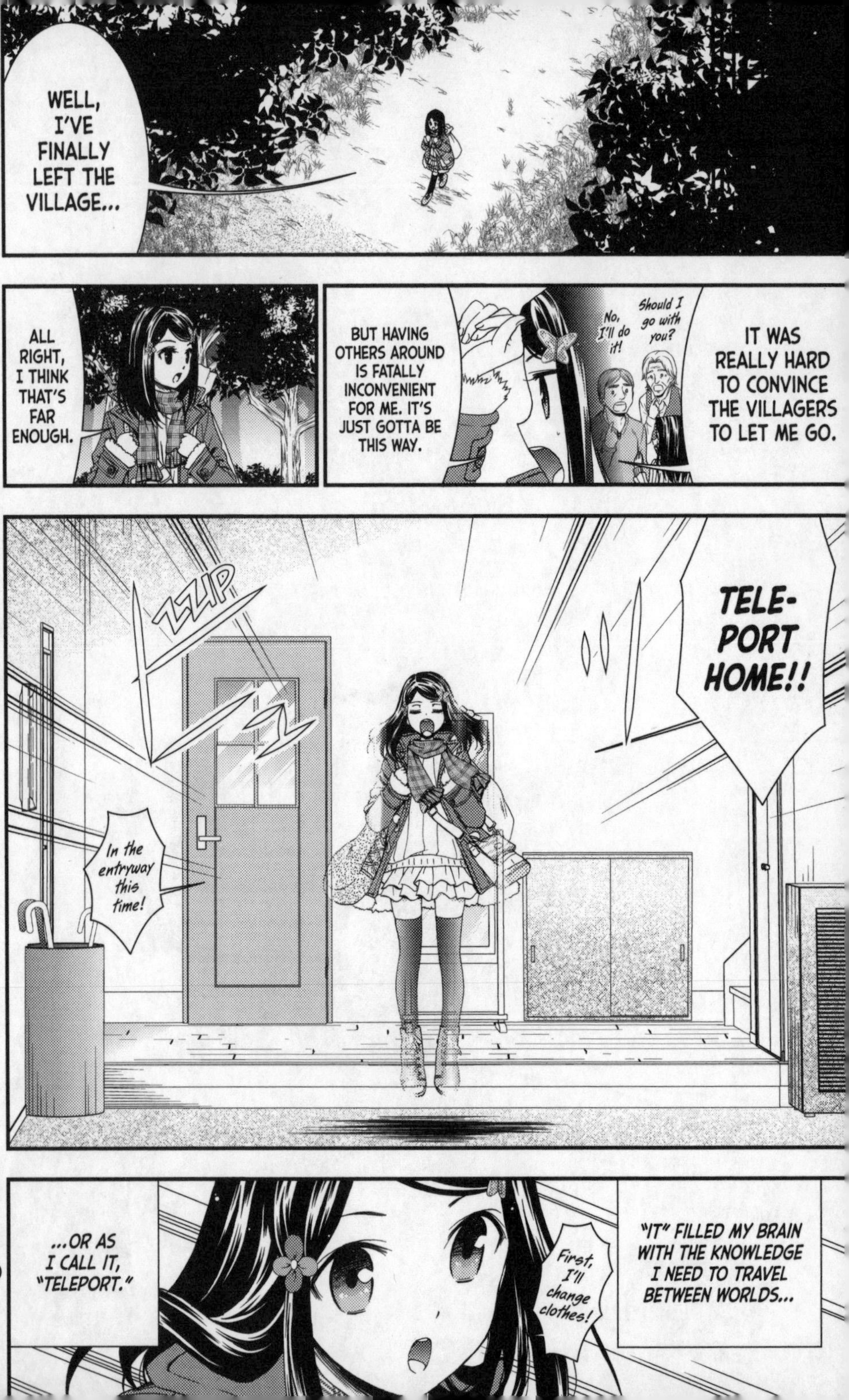
WELL, I'VE FINALLY LEFT THE VILLAGE...
IT WAS REALLY HARD TO CONVINCE THE VILLAGERS TO LET ME GO.
Should I go with you?
No, I'll do it!
BUT HAVING OTHERS AROUND IS FATALLY INCONVENIENT FOR ME. IT'S JUST GOTTA BE THIS WAY.
ALL RIGHT, I THINK THAT'S FAR ENOUGH.
TELE-PORT HOME!!
ZZIP
In the entryway this time!
"IT" FILLED MY BRAIN WITH THE KNOWLEDGE I NEED TO TRAVEL BETWEEN WORLDS...
First, I'll change clothes!
...OR AS I CALL IT, "TELEPORT."

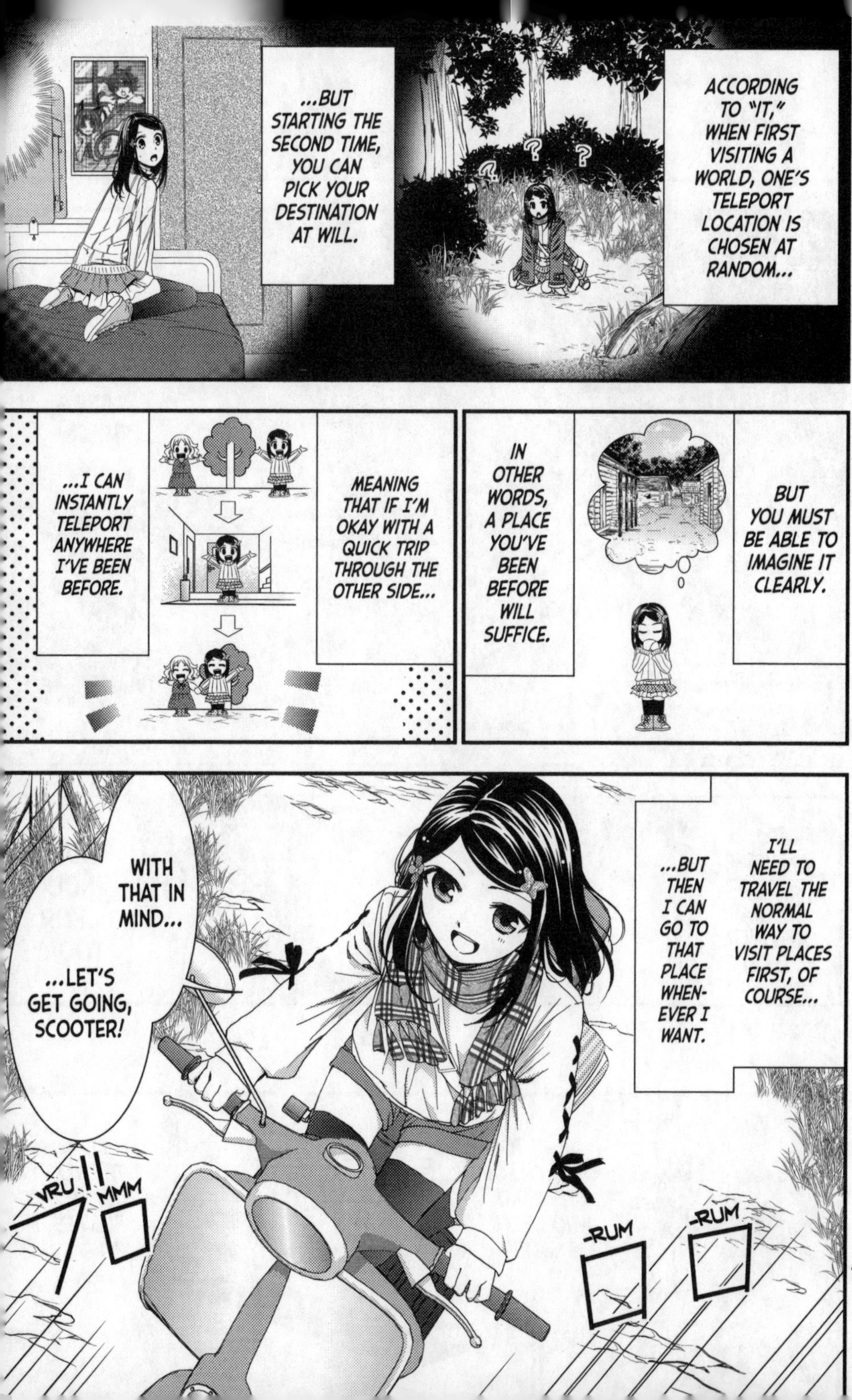
ACCORDING TO "IT," WHEN FIRST VISITING A WORLD, ONE'S TELEPORT LOCATION IS CHOSEN AT RANDOM...
...BUT STARTING THE SECOND TIME, YOU CAN PICK YOUR DESTINATION AT WILL.
BUT YOU MUST BE ABLE TO IMAGINE IT CLEARLY.
IN OTHER WORDS, A PLACE YOU'VE BEEN BEFORE WILL SUFFICE.
MEANING THAT IF I'M OKAY WITH A QUICK TRIP THROUGH THE OTHER SIDE...
...I CAN INSTANTLY TELEPORT ANYWHERE I'VE BEEN BEFORE.
I'LL NEED TO TRAVEL THE NORMAL WAY TO VISIT PLACES FIRST, OF COURSE...
...BUT THEN I CAN GO TO THAT PLACE WHENEVER I WANT.
WITH THAT IN MIND...
...LET'S GET GOING, SCOOTER!
-RUM
-RUM
VRUMMM

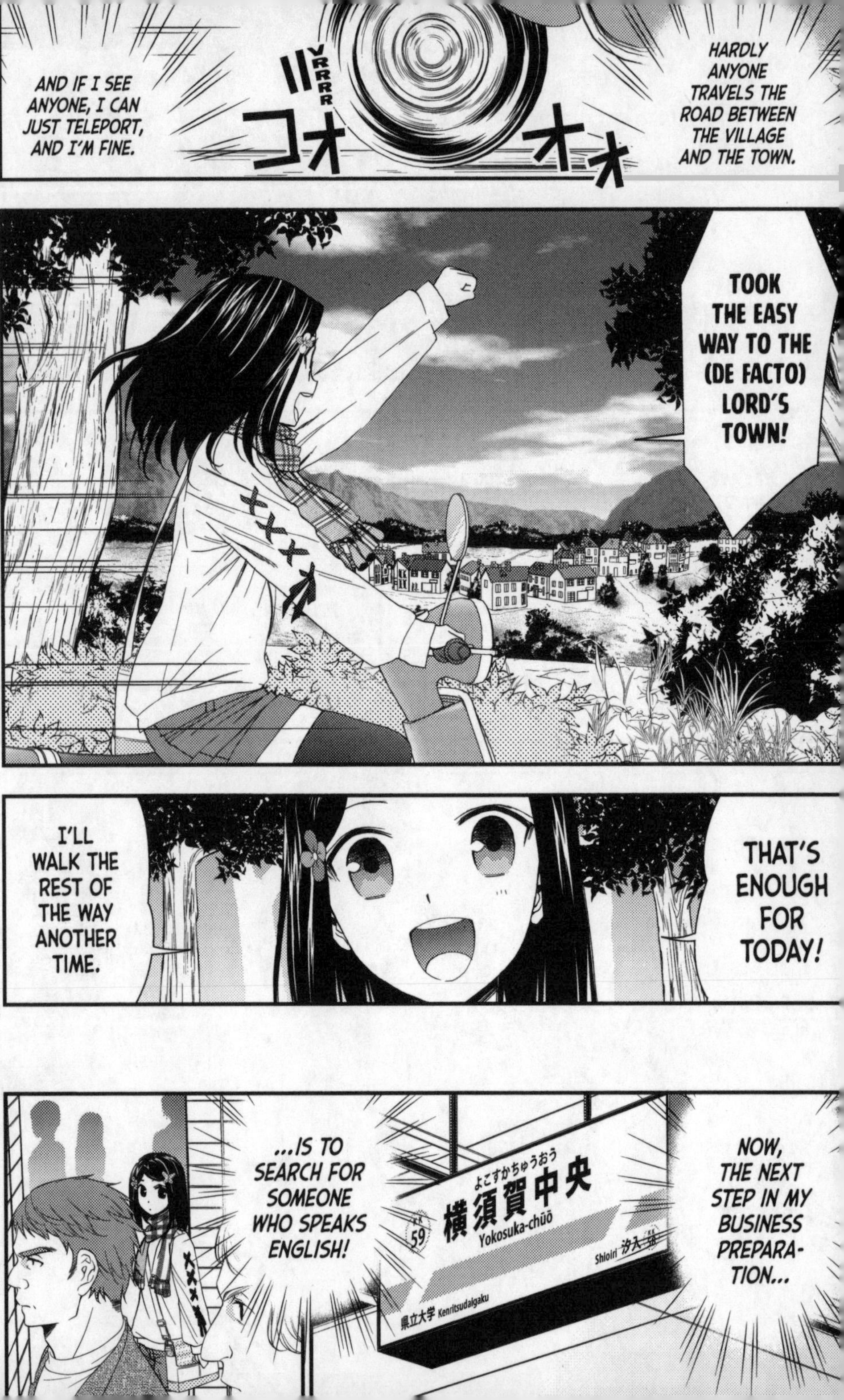
HARDLY ANYONE TRAVELS THE ROAD BETWEEN THE VILLAGE AND THE TOWN.
VRRRR
コオオオ
AND IF I SEE ANYONE, I CAN JUST TELEPORT, AND I'M FINE.
TOOK THE EASY WAY TO THE (DE FACTO) LORD'S TOWN!
THAT'S ENOUGH FOR TODAY!
I'LL WALK THE REST OF THE WAY ANOTHER TIME.
NOW, THE NEXT STEP IN MY BUSINESS PREPARATION...
...IS TO SEARCH FOR SOMEONE WHO SPEAKS ENGLISH!
よこすかちゅうおう
横須賀中央
Yokosuka-chūō
59
Shioiri 汐入
県立大学 Kenritsudaigaku

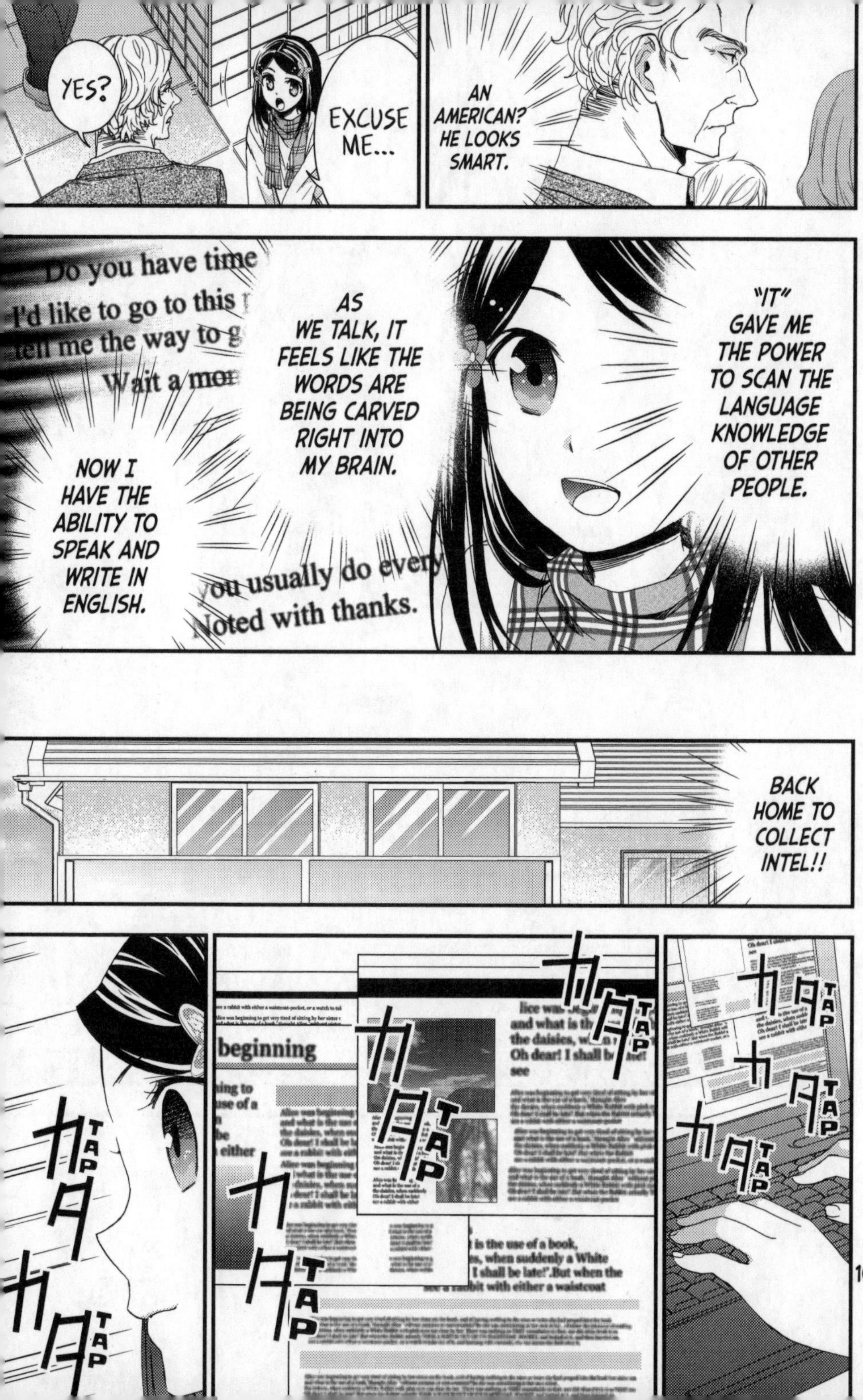
AN AMERICAN? HE LOOKS SMART.
EXCUSE ME...
YES?
"IT" GAVE ME THE POWER TO SCAN THE LANGUAGE KNOWLEDGE OF OTHER PEOPLE.
AS WE TALK, IT FEELS LIKE THE WORDS ARE BEING CARVED RIGHT INTO MY BRAIN.
NOW I HAVE THE ABILITY TO SPEAK AND WRITE IN ENGLISH.
Do you have time
Noted with thanks.
BACK HOME TO COLLECT INTEL!!
カタ TAP
カタ TAP
カタ TAP
カタ TAP
カタ TAP
カタ TAP
カタ TAP
カタ TAP

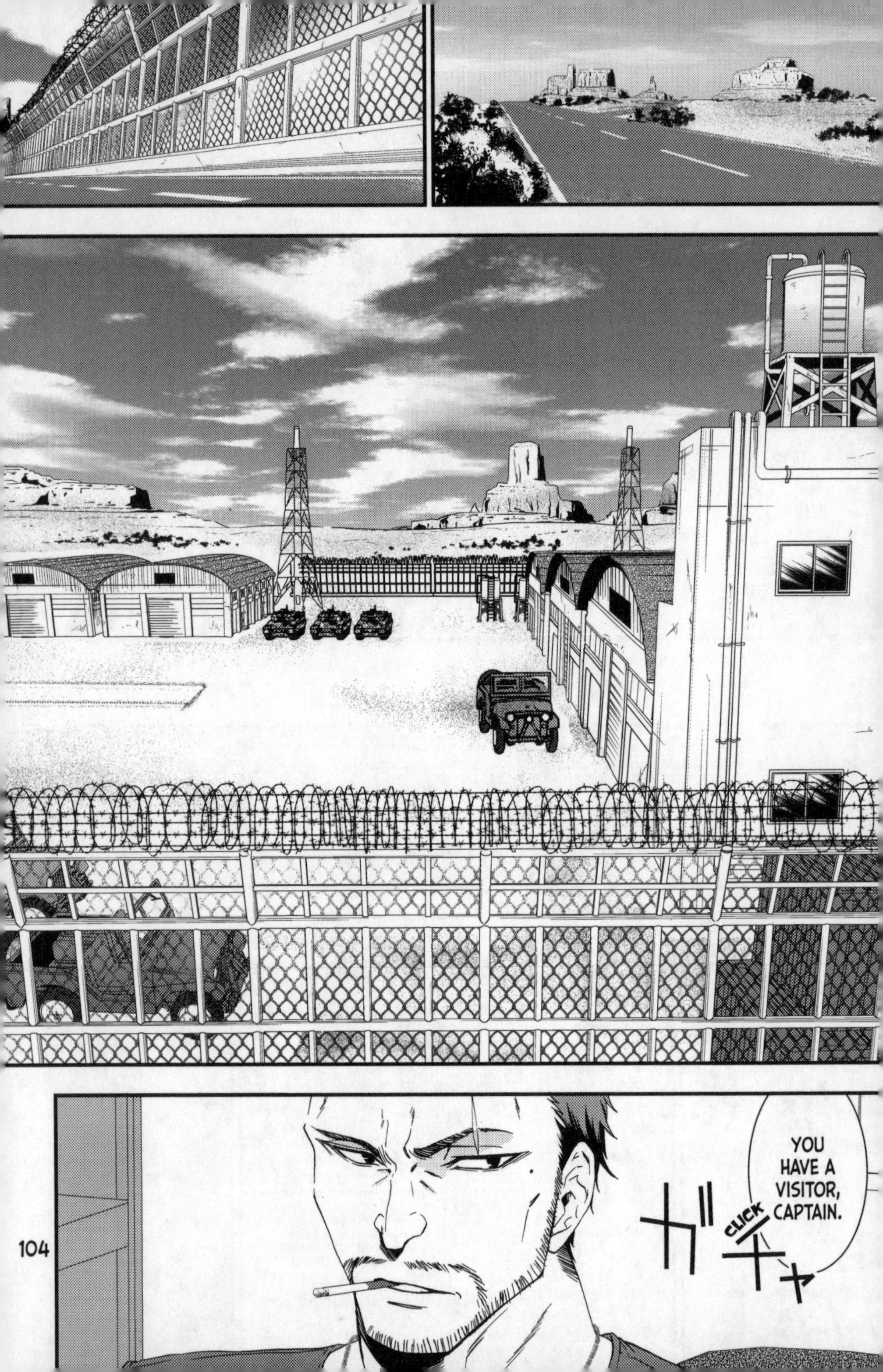
YOU HAVE A VISITOR, CAPTAIN.
ガチャ
CLICK

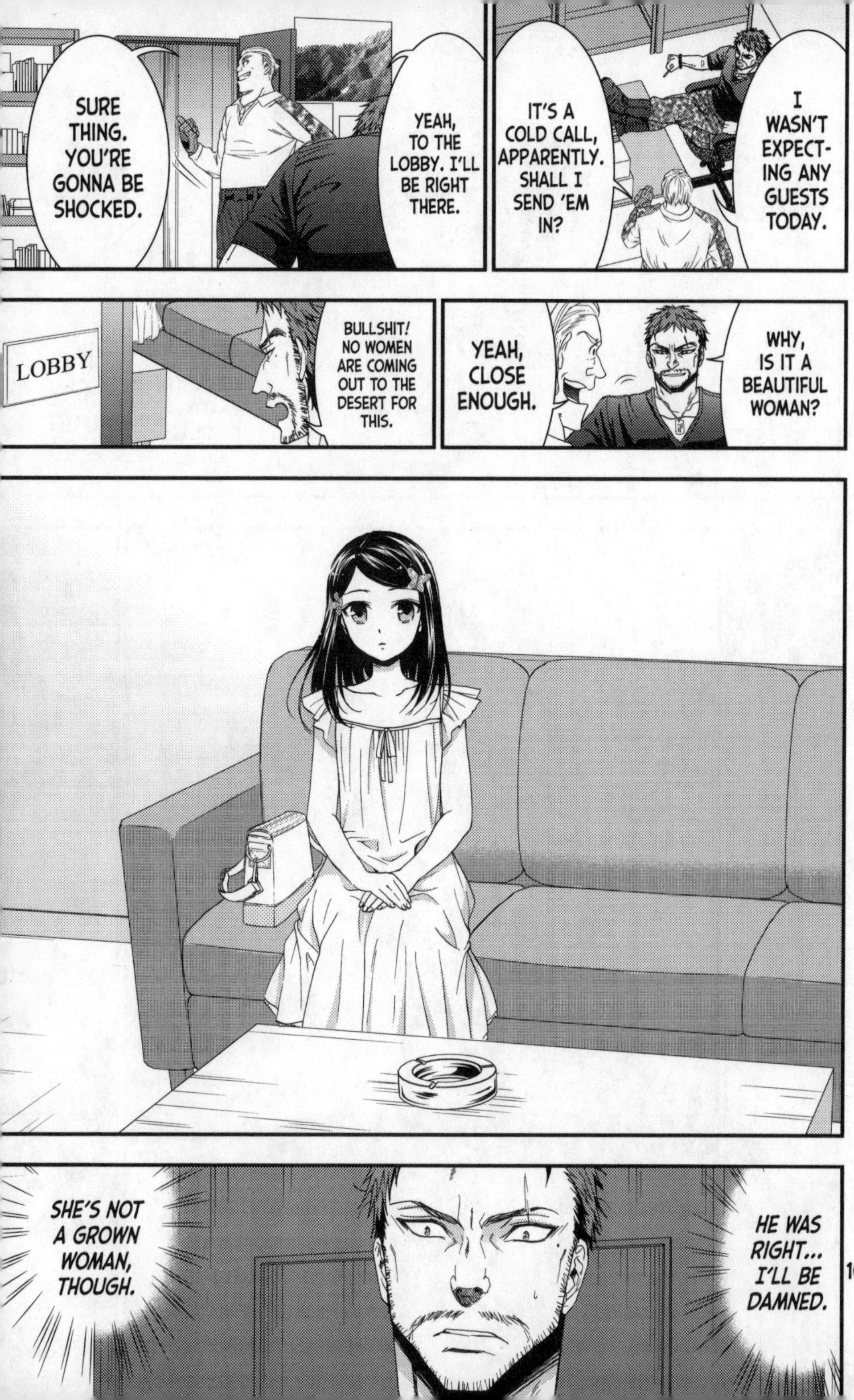
I WASN'T EXPECTING ANY GUESTS TODAY.
IT'S A COLD CALL, APPARENTLY. SHALL I SEND 'EM IN?
YEAH, TO THE LOBBY. I'LL BE RIGHT THERE.
SURE THING. YOU'RE GONNA BE SHOCKED.
WHY, IS IT A BEAUTIFUL WOMAN?
YEAH, CLOSE ENOUGH.
BULLSHIT! NO WOMEN ARE COMING OUT TO THE DESERT FOR THIS.
LOBBY
HE WAS RIGHT... I'LL BE DAMNED.
SHE'S NOT A GROWN WOMAN, THOUGH.

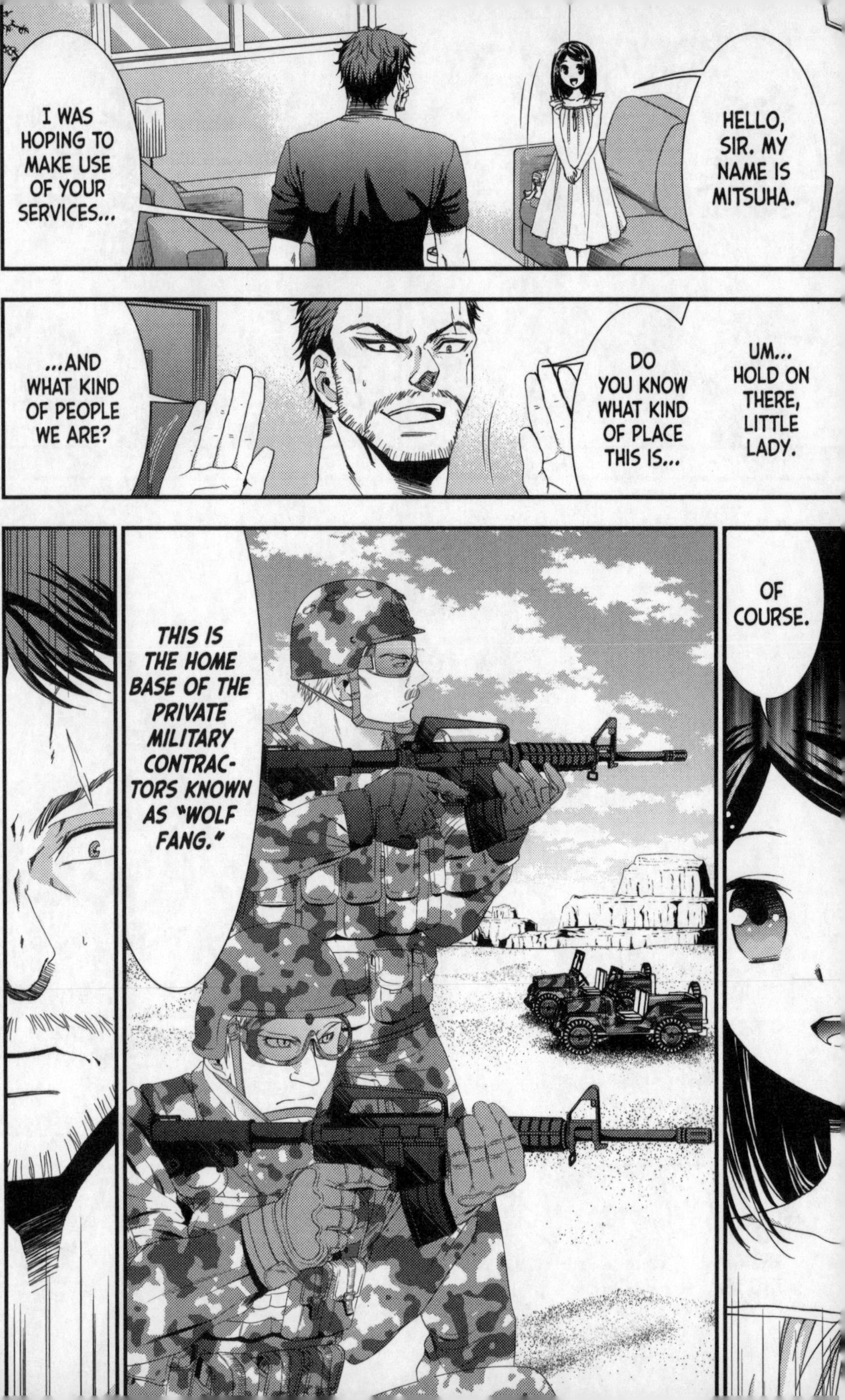
HELLO, SIR. MY NAME IS MITSUHA.
I WAS HOPING TO MAKE USE OF YOUR SERVICES...
UM... HOLD ON THERE, LITTLE LADY.
DO YOU KNOW WHAT KIND OF PLACE THIS IS...
...AND WHAT KIND OF PEOPLE WE ARE?
OF COURSE.
THIS IS THE HOME BASE OF THE PRIVATE MILITARY CONTRAC-TORS KNOWN AS "WOLF FANG."

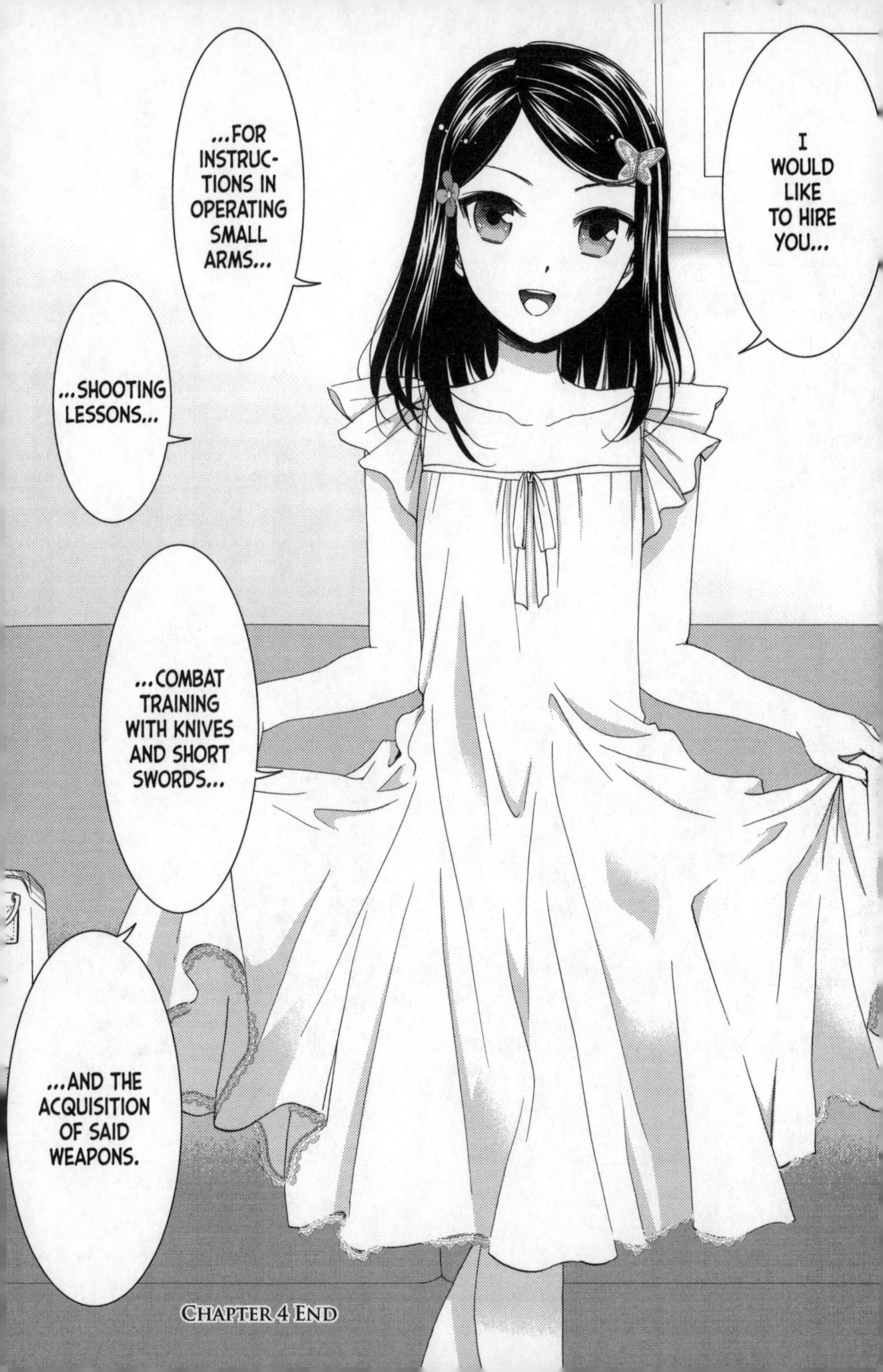
I WOULD LIKE TO HIRE YOU...
...FOR INSTRUC-TIONS IN OPERATING SMALL ARMS...
...SHOOTING LESSONS...
...COMBAT TRAINING WITH KNIVES AND SHORT SWORDS...
...AND THE ACQUISITION OF SAID WEAPONS.
CHAPTER 4 END

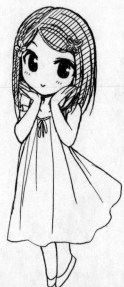

To Japan and its people, I am still Mitsuha Yamano.

But in other places and with other people, I'm just a pretty little foreign girl named Mitsuha from a noble family.

♥

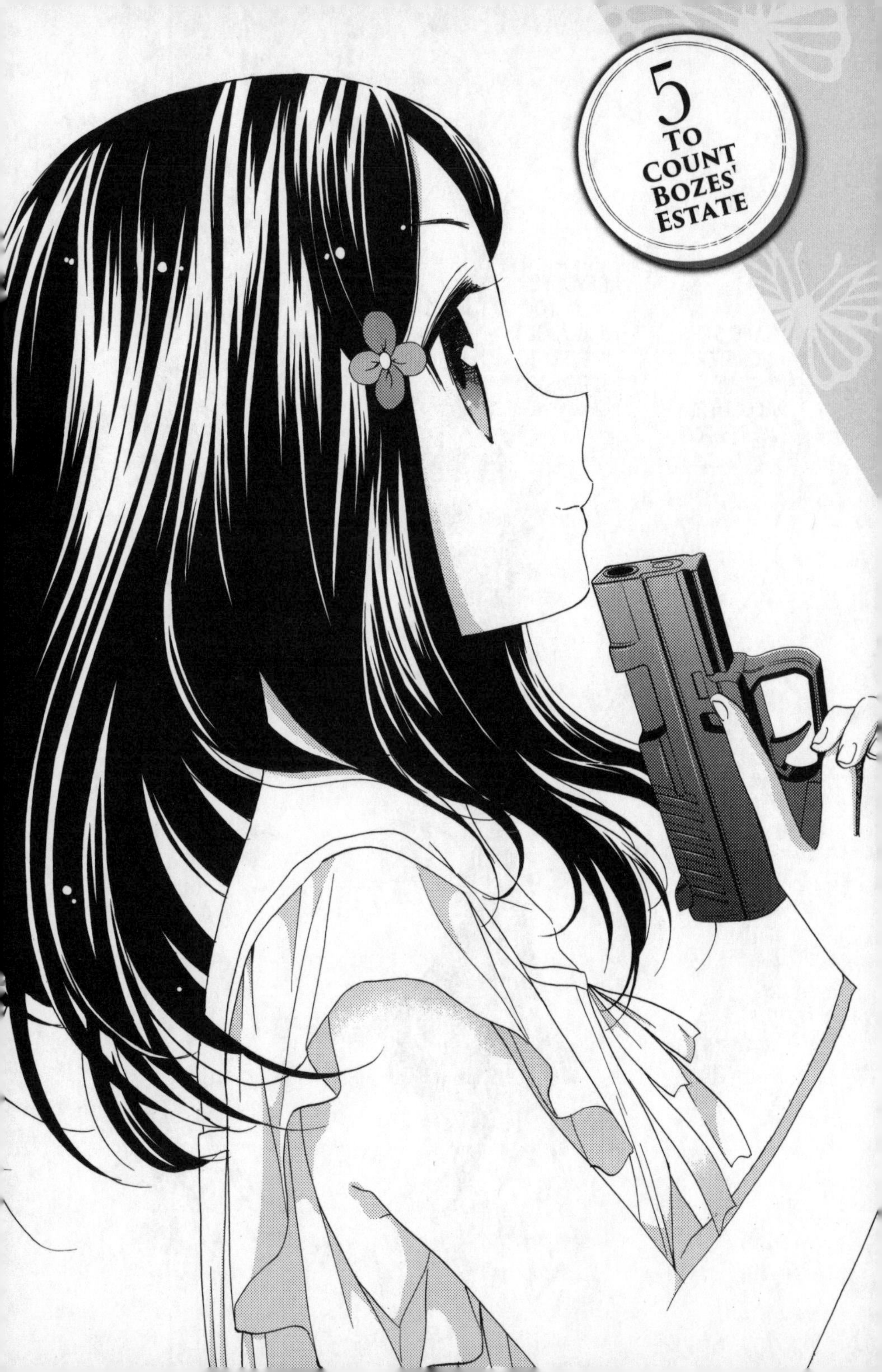
5
To Count Bozes' Estate

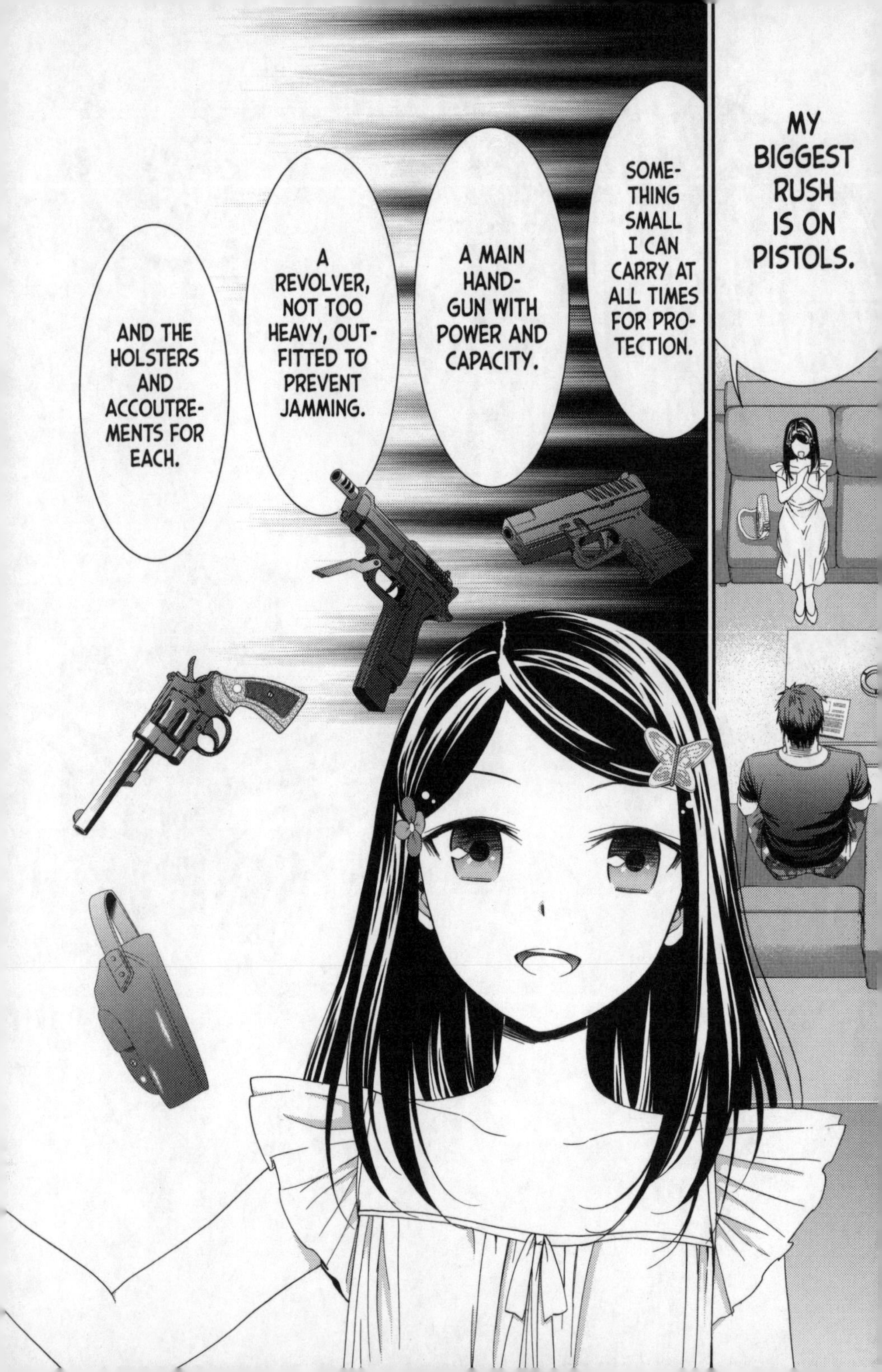
MY BIGGEST RUSH IS ON PISTOLS.
SOME-THING SMALL I CAN CARRY AT ALL TIMES FOR PRO-TECTION.
A MAIN HAND-GUN WITH POWER AND CAPACITY.
A REVOLVER, NOT TOO HEAVY, OUT-FITTED TO PREVENT JAMMING.
AND THE HOLSTERS AND ACCOUTRE-MENTS FOR EACH.

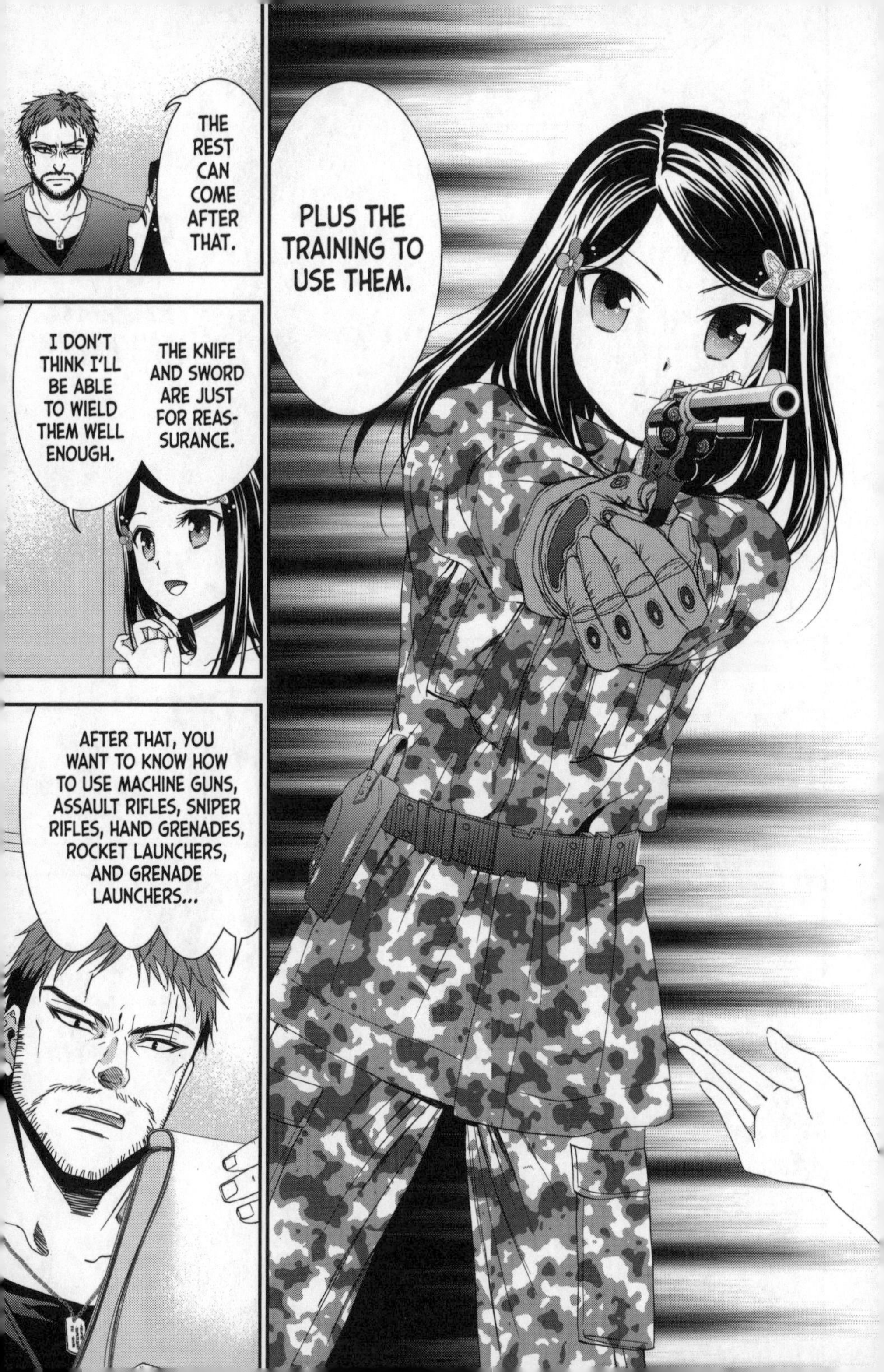
PLUS THE TRAINING TO USE THEM.
THE REST CAN COME AFTER THAT.
THE KNIFE AND SWORD ARE JUST FOR REAS-SURANCE.
I DON'T THINK I'LL BE ABLE TO WIELD THEM WELL ENOUGH.
AFTER THAT, YOU WANT TO KNOW HOW TO USE MACHINE GUNS, ASSAULT RIFLES, SNIPER RIFLES, HAND GRENADES, ROCKET LAUNCHERS, AND GRENADE LAUNCHERS...

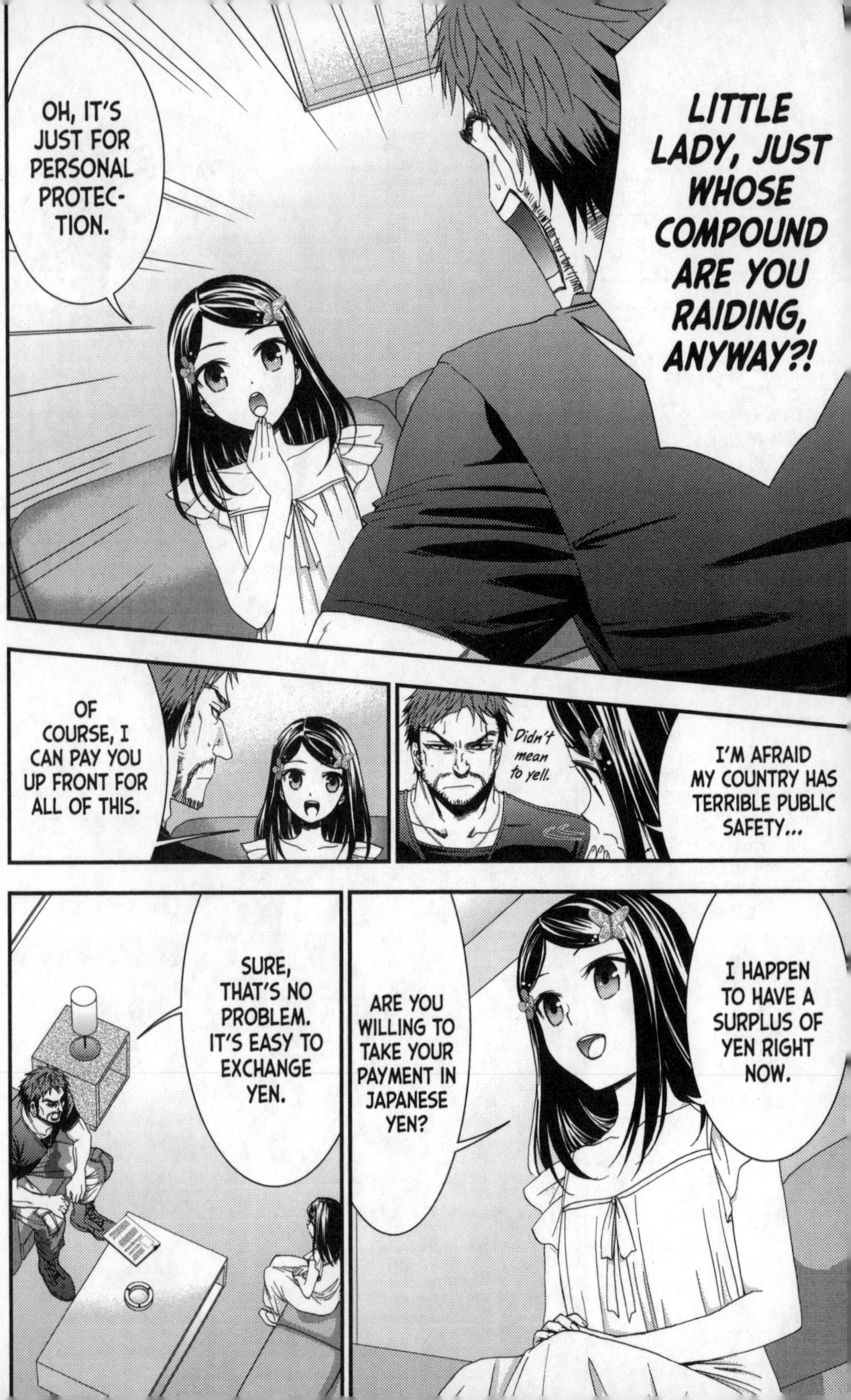
LITTLE LADY, JUST WHOSE COMPOUND ARE YOU RAIDING, ANYWAY?!
OH, IT'S JUST FOR PERSONAL PROTEC-TION.
I'M AFRAID MY COUNTRY HAS TERRIBLE PUBLIC SAFETY...
Didn't mean to yell.
OF COURSE, I CAN PAY YOU UP FRONT FOR ALL OF THIS.
I HAPPEN TO HAVE A SURPLUS OF YEN RIGHT NOW.
ARE YOU WILLING TO TAKE YOUR PAYMENT IN JAPANESE YEN?
SURE, THAT'S NO PROBLEM. IT'S EASY TO EXCHANGE YEN.

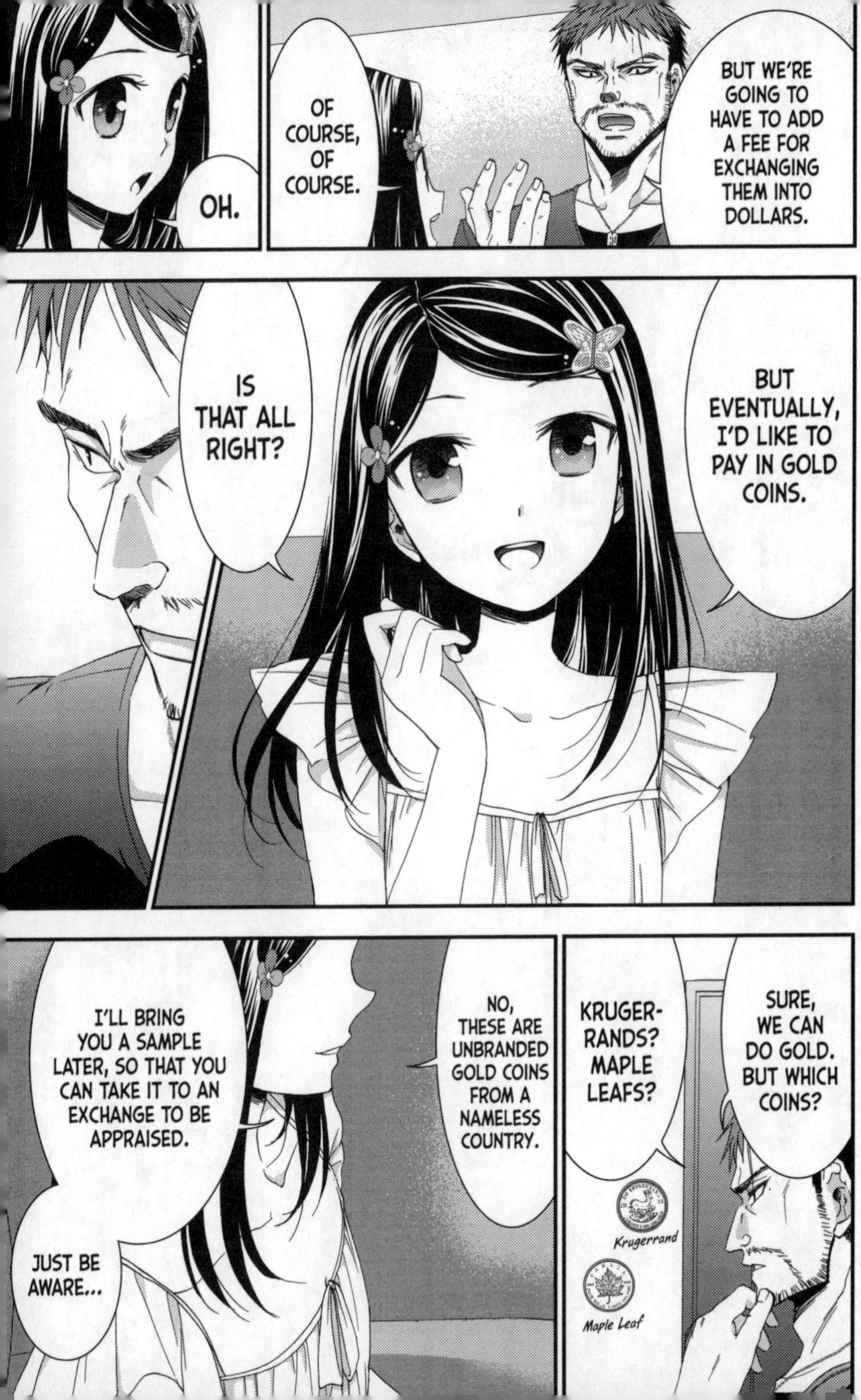
BUT WE'RE GOING TO HAVE TO ADD A FEE FOR EXCHANGING THEM INTO DOLLARS.
OF COURSE, OF COURSE.
OH.
BUT EVENTUALLY, I'D LIKE TO PAY IN GOLD COINS.
IS THAT ALL RIGHT?
SURE, WE CAN DO GOLD. BUT WHICH COINS?
KRUGER-RANDS? MAPLE LEAFS?
Krugerrand
Maple Leaf
NO, THESE ARE UNBRANDED GOLD COINS FROM A NAMELESS COUNTRY.
I'LL BRING YOU A SAMPLE LATER, SO THAT YOU CAN TAKE IT TO AN EXCHANGE TO BE APPRAISED.
JUST BE AWARE...

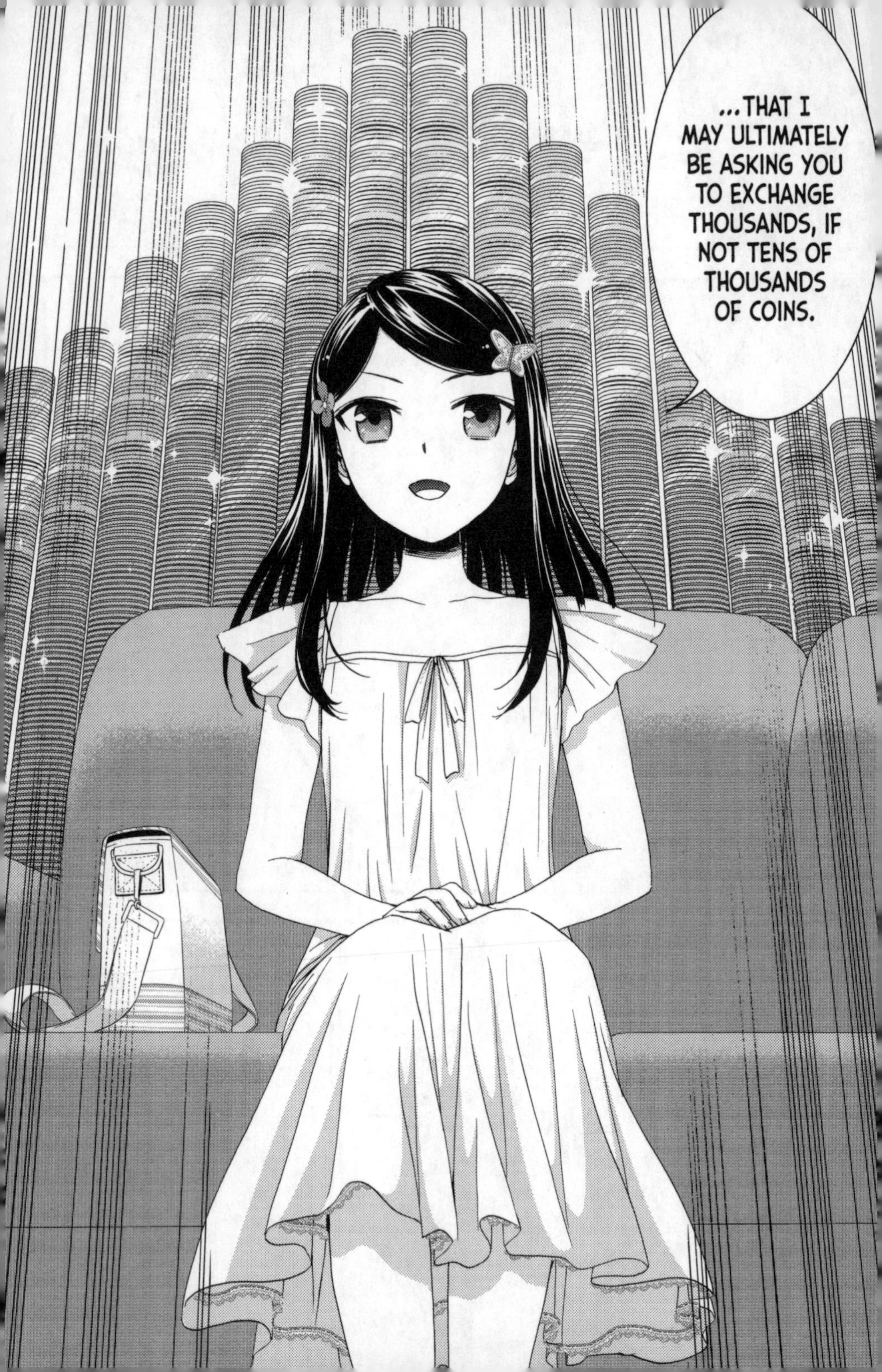
...THAT I MAY ULTIMATELY BE ASKING YOU TO EXCHANGE THOUSANDS, IF NOT TENS OF THOUSANDS OF COINS.

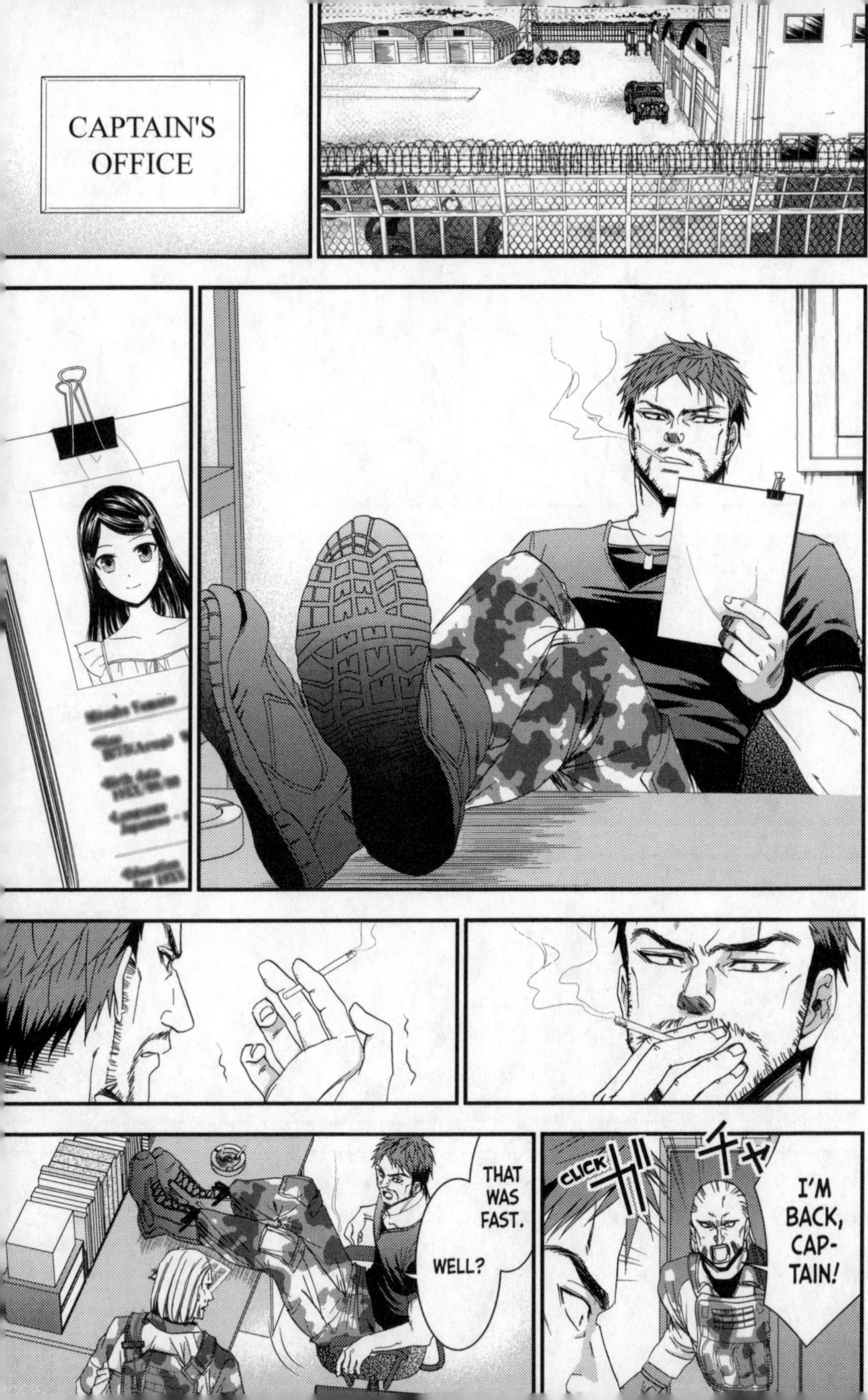
CAPTAIN'S OFFICE
CLICK
ガ
チャ
I'M BACK, CAP-TAIN!
THAT WAS FAST.
WELL?

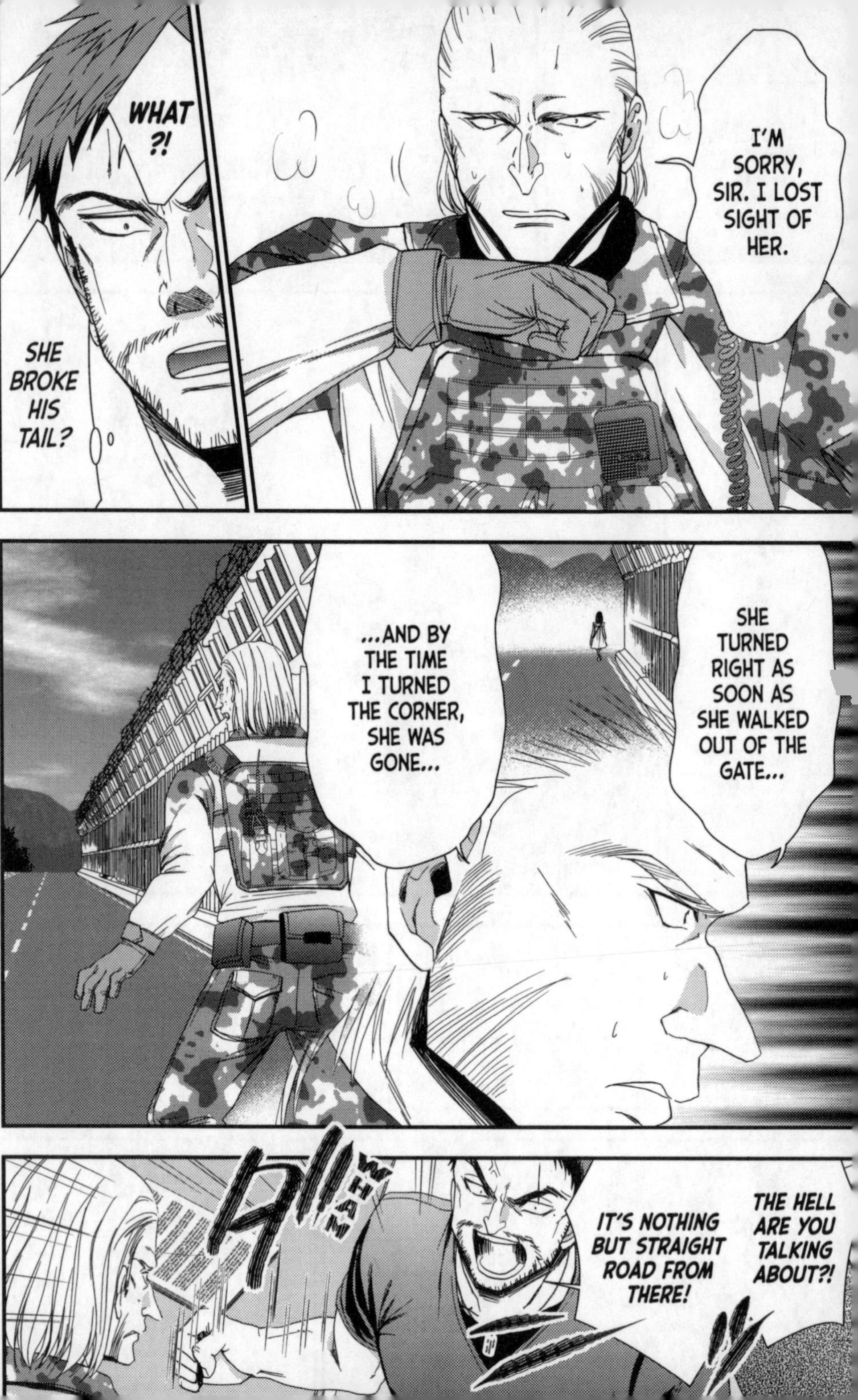

I'M SORRY, SIR. I LOST SIGHT OF HER.
WHAT?!
SHE BROKE HIS TAIL?
SHE TURNED RIGHT AS SOON AS SHE WALKED OUT OF THE GATE...
...AND BY THE TIME I TURNED THE CORNER, SHE WAS GONE...
WHAM
THE HELL ARE YOU TALKING ABOUT?!
IT'S NOTHING BUT STRAIGHT ROAD FROM THERE!

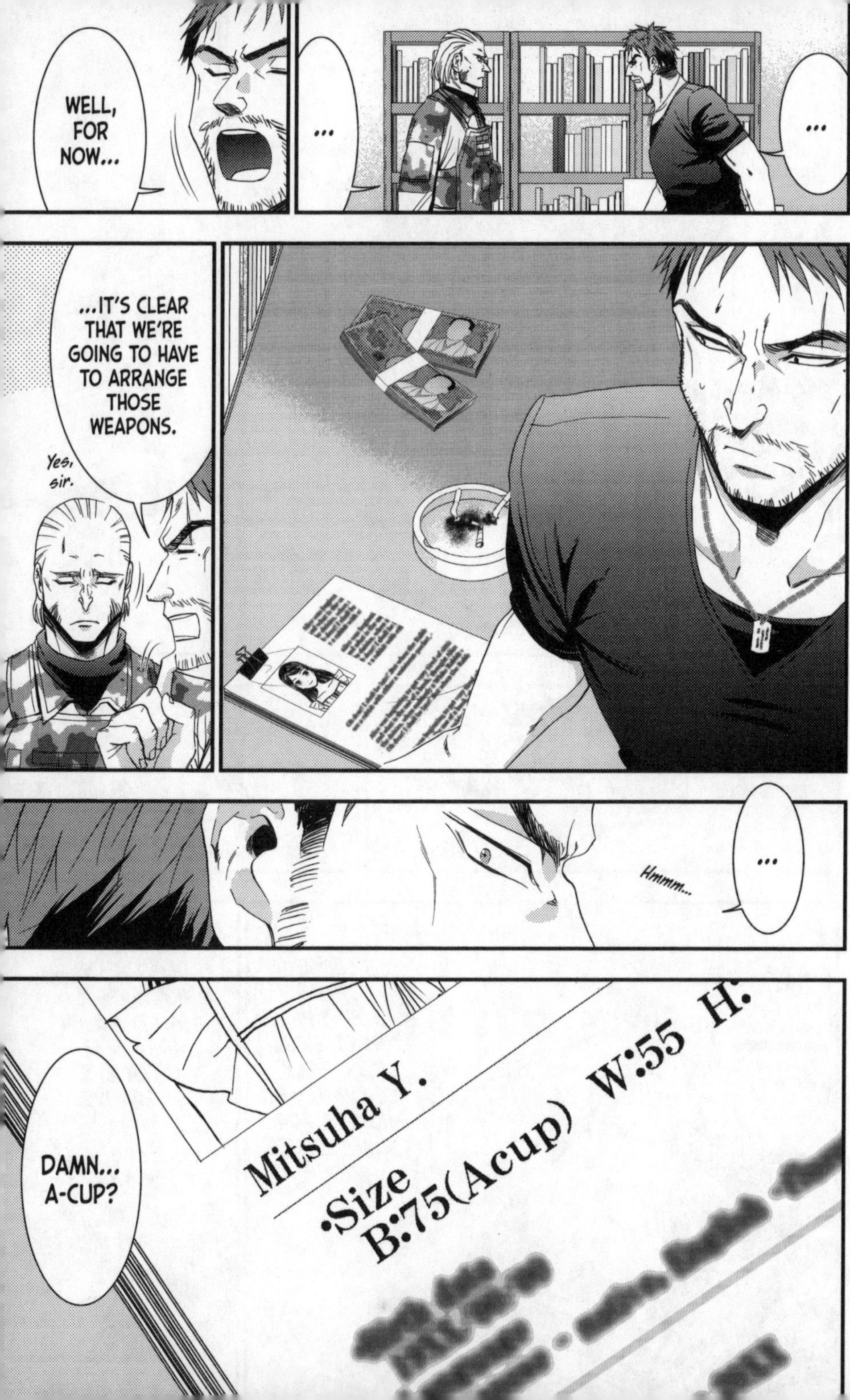
...
...
WELL, FOR NOW...
...IT'S CLEAR THAT WE'RE GOING TO HAVE TO ARRANGE THOSE WEAPONS.
Yes, sir.
...
Hmmm...
Mitsuha Y.
•Size
B:75(Acup) W:55 H:
DAMN... A-CUP?

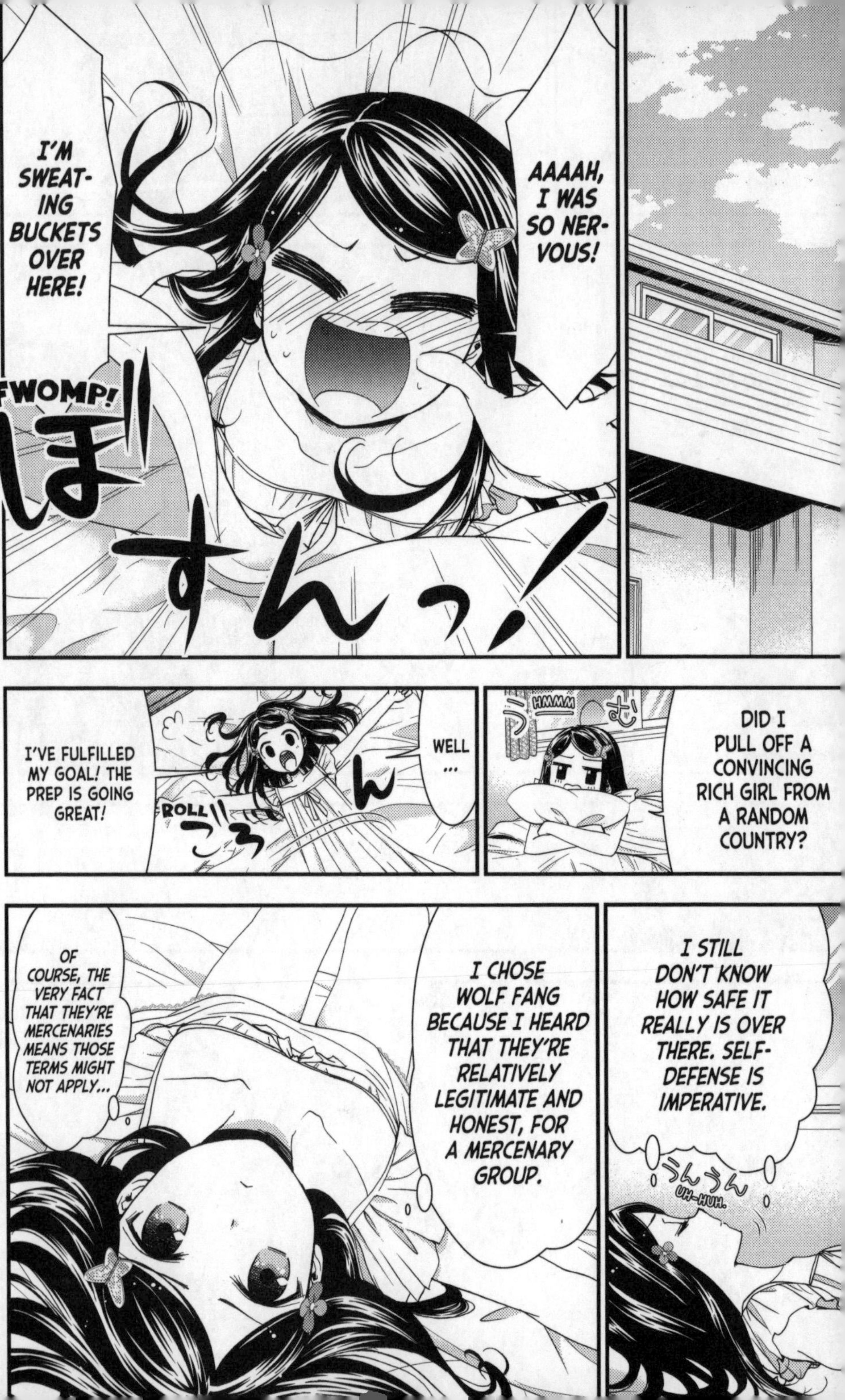
AAAAH, I WAS SO NERVOUS!
I'M SWEATING BUCKETS OVER HERE!
FWOMP!
ぼすんっ!
HMMM
DID I PULL OFF A CONVINCING RICH GIRL FROM A RANDOM COUNTRY?
WELL ...
ん
I'VE FULFILLED MY GOAL! THE PREP IS GOING GREAT!
ROLL
ごろ
I STILL DON'T KNOW HOW SAFE IT REALLY IS OVER THERE. SELF-DEFENSE IS IMPERATIVE.
うんうん
UH-HUH.
I CHOSE WOLF FANG BECAUSE I HEARD THAT THEY'RE RELATIVELY LEGITIMATE AND HONEST, FOR A MERCENARY GROUP.
OF COURSE, THE VERY FACT THAT THEY'RE MERCENARIES MEANS THOSE TERMS MIGHT NOT APPLY...

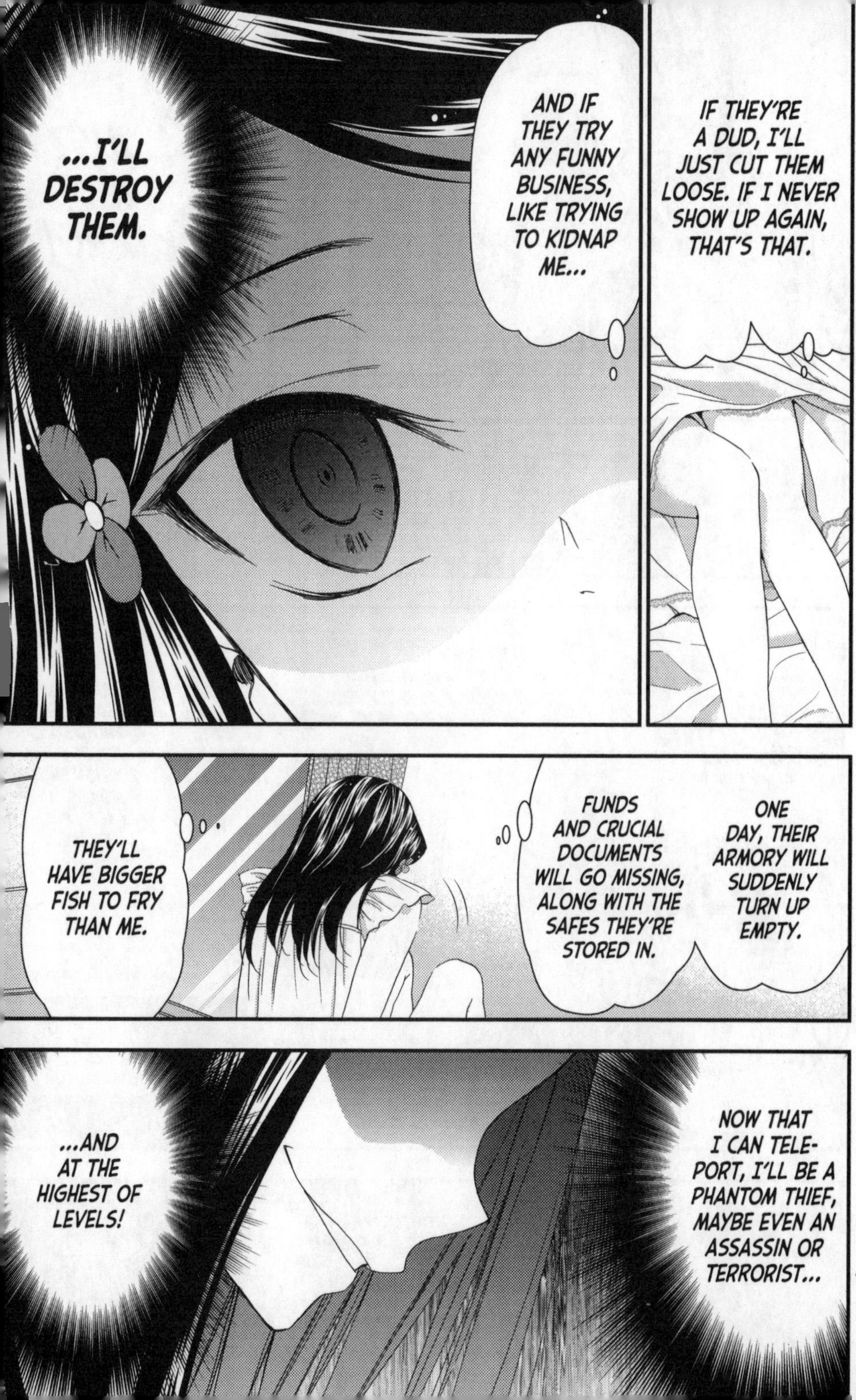
IF THEY'RE A DUD, I'LL JUST CUT THEM LOOSE. IF I NEVER SHOW UP AGAIN, THAT'S THAT.
AND IF THEY TRY ANY FUNNY BUSINESS, LIKE TRYING TO KIDNAP ME...
...I'LL DESTROY THEM.
ONE DAY, THEIR ARMORY WILL SUDDENLY TURN UP EMPTY.
FUNDS AND CRUCIAL DOCUMENTS WILL GO MISSING, ALONG WITH THE SAFES THEY'RE STORED IN.
THEY'LL HAVE BIGGER FISH TO FRY THAN ME.
NOW THAT I CAN TELE-PORT, I'LL BE A PHANTOM THIEF, MAYBE EVEN AN ASSASSIN OR TERRORIST...
...AND AT THE HIGHEST OF LEVELS!

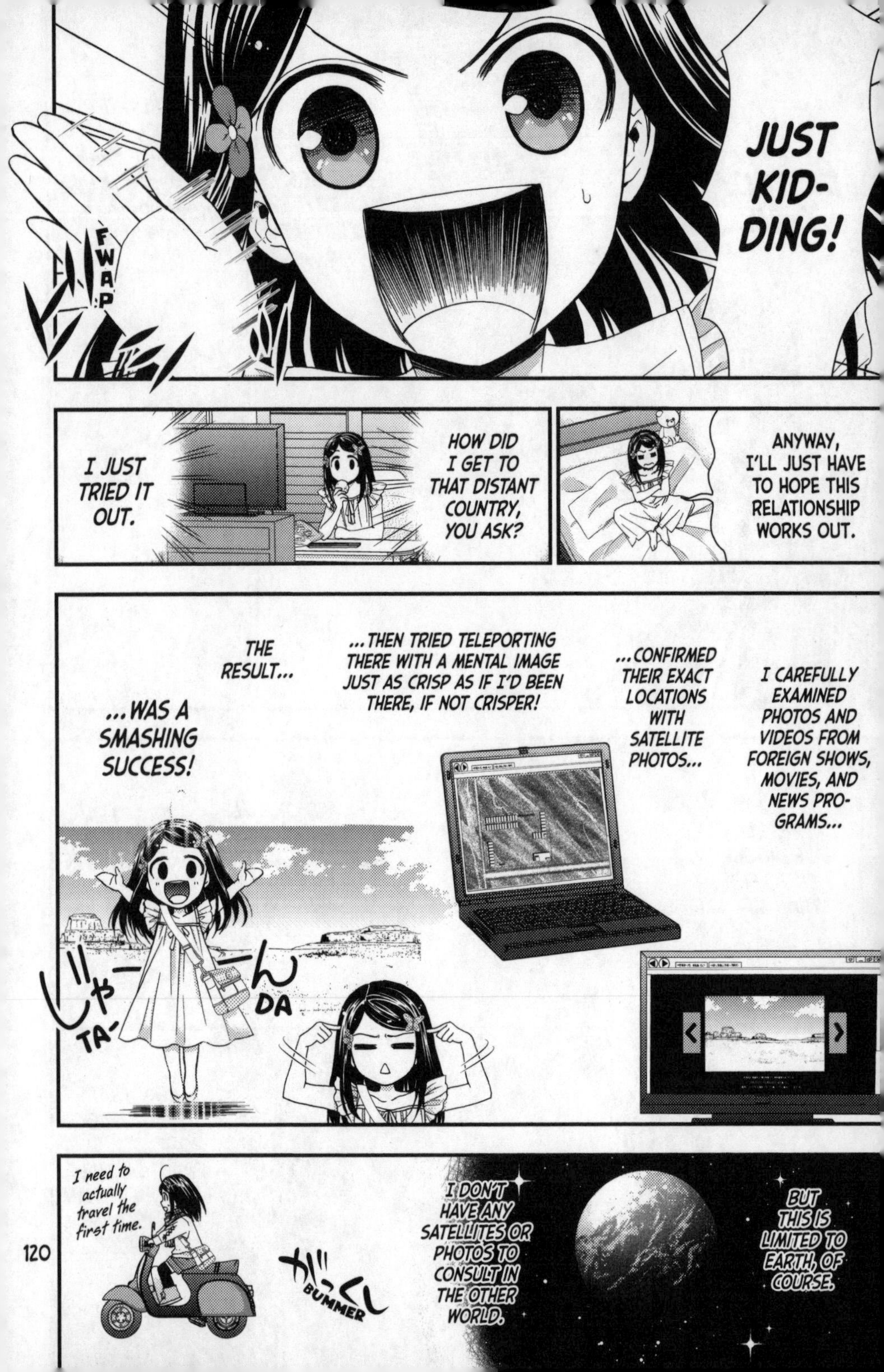
JUST KID-DING!
FWAP
ANYWAY, I'LL JUST HAVE TO HOPE THIS RELATIONSHIP WORKS OUT.
HOW DID I GET TO THAT DISTANT COUNTRY, YOU ASK?
I JUST TRIED IT OUT.
I CAREFULLY EXAMINED PHOTOS AND VIDEOS FROM FOREIGN SHOWS, MOVIES, AND NEWS PRO-GRAMS...
...CONFIRMED THEIR EXACT LOCATIONS WITH SATELLITE PHOTOS...
...THEN TRIED TELEPORTING THERE WITH A MENTAL IMAGE JUST AS CRISP AS IF I'D BEEN THERE, IF NOT CRISPER!
THE RESULT...
...WAS A SMASHING SUCCESS!
じゃーん
TA-
DA
BUT THIS IS LIMITED TO EARTH, OF COURSE.
I DON'T HAVE ANY SATELLITES OR PHOTOS TO CONSULT IN THE OTHER WORLD.
がっくし
BUMMER
I need to actually travel the first time.

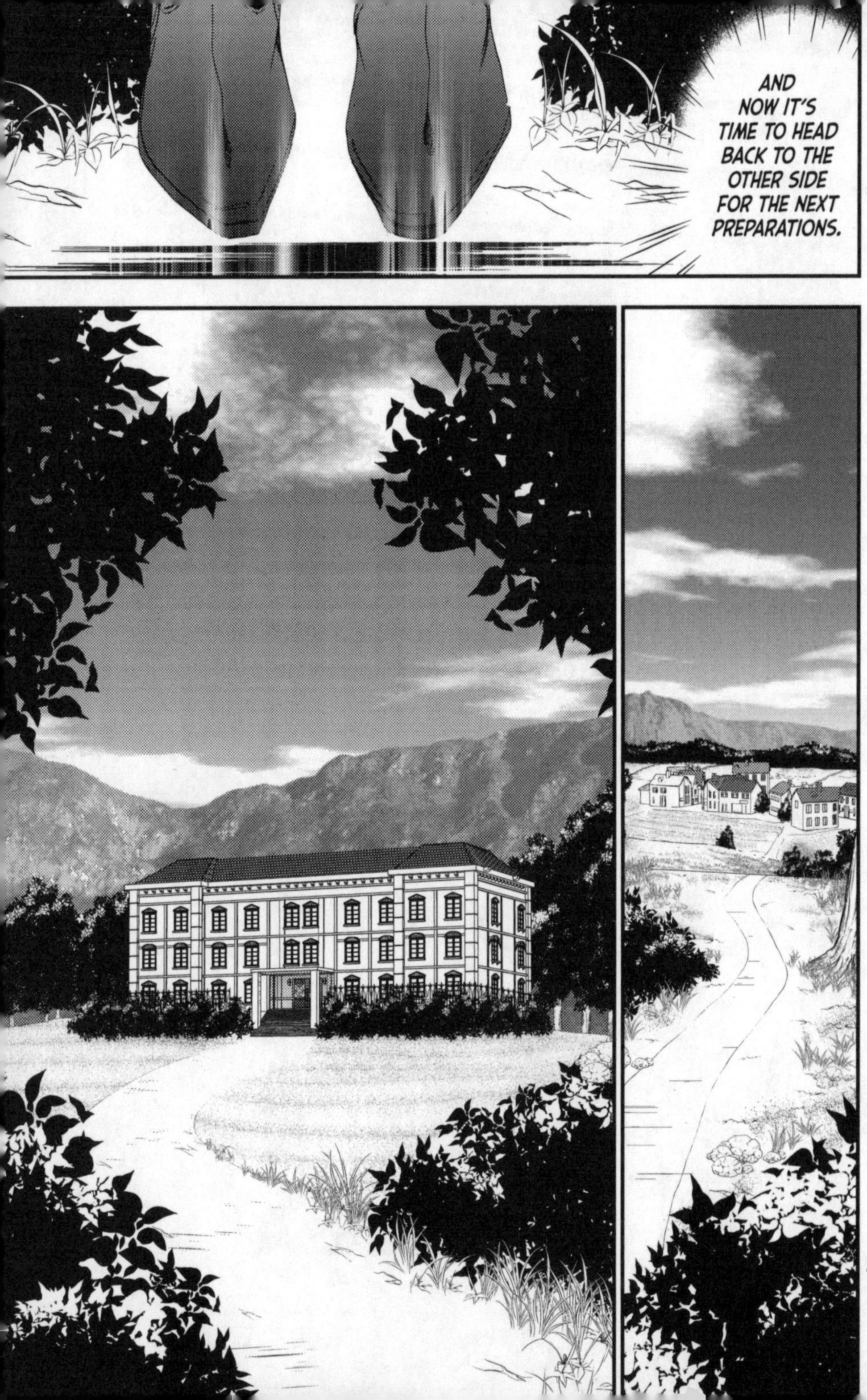
AND NOW IT'S TIME TO HEAD BACK TO THE OTHER SIDE FOR THE NEXT PREPARATIONS.

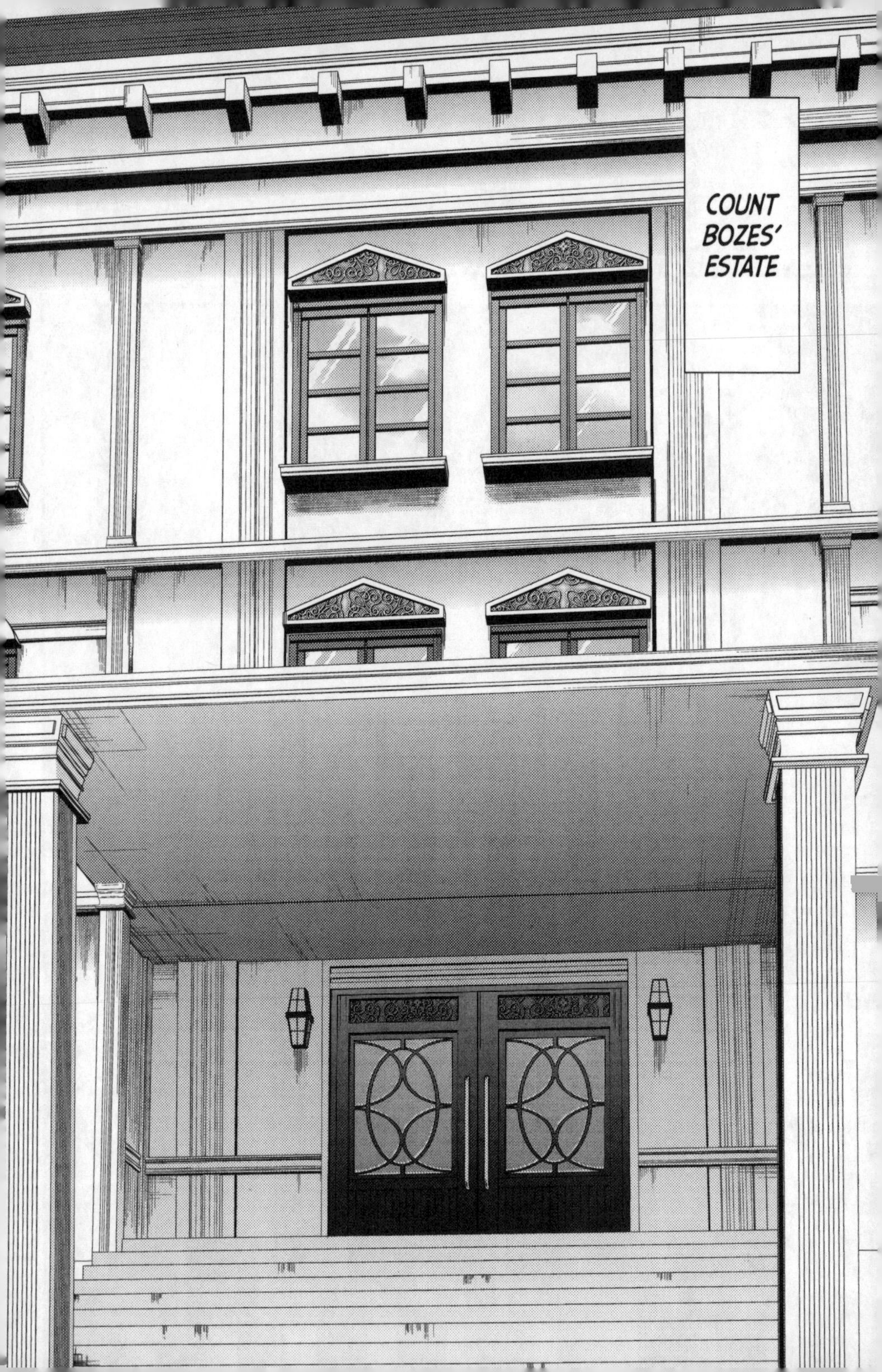
COUNT BOZES' ESTATE

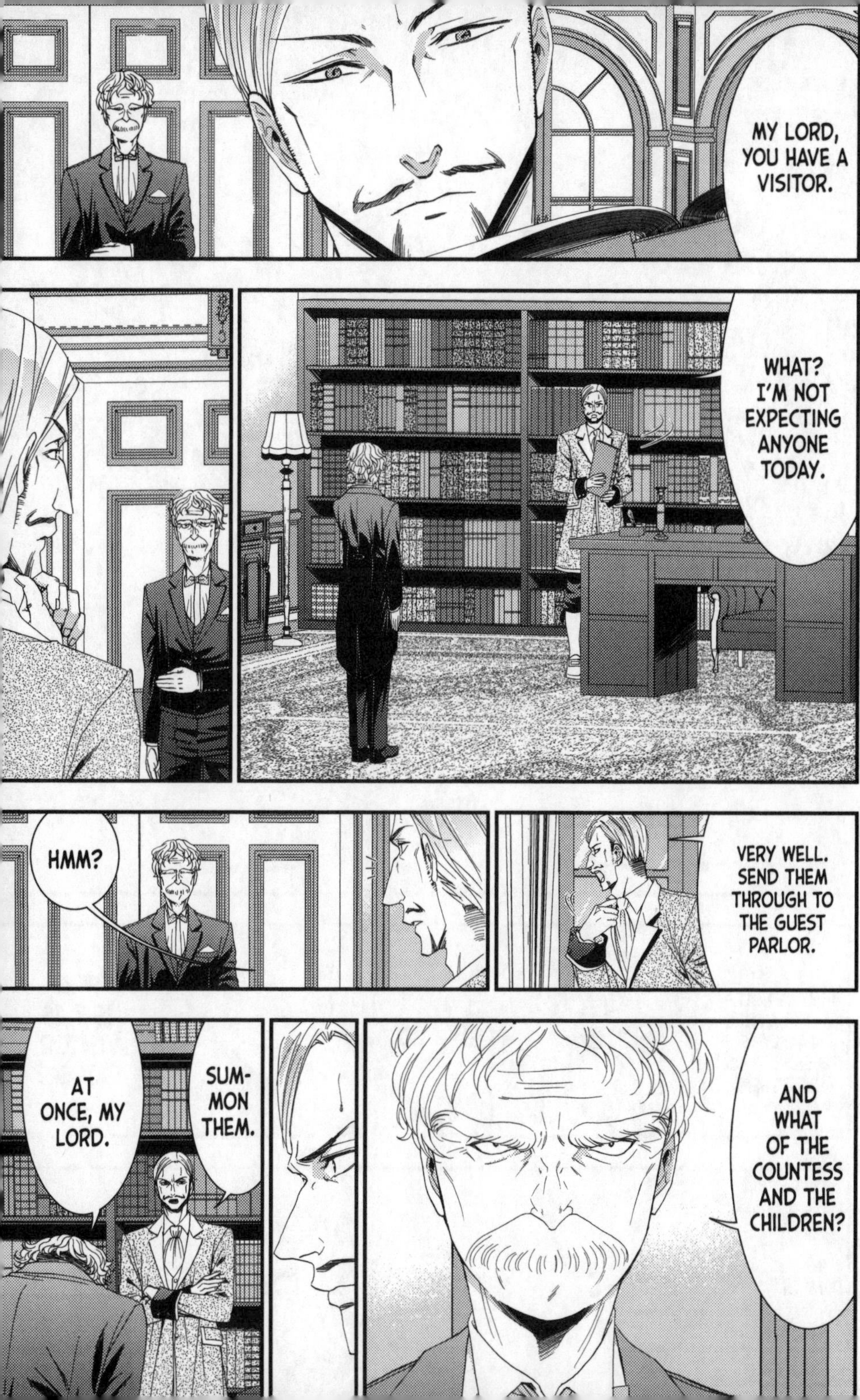
MY LORD, YOU HAVE A VISITOR.
WHAT? I'M NOT EXPECTING ANYONE TODAY.
VERY WELL. SEND THEM THROUGH TO THE GUEST PARLOR.
HMM?
AND WHAT OF THE COUNTESS AND THE CHILDREN?
SUM-MON THEM.
AT ONCE, MY LORD.

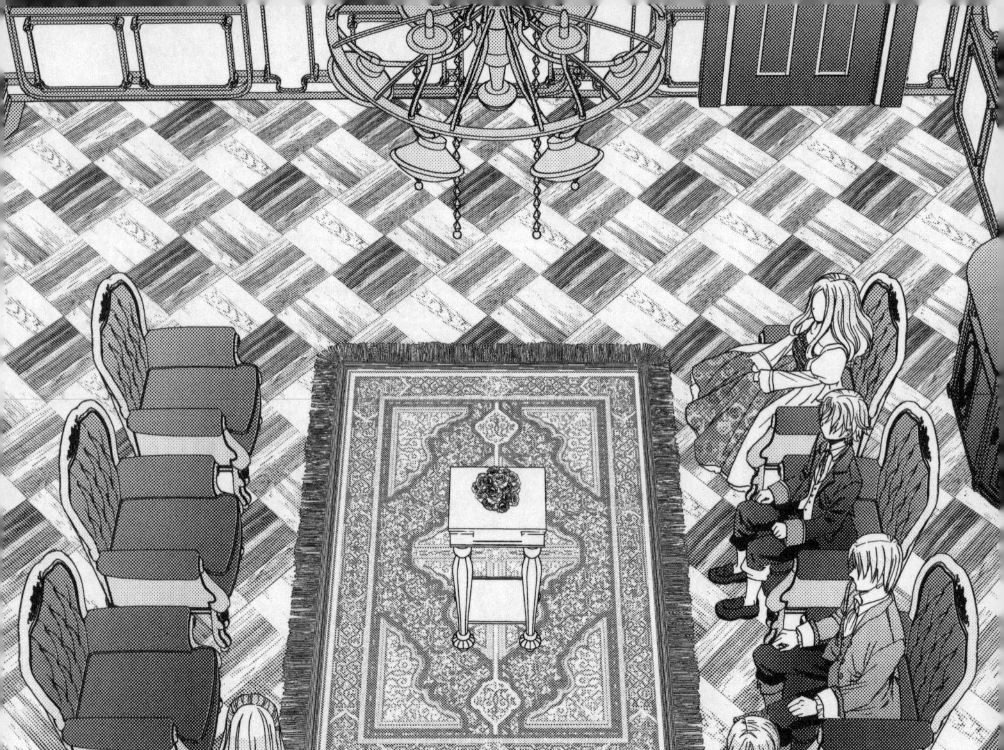

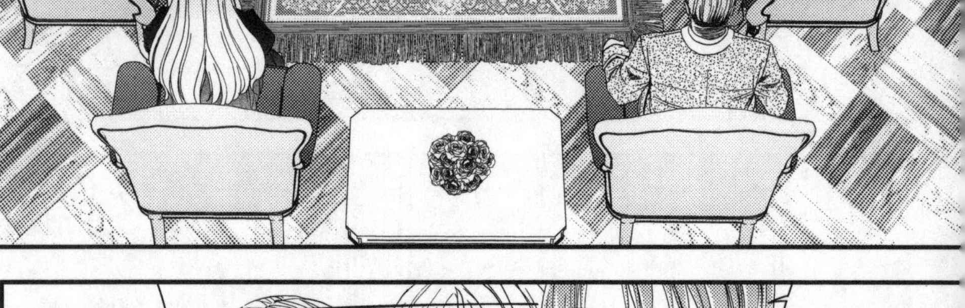
WHO IS THIS VISITOR, FATHER?
THEY MUST BE IMPORTANT, IF THE ENTIRE FAMILY IS REQUIRED TO GREET THEM...

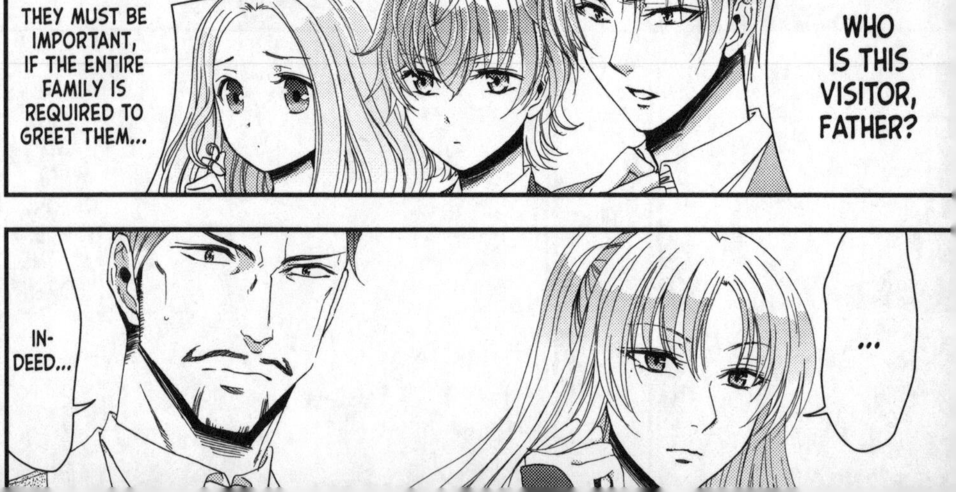
...
IN-DEED...

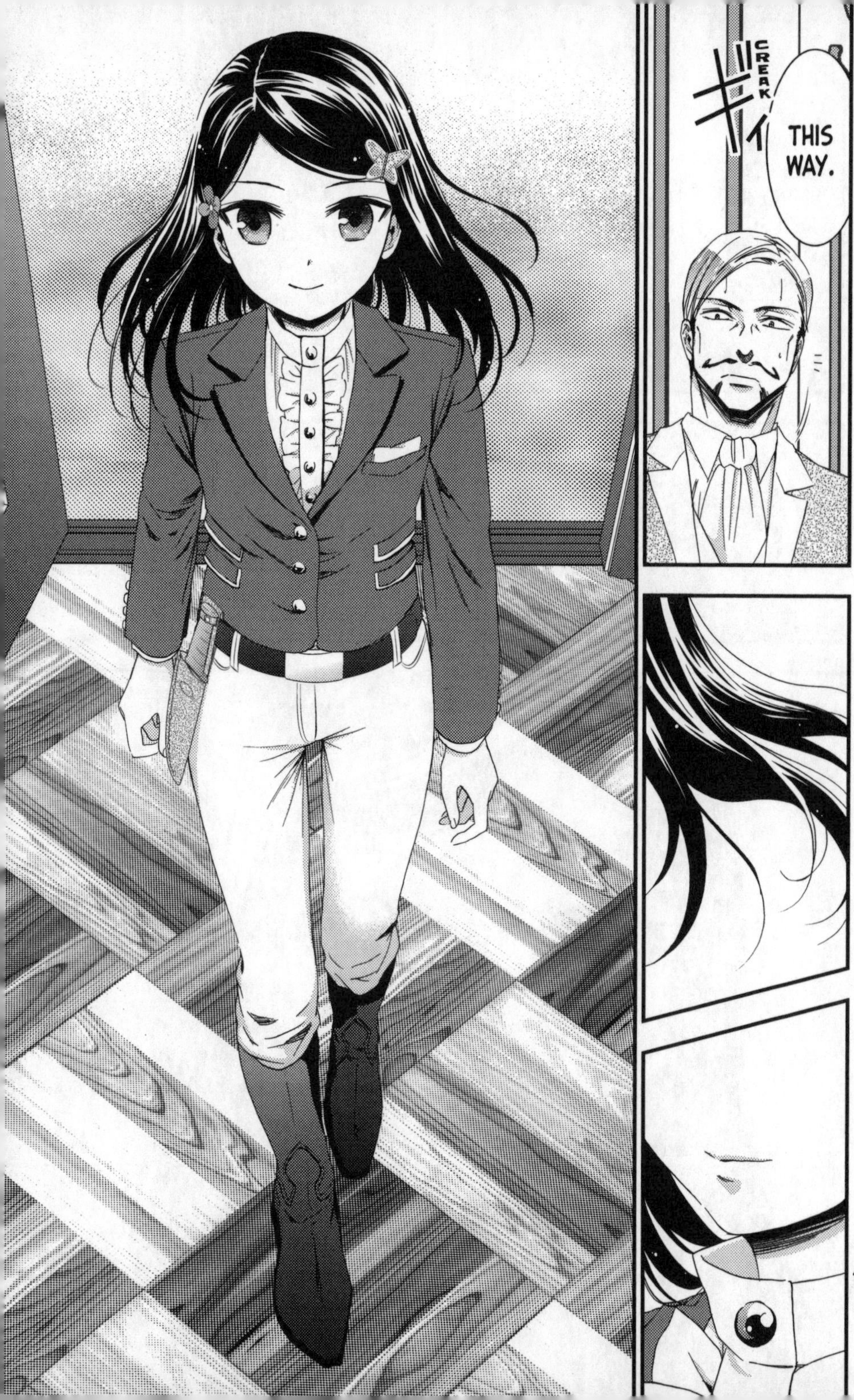
ギイ
CREAK
THIS WAY.

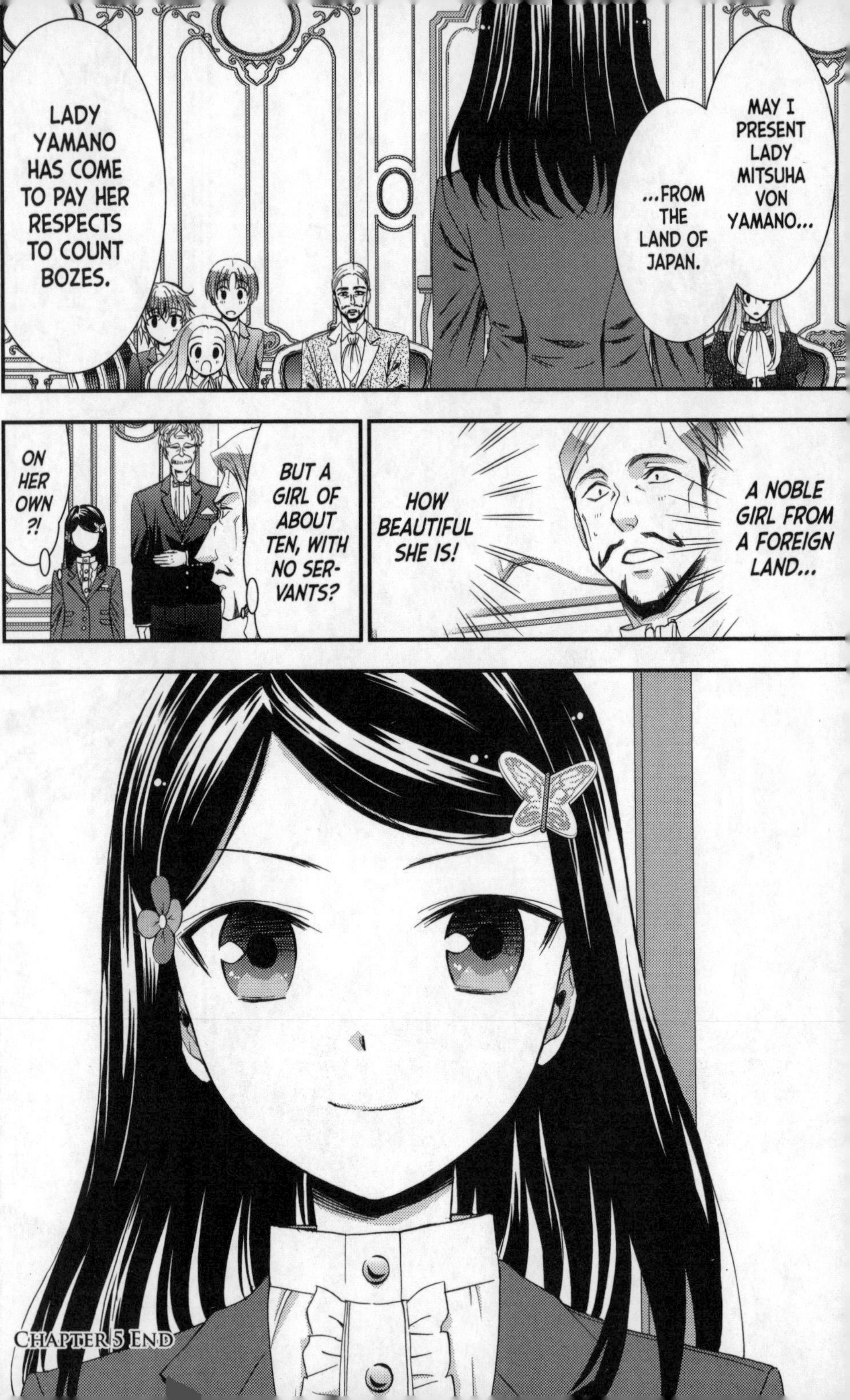
MAY I PRESENT LADY MITSUHA VON YAMANO...
...FROM THE LAND OF JAPAN.
LADY YAMANO HAS COME TO PAY HER RESPECTS TO COUNT BOZES.
A NOBLE GIRL FROM A FOREIGN LAND...
HOW BEAUTIFUL SHE IS!
BUT A GIRL OF ABOUT TEN, WITH NO SERVANTS?
ON HER OWN?!
CHAPTER 5 END

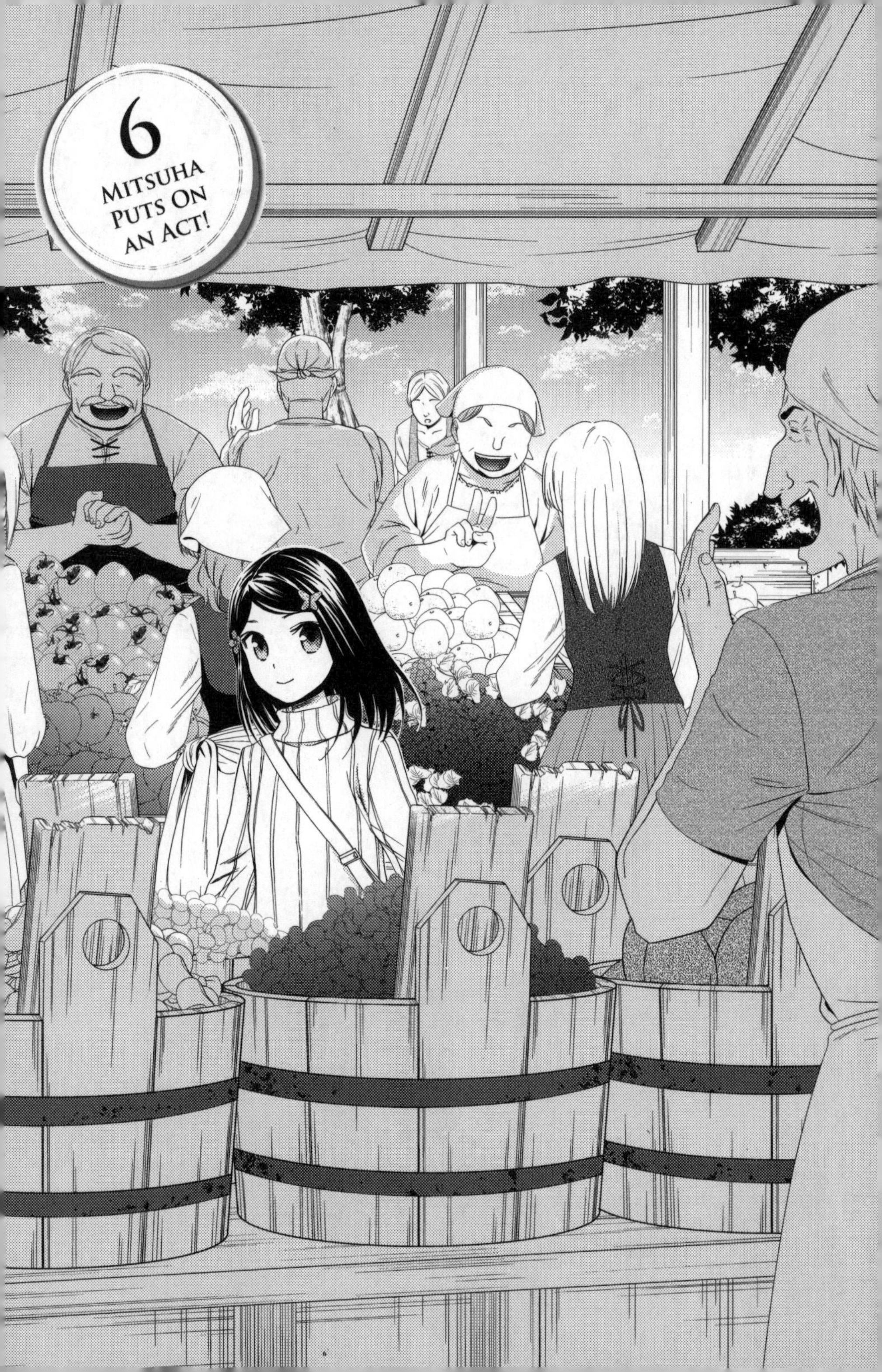
6
Mitsuha Puts On an Act!

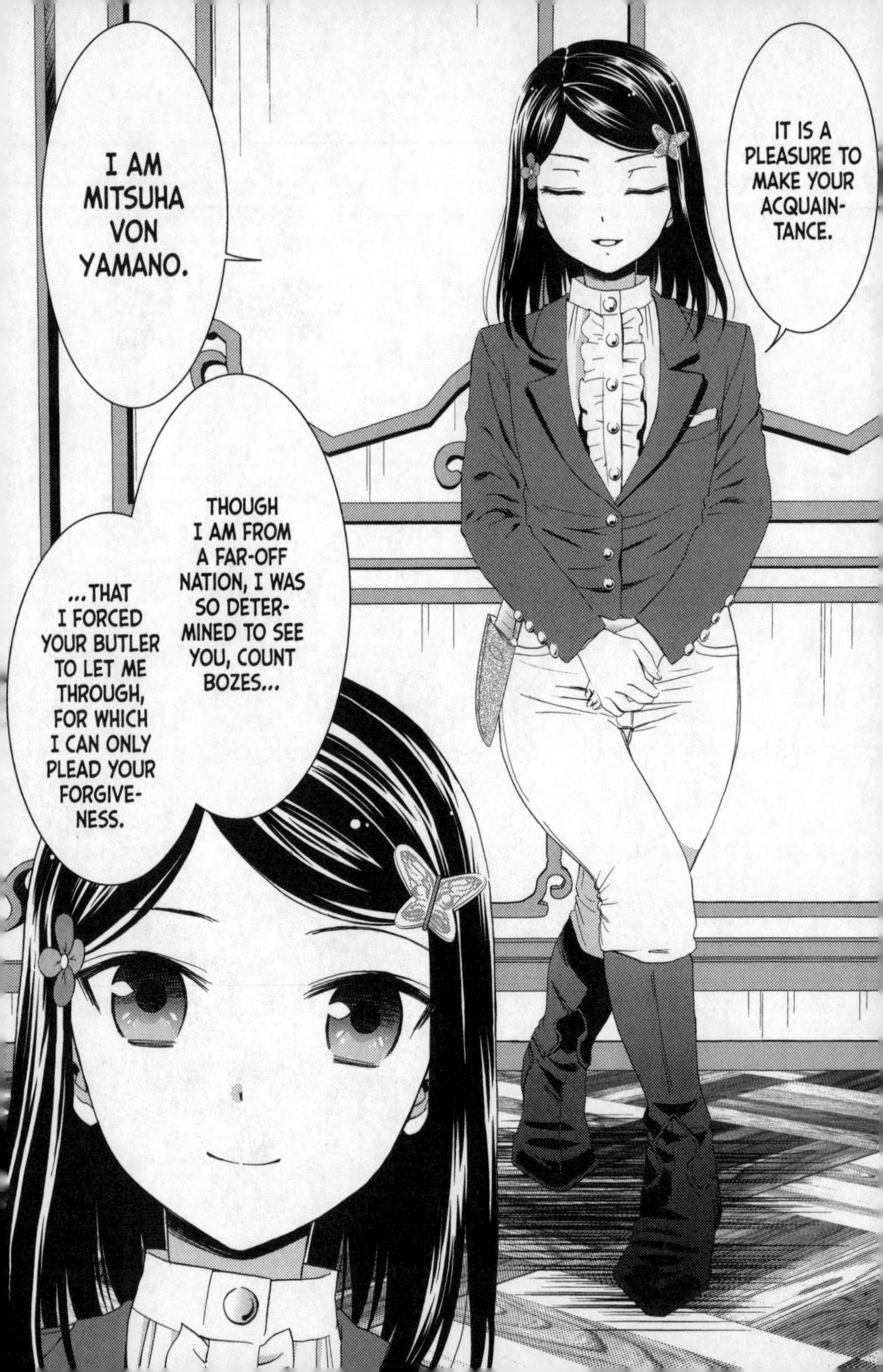
IT IS A PLEASURE TO MAKE YOUR ACQUAINTANCE.
I AM MITSUHA VON YAMANO.
THOUGH I AM FROM A FAR-OFF NATION, I WAS SO DETERMINED TO SEE YOU, COUNT BOZES...
...THAT I FORCED YOUR BUTLER TO LET ME THROUGH, FOR WHICH I CAN ONLY PLEAD YOUR FORGIVENESS.

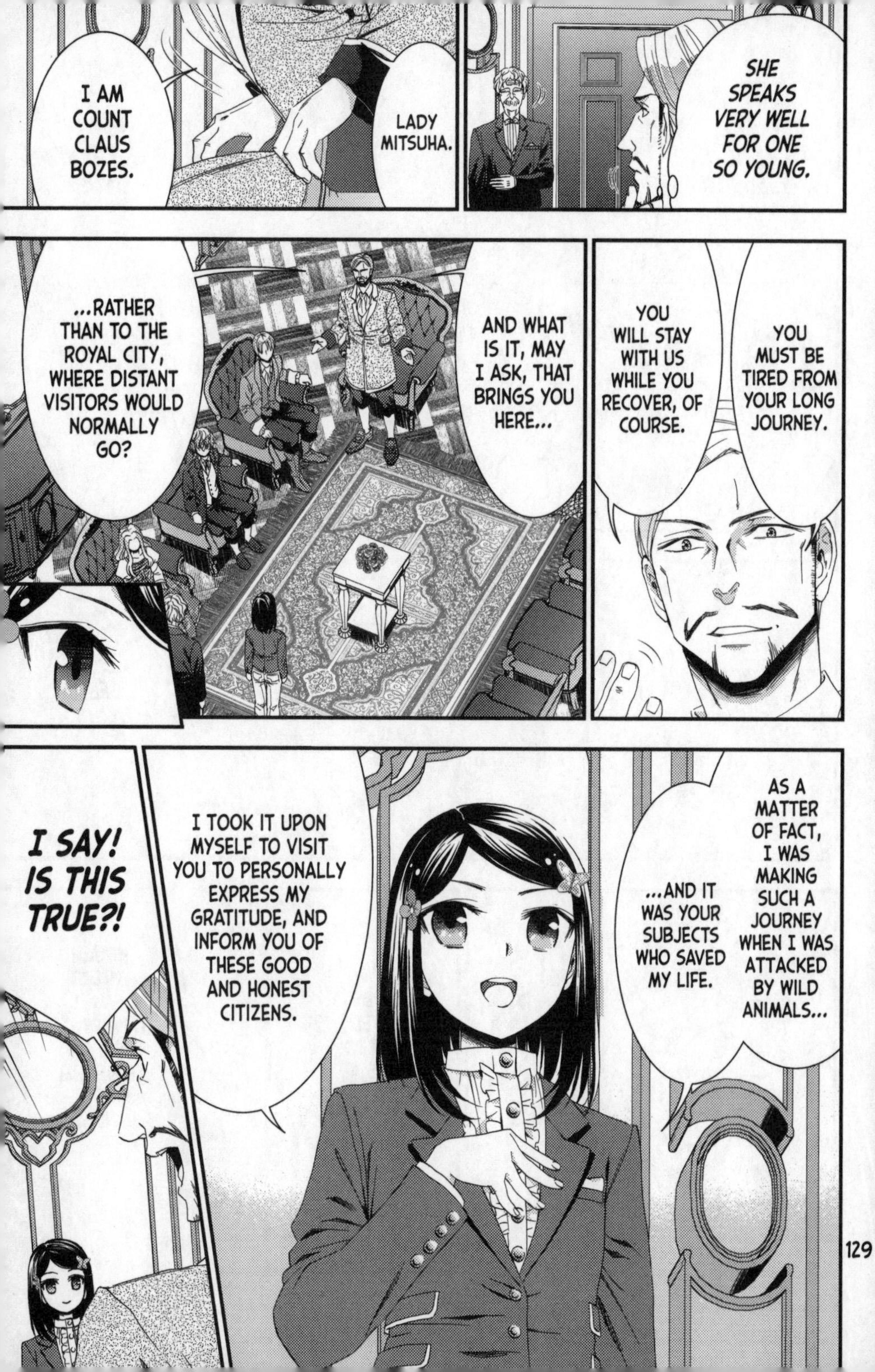
SHE SPEAKS VERY WELL FOR ONE SO YOUNG.
LADY MITSUHA.
I AM COUNT CLAUS BOZES.
YOU MUST BE TIRED FROM YOUR LONG JOURNEY.
YOU WILL STAY WITH US WHILE YOU RECOVER, OF COURSE.
AND WHAT IS IT, MAY I ASK, THAT BRINGS YOU HERE...
...RATHER THAN TO THE ROYAL CITY, WHERE DISTANT VISITORS WOULD NORMALLY GO?
AS A MATTER OF FACT, I WAS MAKING SUCH A JOURNEY WHEN I WAS ATTACKED BY WILD ANIMALS...
...AND IT WAS YOUR SUBJECTS WHO SAVED MY LIFE.
I TOOK IT UPON MYSELF TO VISIT YOU TO PERSONALLY EXPRESS MY GRATITUDE, AND INFORM YOU OF THESE GOOD AND HONEST CITIZENS.
I SAY! IS THIS TRUE?!

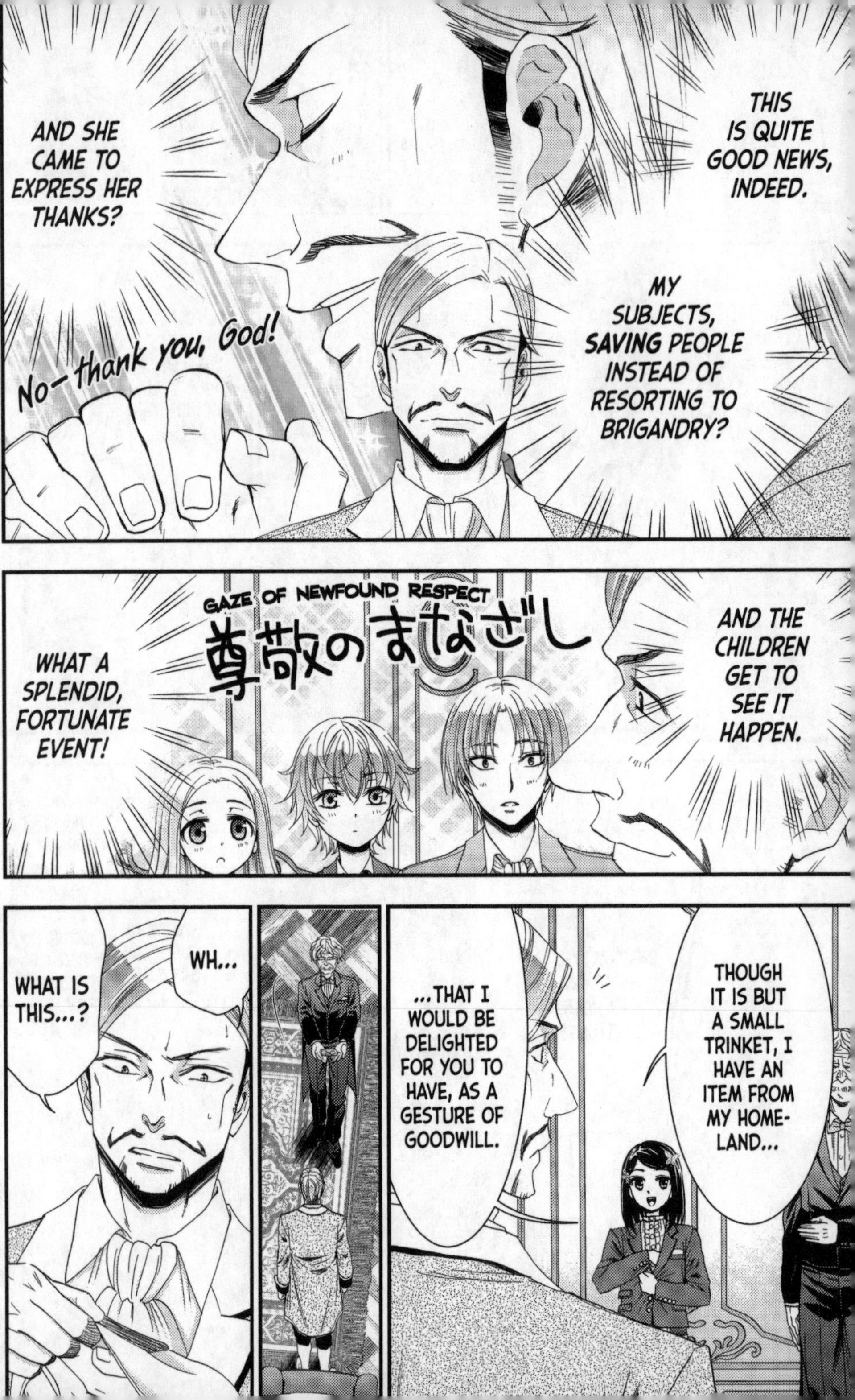
THIS IS QUITE GOOD NEWS, INDEED.
MY SUBJECTS, SAVING PEOPLE INSTEAD OF RESORTING TO BRIGANDRY?
AND SHE CAME TO EXPRESS HER THANKS?
No—thank you, God!
AND THE CHILDREN GET TO SEE IT HAPPEN.
GAZE OF NEWFOUND RESPECT
尊敬のまなざし
WHAT A SPLENDID, FORTUNATE EVENT!
THOUGH IT IS BUT A SMALL TRINKET, I HAVE AN ITEM FROM MY HOME-LAND...
...THAT I WOULD BE DELIGHTED FOR YOU TO HAVE, AS A GESTURE OF GOODWILL.
WH...
WHAT IS THIS...?

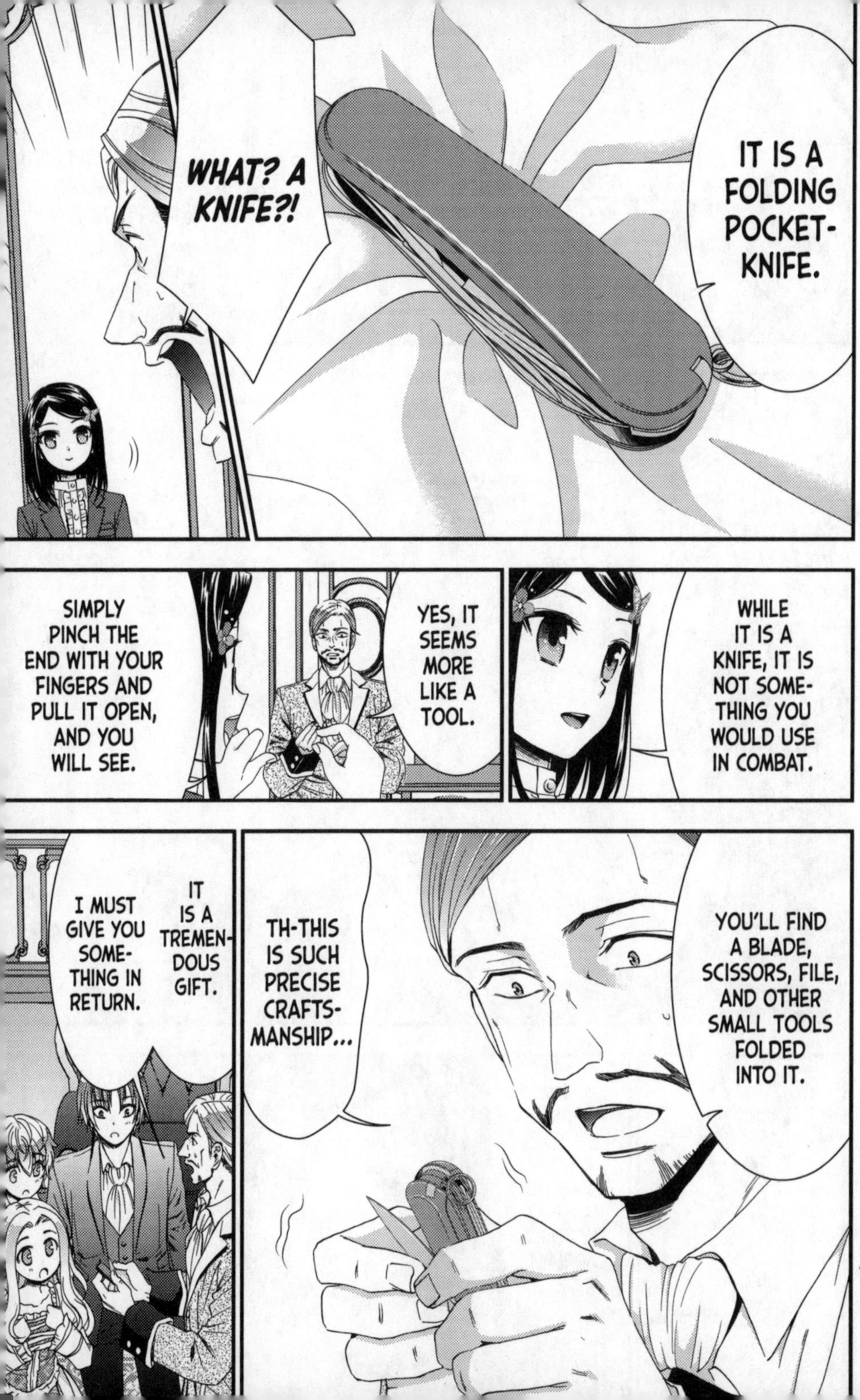
IT IS A FOLDING POCKET-KNIFE.
WHAT? A KNIFE?!
WHILE IT IS A KNIFE, IT IS NOT SOMETHING YOU WOULD USE IN COMBAT.
YES, IT SEEMS MORE LIKE A TOOL.
SIMPLY PINCH THE END WITH YOUR FINGERS AND PULL IT OPEN, AND YOU WILL SEE.
YOU'LL FIND A BLADE, SCISSORS, FILE, AND OTHER SMALL TOOLS FOLDED INTO IT.
TH-THIS IS SUCH PRECISE CRAFTSMANSHIP...
IT IS A TREMENDOUS GIFT.
I MUST GIVE YOU SOMETHING IN RETURN.

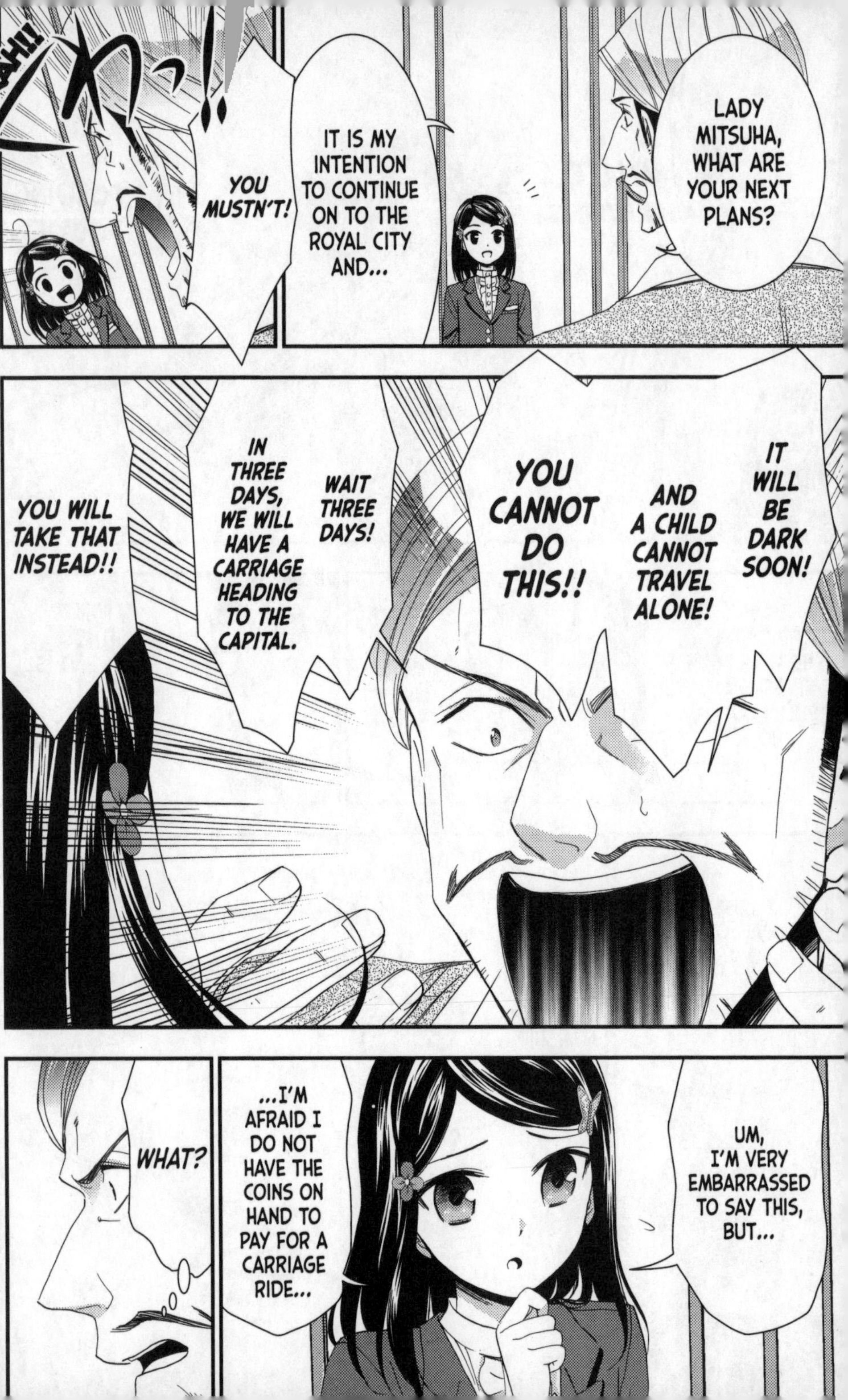
LADY MITSUHA, WHAT ARE YOUR NEXT PLANS?
IT IS MY INTENTION TO CONTINUE ON TO THE ROYAL CITY AND...
YOU MUSTN'T!
GRAH!!
IT WILL BE DARK SOON!
AND A CHILD CANNOT TRAVEL ALONE!
YOU CANNOT DO THIS!!
WAIT THREE DAYS!
IN THREE DAYS, WE WILL HAVE A CARRIAGE HEADING TO THE CAPITAL.
YOU WILL TAKE THAT INSTEAD!!
UM, I'M VERY EMBARRASSED TO SAY THIS, BUT...
...I'M AFRAID I DO NOT HAVE THE COINS ON HAND TO PAY FOR A CARRIAGE RIDE...
WHAT?

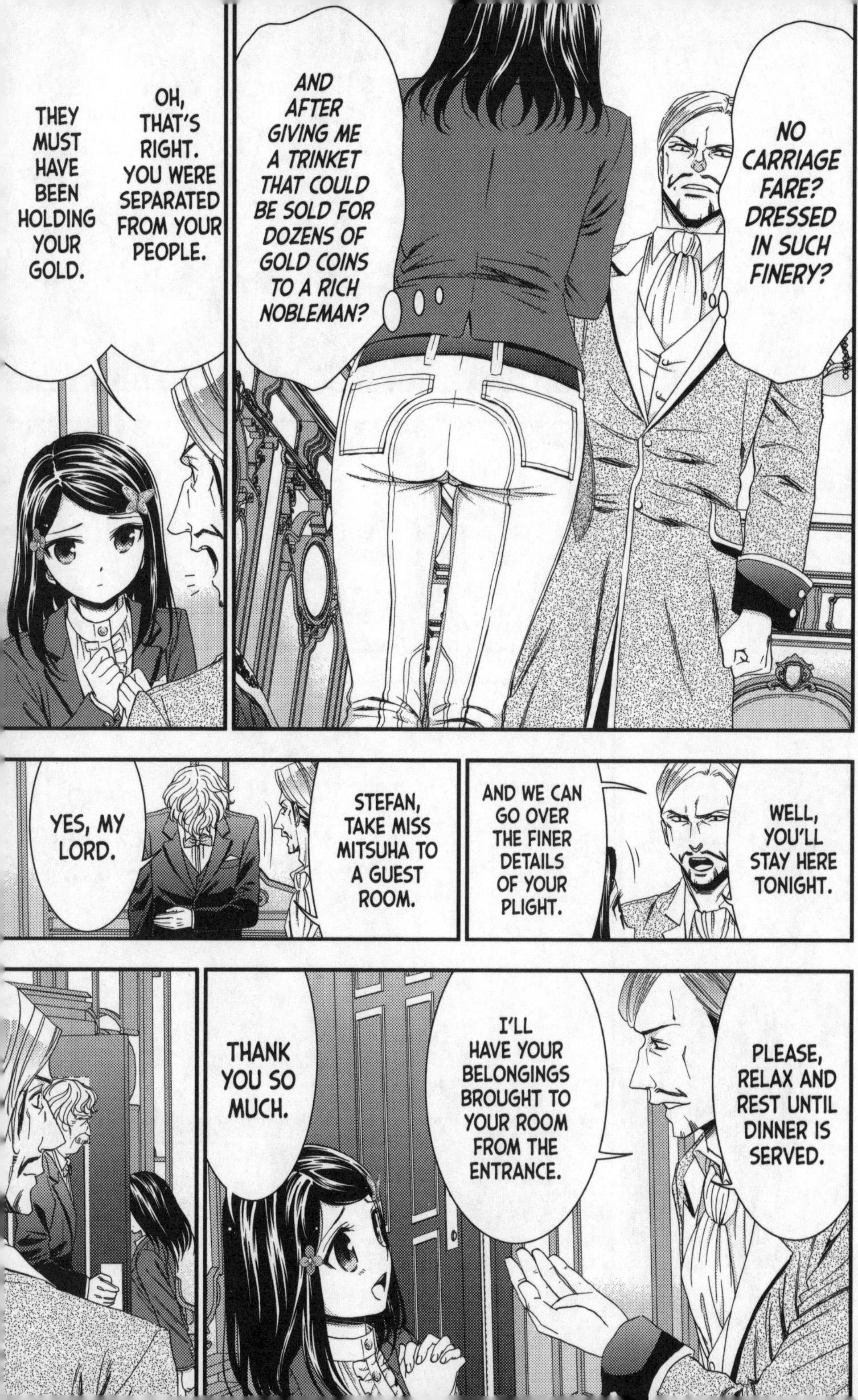
NO CARRIAGE FARE? DRESSED IN SUCH FINERY?
AND AFTER GIVING ME A TRINKET THAT COULD BE SOLD FOR DOZENS OF GOLD COINS TO A RICH NOBLEMAN?
OH, THAT'S RIGHT. YOU WERE SEPARATED FROM YOUR PEOPLE.
THEY MUST HAVE BEEN HOLDING YOUR GOLD.
WELL, YOU'LL STAY HERE TONIGHT.
AND WE CAN GO OVER THE FINER DETAILS OF YOUR PLIGHT.
STEFAN, TAKE MISS MITSUHA TO A GUEST ROOM.
YES, MY LORD.
PLEASE, RELAX AND REST UNTIL DINNER IS SERVED.
I'LL HAVE YOUR BELONGINGS BROUGHT TO YOUR ROOM FROM THE ENTRANCE.
THANK YOU SO MUCH.

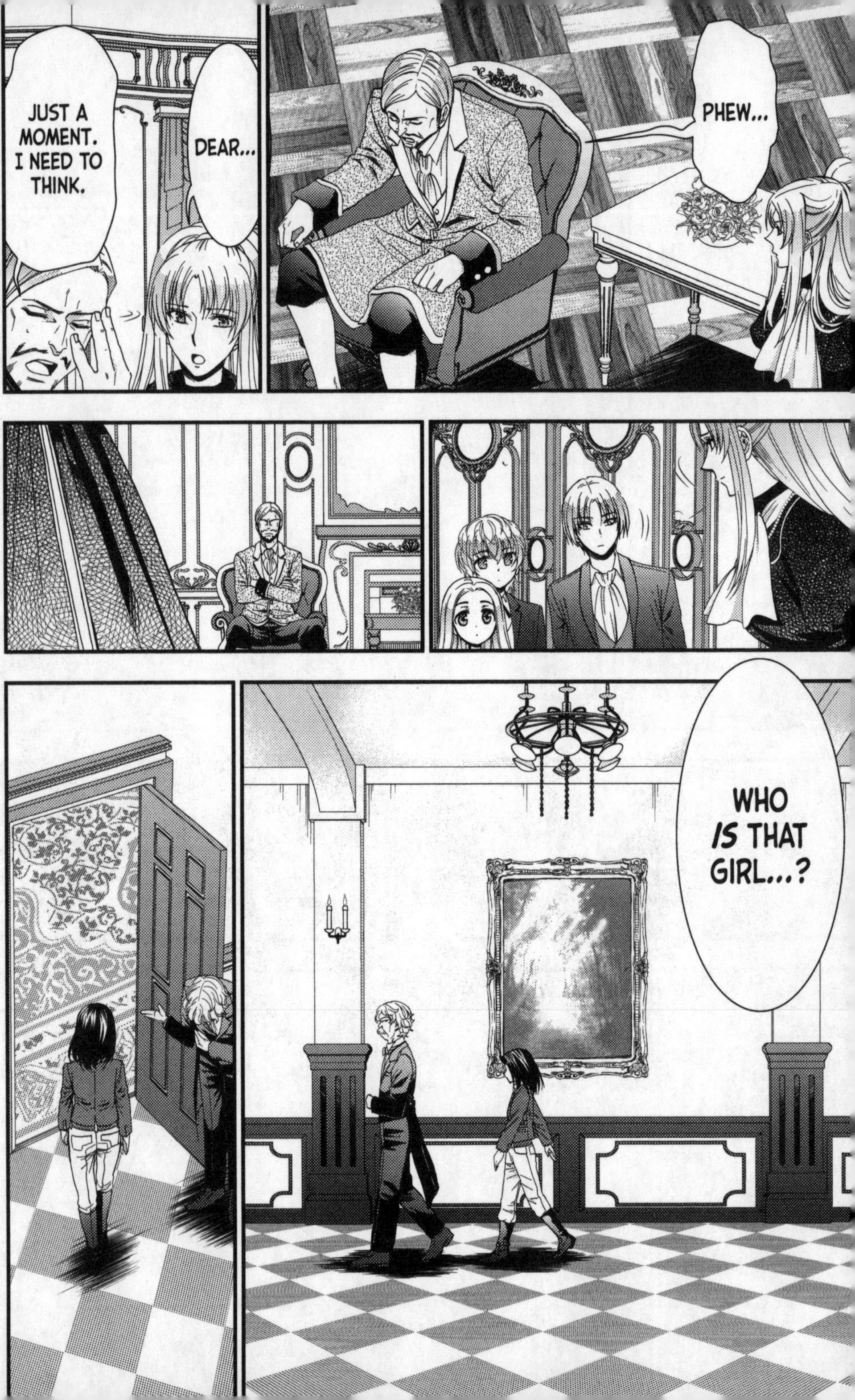
PHEW...
DEAR...
JUST A MOMENT. I NEED TO THINK.
WHO *IS* THAT GIRL...?

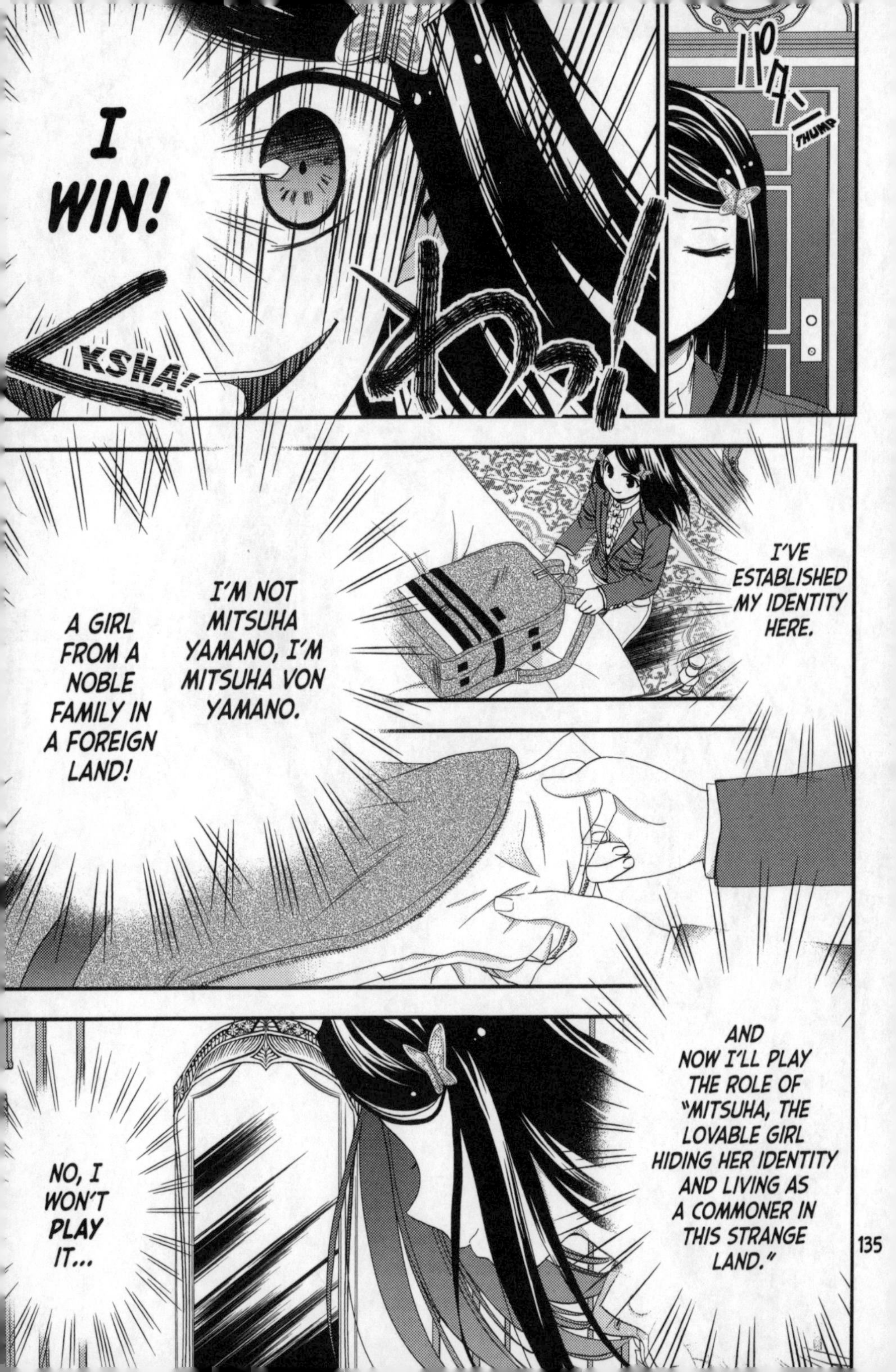
THUMP
KSHA!
I WIN!
I'VE ESTABLISHED MY IDENTITY HERE.
I'M NOT MITSUHA YAMANO, I'M MITSUHA VON YAMANO.
A GIRL FROM A NOBLE FAMILY IN A FOREIGN LAND!
AND NOW I'LL PLAY THE ROLE OF "MITSUHA, THE LOVABLE GIRL HIDING HER IDENTITY AND LIVING AS A COMMONER IN THIS STRANGE LAND."
NO, I WON'T PLAY IT...

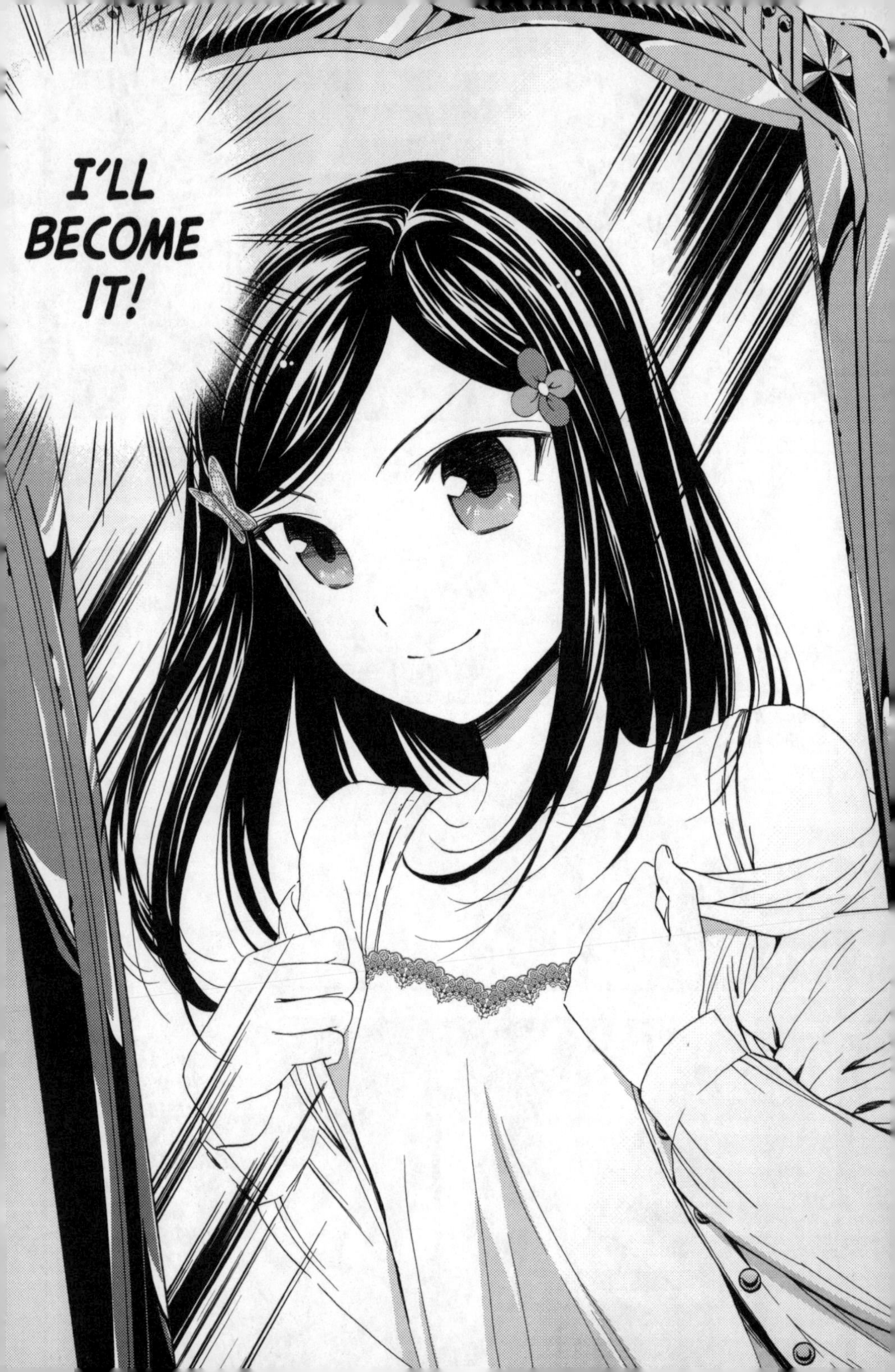
I'LL BECOME IT!

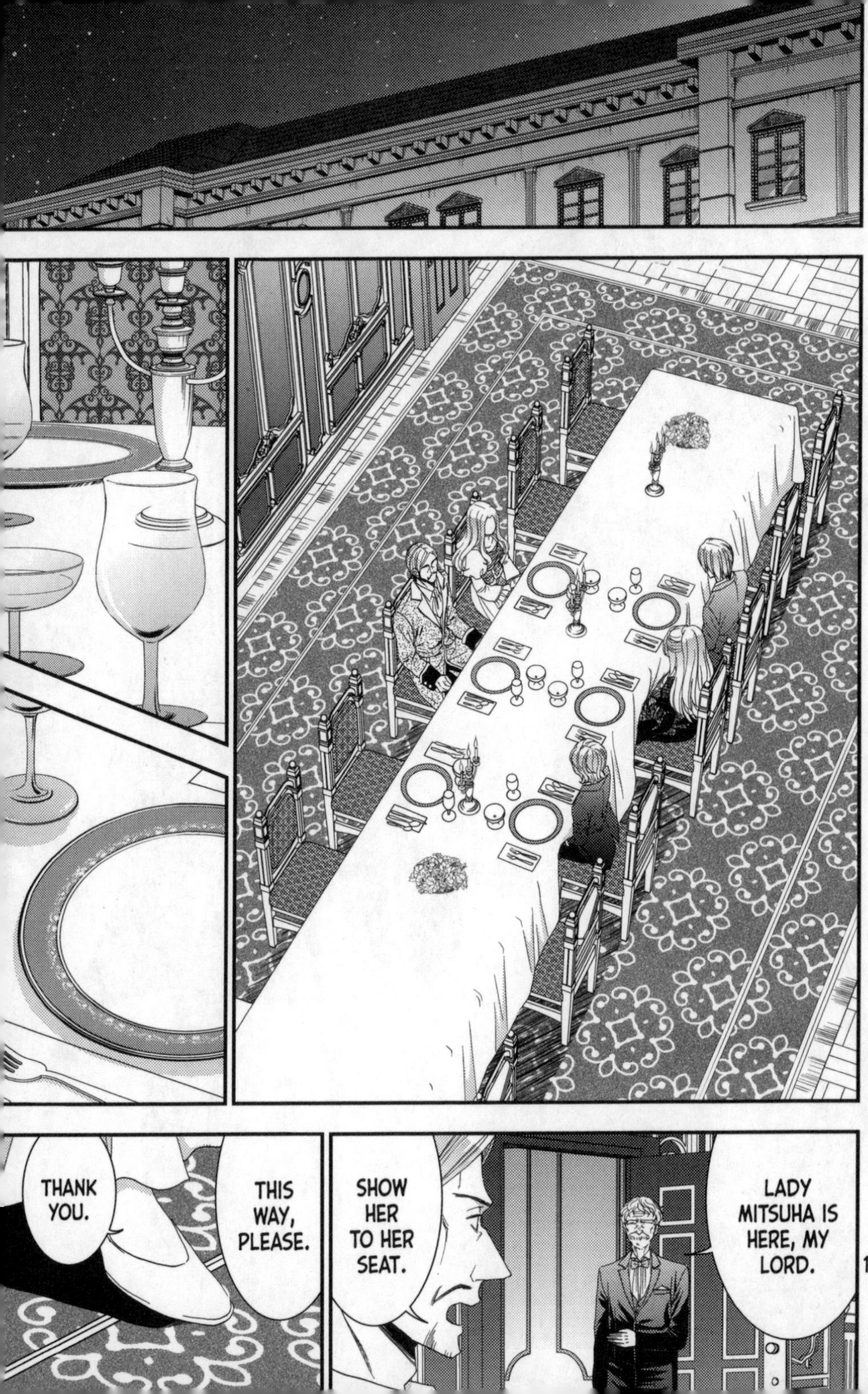
LADY MITSUHA IS HERE, MY LORD.
SHOW HER TO HER SEAT.
THIS WAY, PLEASE.
THANK YOU.

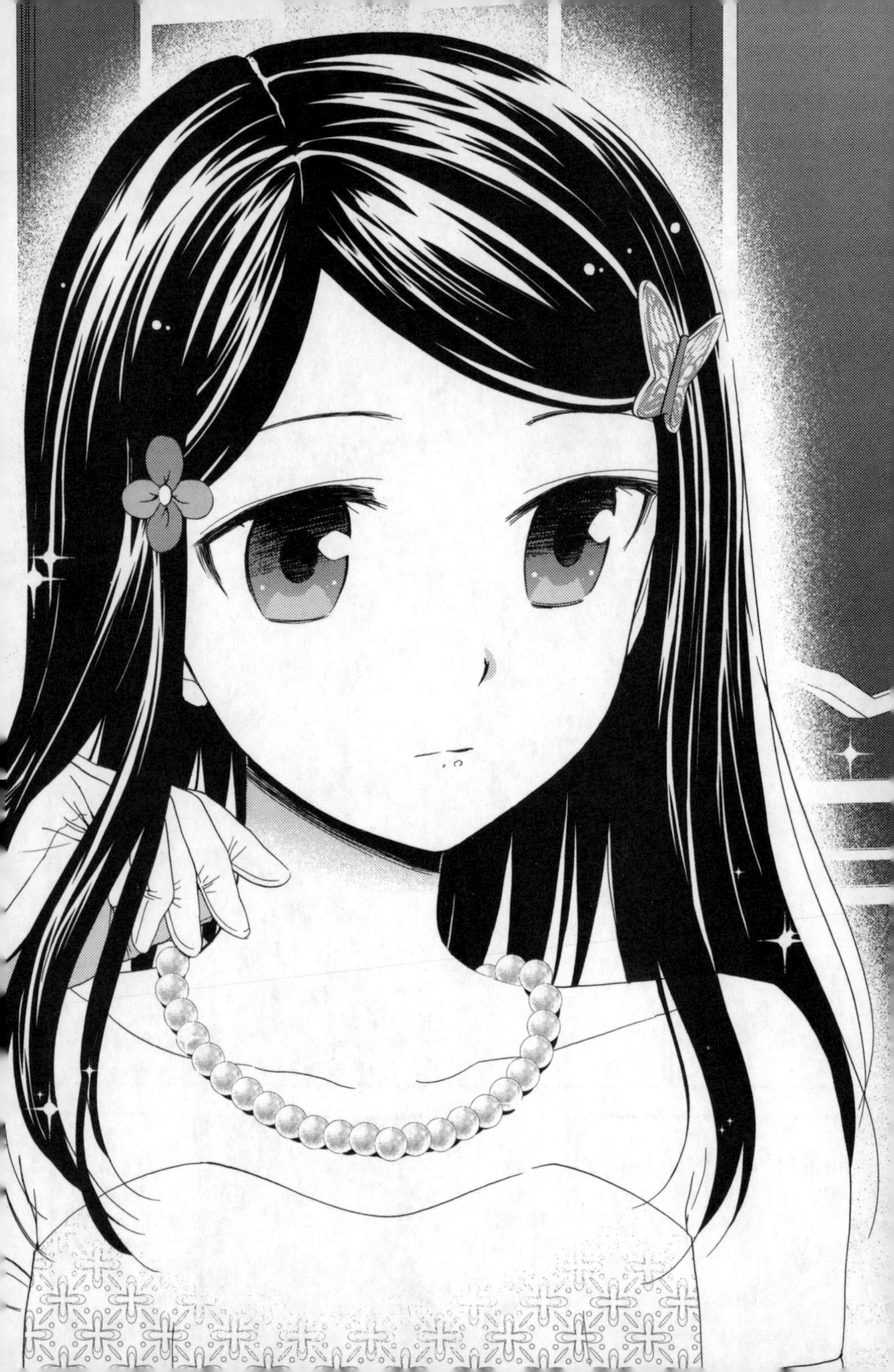

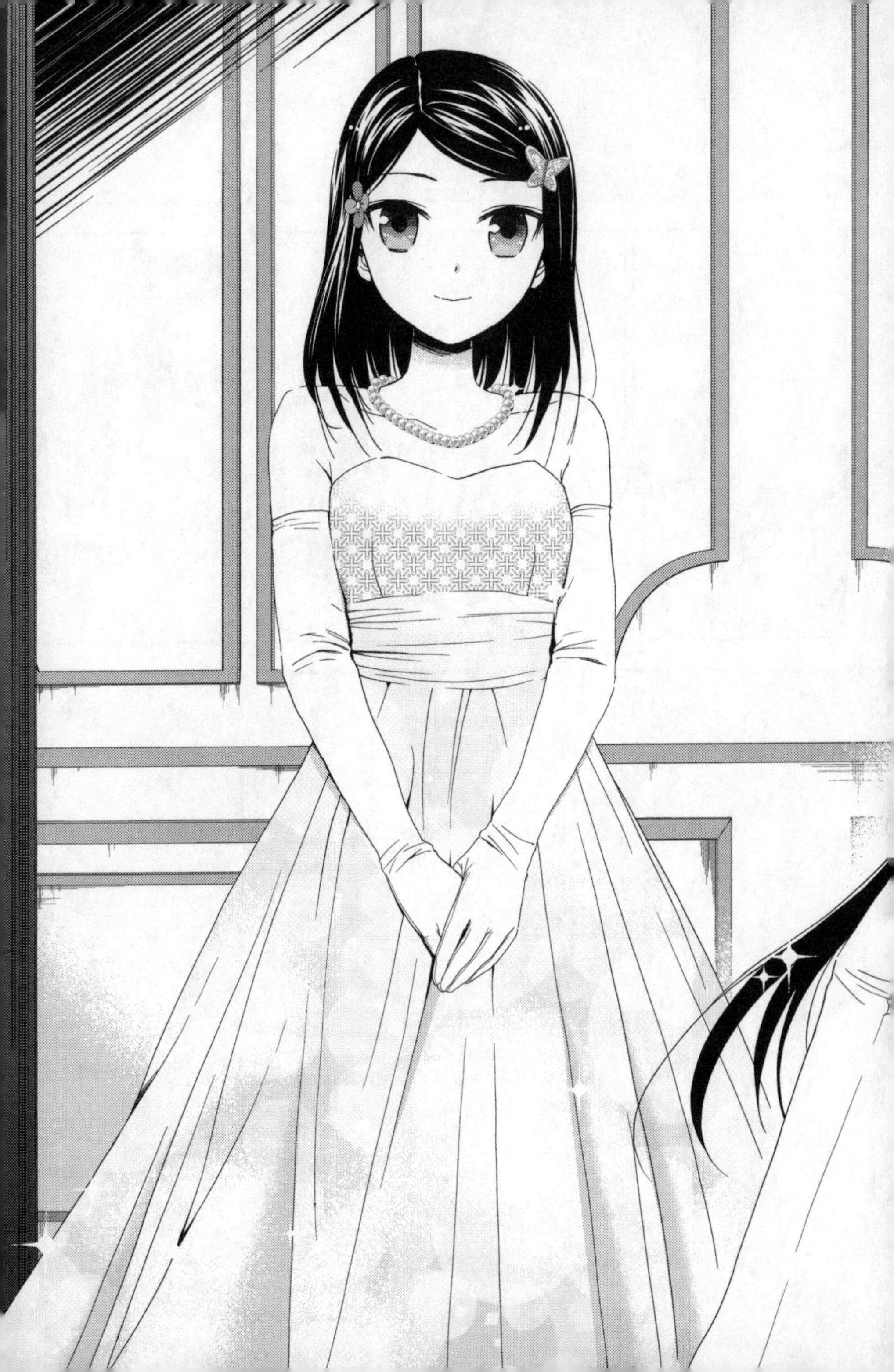

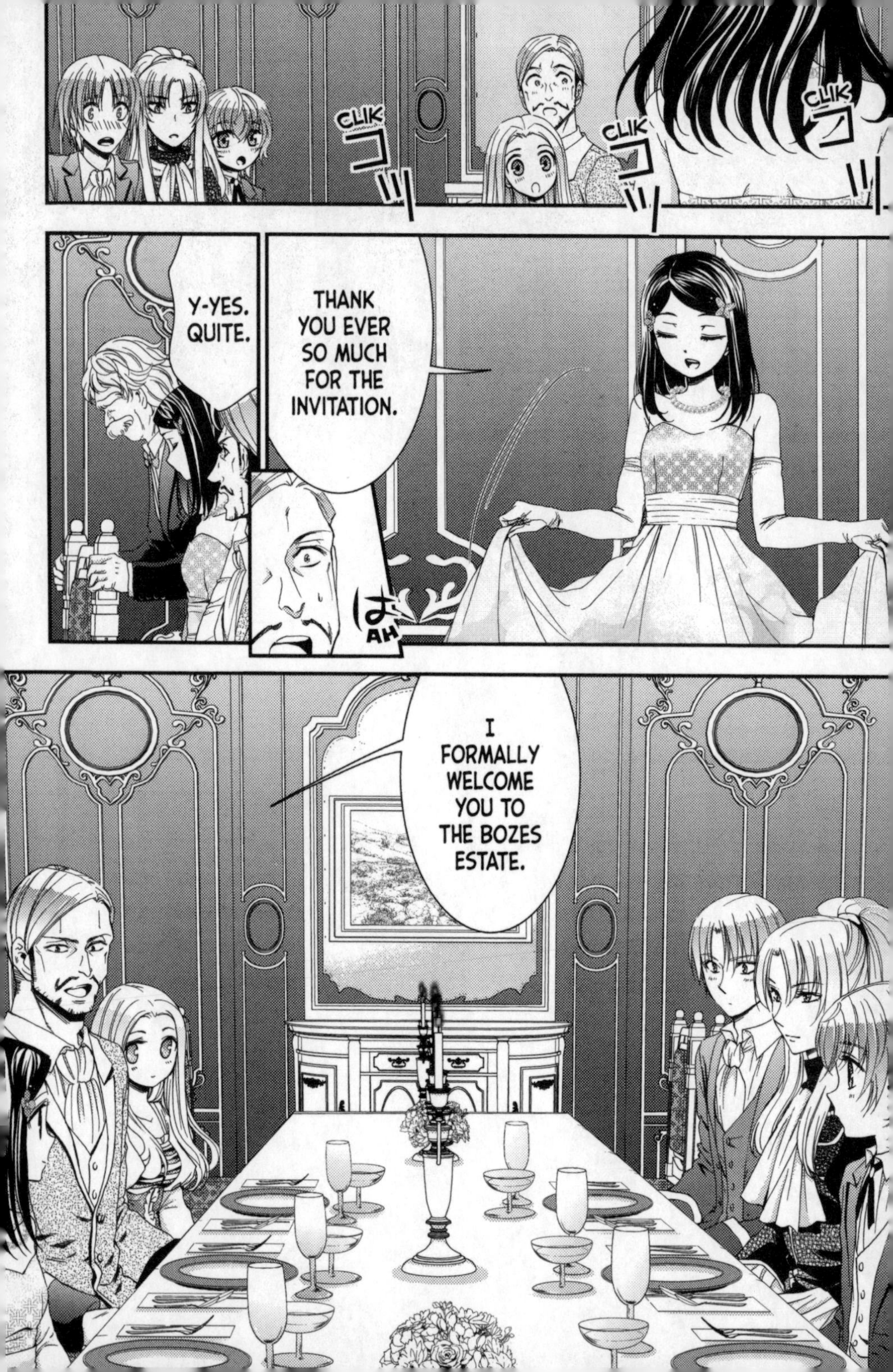
CLIK
CLIK
CLIK
THANK YOU EVER SO MUCH FOR THE INVITATION.
AH
Y-YES. QUITE.
I FORMALLY WELCOME YOU TO THE BOZES ESTATE.

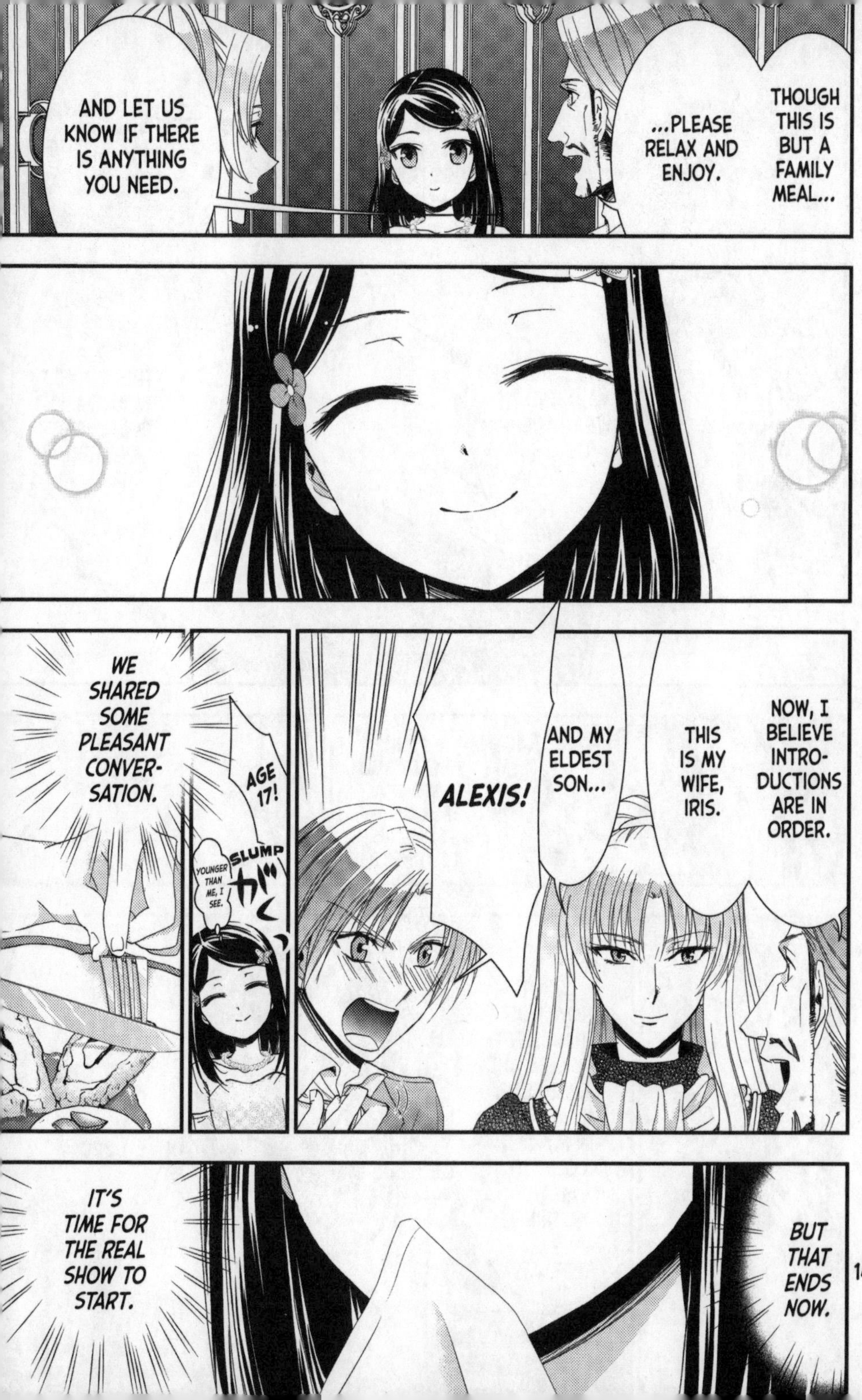
THOUGH THIS IS BUT A FAMILY MEAL...
...PLEASE RELAX AND ENJOY.
AND LET US KNOW IF THERE IS ANYTHING YOU NEED.
NOW, I BELIEVE INTRO-DUCTIONS ARE IN ORDER.
THIS IS MY WIFE, IRIS.
AND MY ELDEST SON...
ALEXIS!
AGE 17!
SLUMP
YOUNGER THAN ME, I SEE.
WE SHARED SOME PLEASANT CONVER-SATION.
BUT THAT ENDS NOW.
IT'S TIME FOR THE REAL SHOW TO START.

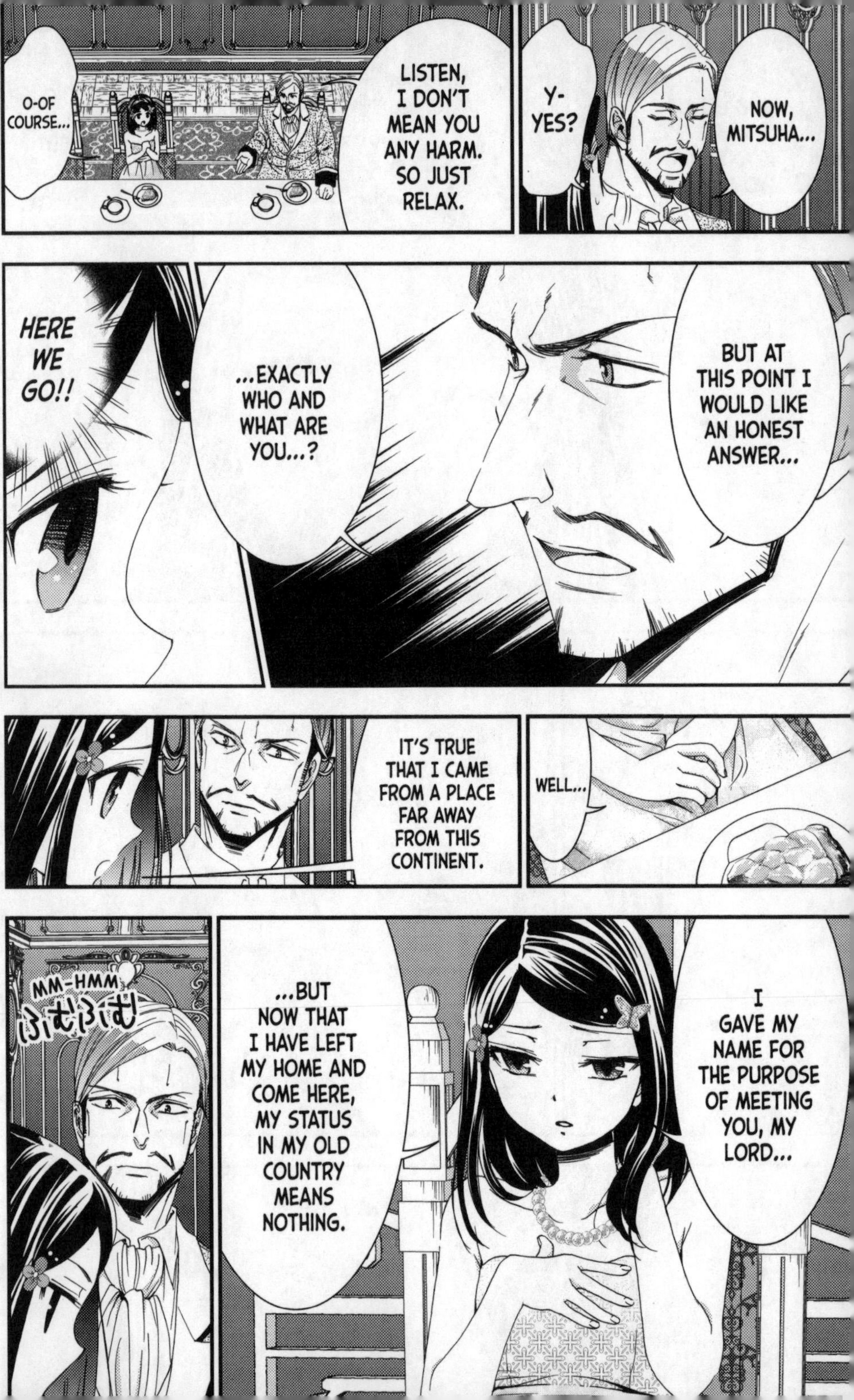
NOW, MITSUHA...
Y-YES?
LISTEN, I DON'T MEAN YOU ANY HARM. SO JUST RELAX.
O-OF COURSE...
BUT AT THIS POINT I WOULD LIKE AN HONEST ANSWER...
...EXACTLY WHO AND WHAT ARE YOU...?
HERE WE GO!!
WELL...
IT'S TRUE THAT I CAME FROM A PLACE FAR AWAY FROM THIS CONTINENT.
I GAVE MY NAME FOR THE PURPOSE OF MEETING YOU, MY LORD...
...BUT NOW THAT I HAVE LEFT MY HOME AND COME HERE, MY STATUS IN MY OLD COUNTRY MEANS NOTHING.
MM-HMM
ふむふむ

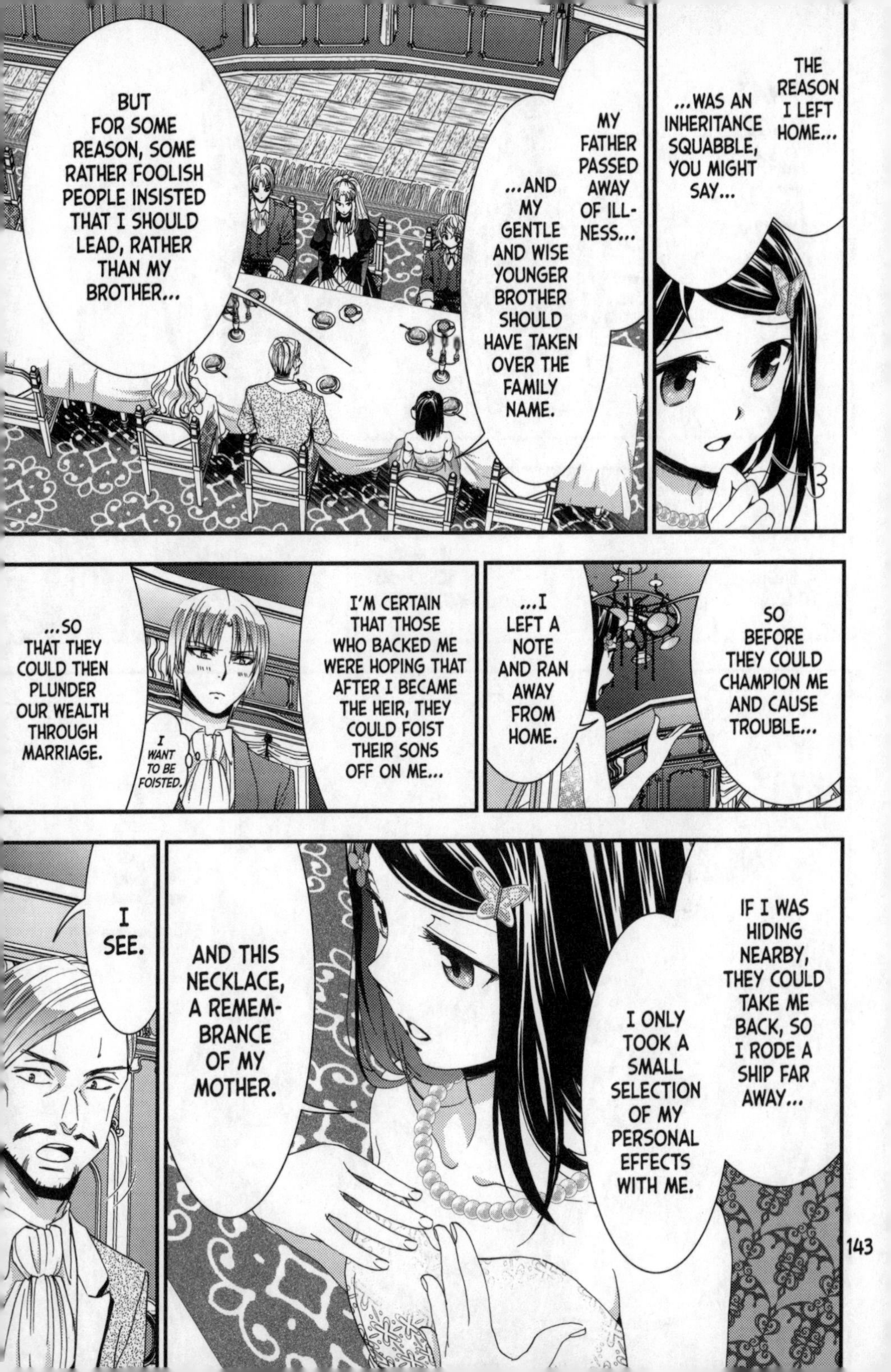
THE REASON I LEFT HOME...
...WAS AN INHERITANCE SQUABBLE, YOU MIGHT SAY...
MY FATHER PASSED AWAY OF ILL-NESS...
...AND MY GENTLE AND WISE YOUNGER BROTHER SHOULD HAVE TAKEN OVER THE FAMILY NAME.
BUT FOR SOME REASON, SOME RATHER FOOLISH PEOPLE INSISTED THAT I SHOULD LEAD, RATHER THAN MY BROTHER...
SO BEFORE THEY COULD CHAMPION ME AND CAUSE TROUBLE...
...I LEFT A NOTE AND RAN AWAY FROM HOME.
I'M CERTAIN THAT THOSE WHO BACKED ME WERE HOPING THAT AFTER I BECAME THE HEIR, THEY COULD FOIST THEIR SONS OFF ON ME...
...SO THAT THEY COULD THEN PLUNDER OUR WEALTH THROUGH MARRIAGE.
I WANT TO BE FOISTED.
IF I WAS HIDING NEARBY, THEY COULD TAKE ME BACK, SO I RODE A SHIP FAR AWAY...
I ONLY TOOK A SMALL SELECTION OF MY PERSONAL EFFECTS WITH ME.
AND THIS NECKLACE, A REMEM-BRANCE OF MY MOTHER.
I SEE.

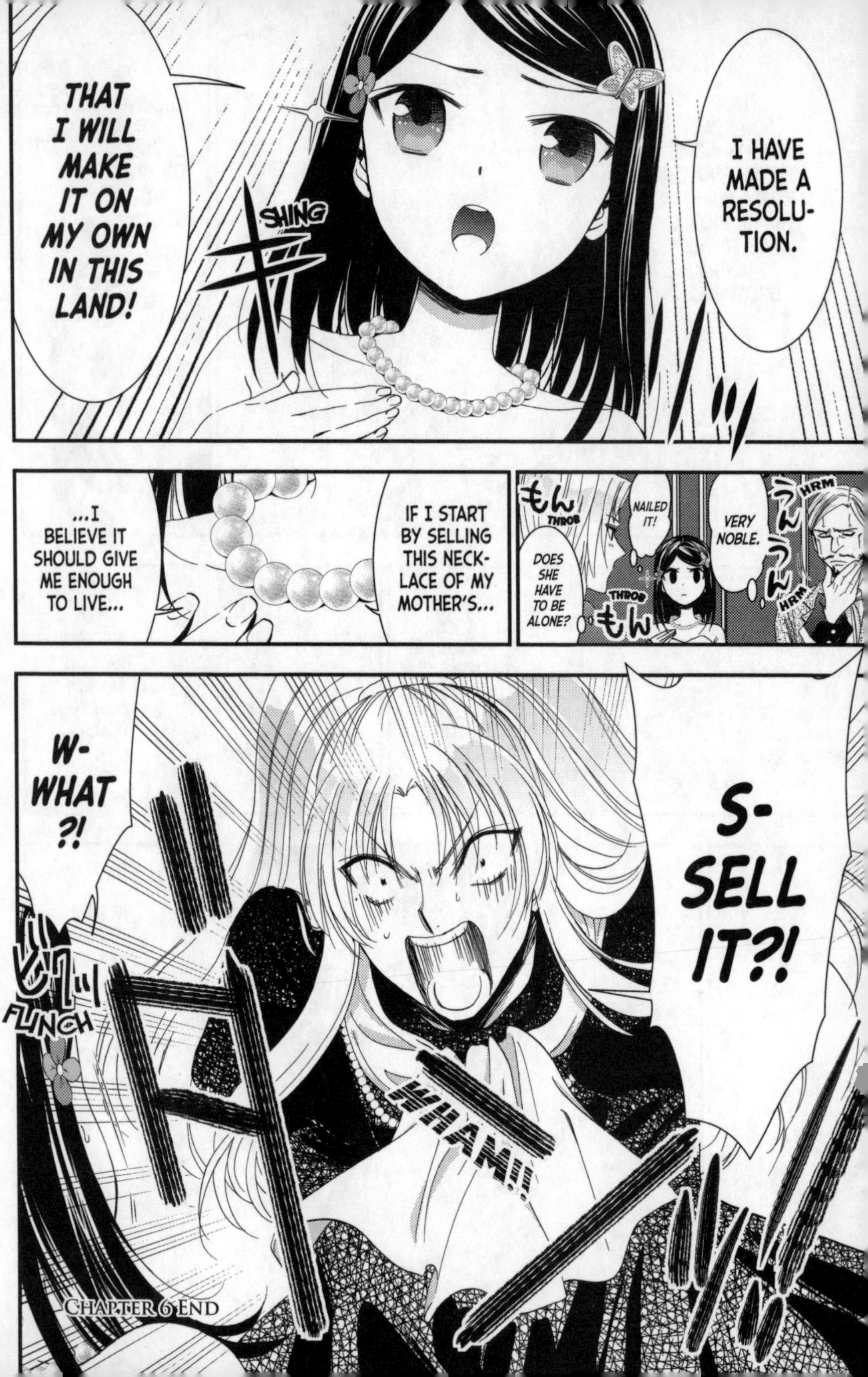
I HAVE MADE A RESOLUTION.
SHING
THAT I WILL MAKE IT ON MY OWN IN THIS LAND!
うん HRM
うん HRM
VERY NOBLE.
NAILED IT!
もん THROB
もん THROB
DOES SHE HAVE TO BE ALONE?
IF I START BY SELLING THIS NECKLACE OF MY MOTHER'S...
...I BELIEVE IT SHOULD GIVE ME ENOUGH TO LIVE...
S-SELL IT?!
WHAM!!
W-WHAT?!
FLINCH
CHAPTER 6 END

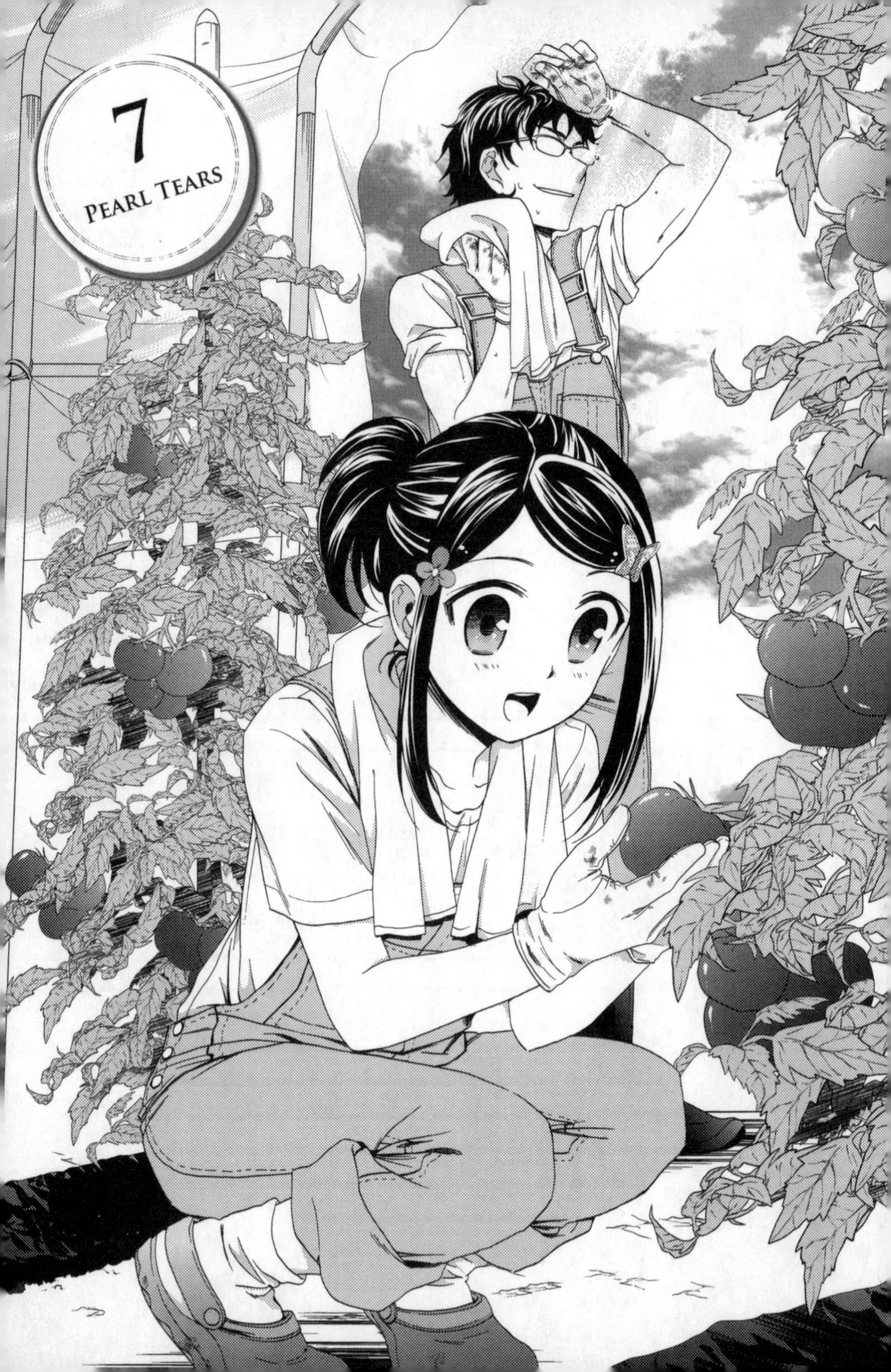
7
Pearl Tears

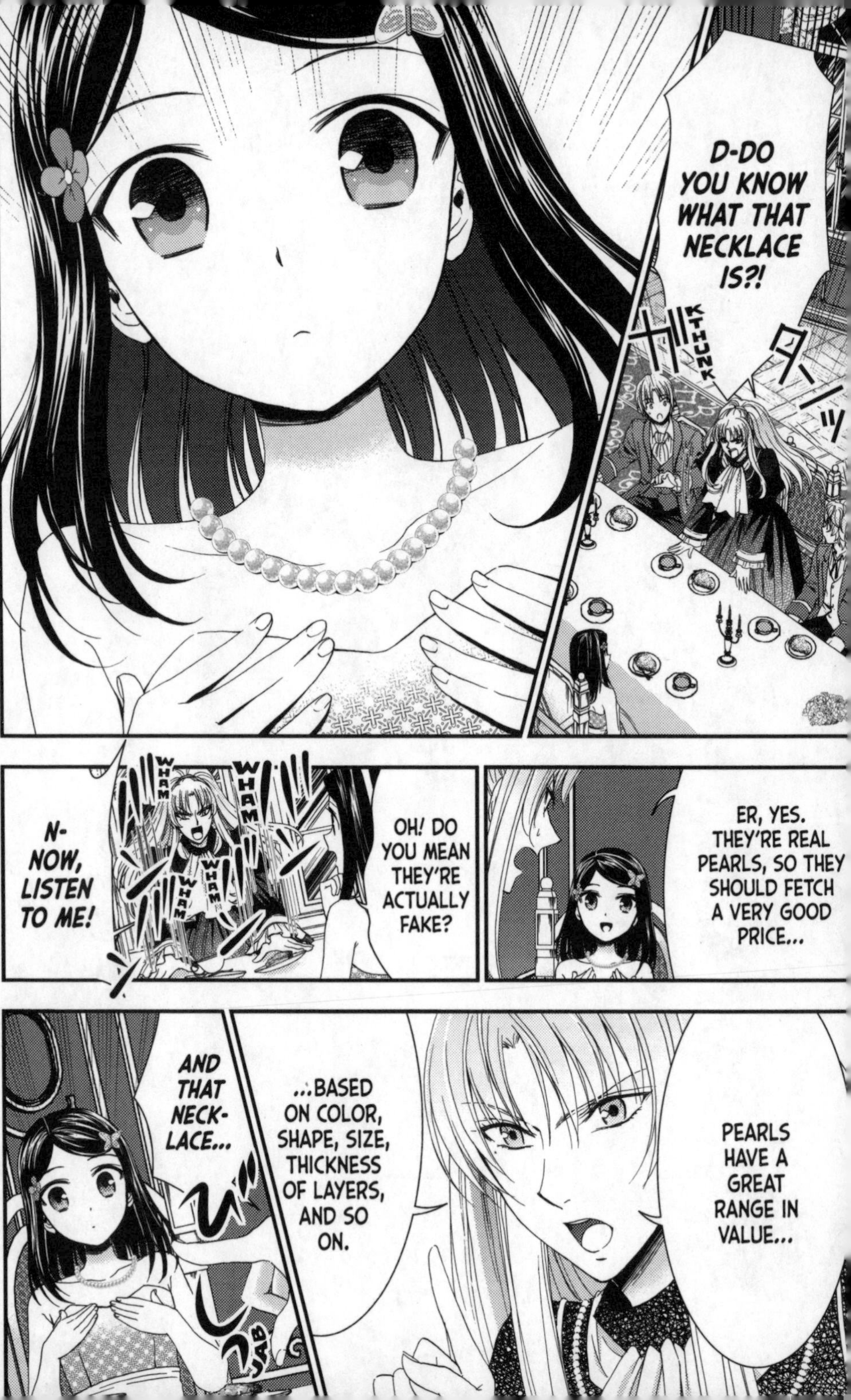
D-DO YOU KNOW WHAT THAT NECKLACE IS?!
KTHUNK
ER, YES. THEY'RE REAL PEARLS, SO THEY SHOULD FETCH A VERY GOOD PRICE...
OH! DO YOU MEAN THEY'RE ACTUALLY FAKE?
WHAM
WHAM
WHAM
WHAM
N-NOW, LISTEN TO ME!
PEARLS HAVE A GREAT RANGE IN VALUE...
...BASED ON COLOR, SHAPE, SIZE, THICKNESS OF LAYERS, AND SO ON.
AND THAT NECK-LACE...
JAB

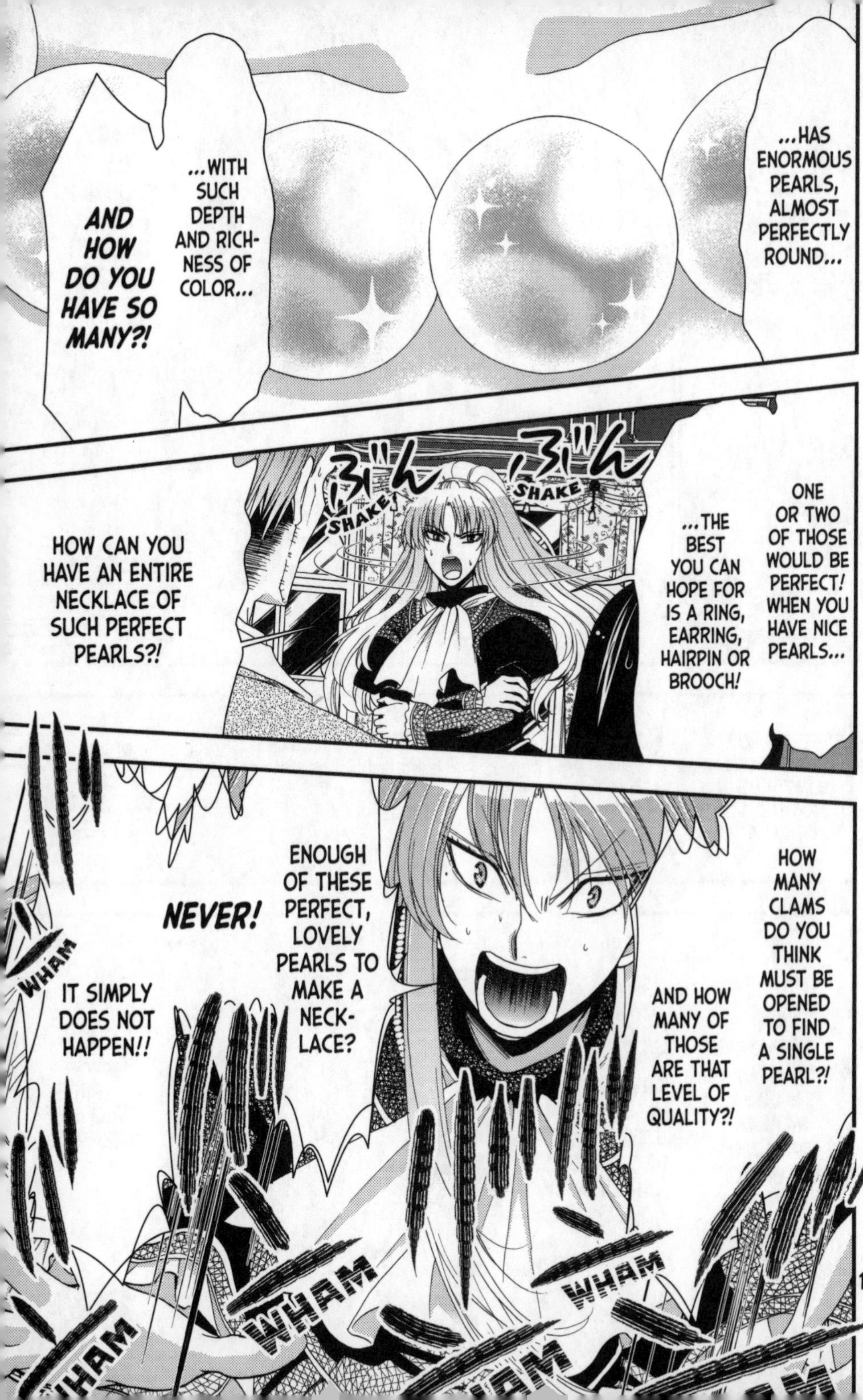
...HAS ENORMOUS PEARLS, ALMOST PERFECTLY ROUND...
...WITH SUCH DEPTH AND RICHNESS OF COLOR...
AND HOW DO YOU HAVE SO MANY?!
ONE OR TWO OF THOSE WOULD BE PERFECT! WHEN YOU HAVE NICE PEARLS...
...THE BEST YOU CAN HOPE FOR IS A RING, EARRING, HAIRPIN OR BROOCH!
ぶん
SHAKE
ぶん
SHAKE
HOW CAN YOU HAVE AN ENTIRE NECKLACE OF SUCH PERFECT PEARLS?!
HOW MANY CLAMS DO YOU THINK MUST BE OPENED TO FIND A SINGLE PEARL?!
AND HOW MANY OF THOSE ARE THAT LEVEL OF QUALITY?!
ENOUGH OF THESE PERFECT, LOVELY PEARLS TO MAKE A NECKLACE?
NEVER!
IT SIMPLY DOES NOT HAPPEN!!
WHAM
WHAM
WHAM
WHAM
WHAM

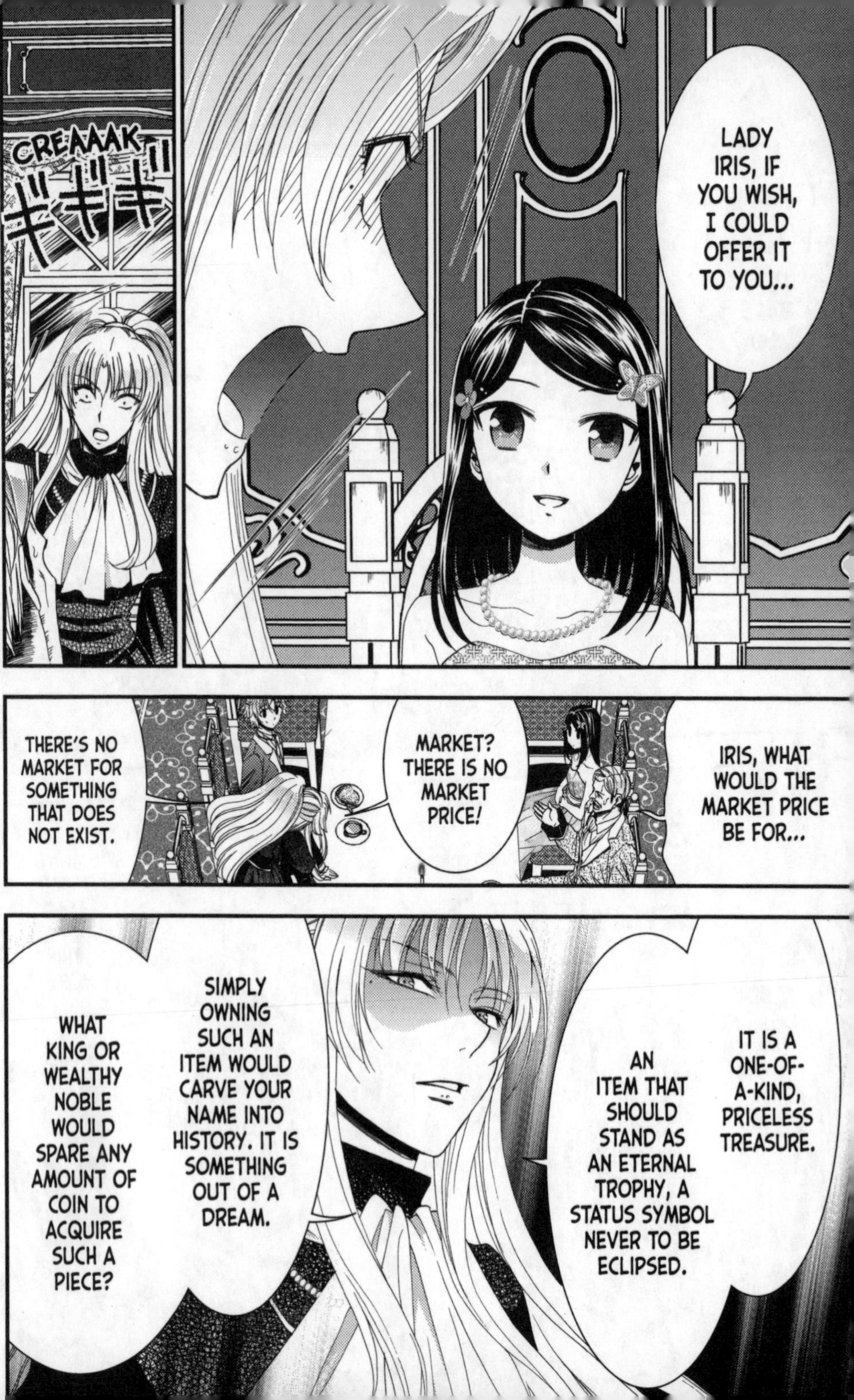
LADY IRIS, IF YOU WISH, I COULD OFFER IT TO YOU...
CREAAK
ギギギ
IRIS, WHAT WOULD THE MARKET PRICE BE FOR...
MARKET? THERE IS NO MARKET PRICE!
THERE'S NO MARKET FOR SOMETHING THAT DOES NOT EXIST.
IT IS A ONE-OF-A-KIND, PRICELESS TREASURE.
AN ITEM THAT SHOULD STAND AS AN ETERNAL TROPHY, A STATUS SYMBOL NEVER TO BE ECLIPSED.
SIMPLY OWNING SUCH AN ITEM WOULD CARVE YOUR NAME INTO HISTORY. IT IS SOMETHING OUT OF A DREAM.
WHAT KING OR WEALTHY NOBLE WOULD SPARE ANY AMOUNT OF COIN TO ACQUIRE SUCH A PIECE?

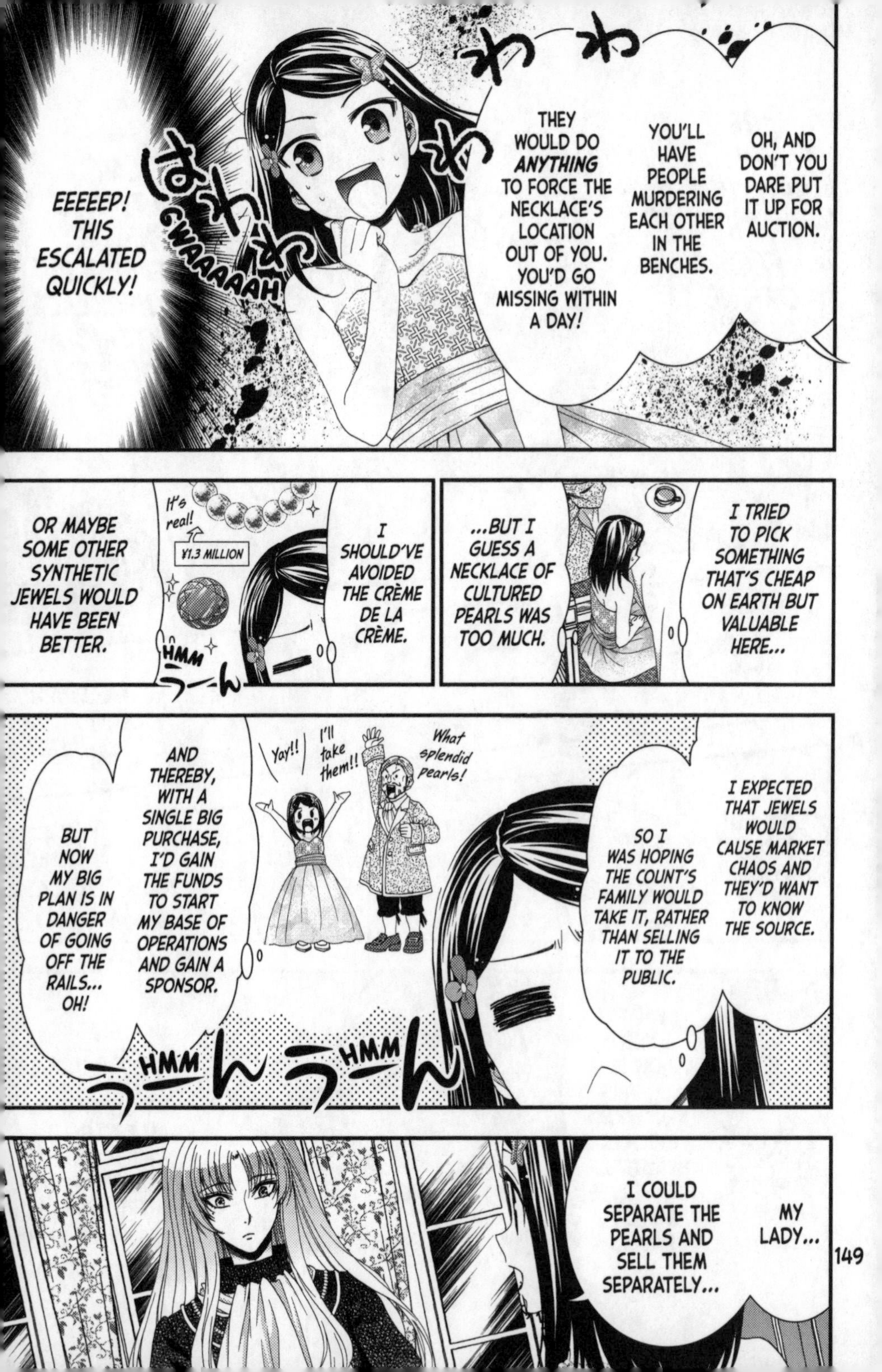
OH, AND DON'T YOU DARE PUT IT UP FOR AUCTION.
YOU'LL HAVE PEOPLE MURDERING EACH OTHER IN THE BENCHES.
THEY WOULD DO *ANYTHING* TO FORCE THE NECKLACE'S LOCATION OUT OF YOU. YOU'D GO MISSING WITHIN A DAY!
わわ
はわわ
GWAAAAAH
EEEEEP! THIS ESCALATED QUICKLY!
I TRIED TO PICK SOMETHING THAT'S CHEAP ON EARTH BUT VALUABLE HERE...
...BUT I GUESS A NECKLACE OF CULTURED PEARLS WAS TOO MUCH.
I SHOULD'VE AVOIDED THE CRÈME DE LA CRÈME.
It's real!
¥1.3 MILLION
HMM
うーん
OR MAYBE SOME OTHER SYNTHETIC JEWELS WOULD HAVE BEEN BETTER.
I EXPECTED THAT JEWELS WOULD CAUSE MARKET CHAOS AND THEY'D WANT TO KNOW THE SOURCE.
SO I WAS HOPING THE COUNT'S FAMILY WOULD TAKE IT, RATHER THAN SELLING IT TO THE PUBLIC.
What splendid pearls!
I'll take them!!
Yay!!
AND THEREBY, WITH A SINGLE BIG PURCHASE, I'D GAIN THE FUNDS TO START MY BASE OF OPERATIONS AND GAIN A SPONSOR.
BUT NOW MY BIG PLAN IS IN DANGER OF GOING OFF THE RAILS... OH!
HMM
うーん
HMM
うーん
MY LADY...
I COULD SEPARATE THE PEARLS AND SELL THEM SEPARATELY...

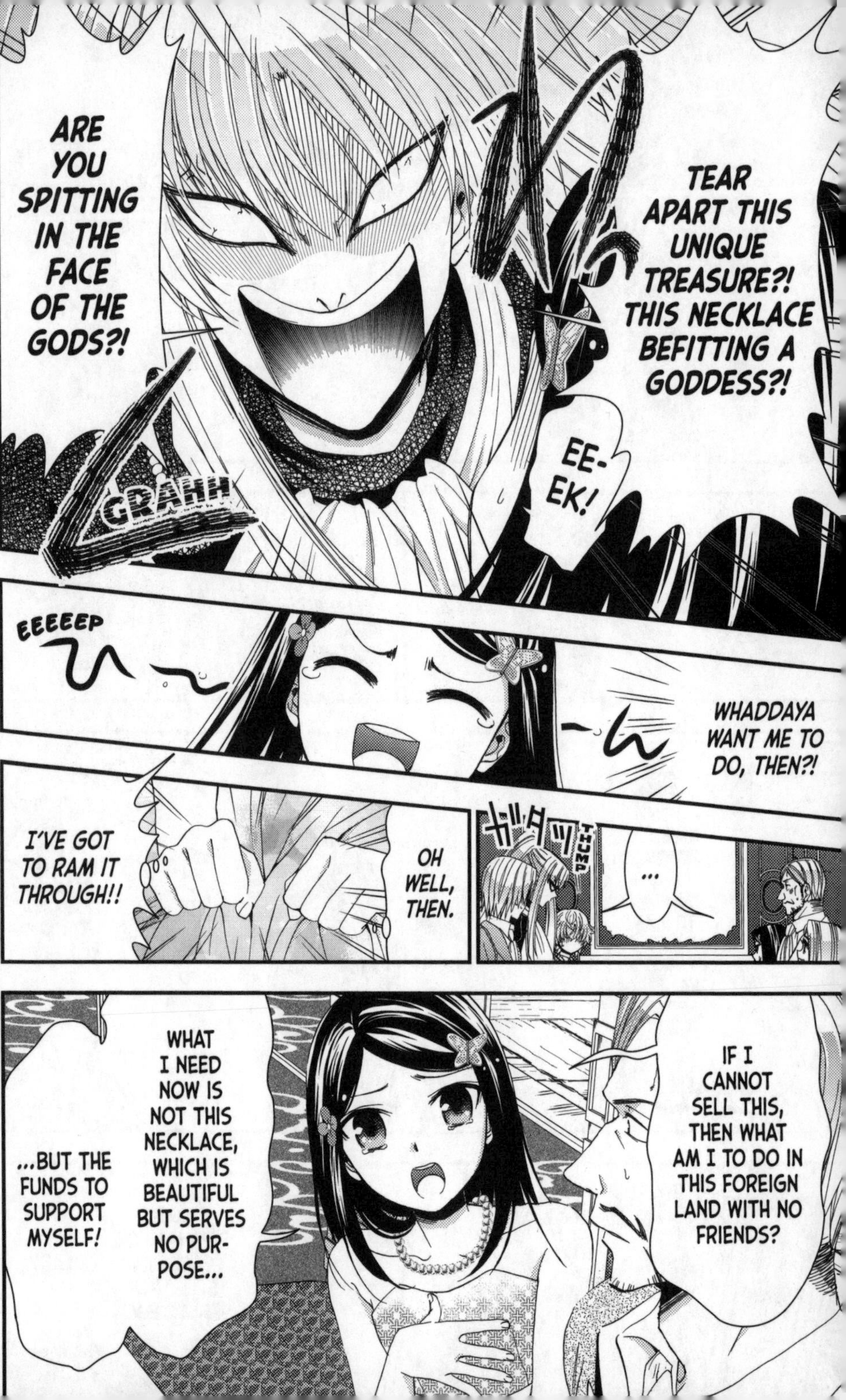

TEAR APART THIS UNIQUE TREASURE?! THIS NECKLACE BEFITTING A GODDESS?!
ARE YOU SPITTING IN THE FACE OF THE GODS?!
EE-EK!
GRAHH
WHADDAYA WANT ME TO DO, THEN?!
EEEEEP
THUMP
...
OH WELL, THEN.
I'VE GOT TO RAM IT THROUGH!!
IF I CANNOT SELL THIS, THEN WHAT AM I TO DO IN THIS FOREIGN LAND WITH NO FRIENDS?
WHAT I NEED NOW IS NOT THIS NECKLACE, WHICH IS BEAUTIFUL BUT SERVES NO PURPOSE...
...BUT THE FUNDS TO SUPPORT MYSELF!

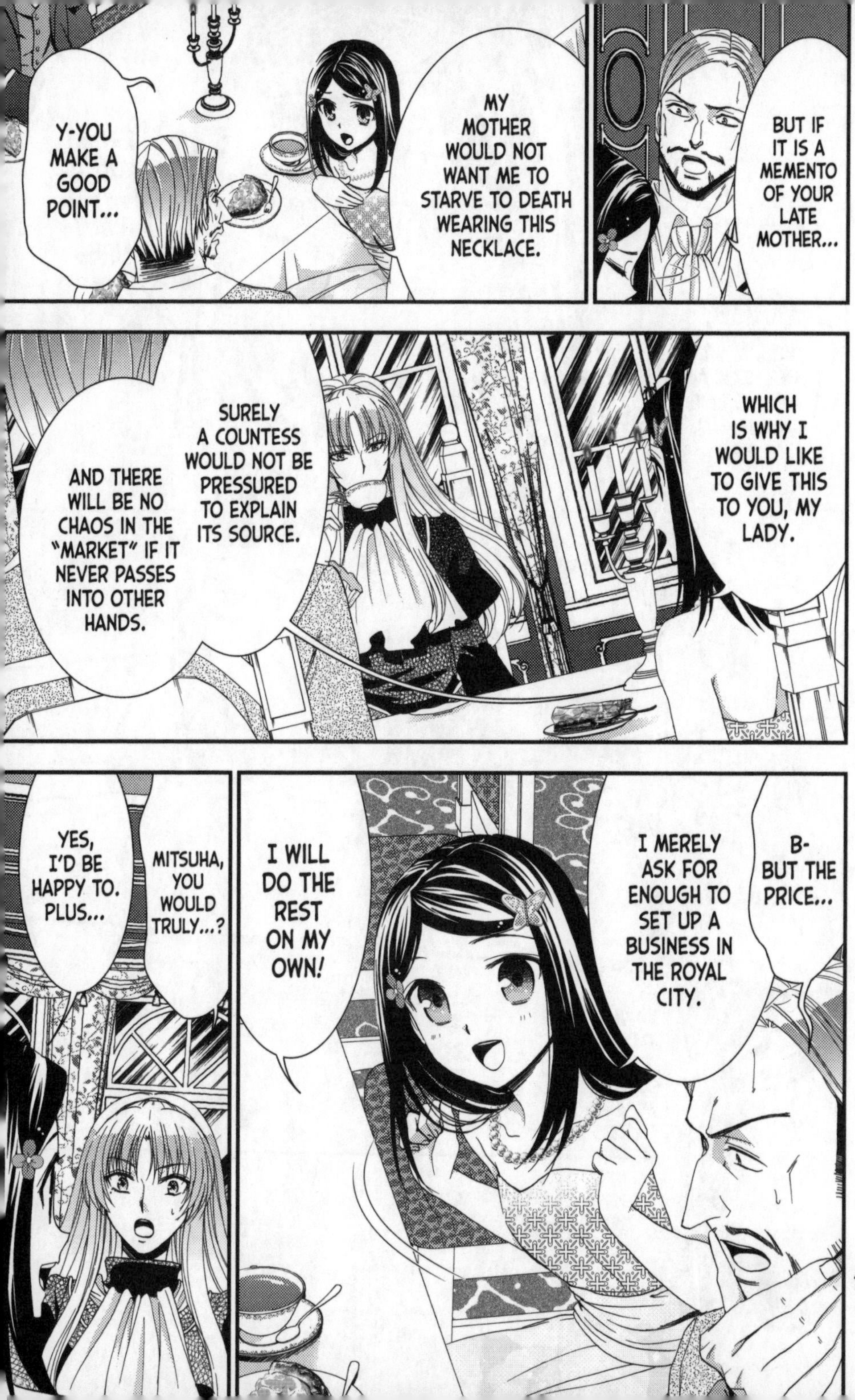
BUT IF IT IS A MEMENTO OF YOUR LATE MOTHER...
MY MOTHER WOULD NOT WANT ME TO STARVE TO DEATH WEARING THIS NECKLACE.
Y-YOU MAKE A GOOD POINT...
WHICH IS WHY I WOULD LIKE TO GIVE THIS TO YOU, MY LADY.
SURELY A COUNTESS WOULD NOT BE PRESSURED TO EXPLAIN ITS SOURCE.
AND THERE WILL BE NO CHAOS IN THE "MARKET" IF IT NEVER PASSES INTO OTHER HANDS.
B- BUT THE PRICE...
I MERELY ASK FOR ENOUGH TO SET UP A BUSINESS IN THE ROYAL CITY.
I WILL DO THE REST ON MY OWN!
MITSUHA, YOU WOULD TRULY...?
YES, I'D BE HAPPY TO. PLUS...

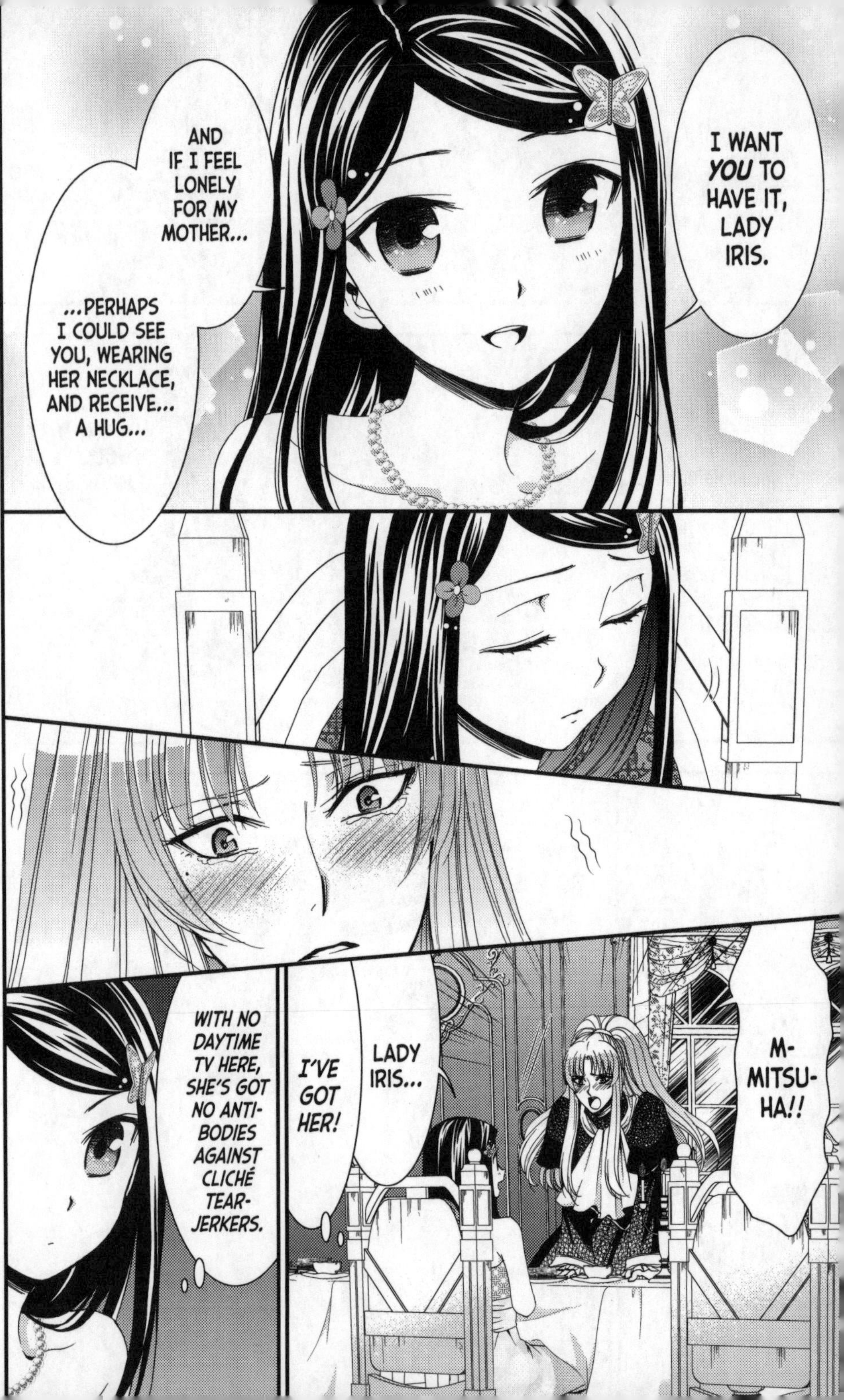
I WANT *YOU* TO HAVE IT, LADY IRIS.
AND IF I FEEL LONELY FOR MY MOTHER...
...PERHAPS I COULD SEE YOU, WEARING HER NECKLACE, AND RECEIVE... A HUG...
M-MITSU-HA!!
LADY IRIS...
I'VE GOT HER!
WITH NO DAYTIME TV HERE, SHE'S GOT NO ANTI-BODIES AGAINST CLICHÉ TEAR-JERKERS.

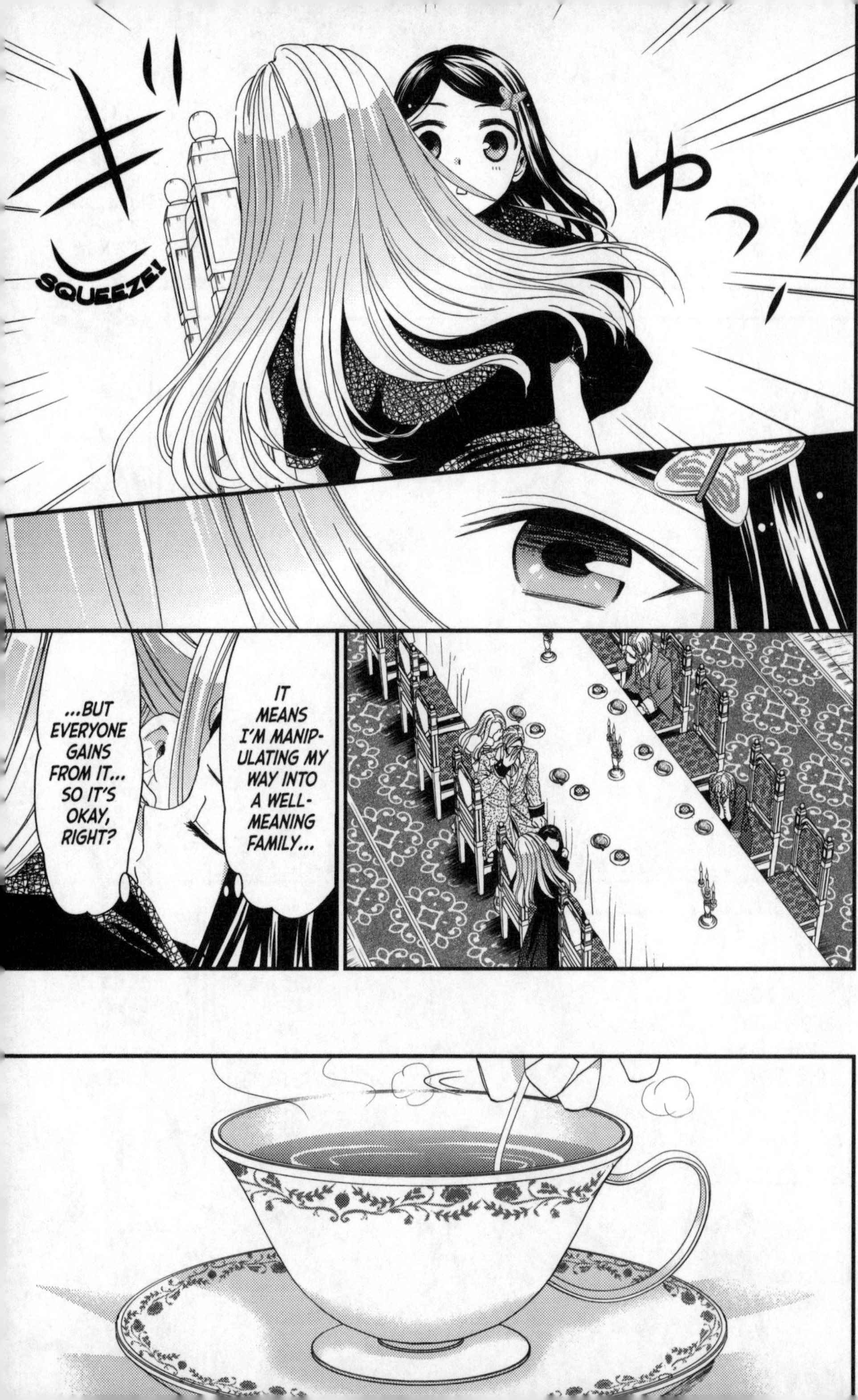
ぎゅっ!
SQUEEZE!
IT MEANS I'M MANIPULATING MY WAY INTO A WELL-MEANING FAMILY...
...BUT EVERYONE GAINS FROM IT... SO IT'S OKAY, RIGHT?

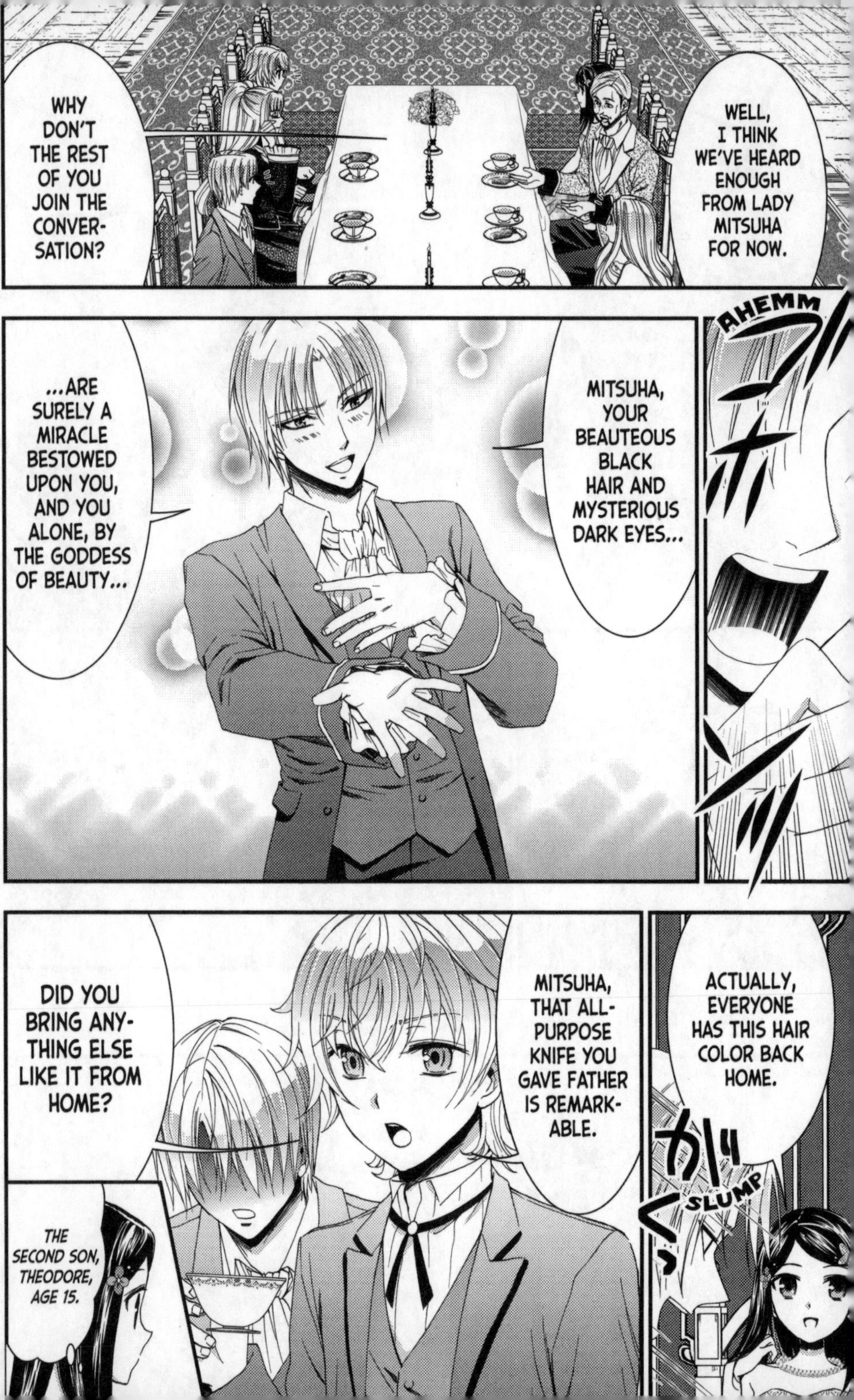
WELL, I THINK WE'VE HEARD ENOUGH FROM LADY MITSUHA FOR NOW.
WHY DON'T THE REST OF YOU JOIN THE CONVERSATION?
AHEMM
MITSUHA, YOUR BEAUTEOUS BLACK HAIR AND MYSTERIOUS DARK EYES...
...ARE SURELY A MIRACLE BESTOWED UPON YOU, AND YOU ALONE, BY THE GODDESS OF BEAUTY...
ACTUALLY, EVERYONE HAS THIS HAIR COLOR BACK HOME.
SLUMP
MITSUHA, THAT ALL-PURPOSE KNIFE YOU GAVE FATHER IS REMARKABLE.
DID YOU BRING ANYTHING ELSE LIKE IT FROM HOME?
THE SECOND SON, THEODORE, AGE 15.

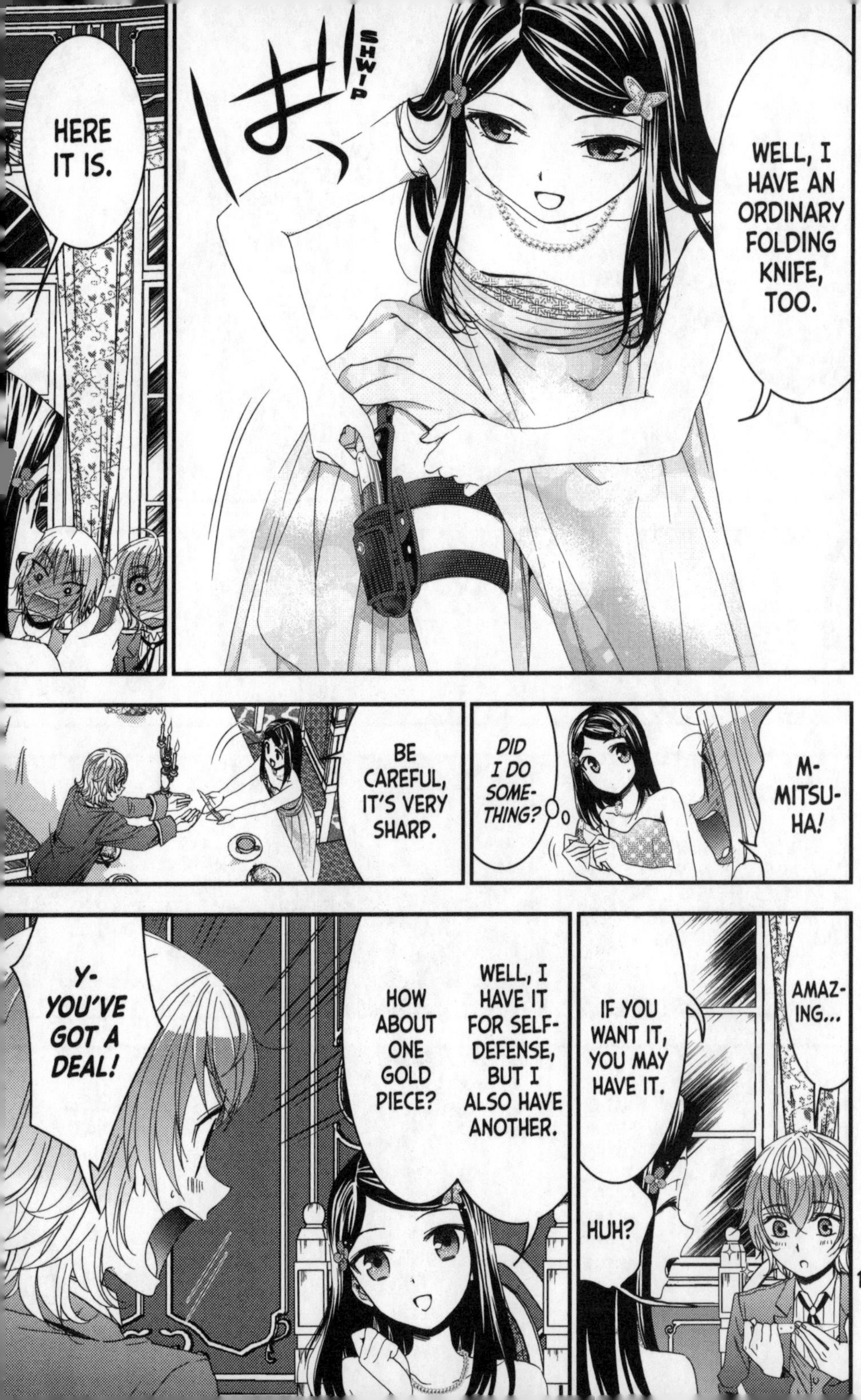
WELL, I HAVE AN ORDINARY FOLDING KNIFE, TOO.
ばっ
SHWIP
HERE IT IS.
M-MITSU-HA!
DID I DO SOME-THING?
BE CAREFUL, IT'S VERY SHARP.
AMAZ-ING...
IF YOU WANT IT, YOU MAY HAVE IT.
HUH?
WELL, I HAVE IT FOR SELF-DEFENSE, BUT I ALSO HAVE ANOTHER.
HOW ABOUT ONE GOLD PIECE?
Y-YOU'VE GOT A DEAL!

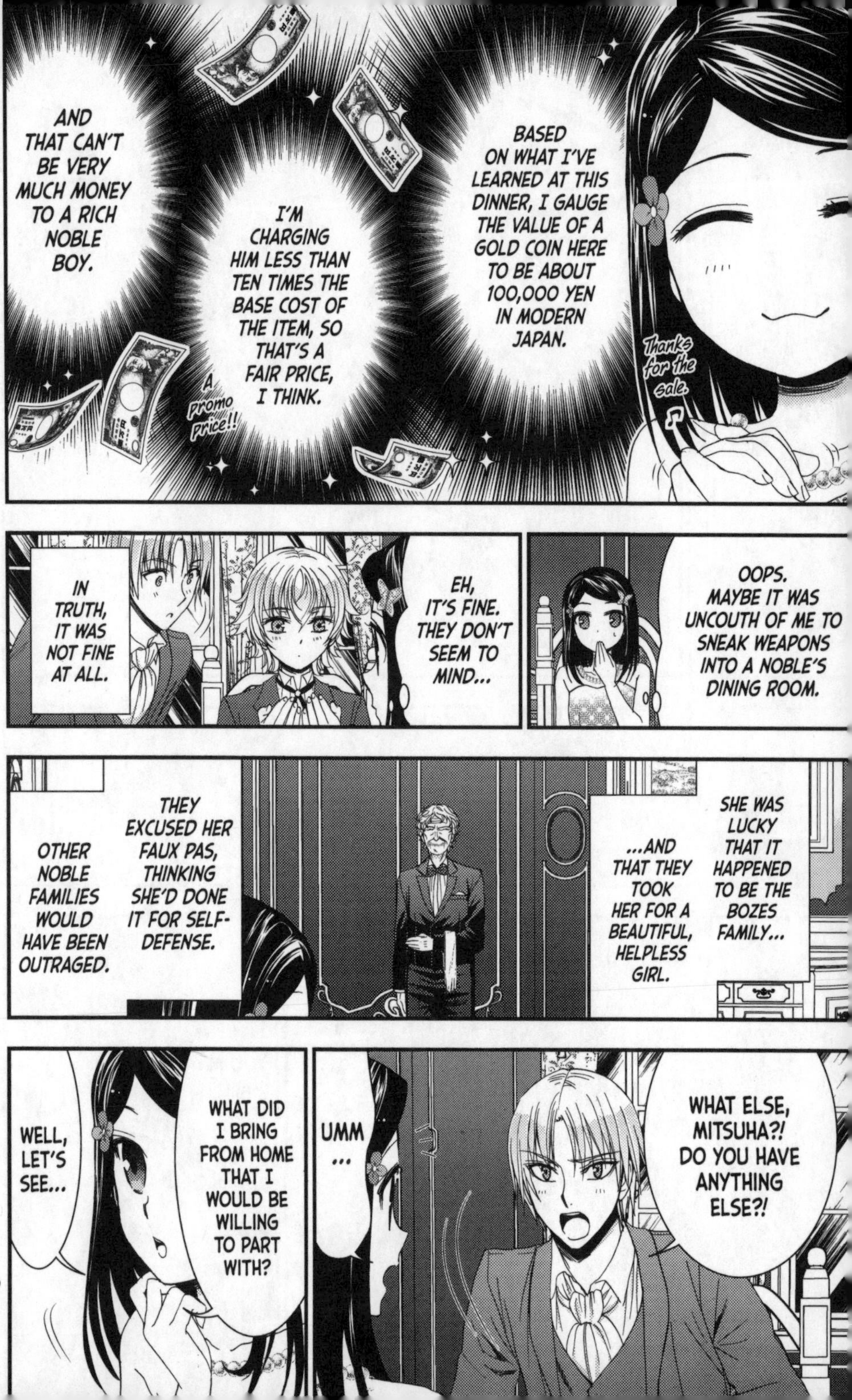
BASED ON WHAT I'VE LEARNED AT THIS DINNER, I GAUGE THE VALUE OF A GOLD COIN HERE TO BE ABOUT 100,000 YEN IN MODERN JAPAN.
Thanks for the sale. ♪
I'M CHARGING HIM LESS THAN TEN TIMES THE BASE COST OF THE ITEM, SO THAT'S A FAIR PRICE, I THINK.
A Promo Price!!
AND THAT CAN'T BE VERY MUCH MONEY TO A RICH NOBLE BOY.
OOPS. MAYBE IT WAS UNCOUTH OF ME TO SNEAK WEAPONS INTO A NOBLE'S DINING ROOM.
EH, IT'S FINE. THEY DON'T SEEM TO MIND...
IN TRUTH, IT WAS NOT FINE AT ALL.
SHE WAS LUCKY THAT IT HAPPENED TO BE THE BOZES FAMILY...
...AND THAT THEY TOOK HER FOR A BEAUTIFUL, HELPLESS GIRL.
THEY EXCUSED HER FAUX PAS, THINKING SHE'D DONE IT FOR SELF-DEFENSE.
OTHER NOBLE FAMILIES WOULD HAVE BEEN OUTRAGED.
WHAT ELSE, MITSUHA?! DO YOU HAVE ANYTHING ELSE?!
UMM ...
WHAT DID I BRING FROM HOME THAT I WOULD BE WILLING TO PART WITH?
WELL, LET'S SEE...

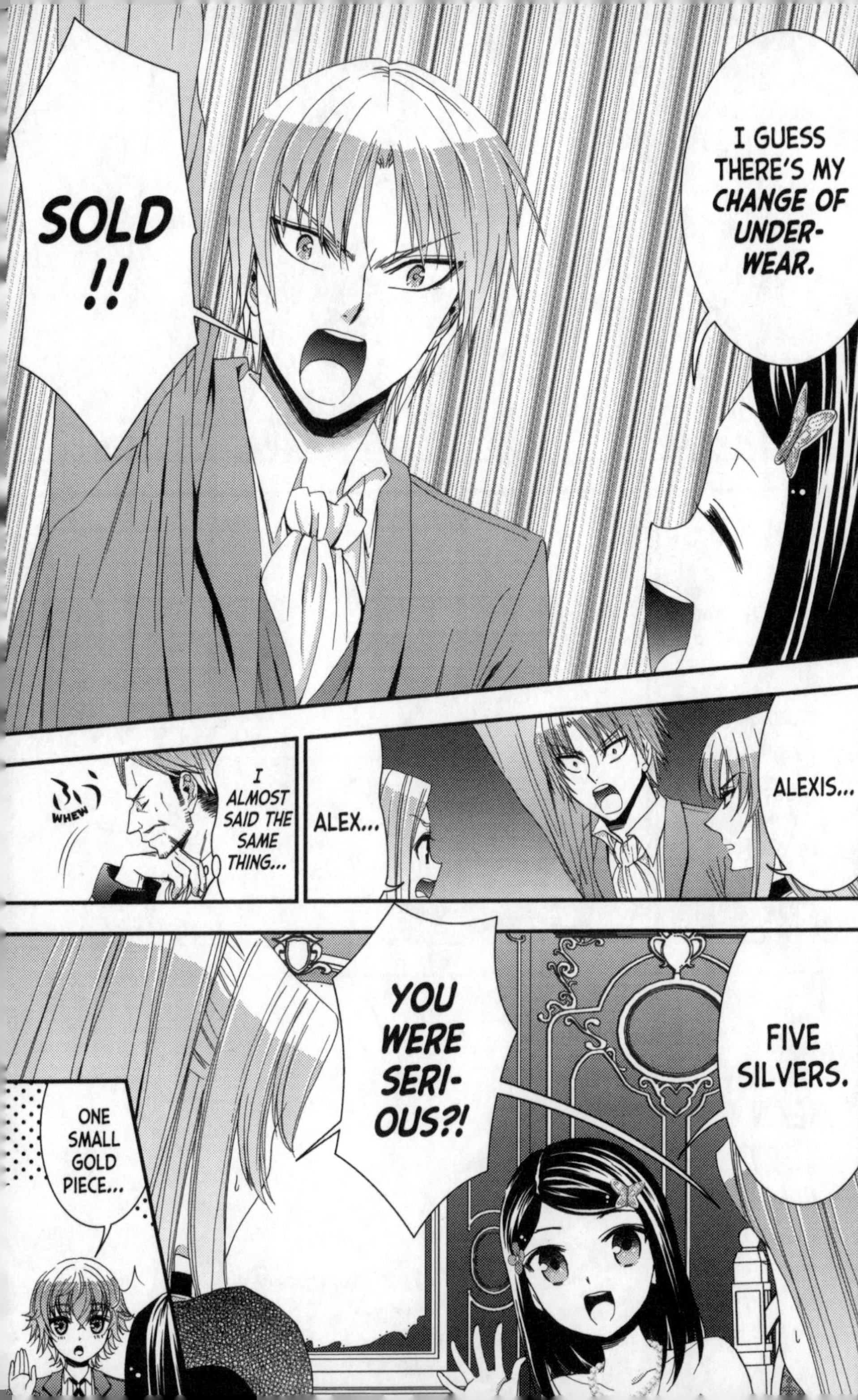
I GUESS THERE'S MY CHANGE OF UNDER-WEAR.
SOLD !!
ALEXIS...
ALEX...
I ALMOST SAID THE SAME THING...
ふう
WHEW
FIVE SILVERS.
YOU WERE SERI-OUS?!
ONE SMALL GOLD PIECE...

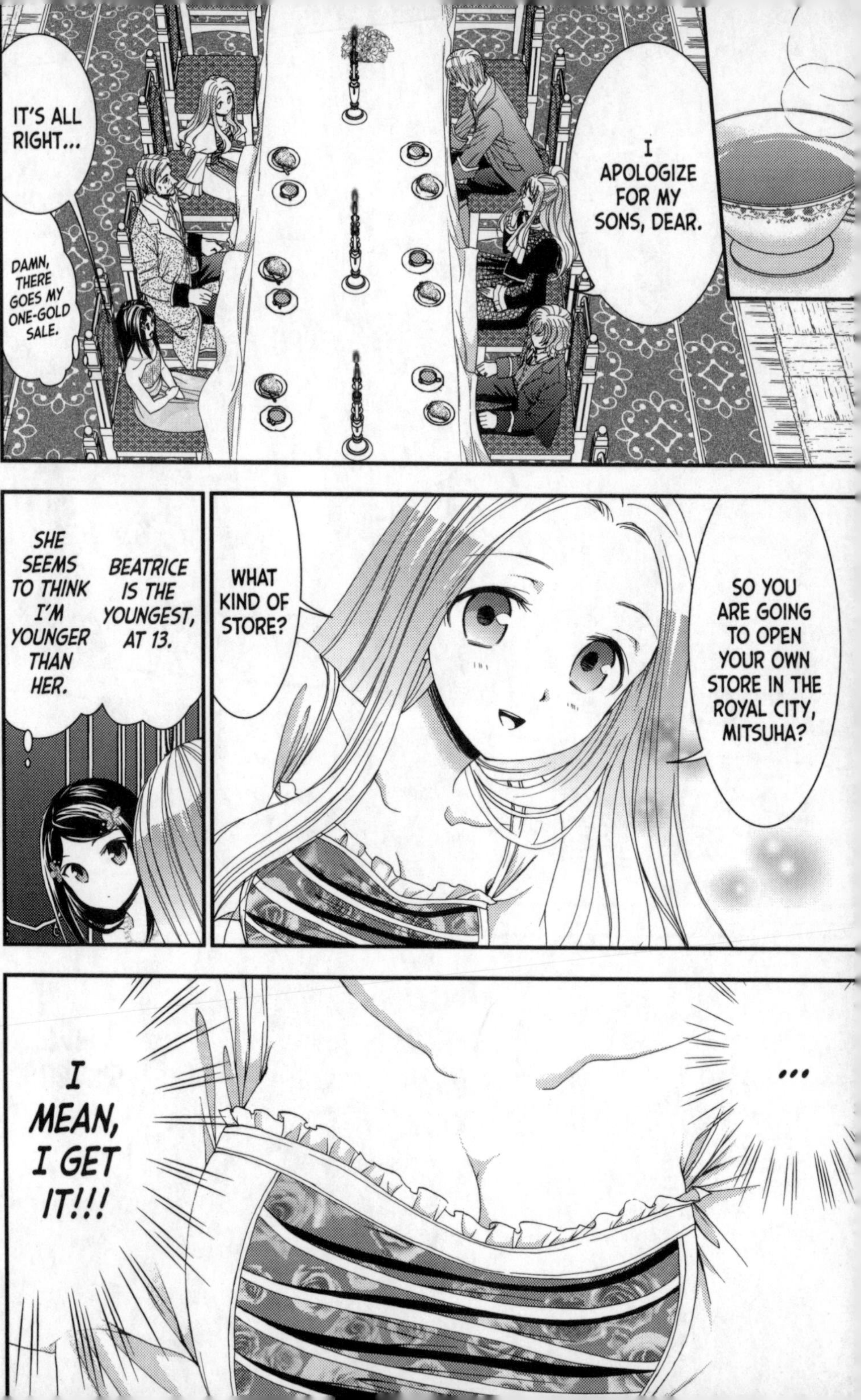
I APOLOGIZE FOR MY SONS, DEAR.
IT'S ALL RIGHT...
DAMN, THERE GOES MY ONE-GOLD SALE.
SO YOU ARE GOING TO OPEN YOUR OWN STORE IN THE ROYAL CITY, MITSUHA?
WHAT KIND OF STORE?
BEATRICE IS THE YOUNGEST, AT 13.
SHE SEEMS TO THINK I'M YOUNGER THAN HER.
...
I MEAN, I GET IT!!!

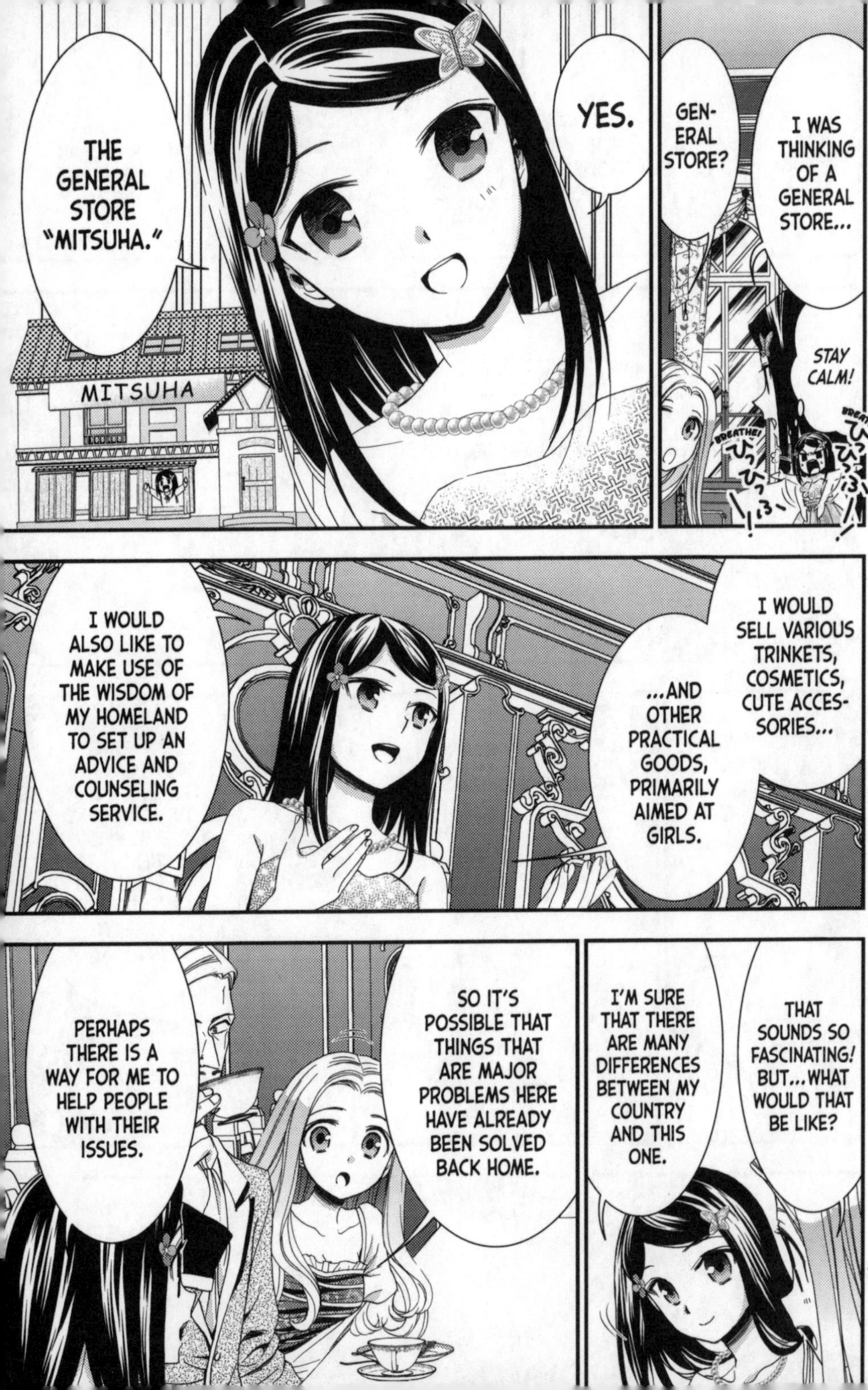
I WAS THINKING OF A GENERAL STORE...
GEN-ERAL STORE?
STAY CALM!
BREATHE!
BREATHE!
YES.
THE GENERAL STORE "MITSUHA."
MITSUHA
I WOULD SELL VARIOUS TRINKETS, COSMETICS, CUTE ACCES-SORIES...
...AND OTHER PRACTICAL GOODS, PRIMARILY AIMED AT GIRLS.
I WOULD ALSO LIKE TO MAKE USE OF THE WISDOM OF MY HOMELAND TO SET UP AN ADVICE AND COUNSELING SERVICE.
THAT SOUNDS SO FASCINATING! BUT...WHAT WOULD THAT BE LIKE?
I'M SURE THAT THERE ARE MANY DIFFERENCES BETWEEN MY COUNTRY AND THIS ONE.
SO IT'S POSSIBLE THAT THINGS THAT ARE MAJOR PROBLEMS HERE HAVE ALREADY BEEN SOLVED BACK HOME.
PERHAPS THERE IS A WAY FOR ME TO HELP PEOPLE WITH THEIR ISSUES.

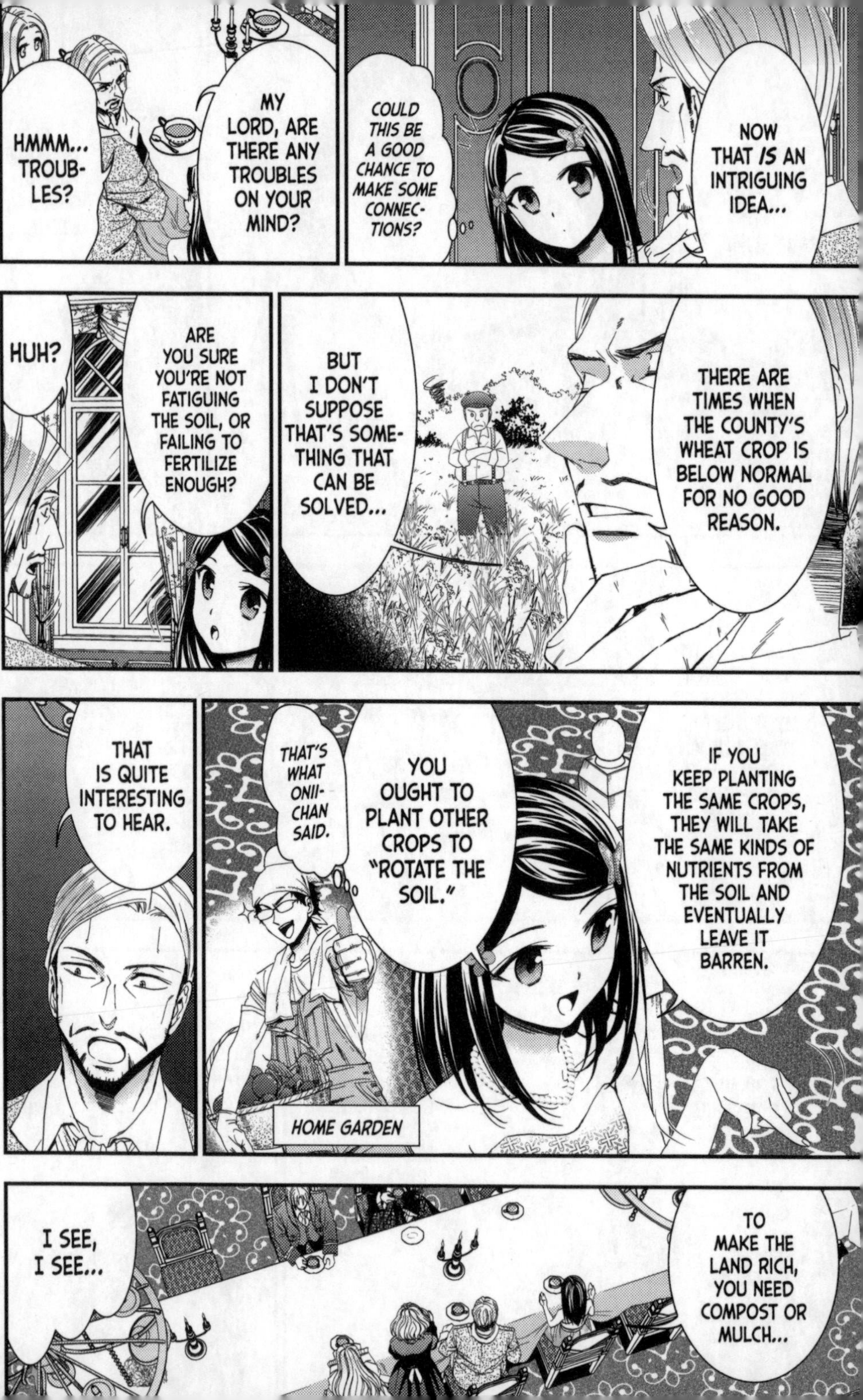
NOW THAT IS AN INTRIGUING IDEA...
COULD THIS BE A GOOD CHANCE TO MAKE SOME CONNECTIONS?
MY LORD, ARE THERE ANY TROUBLES ON YOUR MIND?
HMMM... TROUBLES?
THERE ARE TIMES WHEN THE COUNTY'S WHEAT CROP IS BELOW NORMAL FOR NO GOOD REASON.
BUT I DON'T SUPPOSE THAT'S SOMETHING THAT CAN BE SOLVED...
ARE YOU SURE YOU'RE NOT FATIGUING THE SOIL, OR FAILING TO FERTILIZE ENOUGH?
HUH?
IF YOU KEEP PLANTING THE SAME CROPS, THEY WILL TAKE THE SAME KINDS OF NUTRIENTS FROM THE SOIL AND EVENTUALLY LEAVE IT BARREN.
YOU OUGHT TO PLANT OTHER CROPS TO "ROTATE THE SOIL."
THAT'S WHAT ONII-CHAN SAID.
HOME GARDEN
THAT IS QUITE INTERESTING TO HEAR.
TO MAKE THE LAND RICH, YOU NEED COMPOST OR MULCH...
I SEE, I SEE...

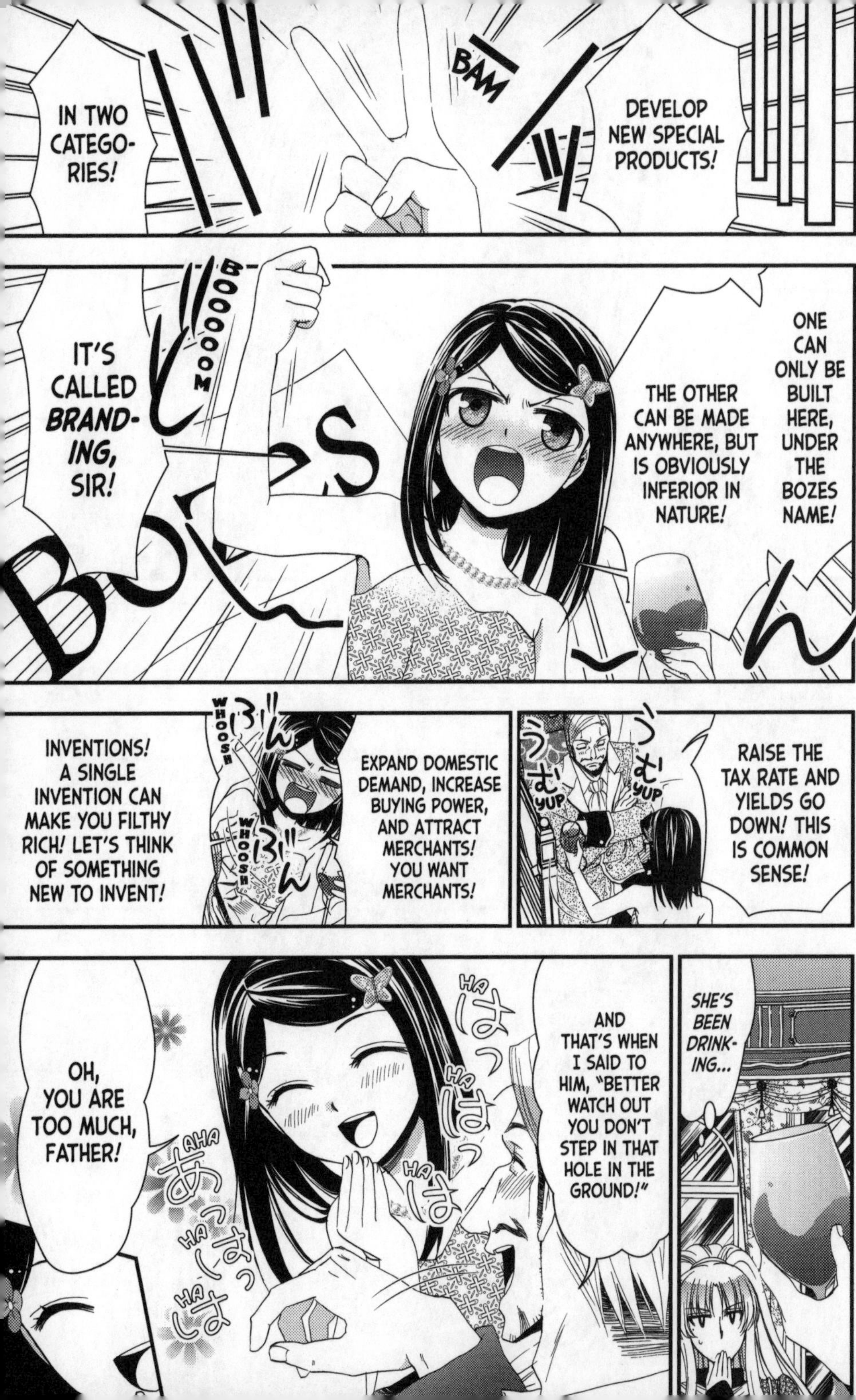
DEVELOP NEW SPECIAL PRODUCTS!
BAM
IN TWO CATEGO-RIES!
ONE CAN ONLY BE BUILT HERE, UNDER THE BOZES NAME!
THE OTHER CAN BE MADE ANYWHERE, BUT IS OBVIOUSLY INFERIOR IN NATURE!
BOOOOOOM
IT'S CALLED *BRAND-ING*, SIR!
YUP
YUP
RAISE THE TAX RATE AND YIELDS GO DOWN! THIS IS COMMON SENSE!
EXPAND DOMESTIC DEMAND, INCREASE BUYING POWER, AND ATTRACT MERCHANTS! YOU WANT MERCHANTS!
WHOOSH
WHOOSH
INVENTIONS! A SINGLE INVENTION CAN MAKE YOU FILTHY RICH! LET'S THINK OF SOMETHING NEW TO INVENT!
SHE'S BEEN DRINK-ING...
AND THAT'S WHEN I SAID TO HIM, "BETTER WATCH OUT YOU DON'T STEP IN THAT HOLE IN THE GROUND!"
HA
HA
HA
OH, YOU ARE TOO MUCH, FATHER!
AHA
HA
HA

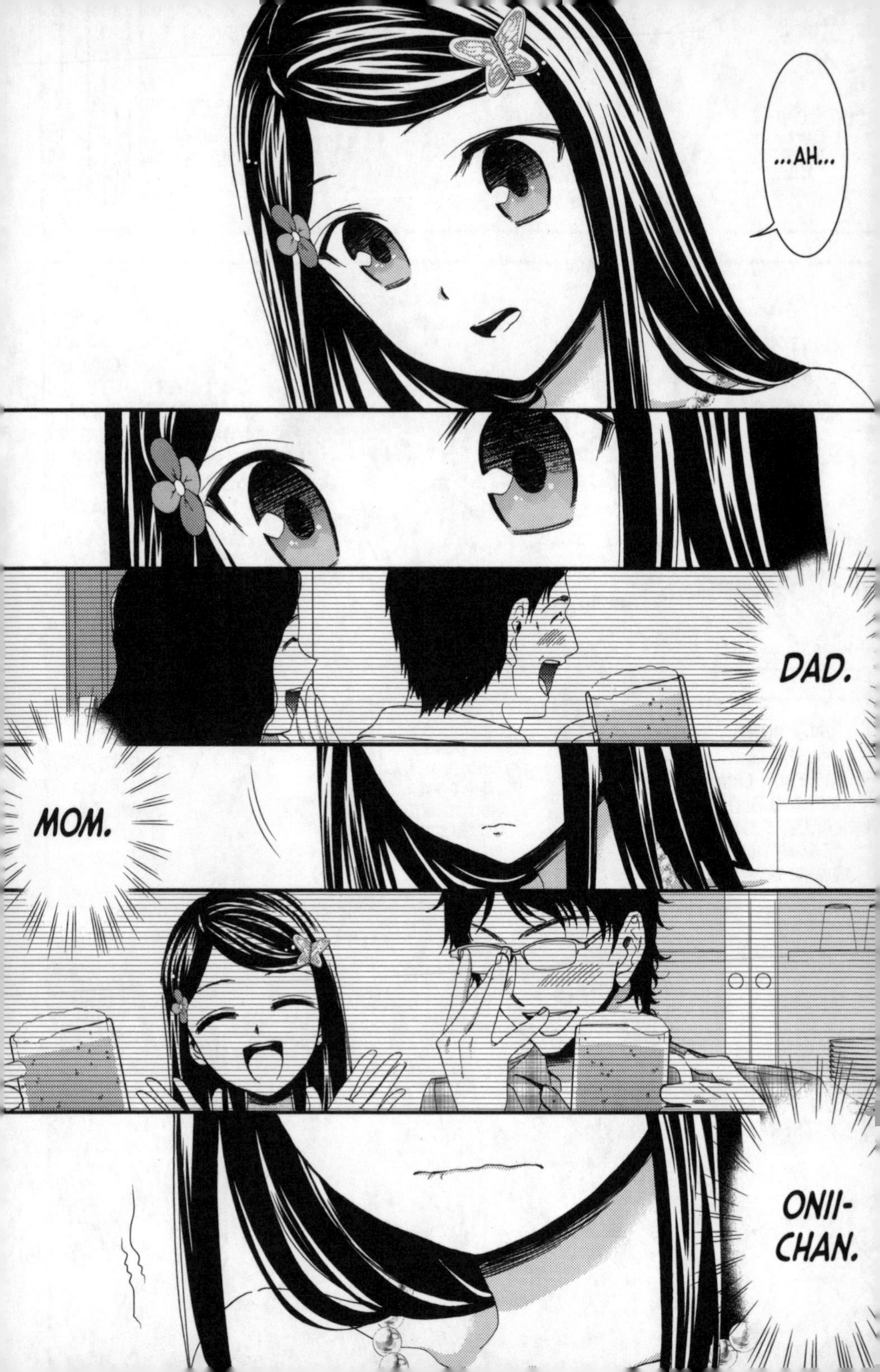
...AH...
DAD.
MOM.
ONII-CHAN.

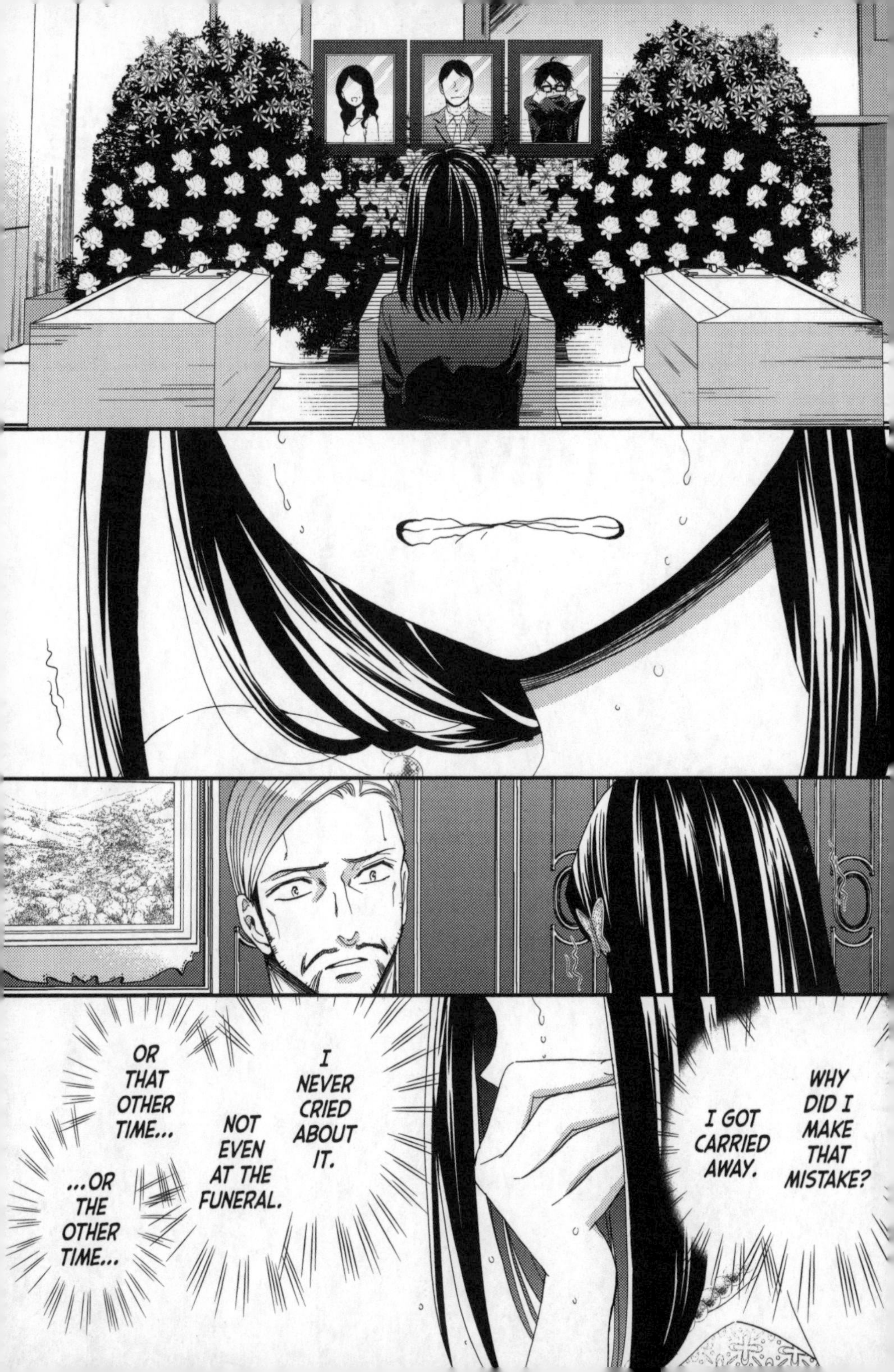
WHY DID I MAKE THAT MISTAKE?
I GOT CARRIED AWAY.
I NEVER CRIED ABOUT IT.
NOT EVEN AT THE FUNERAL.
OR THAT OTHER TIME...
...OR THE OTHER TIME...

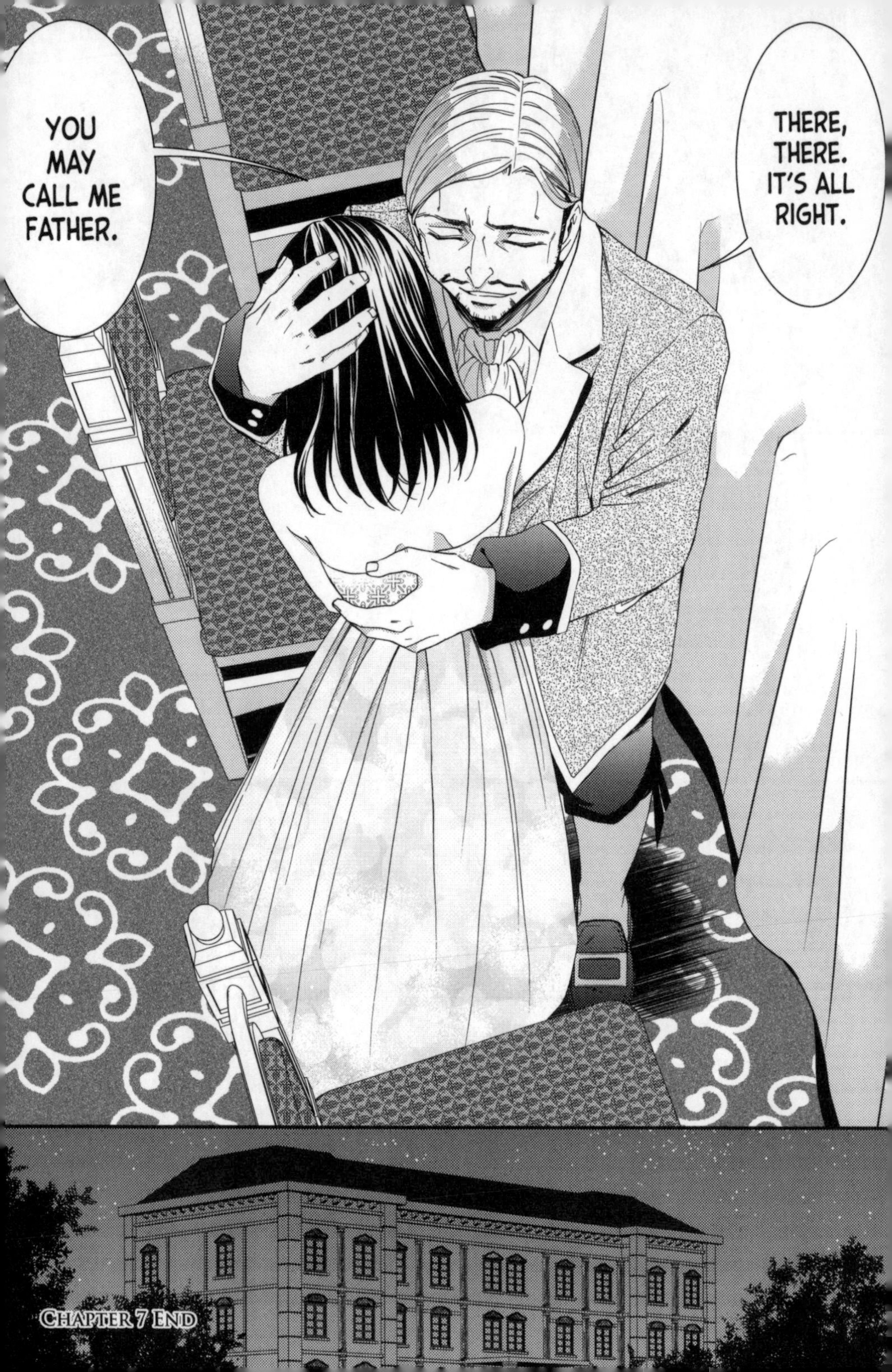
THERE, THERE. IT'S ALL RIGHT.
YOU MAY CALL ME FATHER.
CHAPTER 7 END

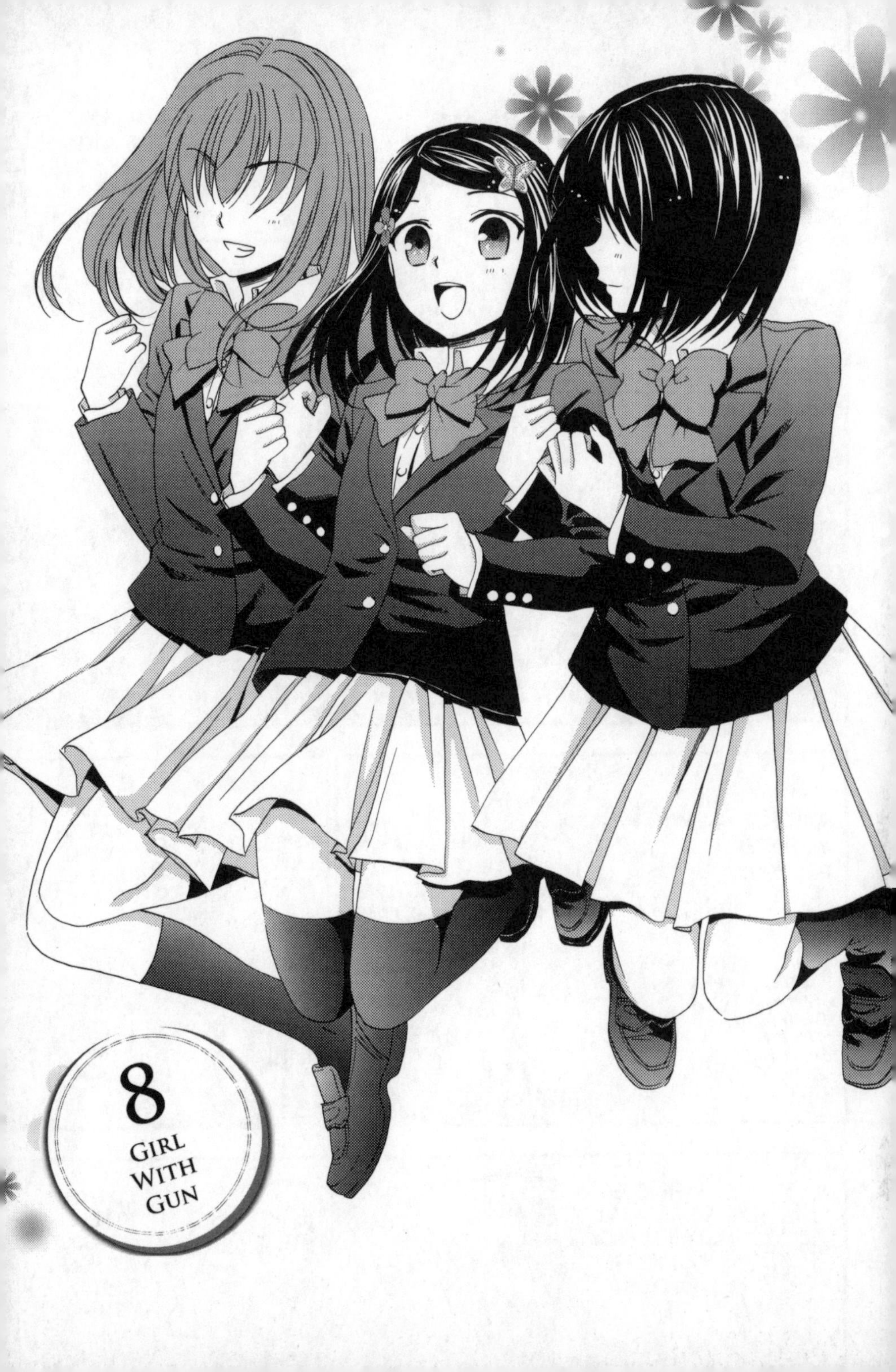

8
Girl With Gun

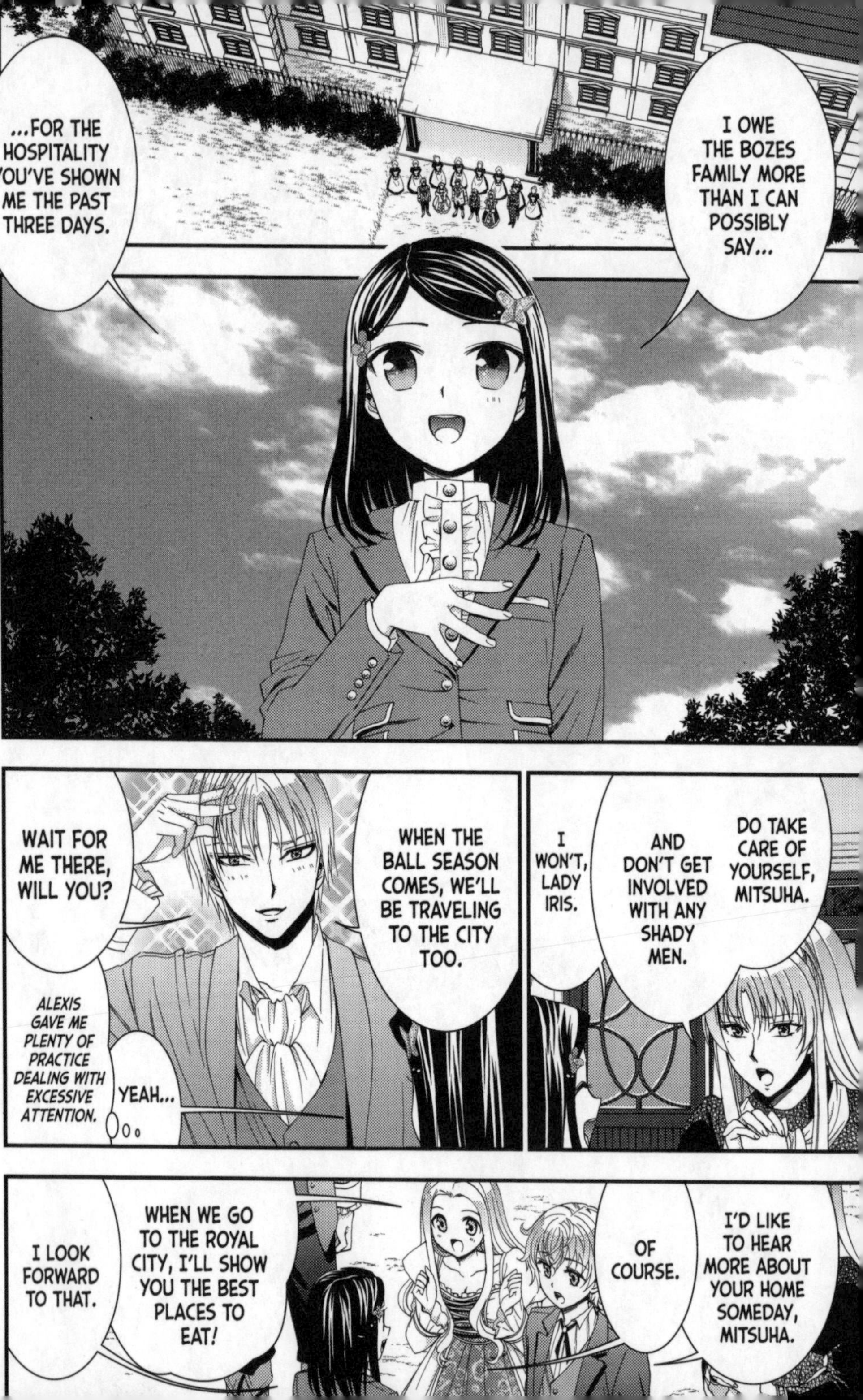
I OWE THE BOZES FAMILY MORE THAN I CAN POSSIBLY SAY...
...FOR THE HOSPITALITY YOU'VE SHOWN ME THE PAST THREE DAYS.
DO TAKE CARE OF YOURSELF, MITSUHA.
AND DON'T GET INVOLVED WITH ANY SHADY MEN.
I WON'T, LADY IRIS.
WHEN THE BALL SEASON COMES, WE'LL BE TRAVELING TO THE CITY TOO.
WAIT FOR ME THERE, WILL YOU?
YEAH...
ALEXIS GAVE ME PLENTY OF PRACTICE DEALING WITH EXCESSIVE ATTENTION.
I'D LIKE TO HEAR MORE ABOUT YOUR HOME SOMEDAY, MITSUHA.
OF COURSE.
WHEN WE GO TO THE ROYAL CITY, I'LL SHOW YOU THE BEST PLACES TO EAT!
I LOOK FORWARD TO THAT.

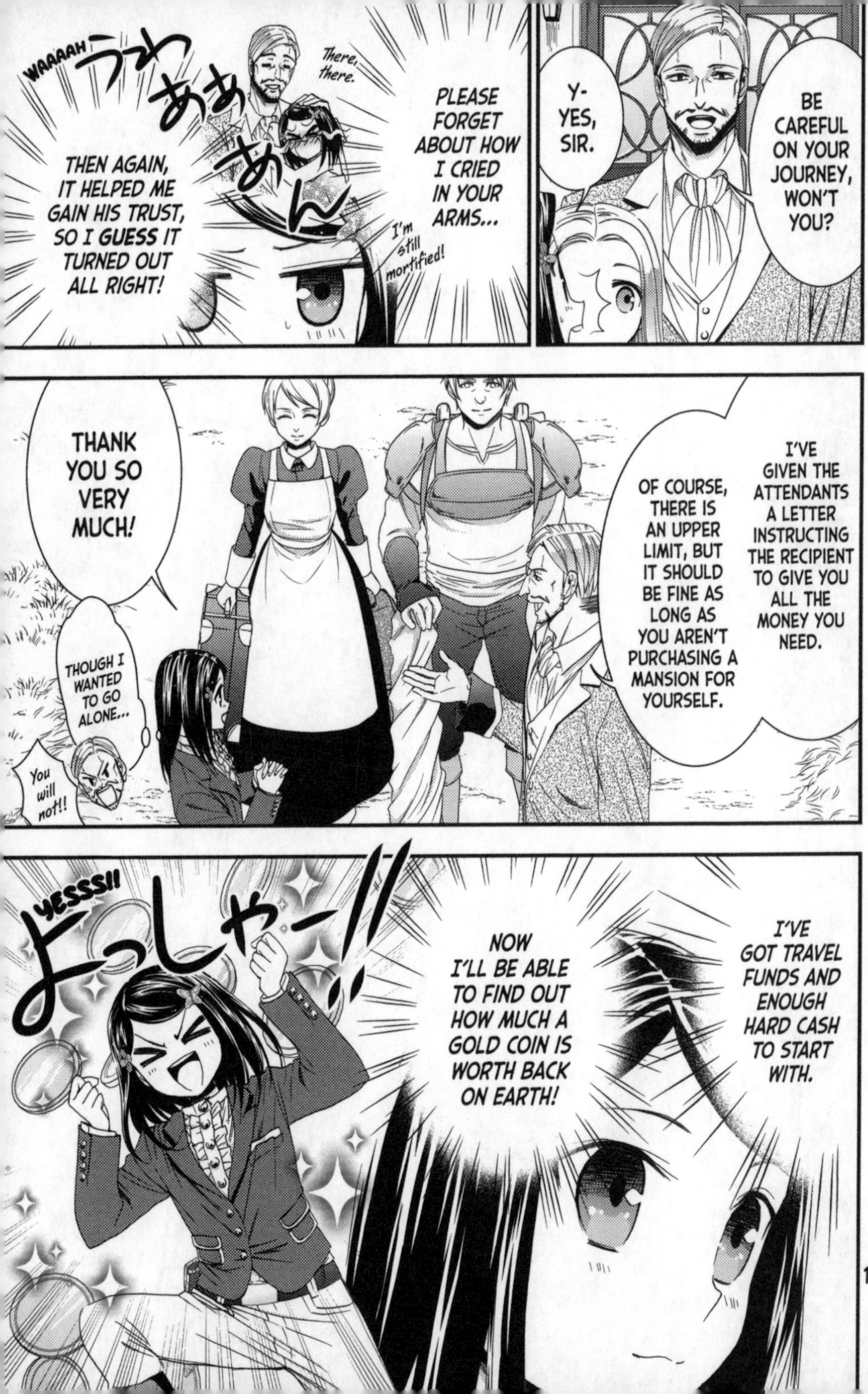
BE CAREFUL ON YOUR JOURNEY, WON'T YOU?
Y-YES, SIR.
PLEASE FORGET ABOUT HOW I CRIED IN YOUR ARMS...
I'm still mortified!
WAAAAH
うわああああん
There, there.
THEN AGAIN, IT HELPED ME GAIN HIS TRUST, SO I GUESS IT TURNED OUT ALL RIGHT!
I'VE GIVEN THE ATTENDANTS A LETTER INSTRUCTING THE RECIPIENT TO GIVE YOU ALL THE MONEY YOU NEED.
OF COURSE, THERE IS AN UPPER LIMIT, BUT IT SHOULD BE FINE AS LONG AS YOU AREN'T PURCHASING A MANSION FOR YOURSELF.
THANK YOU SO VERY MUCH!
THOUGH I WANTED TO GO ALONE...
You will not!!
I'VE GOT TRAVEL FUNDS AND ENOUGH HARD CASH TO START WITH.
NOW I'LL BE ABLE TO FIND OUT HOW MUCH A GOLD COIN IS WORTH BACK ON EARTH!
YESSS!!
よっしゃー!!

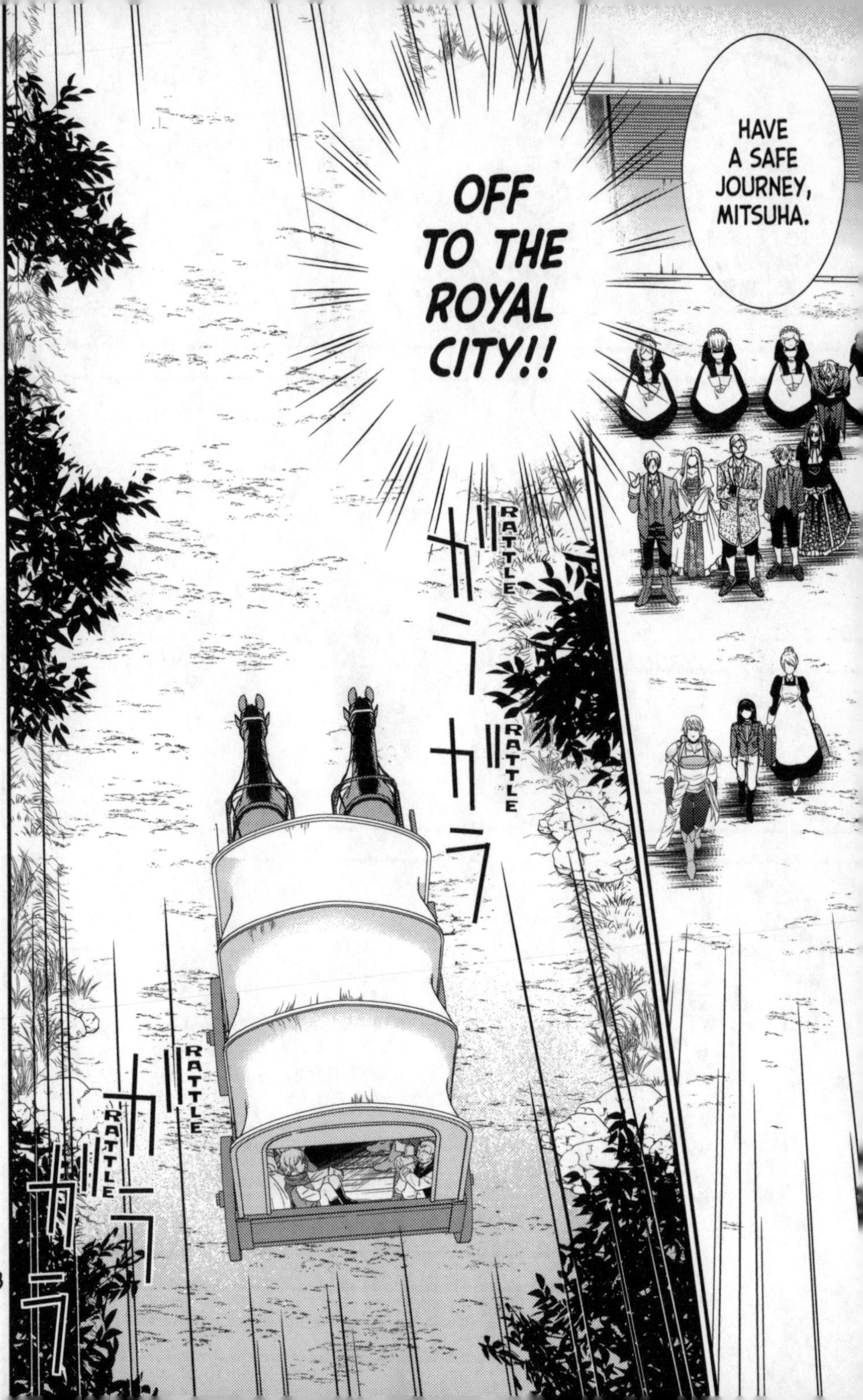
HAVE A SAFE JOURNEY, MITSUHA.
OFF TO THE ROYAL CITY!!
RATTLE
RATTLE
RATTLE
RATTLE

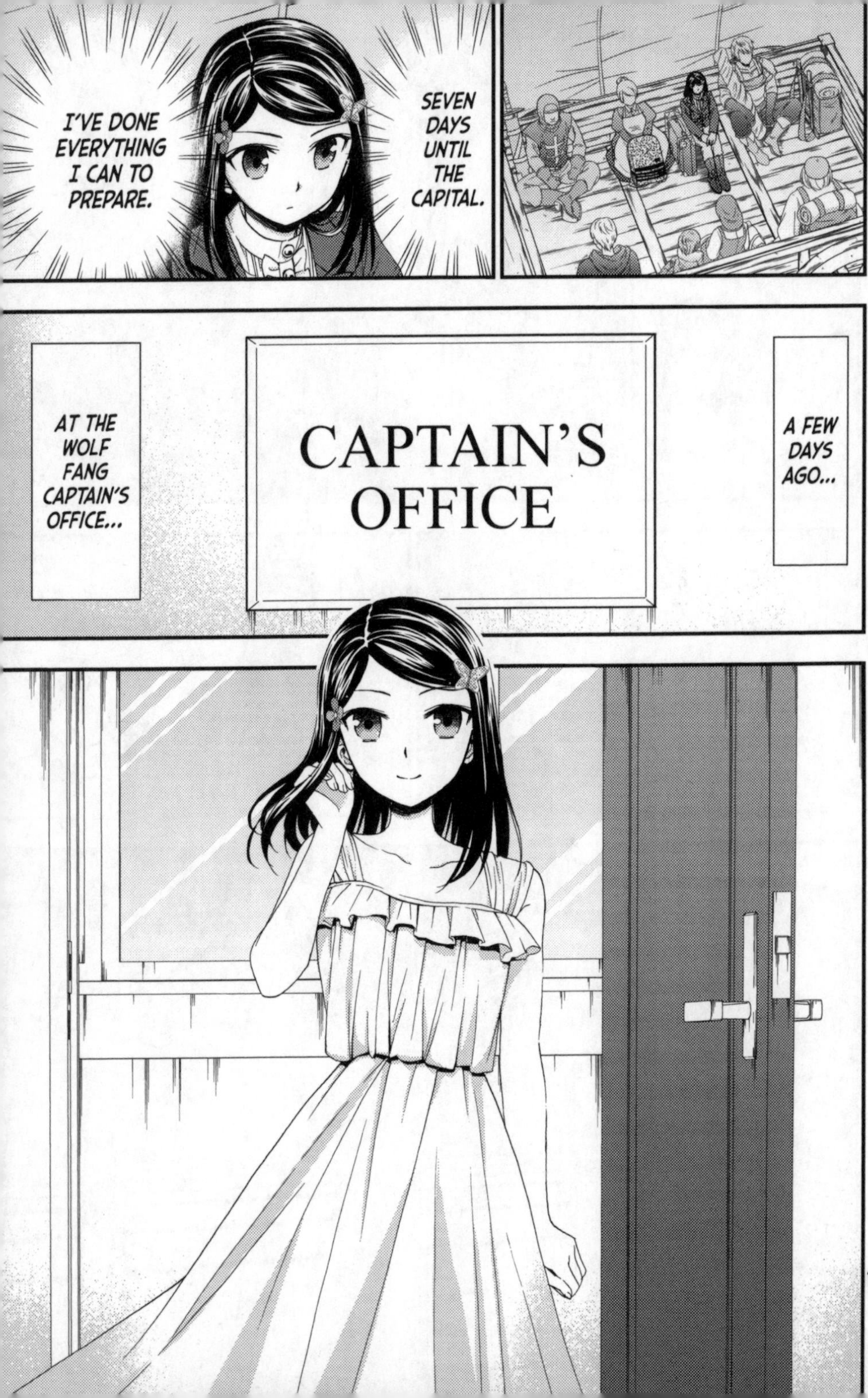
SEVEN DAYS UNTIL THE CAPITAL.
I'VE DONE EVERYTHING I CAN TO PREPARE.
A FEW DAYS AGO...
CAPTAIN'S OFFICE
AT THE WOLF FANG CAPTAIN'S OFFICE...

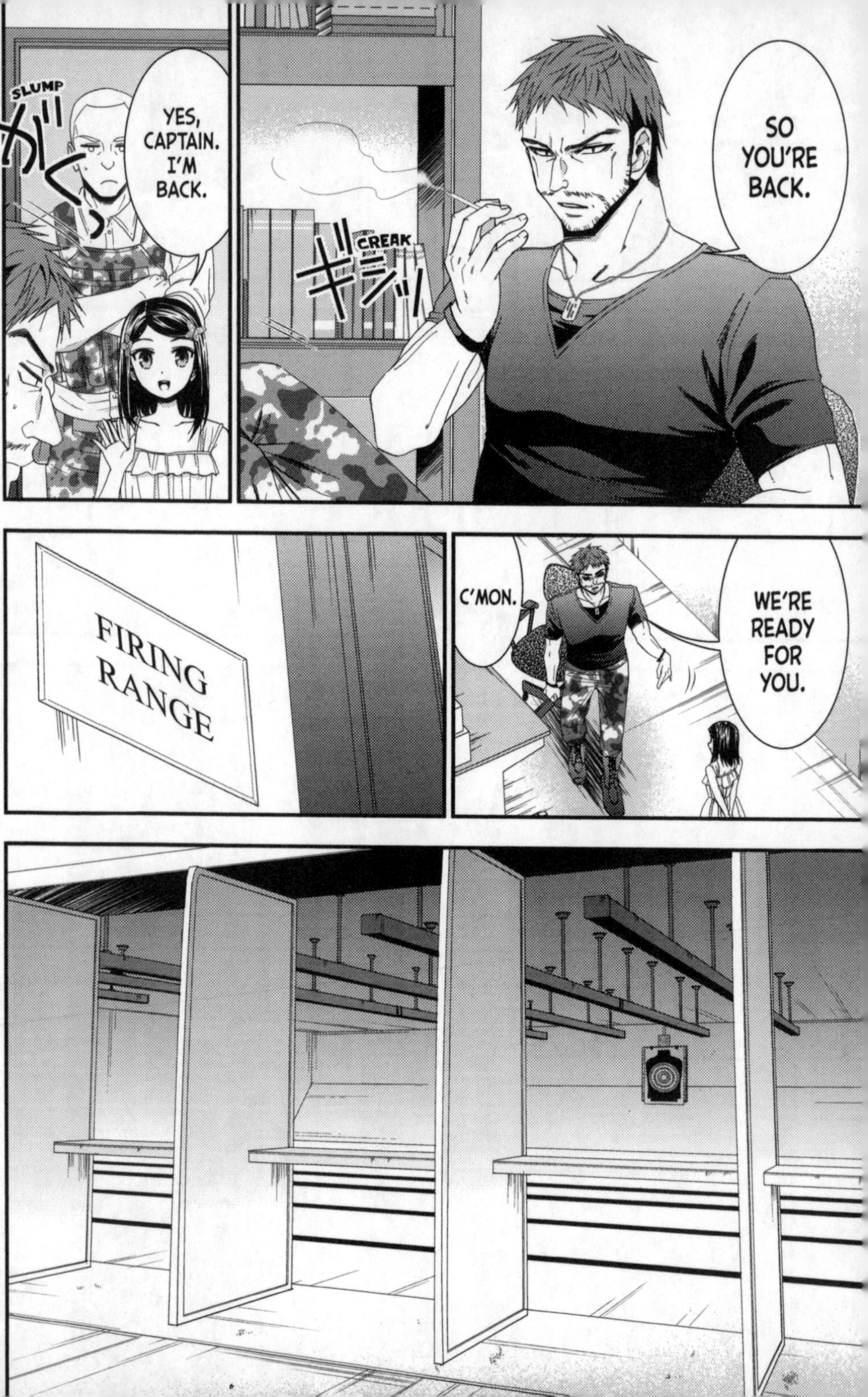
SO YOU'RE BACK.
CREAK
ギシッ
SLUMP
がくっ
YES, CAPTAIN. I'M BACK.
WE'RE READY FOR YOU.
C'MON.
FIRING RANGE

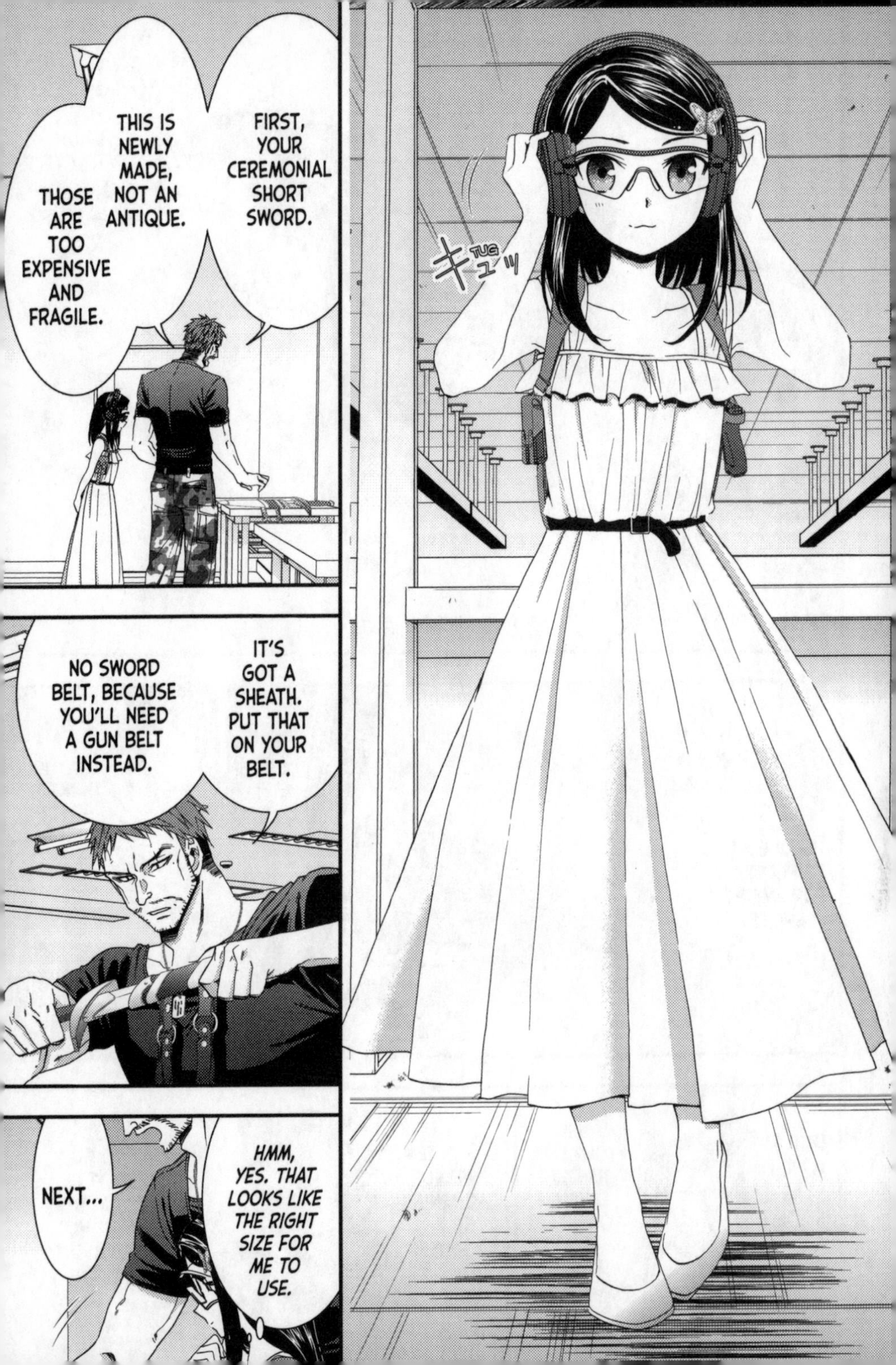
キュッ
TUG
FIRST, YOUR CEREMONIAL SHORT SWORD.
THIS IS NEWLY MADE, NOT AN ANTIQUE.
THOSE ARE TOO EXPENSIVE AND FRAGILE.
IT'S GOT A SHEATH. PUT THAT ON YOUR BELT.
NO SWORD BELT, BECAUSE YOU'LL NEED A GUN BELT INSTEAD.
HMM, YES. THAT LOOKS LIKE THE RIGHT SIZE FOR ME TO USE.
NEXT...

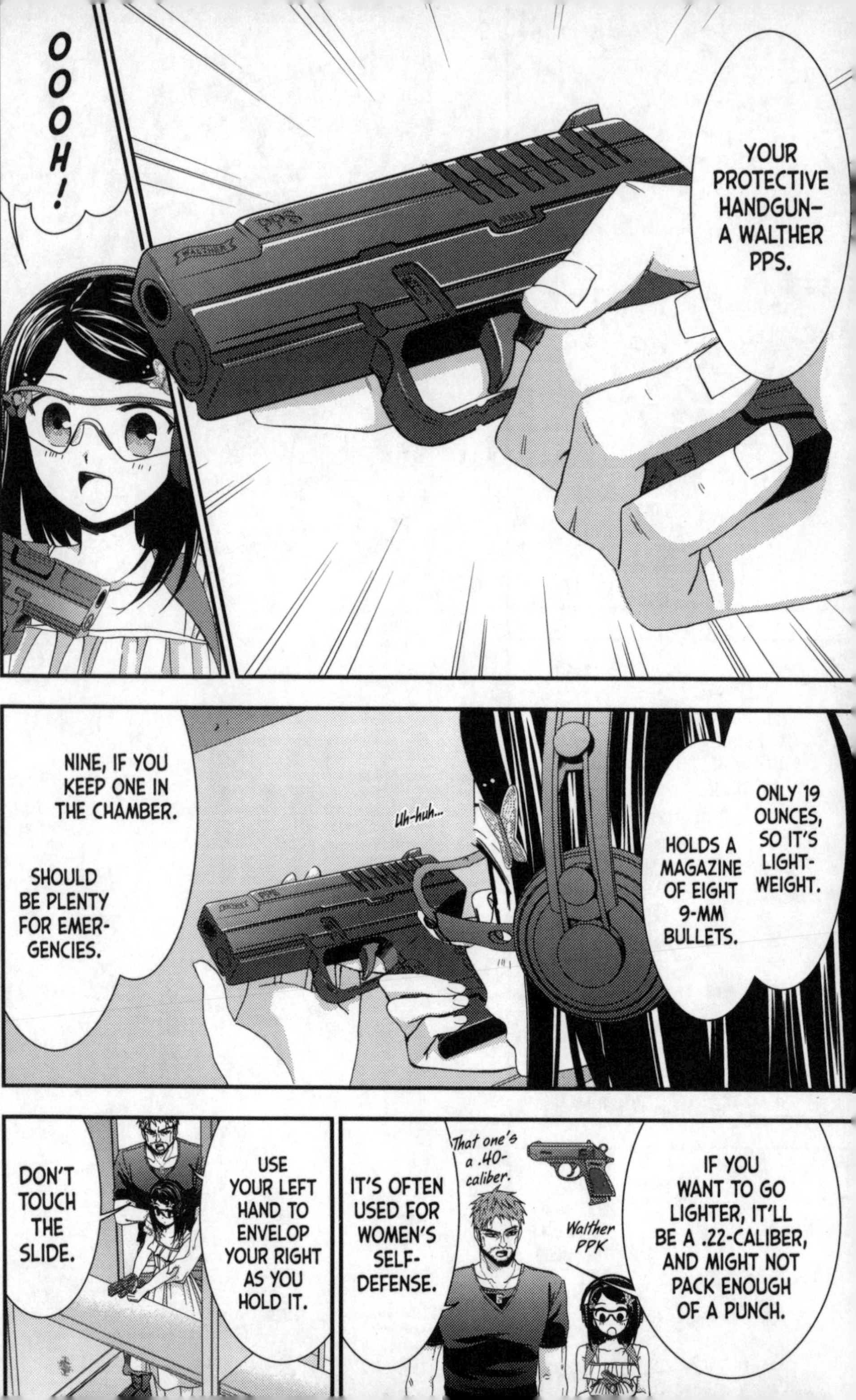
YOUR PROTECTIVE HANDGUN— A WALTHER PPS.
OOOH!
ONLY 19 OUNCES, SO IT'S LIGHT-WEIGHT.
HOLDS A MAGAZINE OF EIGHT 9-MM BULLETS.
Uh-huh...
NINE, IF YOU KEEP ONE IN THE CHAMBER.
SHOULD BE PLENTY FOR EMER-GENCIES.
IF YOU WANT TO GO LIGHTER, IT'LL BE A .22-CALIBER, AND MIGHT NOT PACK ENOUGH OF A PUNCH.
Walther PPK
That one's a .40-caliber.
IT'S OFTEN USED FOR WOMEN'S SELF-DEFENSE.
USE YOUR LEFT HAND TO ENVELOP YOUR RIGHT AS YOU HOLD IT.
DON'T TOUCH THE SLIDE.

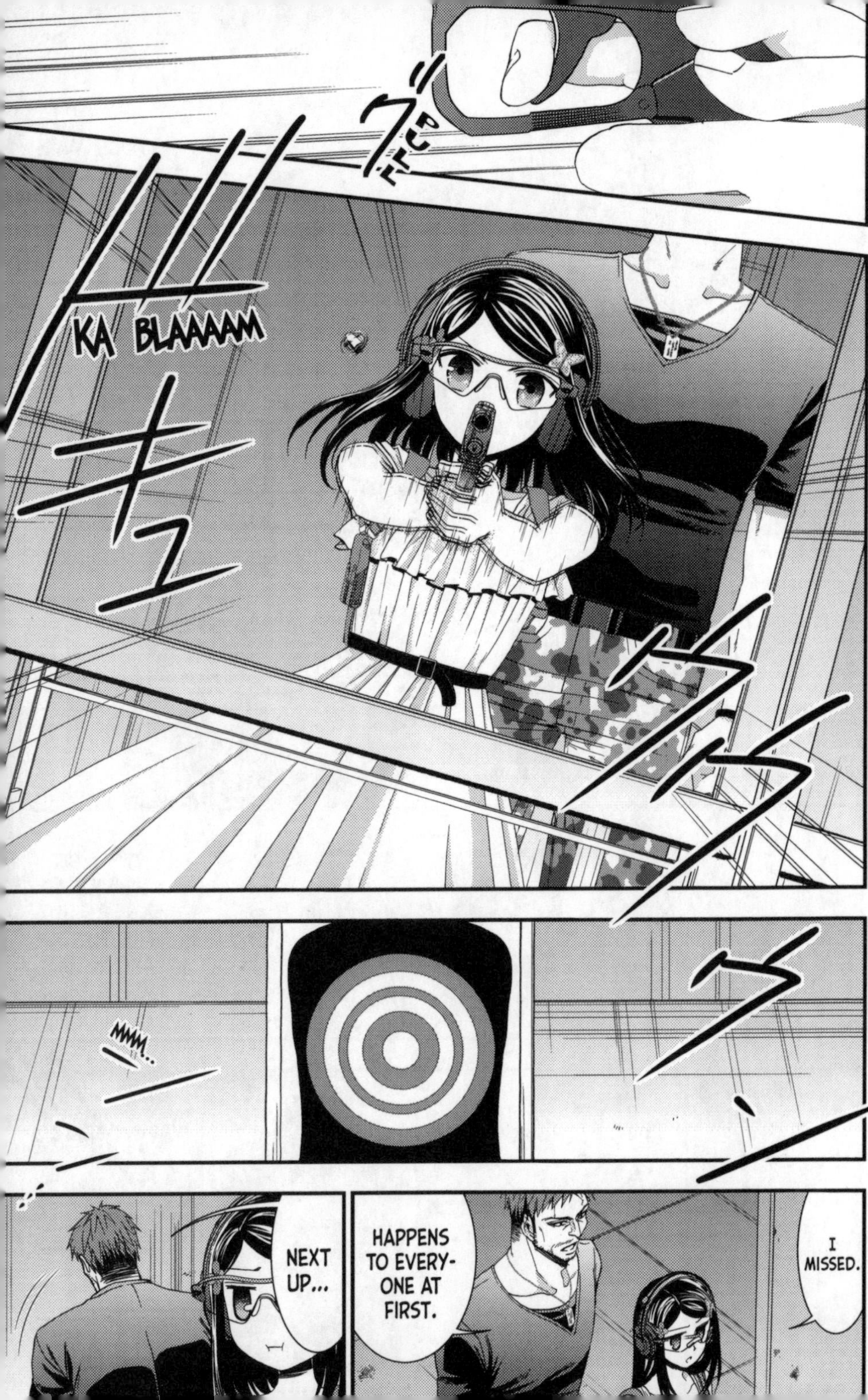
PULL
KA BLAAAM
MMM...
I MISSED.
HAPPENS TO EVERY-ONE AT FIRST.
NEXT UP...

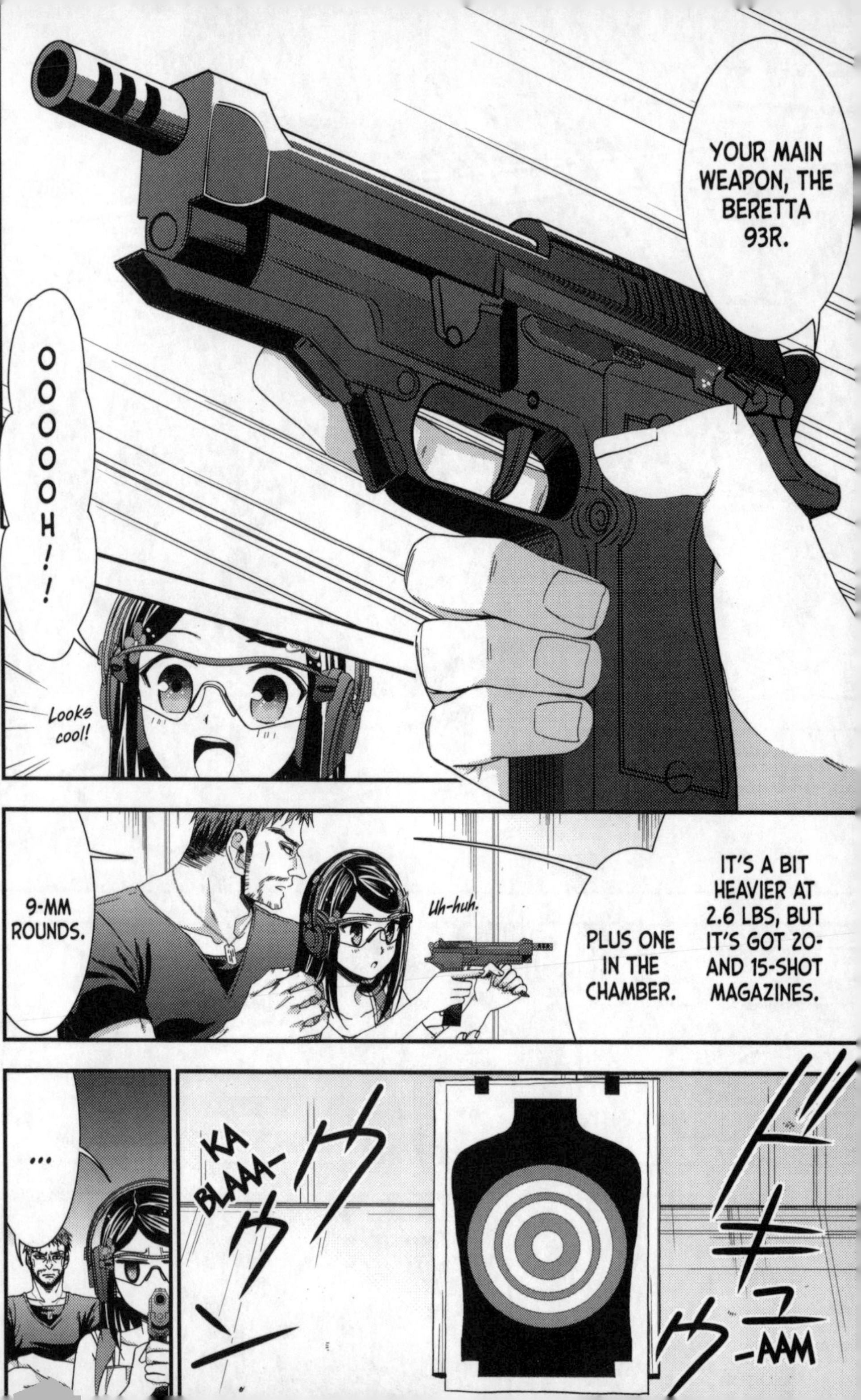
YOUR MAIN WEAPON, THE BERETTA 93R.
OOOOOH!!
Looks cool!
IT'S A BIT HEAVIER AT 2.6 LBS, BUT IT'S GOT 20- AND 15-SHOT MAGAZINES.
PLUS ONE IN THE CHAMBER.
Uh-huh.
9-MM ROUNDS.
-AAM
KA BLAAA-
...

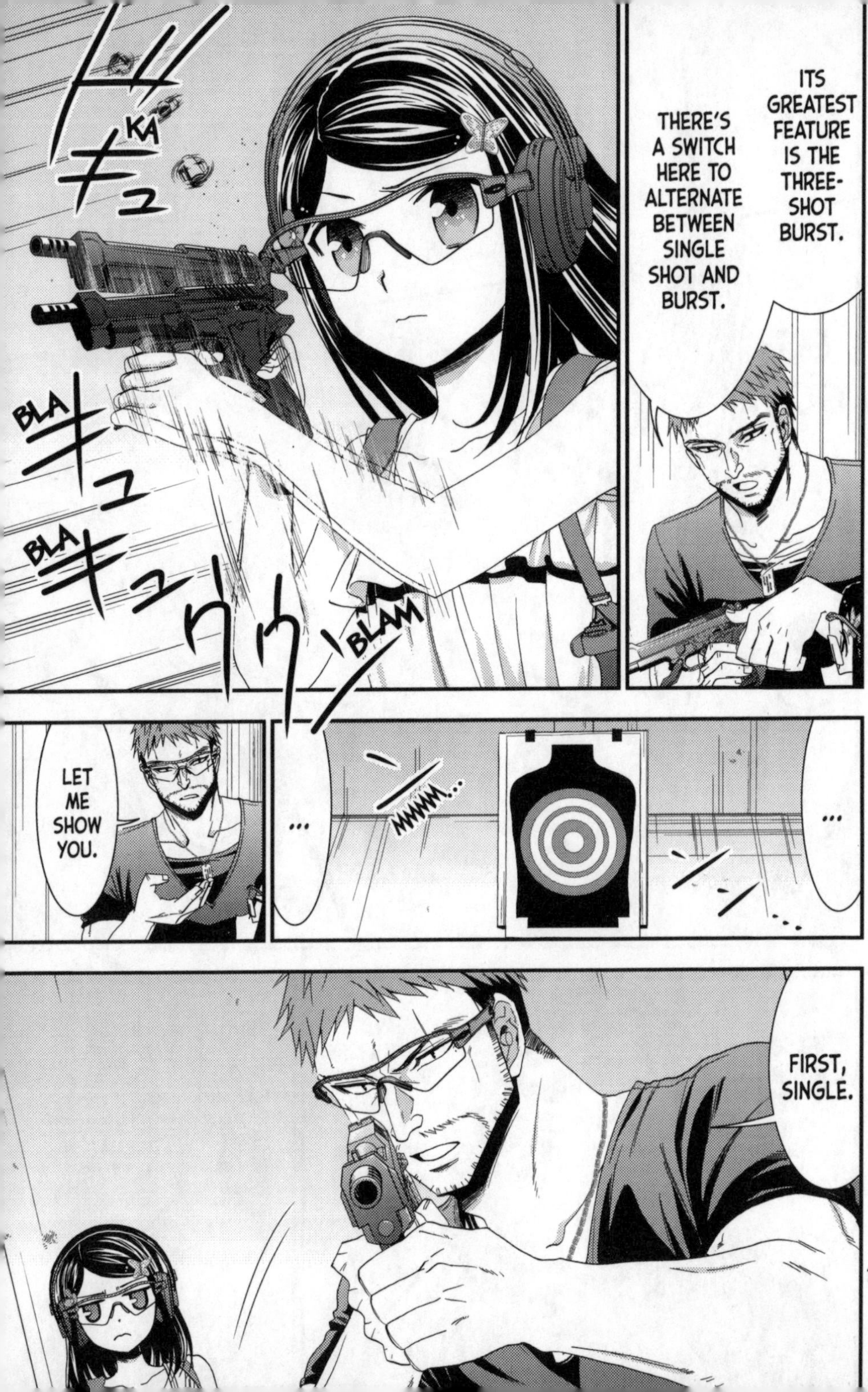
ITS GREATEST FEATURE IS THE THREE-SHOT BURST.
THERE'S A SWITCH HERE TO ALTERNATE BETWEEN SINGLE SHOT AND BURST.
KA
BLA
BLA
BLAM
...
MMMM...
...
LET ME SHOW YOU.
FIRST, SINGLE.

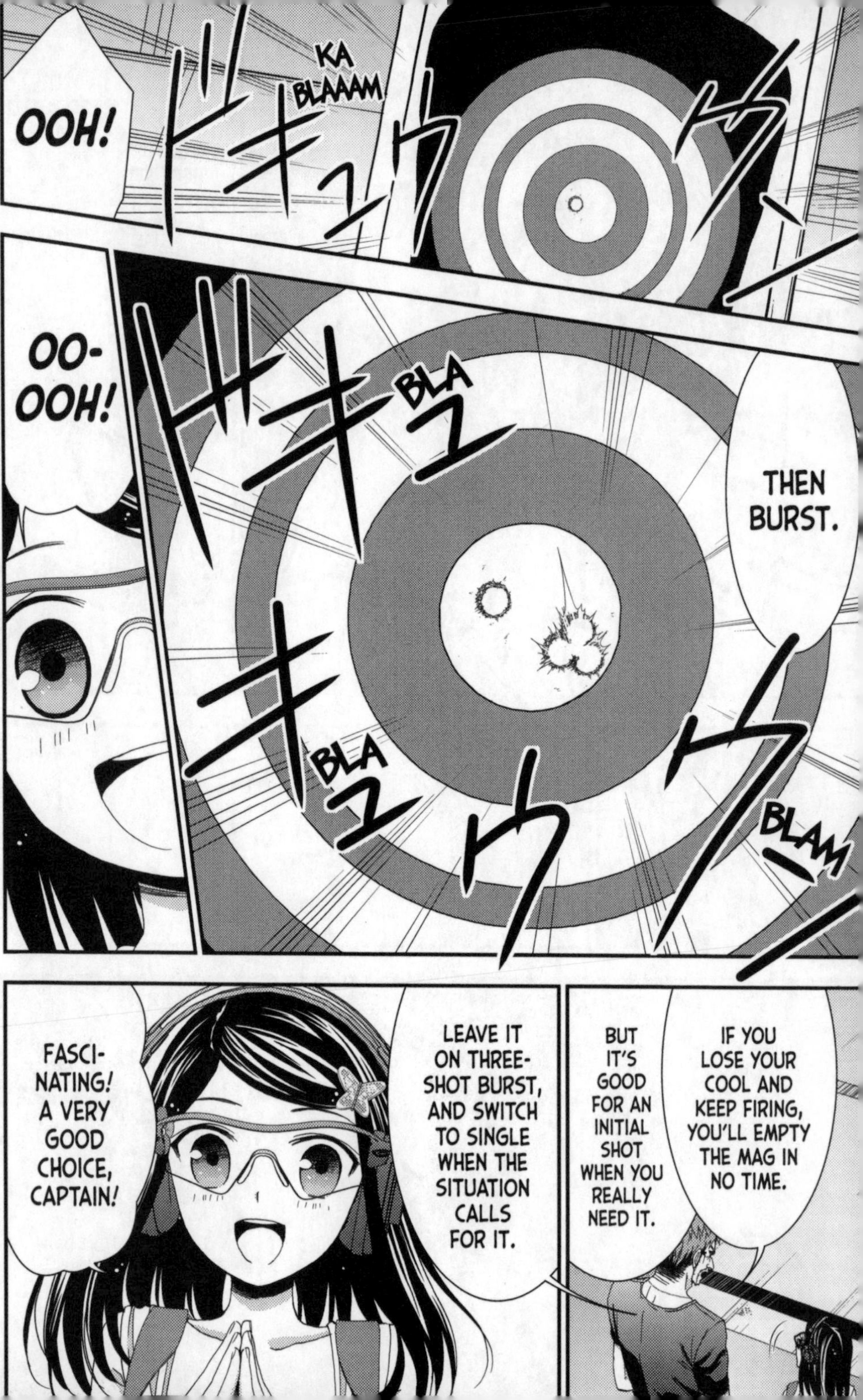
KA BLAAAM
OOH!
THEN BURST.
BLA
BLA
BLAM
OO-OOH!
IF YOU LOSE YOUR COOL AND KEEP FIRING, YOU'LL EMPTY THE MAG IN NO TIME.
BUT IT'S GOOD FOR AN INITIAL SHOT WHEN YOU REALLY NEED IT.
LEAVE IT ON THREE-SHOT BURST, AND SWITCH TO SINGLE WHEN THE SITUATION CALLS FOR IT.
FASCI-NATING! A VERY GOOD CHOICE, CAPTAIN!

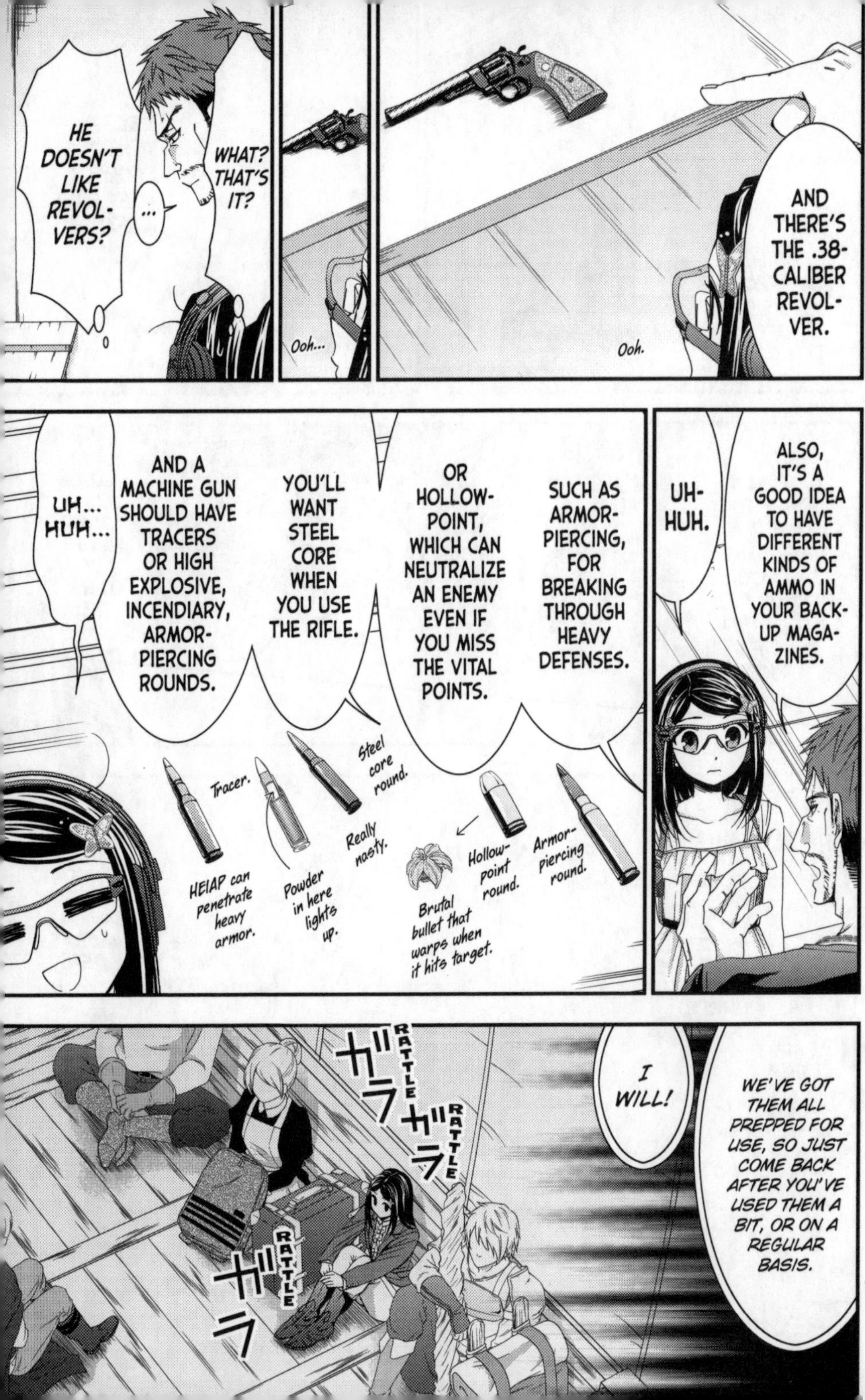
AND THERE'S THE .38-CALIBER REVOLVER.
Ooh.
Ooh...
WHAT? THAT'S IT?
HE DOESN'T LIKE REVOLVERS?
...
ALSO, IT'S A GOOD IDEA TO HAVE DIFFERENT KINDS OF AMMO IN YOUR BACK-UP MAGAZINES.
UH-HUH.
SUCH AS ARMOR-PIERCING, FOR BREAKING THROUGH HEAVY DEFENSES.
OR HOLLOW-POINT, WHICH CAN NEUTRALIZE AN ENEMY EVEN IF YOU MISS THE VITAL POINTS.
YOU'LL WANT STEEL CORE WHEN YOU USE THE RIFLE.
AND A MACHINE GUN SHOULD HAVE TRACERS OR HIGH EXPLOSIVE, INCENDIARY, ARMOR-PIERCING ROUNDS.
UH... HUH...
Armor-piercing round.
Hollow-point round.
Brutal bullet that warps when it hits target.
Steel core round.
Really nasty.
Tracer.
Powder in here lights up.
HEIAP can penetrate heavy armor.
WE'VE GOT THEM ALL PREPPED FOR USE, SO JUST COME BACK AFTER YOU'VE USED THEM A BIT, OR ON A REGULAR BASIS.
I WILL!
ガラ RATTLE
ガラ RATTLE
ガラ RATTLE

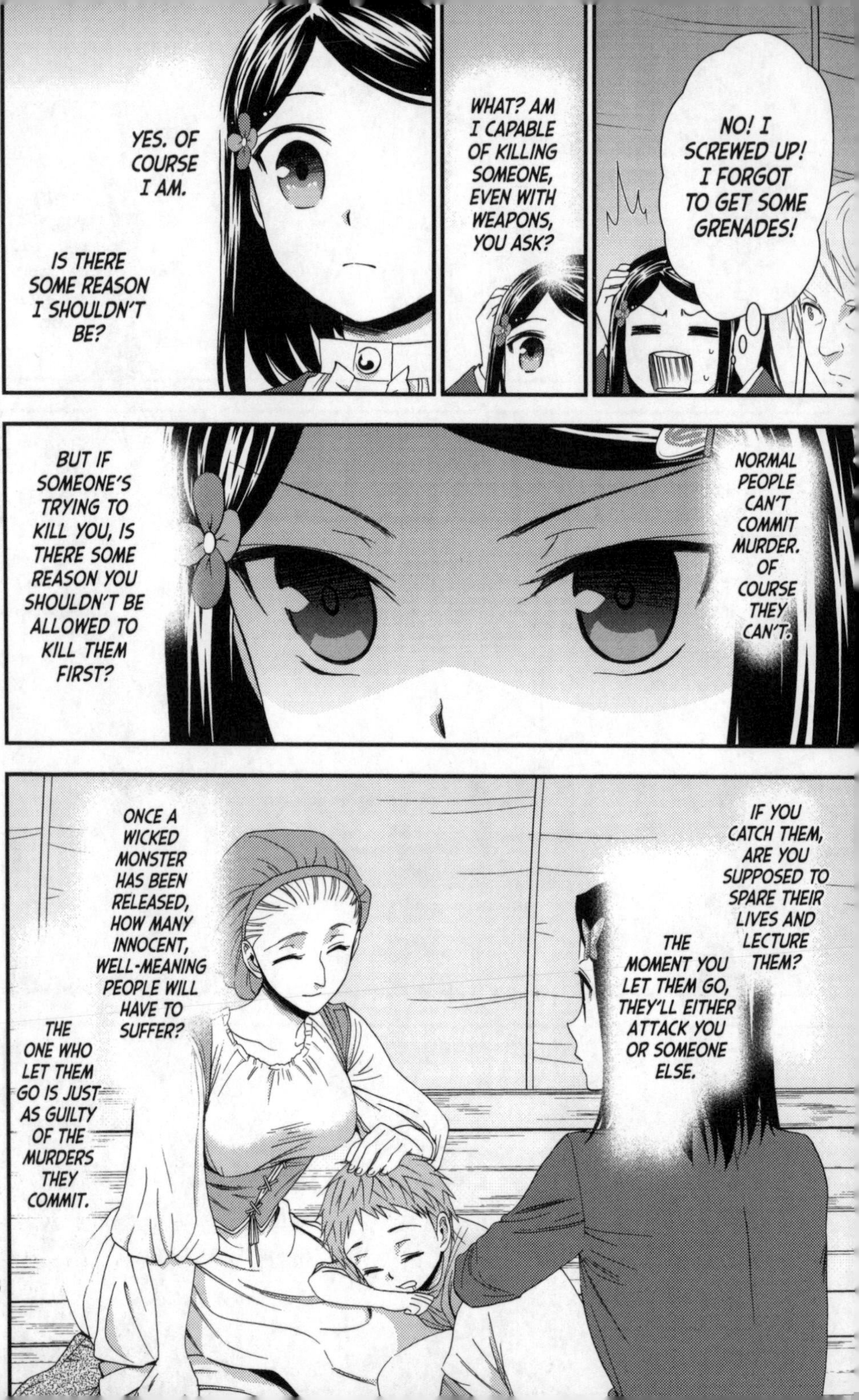
NO! I SCREWED UP! I FORGOT TO GET SOME GRENADES!
WHAT? AM I CAPABLE OF KILLING SOMEONE, EVEN WITH WEAPONS, YOU ASK?
YES. OF COURSE I AM.
IS THERE SOME REASON I SHOULDN'T BE?
NORMAL PEOPLE CAN'T COMMIT MURDER. OF COURSE THEY CAN'T.
BUT IF SOMEONE'S TRYING TO KILL YOU, IS THERE SOME REASON YOU SHOULDN'T BE ALLOWED TO KILL THEM FIRST?
IF YOU CATCH THEM, ARE YOU SUPPOSED TO SPARE THEIR LIVES AND LECTURE THEM?
THE MOMENT YOU LET THEM GO, THEY'LL EITHER ATTACK YOU OR SOMEONE ELSE.
ONCE A WICKED MONSTER HAS BEEN RELEASED, HOW MANY INNOCENT, WELL-MEANING PEOPLE WILL HAVE TO SUFFER?
THE ONE WHO LET THEM GO IS JUST AS GUILTY OF THE MURDERS THEY COMMIT.

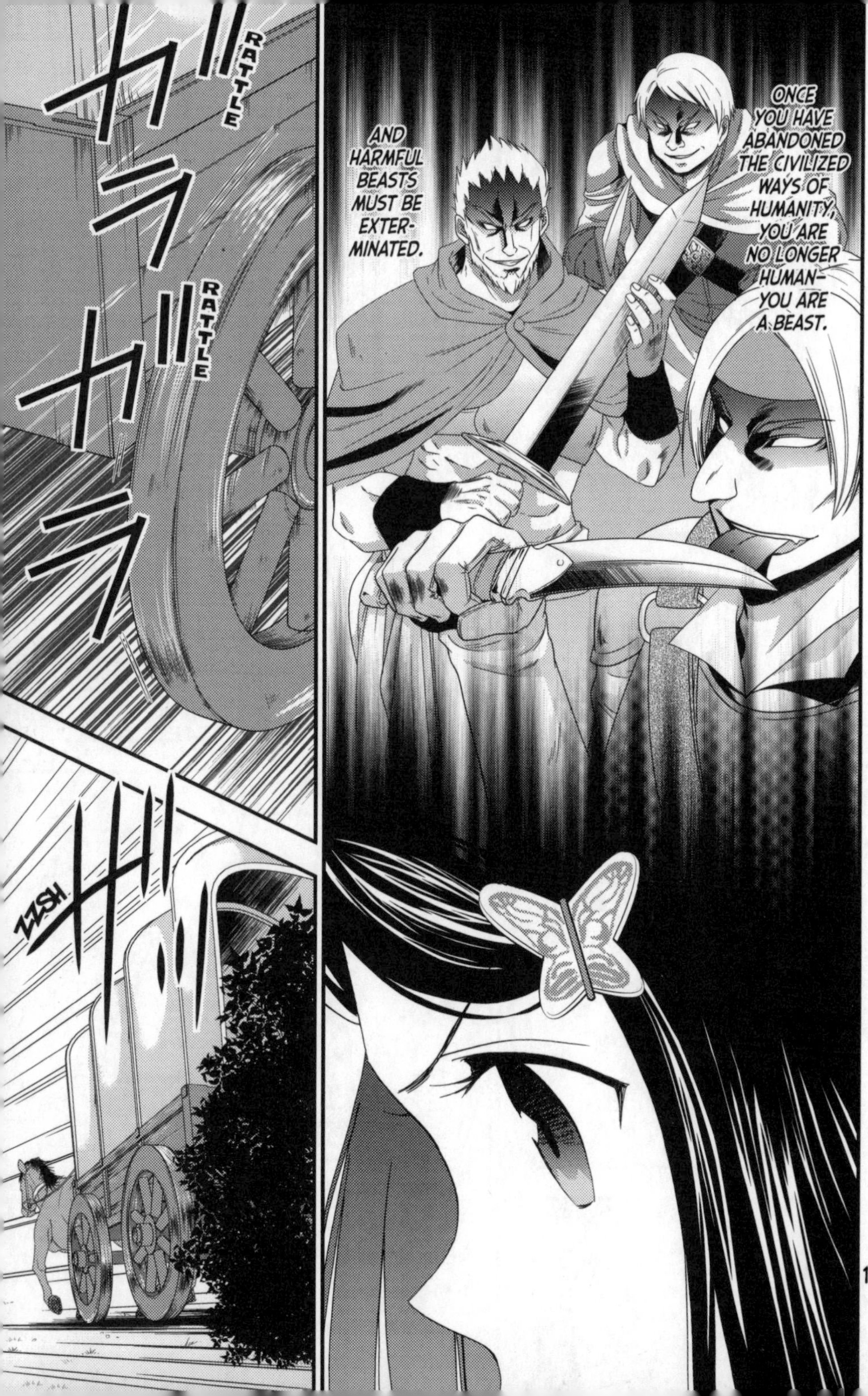
ONCE YOU HAVE ABANDONED THE CIVILIZED WAYS OF HUMANITY, YOU ARE NO LONGER HUMAN— YOU ARE A BEAST.
AND HARMFUL BEASTS MUST BE EXTER-MINATED.
RATTLE
RATTLE
ZZSH

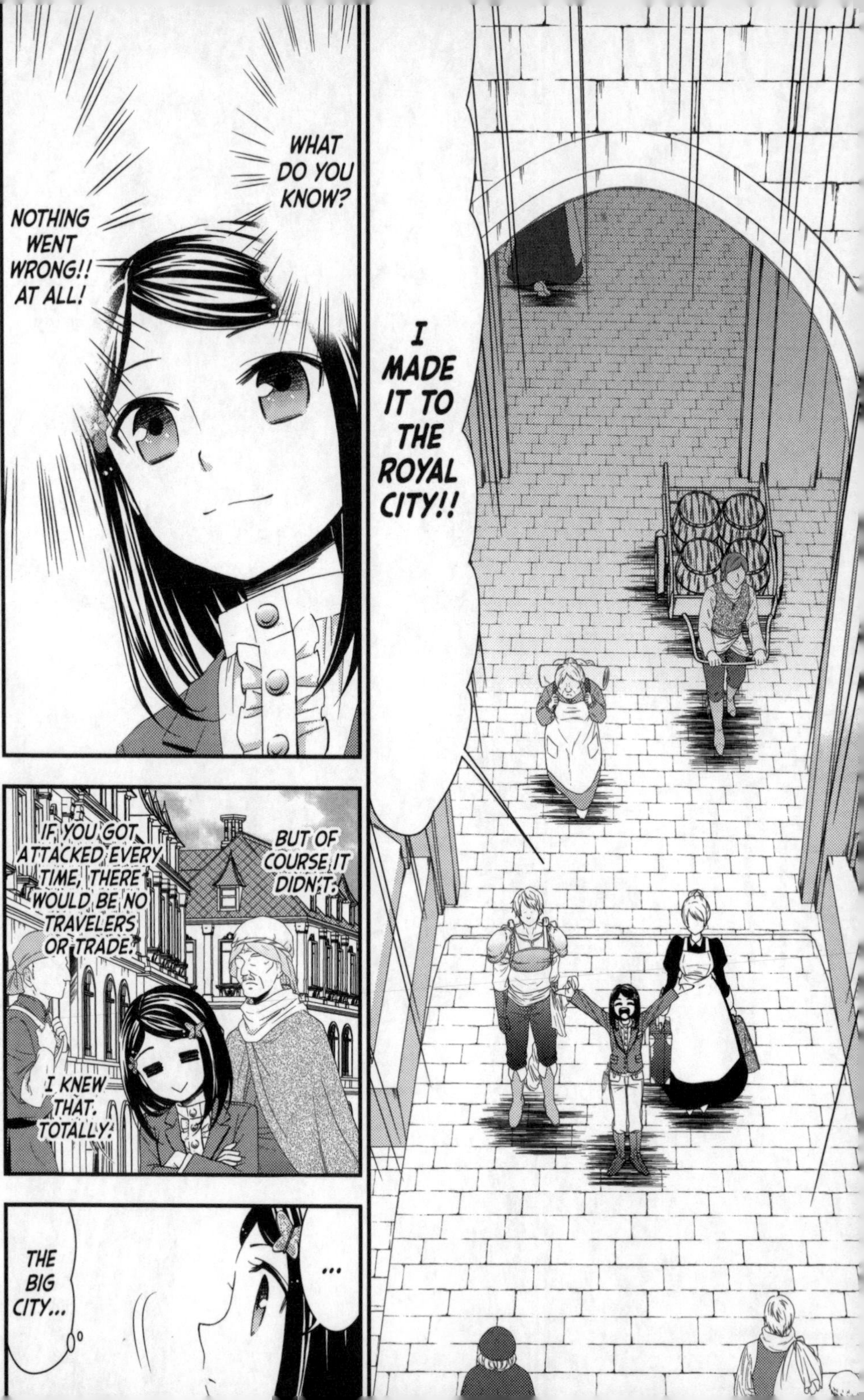
I MADE IT TO THE ROYAL CITY!!
WHAT DO YOU KNOW?
NOTHING WENT WRONG!! AT ALL!
BUT OF COURSE IT DIDN'T.
IF YOU GOT ATTACKED EVERY TIME, THERE WOULD BE NO TRAVELERS OR TRADE.
I KNEW THAT. TOTALLY.
...
THE BIG CITY...

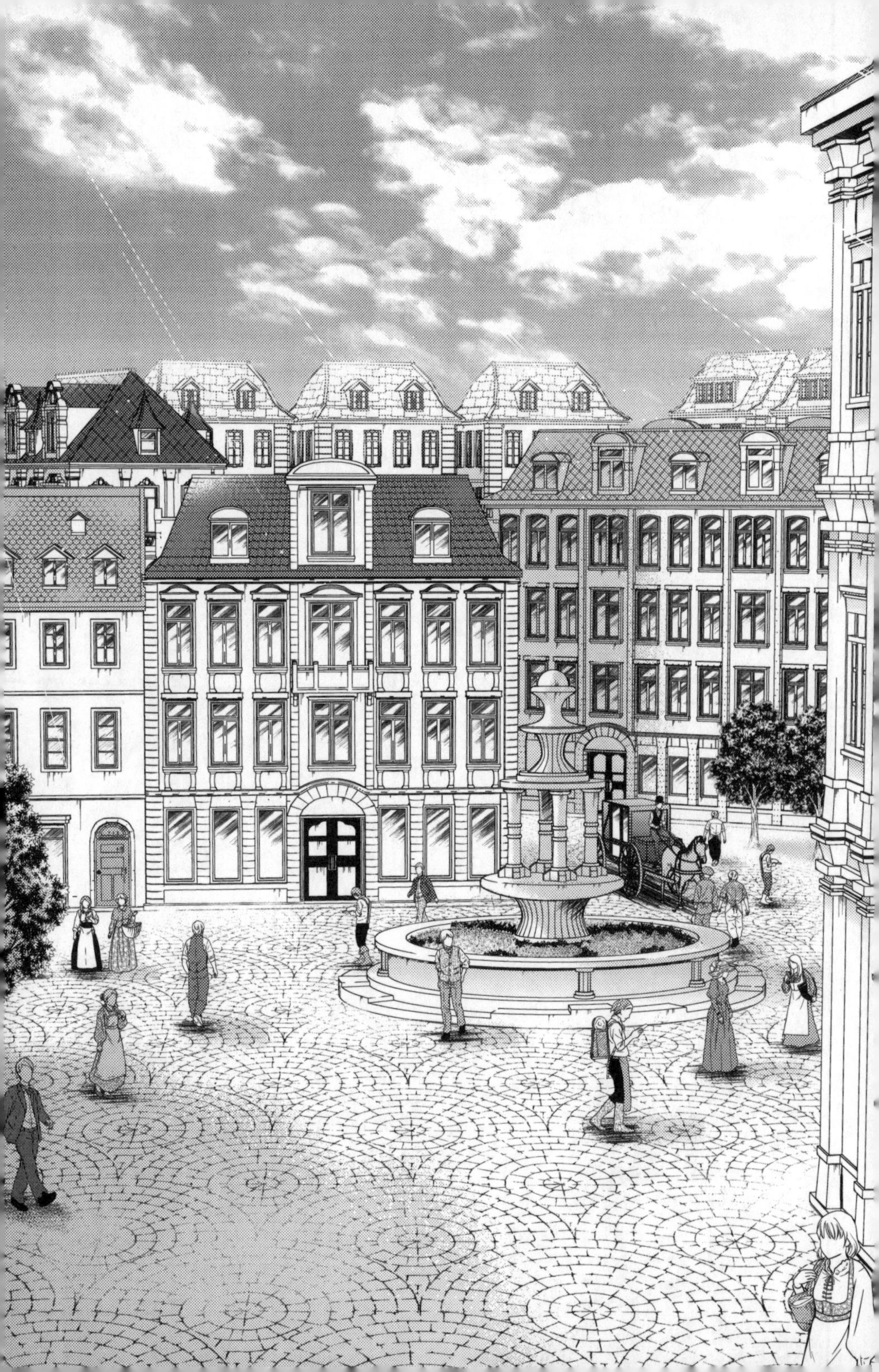

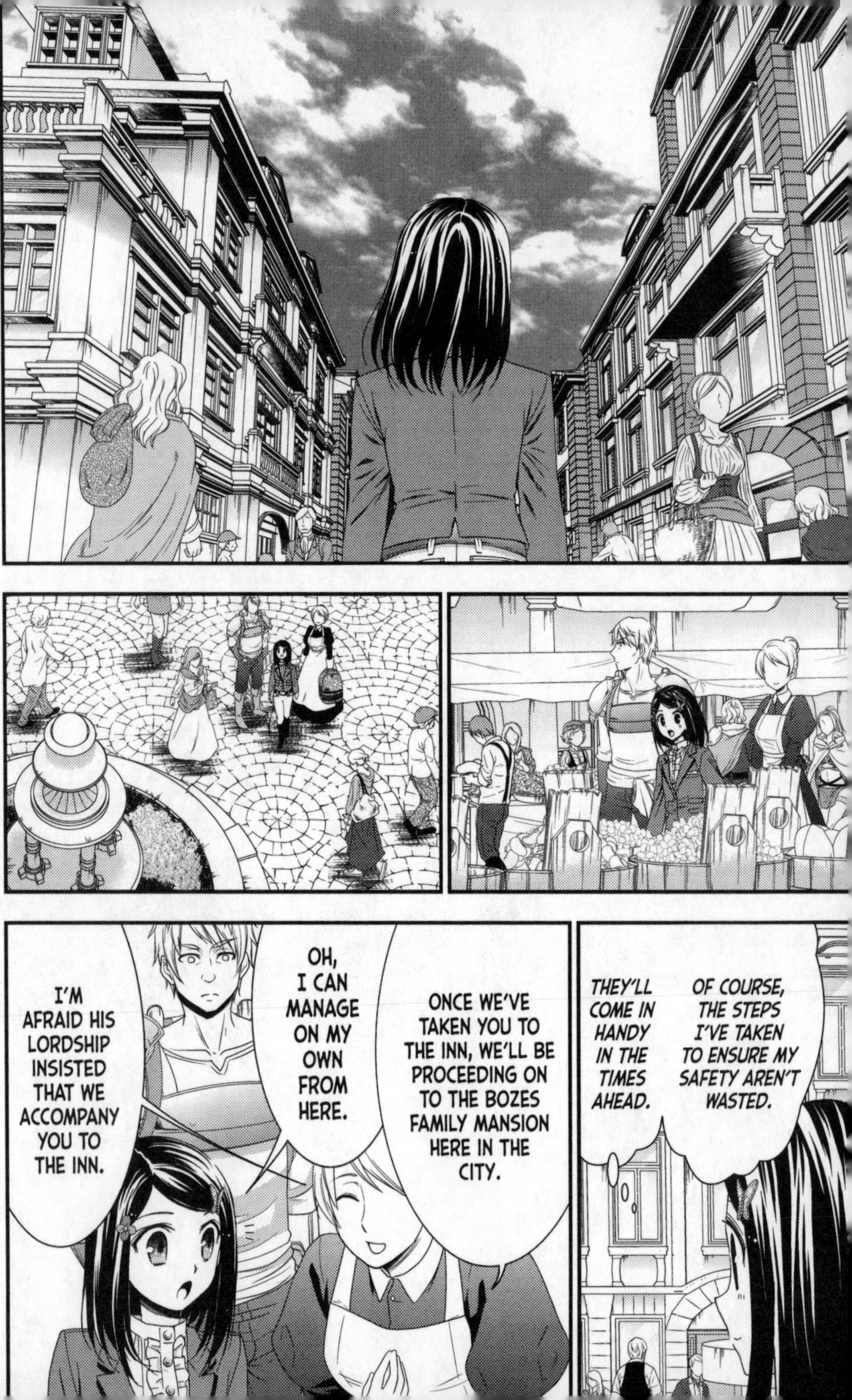
OF COURSE, THE STEPS I'VE TAKEN TO ENSURE MY SAFETY AREN'T WASTED.
THEY'LL COME IN HANDY IN THE TIMES AHEAD.
ONCE WE'VE TAKEN YOU TO THE INN, WE'LL BE PROCEEDING ON TO THE BOZES FAMILY MANSION HERE IN THE CITY.
OH, I CAN MANAGE ON MY OWN FROM HERE.
I'M AFRAID HIS LORDSHIP INSISTED THAT WE ACCOMPANY YOU TO THE INN.

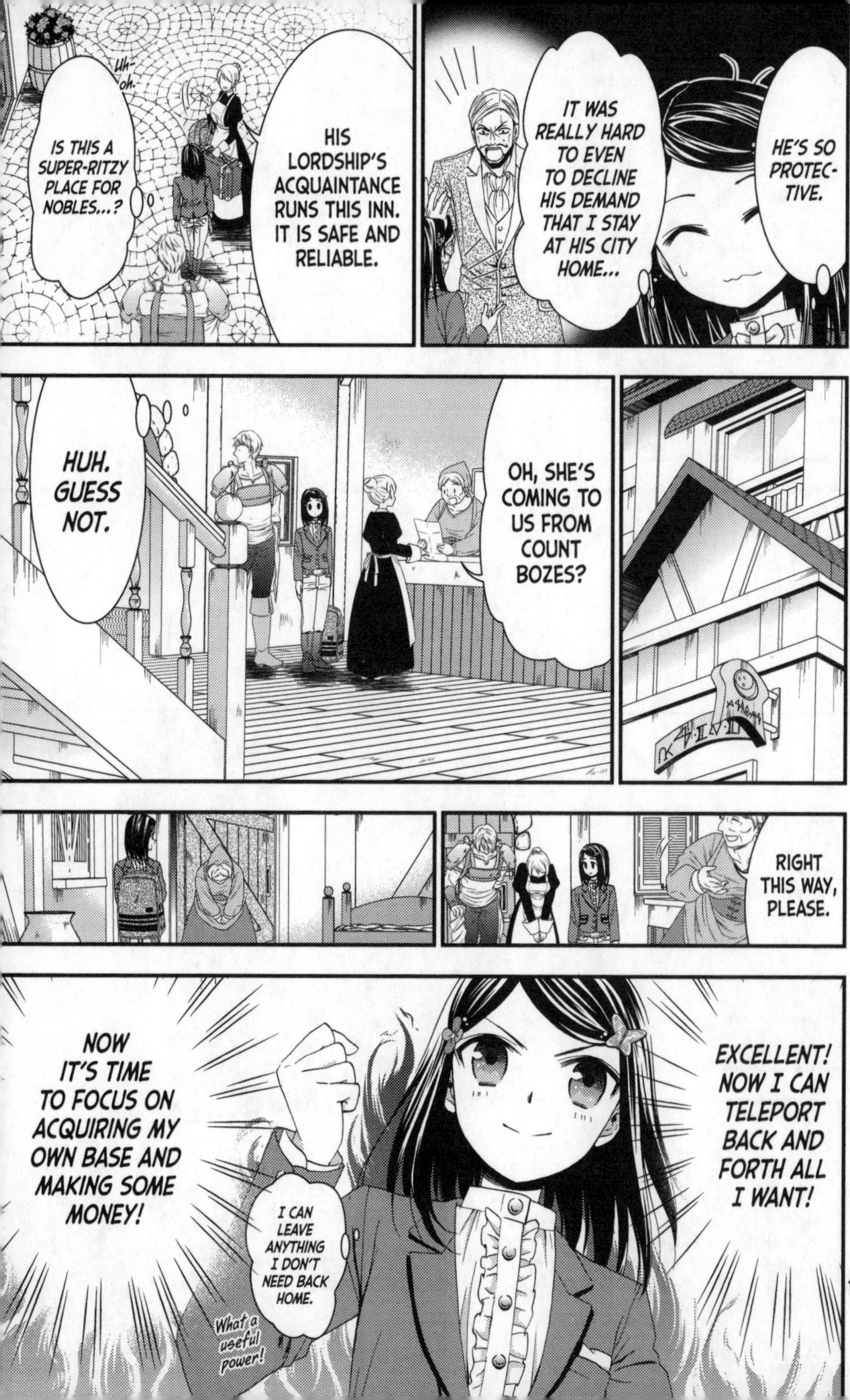
IT WAS REALLY HARD TO EVEN TO DECLINE HIS DEMAND THAT I STAY AT HIS CITY HOME...
HE'S SO PROTEC-TIVE.
HIS LORDSHIP'S ACQUAINTANCE RUNS THIS INN. IT IS SAFE AND RELIABLE.
Uh-oh.
IS THIS A SUPER-RITZY PLACE FOR NOBLES...?
OH, SHE'S COMING TO US FROM COUNT BOZES?
HUH. GUESS NOT.
RIGHT THIS WAY, PLEASE.
EXCELLENT! NOW I CAN TELEPORT BACK AND FORTH ALL I WANT!
I CAN LEAVE ANYTHING I DON'T NEED BACK HOME.
NOW IT'S TIME TO FOCUS ON ACQUIRING MY OWN BASE AND MAKING SOME MONEY!
What a useful power!

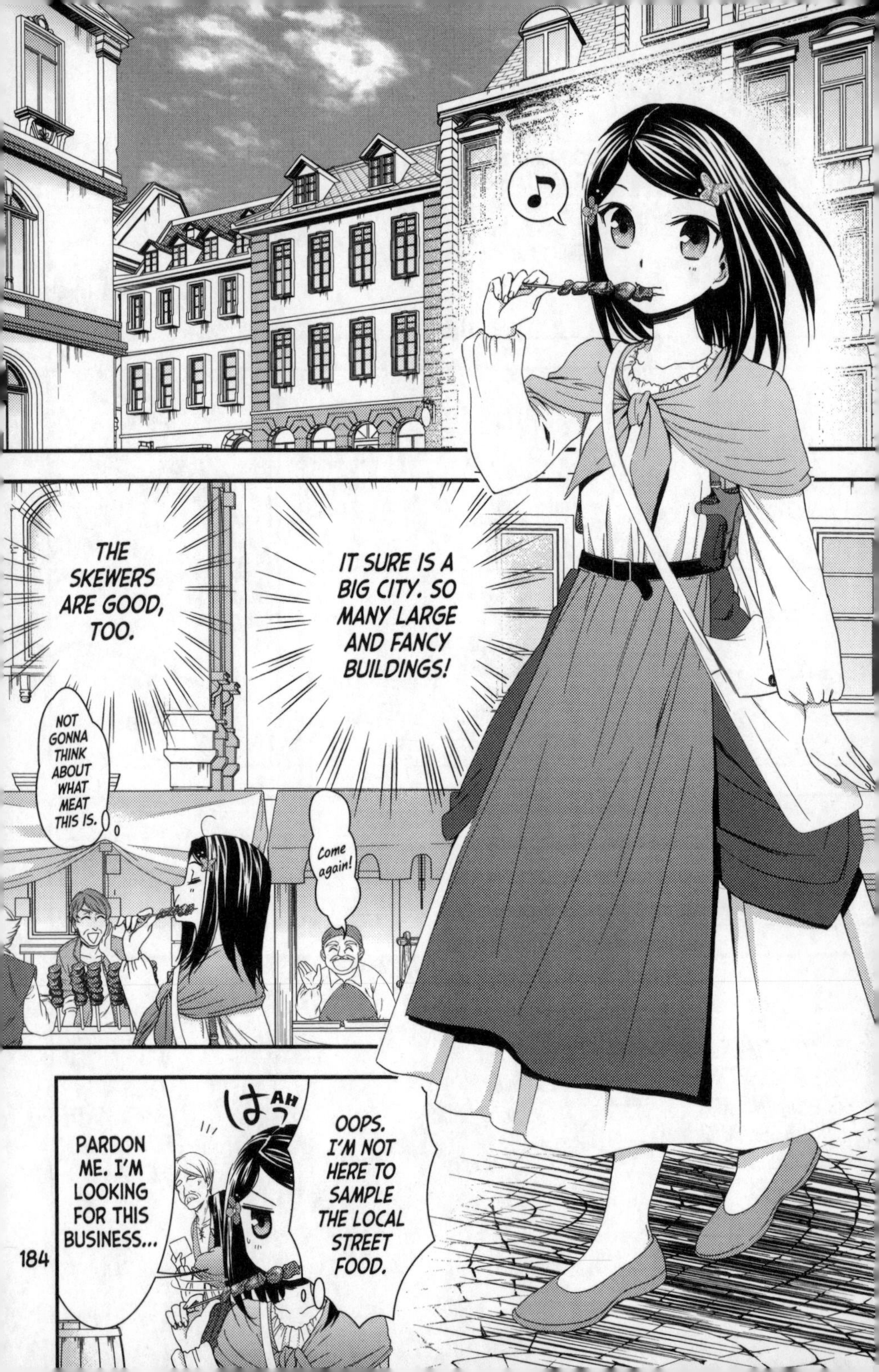
♪
IT SURE IS A BIG CITY. SO MANY LARGE AND FANCY BUILDINGS!
THE SKEWERS ARE GOOD, TOO.
Come again!
NOT GONNA THINK ABOUT WHAT MEAT THIS IS.
はっ AH
OOPS. I'M NOT HERE TO SAMPLE THE LOCAL STREET FOOD.
PARDON ME. I'M LOOKING FOR THIS BUSINESS...

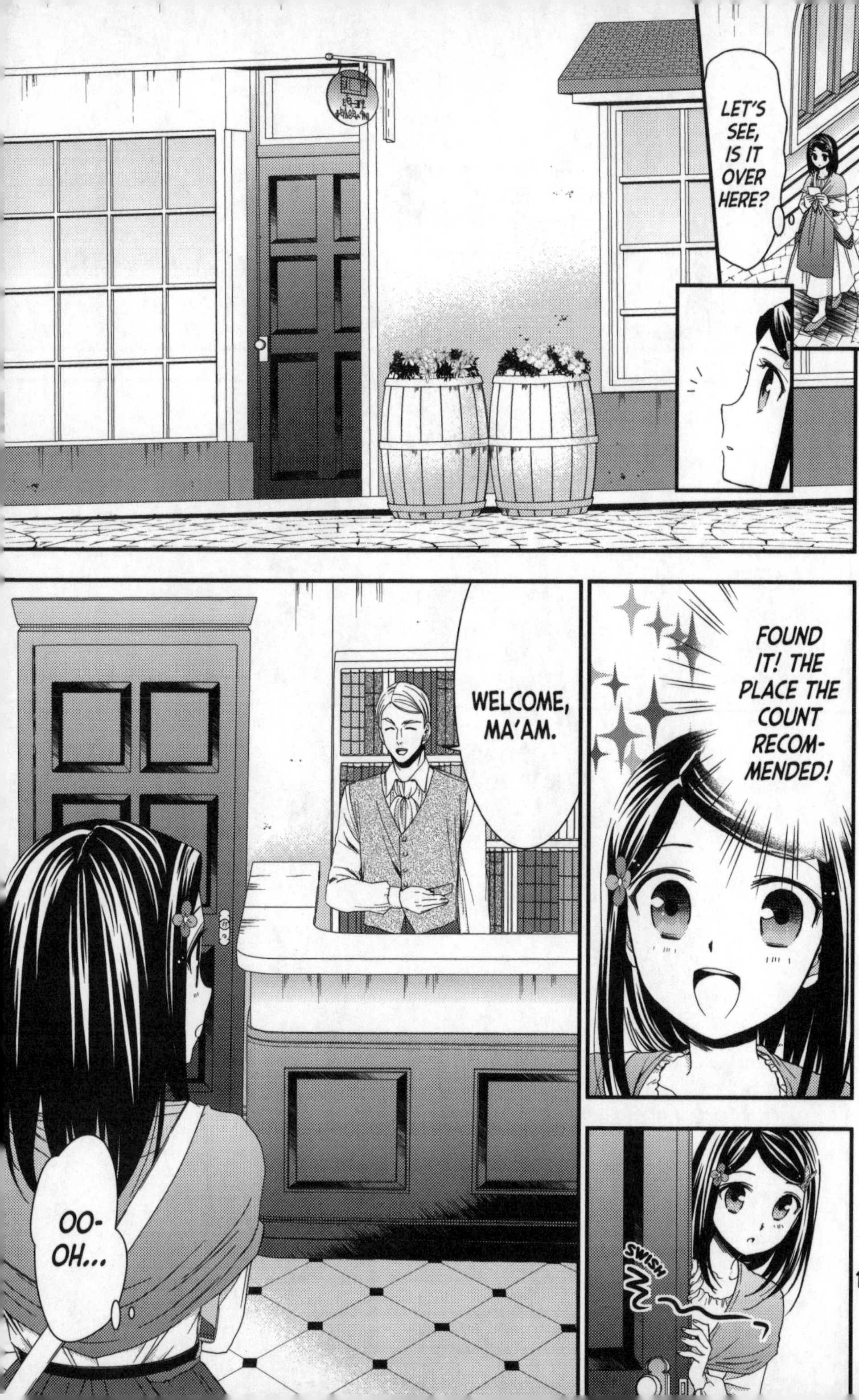
LET'S SEE, IS IT OVER HERE?
FOUND IT! THE PLACE THE COUNT RECOMMENDED!
WELCOME, MA'AM.
SWISH
OO-OH...

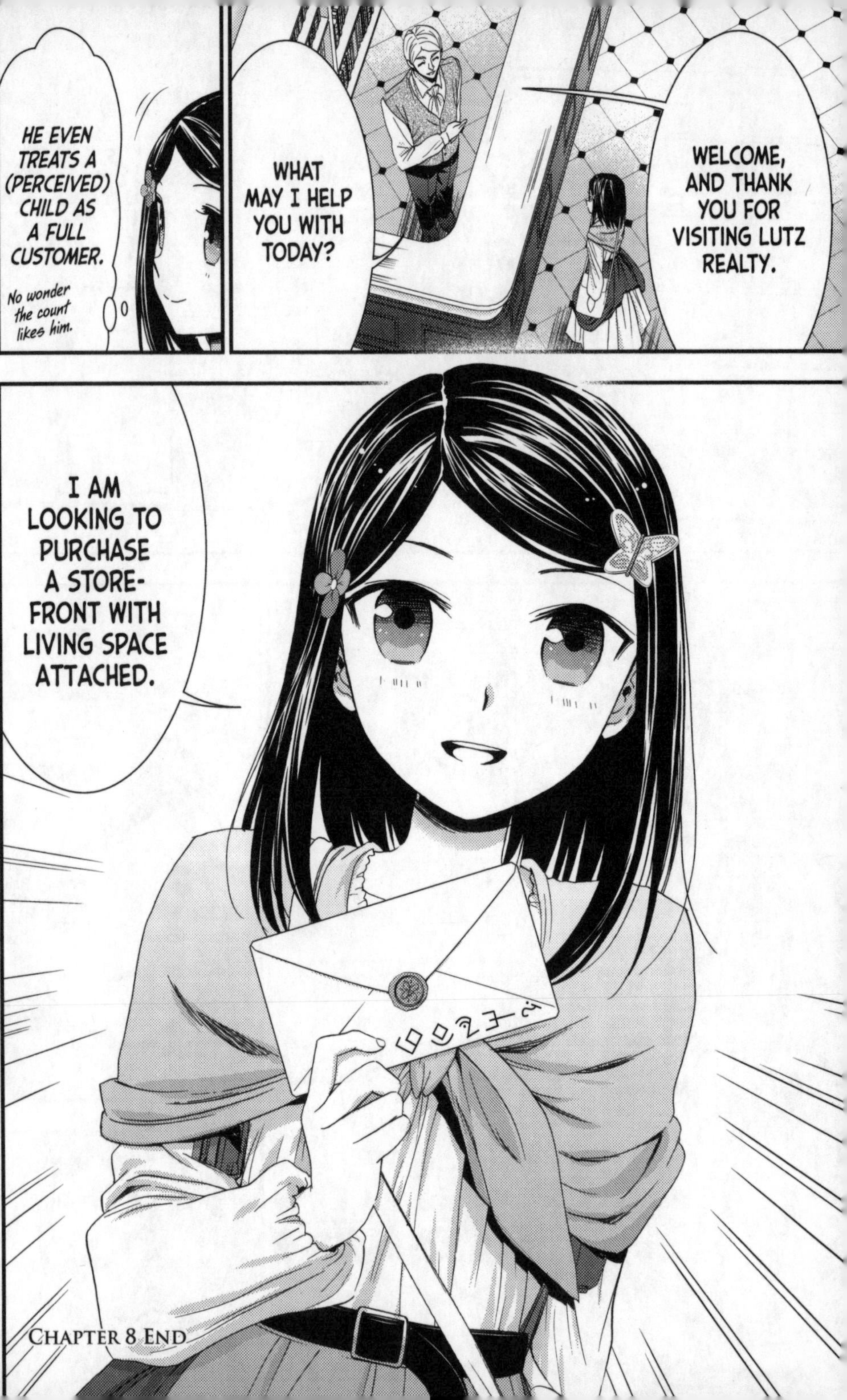
WELCOME, AND THANK YOU FOR VISITING LUTZ REALTY.
WHAT MAY I HELP YOU WITH TODAY?
HE EVEN TREATS A (PERCEIVED) CHILD AS A FULL CUSTOMER.
No wonder the count likes him.
I AM LOOKING TO PURCHASE A STORE-FRONT WITH LIVING SPACE ATTACHED.
CHAPTER 8 END

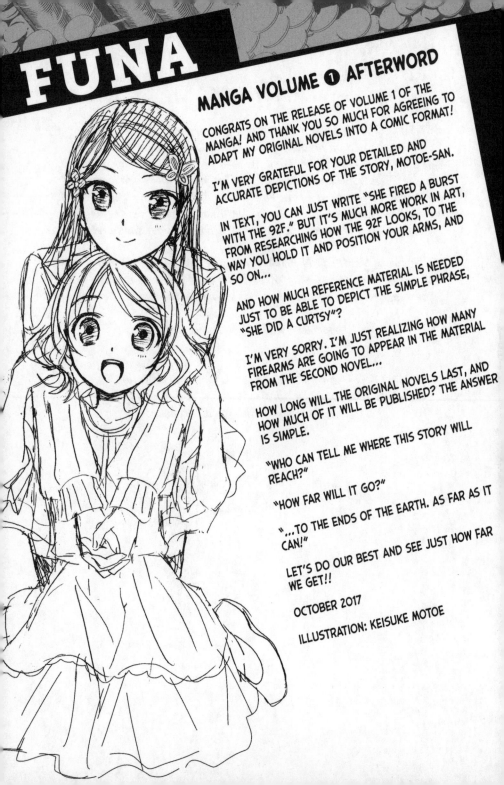

FUNA

MANGA VOLUME ❶ AFTERWORD

CONGRATS ON THE RELEASE OF VOLUME 1 OF THE MANGA! AND THANK YOU SO MUCH FOR AGREEING TO ADAPT MY ORIGINAL NOVELS INTO A COMIC FORMAT!

I'M VERY GRATEFUL FOR YOUR DETAILED AND ACCURATE DEPICTIONS OF THE STORY, MOTOE-SAN.

IN TEXT, YOU CAN JUST WRITE "SHE FIRED A BURST WITH THE 92F." BUT IT'S MUCH MORE WORK IN ART, FROM RESEARCHING HOW THE 92F LOOKS, TO THE WAY YOU HOLD IT AND POSITION YOUR ARMS, AND SO ON...

AND HOW MUCH REFERENCE MATERIAL IS NEEDED JUST TO BE ABLE TO DEPICT THE SIMPLE PHRASE, "SHE DID A CURTSY"?

I'M VERY SORRY. I'M JUST REALIZING HOW MANY FIREARMS ARE GOING TO APPEAR IN THE MATERIAL FROM THE SECOND NOVEL...

HOW LONG WILL THE ORIGINAL NOVELS LAST, AND HOW MUCH OF IT WILL BE PUBLISHED? THE ANSWER IS SIMPLE.

"WHO CAN TELL ME WHERE THIS STORY WILL REACH?"

"HOW FAR WILL IT GO?"

"...TO THE ENDS OF THE EARTH. AS FAR AS IT CAN!"

LET'S DO OUR BEST AND SEE JUST HOW FAR WE GET!!

OCTOBER 2017

ILLUSTRATION: KEISUKE MOTOE

Afterword

Hello, I'm Keisuke Motoe. Thank you very much for reading the manga edition of Saving 80,000 Gold in Another World for My Retirement. Have you enjoyed Mitsuha-chan's action-packed journey so far? This volume was kind of like the preparatory arc leading up to the royal city, so we'll have lots of fun watching her go in the next volume. There are bits that I reluctantly had to cut from the original story, so if it appeals to you, please do check out the novels.

I'm full of gratitude to FUNA-sensei for entrusting his story to me, my editor and assistants for helping me out, and of course, to you readers most of all. I hope you'll join us for the next volume.

September 2017   Keisuke Motoe

Staff
I.Kuma-san, K.E-san, Sakuma-san, Sakurai-san, Teramoto-san, Hiramatsu-san, M.Jima-san, Yamanaka-san. Thank you all so much!

See you later!

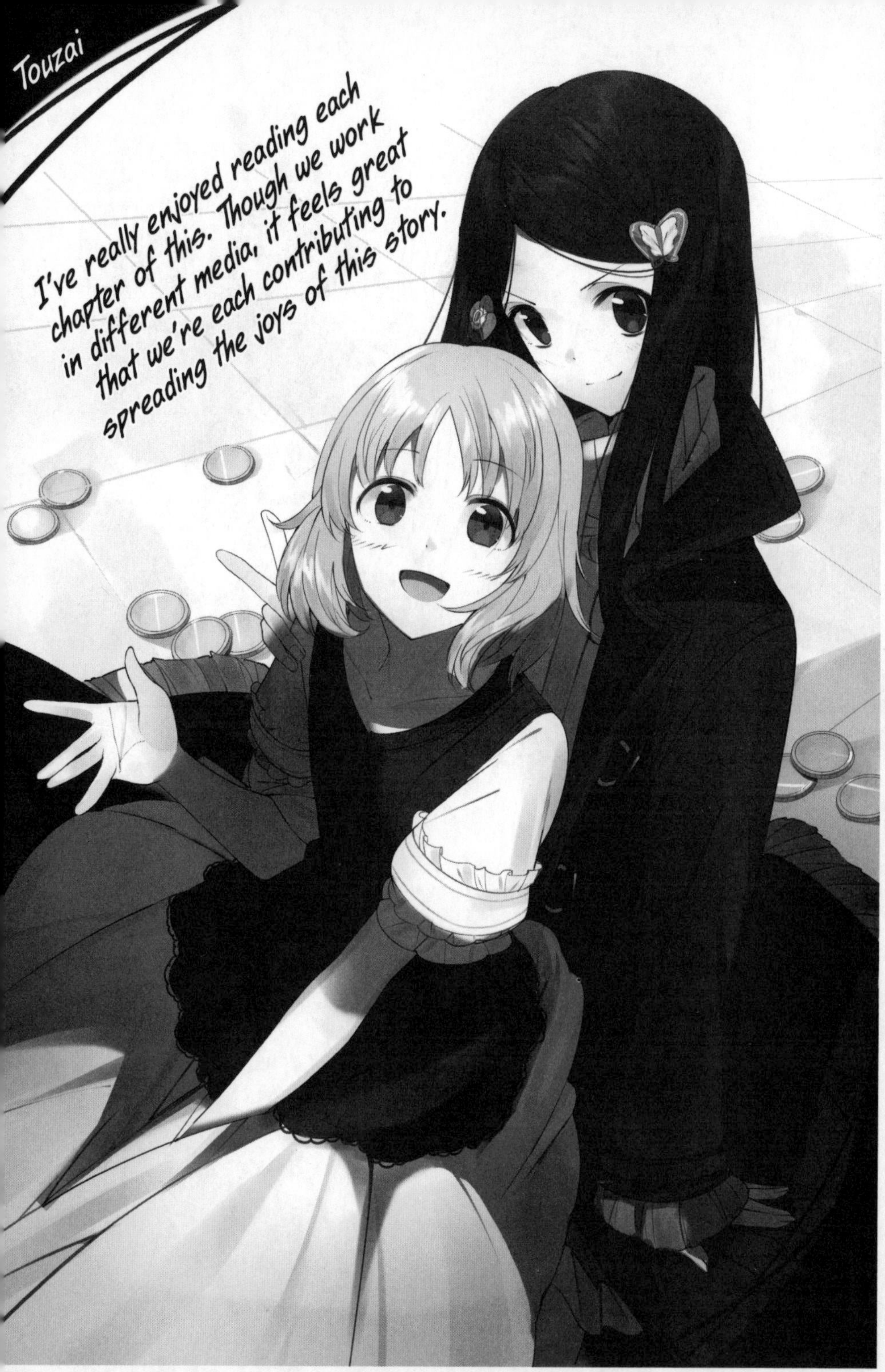
Touzai
I've really enjoyed reading each chapter of this. Though we work in different media, it feels great that we're each contributing to spreading the joys of this story.

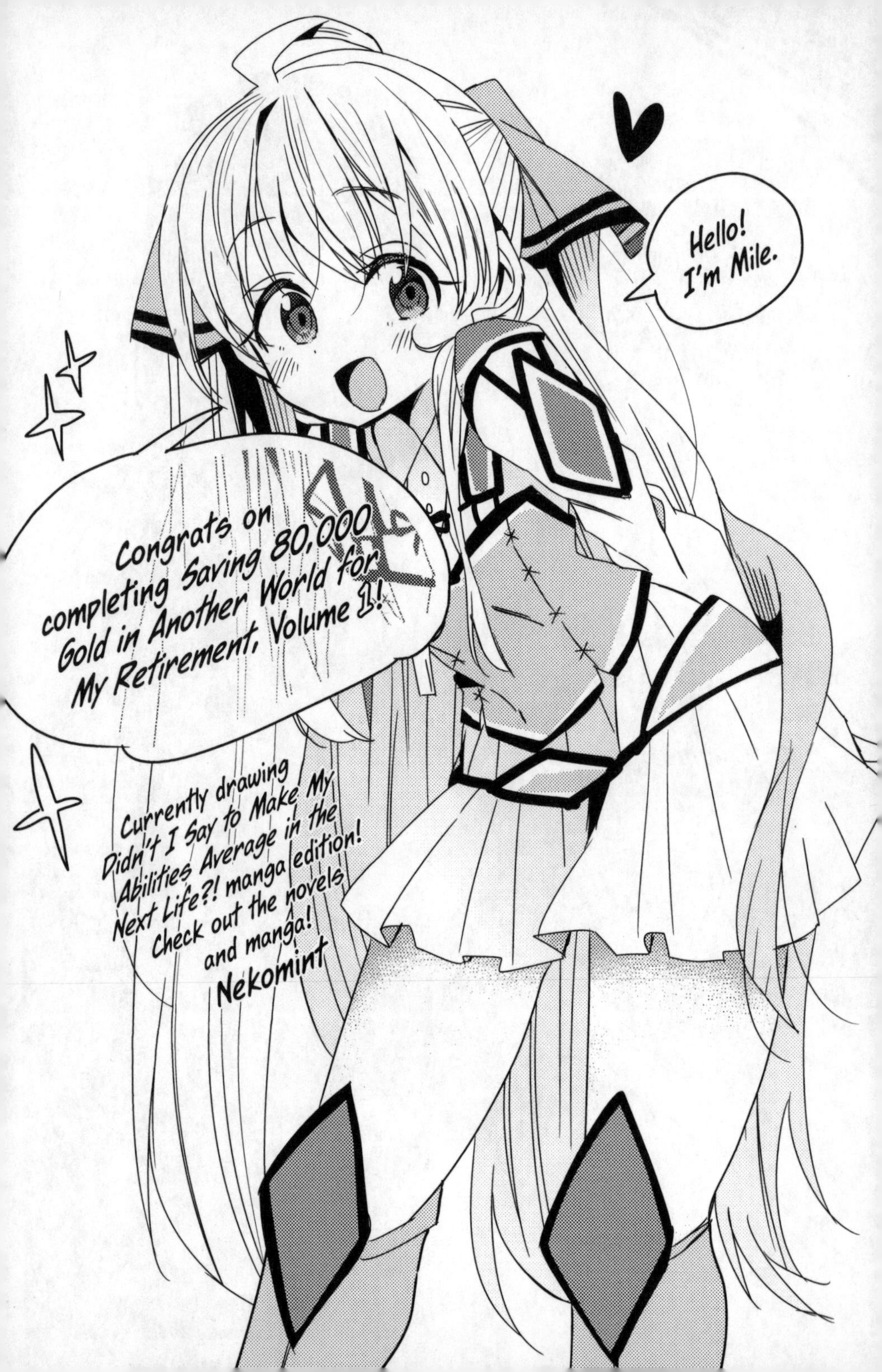
Hello! I'm Mile.
Congrats on completing Saving 80,000 Gold in Another World for My Retirement, Volume 1!
Currently drawing Didn't I Say to Make My Abilities Average in the Next Life?! manga edition! Check out the novels and manga!
Nekomint

Saving 80,000 Gold in Another World for My Retirement

Volume 1

Congratulations!!

This is Kaoru, protagonist of FUNA-sensei's other series, I Shall Survive Using Potions!

Check out the novels and manga edition!

Hibiki Kokonoe

A Kodansha Trade Paperback Original

Saving 80,000 Gold in Another World for My Retirement 1 copyright © 2017 FUNA / Keisuke Motoe / Touzai
English translation copyright © 2023 FUNA / Keisuke Motoe / Touzai

Published in the United States by
Kodansha USA Publishing, LLC, New York.

Publication rights for this English edition arranged through
Kodansha Ltd., Tokyo.

First published in Japan in 2017 by Kodansha Ltd., Tokyo
as *Rougo ni Sonaete Isekai de 8-Man-Mai no Kinka o Tamemasu,* volume 1.

ISBN 978-1-64651-819-7

Printed in the United States of America.

9 8 7 6 5 4 3 2 1

Translation: Stephen Paul
Lettering: Jennifer Skarupa, Dezi Sienty
Editing: Aimee Zink
Kodansha USA Publishing edition cover design by Phil Balsman

Publisher: Kiichiro Sugawara

Director of Publishing Services: Ben Applegate
Director of Publishing Operations: Dave Barrett
Publishing Services Managing Editors: Alanna Ruse, Madison Salters,
with Grace Chen
Senior Production Manager: Angela Zurlo

KODANSHA.US

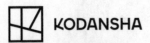 KODANSHA